MW00628615

Iran Unveiled:
How the Revolutionary Guards
Is Turning Theocracy
into Military Dictatorship

Iran Unveiled:
How the Revolutionary Guards
Is Turning Theocracy
into Military Dictatorship

Ali Alfoneh

The AEI Press

Publisher for the American Enterprise Institute

WASHINGTON, D.C.

Distributed by arrangement with the Rowman & Littlefield Publishing Group, 4501 Forbes Boulevard, Suite 200, Lanham, Maryland 20706. To order, call toll free 1-800-462-6420 or 1-717-794-3800. For all other inquiries, please contact AEI Press, 1150 Seventeenth Street, N.W., Washington, D.C. 20036, or call 1-800-862-5801.

Library of Congress Cataloging-in-Publication Data

Alfoneh, Ali.
  Iran unveiled : how the revolutionary guards is turning theocracy into military dictatorship / Ali Alfoneh.
    p. cm.

Includes bibliographical references and index.

  ISBN 978-0-8447-7253-0 (cloth)—ISBN 978-0-8447-7254-7 (pbk.)—
ISBN 978-0-8447-7255-4 (ebook)
  1. Sipah-i Pasdaran-i Inqilab-i Islami (Iran) 2. Iran—History, Military.
3. Civil-military relations—Iran. 4. Iran—Politics and government—1997—
I. Title.

  UA853.I7A44 2013
  955.06—dc23

                                                      2012050830

Printed in the United States of America

Contents

LIST OF ILLUSTRATIONS   viii

ACKNOWLEDGMENTS   xi

1. INTRODUCTION   1
   Notes   5

2. EMERGENCE OF THE GUARDS   6
   2.1. Not One, but Several Guards   6
   2.2. Unification of the Guards, Institutionalization
       of Factionalism   10
   Notes   14

3. THE REVOLUTIONARY GUARDS' ROLE IN DOMESTIC POLITICS   16
   3.1. Legal Framework   17
   3.2. A History of Politicization   19
   3.3. Conclusion   38
   Notes   38

4. THE IRGC AS AN INTERNAL SECURITY ORGANIZATION IN
   CONTEMPORARY IRAN   47
   4.1. Formal Merger of the IRGC with the Basij   48
   4.2. The Mosaic Doctrine   50
   4.3. Conclusion   56
   Notes   57

5. COLLAPSE OF THE COMMISSARIAT   79
   5.1. Legal Framework   79
   5.2. Early History and Establishment   84
   5.3. Khomeini's Commissars   87
   5.4. Khamenei's Commissars   117

5.5. Conclusion *128*
Notes *128*

6. **Dysfunctional Ideological/Political Indoctrination in the IRGC**   **150**
    6.1. The Legal Framework and Institutions *151*
    6.2. Early Attempts at Ideological/Political Indoctrination in the IRGC *152*
    6.3. Indoctrinating to Intervene *156*
    6.4. Contradictions and Implications *159*
    6.5. Conclusion *161*
    Notes *161*

7. **The Economic Empire of the IRGC**   **165**
    7.1. Twisting of the Legal Framework *166*
    7.2. From Military Industries to the Production of Consumer Goods *168*
    7.3. From Social Housing to Real Estate Speculation in Dubai *169*
    7.4. The IRGC as a Contractor: Enemy of the Private Sector *171*
    7.5. Chain Stores of the Guards: Competition with the Traditional Bazaar *173*
    7.6. The IRGC and Telecommunications: Elimination of Domestic and Foreign Competition *175*
    7.7. The IRGC and the Oil and Gas Sector *175*
    7.8. The IRGC on the Tehran Stock Exchange *179*
    7.9. The IRGC and Smuggling *189*
    7.10. Conclusion *191*
    Notes *192*

8. **The Revolutionary Guards and the Export of the Revolution**   **204**
    8.1. The Ideological Foundations of the Export of the Revolution *204*
    8.2. Practical Foundations of the Export of the Revolution: Iranian Revolutionaries as Members of a World Revolutionary Movement *206*

8.3. Export of the Revolution as a National Security Doctrine
and an Instrument of Domestic Power Struggle   *211*

8.4. Exporting the Revolution   *214*

8.5. Conclusion: Practical Benefits of the Export
of the Revolution for the IRGC   *235*

Notes   *237*

9. CONCLUSION   246

INDEX   251

ABOUT THE AUTHOR   267

List of Illustrations

FIGURES

2-1   Attempted Reconstruction of the Organizational Chart
       of the IRGC as of April 22, 1979   13
7-1   Value of Privatized State-Owned Enterprises in Iran,
       1991–2008   180
7-2   Percentage of Assets Purchased through Privatization
       of State-Owned Enterprises in Iran, 2005–2009,
       by Purchasing Sector   181

TABLES

2-1   Islamist Khomeini Loyalists at the Eve of the Revolution   7
2-2   Composition and Leading Members of the Umbrella
       Organization Holy Warriors of the Islamic Revolution   9
2-3   Factions Negotiating Unification of the Guards in 1979   12
4-1   IRGC Organizational Structure at General Governorate
       Level as of July 2008   51
5-1   Representatives of Grand Ayatollah Khomeini and
       Ayatollah Khamenei to the IRGC, 1979–2011   81
5-2   Representatives of the Supreme Leader in the IRGC   83
5-3   Representatives of the Supreme Leader to the IRGC
       at the Provincial Level   85
7-1   Main Subsidiaries of the Mehr Finance and Credit
       Institution (Formerly the Basij Cooperative
       Foundation)   182
7-2   Subsidiaries of the Mehr Finance and Credit Institution   183
7-3   Companies Entirely or Partially Owned by Mehr-e
       Eghtesad-e Iranian Investment Company   184

7-4   Companies and Investment Institutes Entirely or Partially
        Owned by the IRGC Cooperative Foundation as of
        May 31, 2010 *187*

On the cover: This image depicts the IRGC logo. At the base of the coat of arms, the number 1357 refers to the year 1979, which not only commemorates the year of the revolution in Iran, the establishment of the Islamic Republic, and the emergence of the IRGC but also heralds the beginning of a new era of world revolution. The centerpiece of the logo shows strong arms holding an AK-47, the emblematic weapon of revolutionary armies in the 1960s and 1970s. The arms are shaped in the form of the Arabic word *La*, a reference to the first article of the faith in Islam, *La Ilaha Ilallah* (there is no God but Allah). The Islamist character of the IRGC is further signified by a book that symbolizes the Quran. The Arabic text at the top of the logo reads, "And make ready for them whatever force you can." The text is from verse 60 of the "Sura al-Anfal," which—not quoted on the coat of arms—subsequently reads: "to frighten [terrorize] thereby the enemy of Allah and your enemy and others besides them, whom you know not—Allah knows them." There is also an olive branch, which does not play a prominent role in the logo, and a globe, which does. As demonstrated by its coat of arms, the IRGC is clearly a military organization that serves as the vanguard of an Islamist world revolution—a permanent revolution that never managed to seize control over the Islamic world but helped the IRGC seize control over Iran.

Acknowledgments

This book, and the articles on the Islamic Revolutionary Guards Corps (IRGC) published in the American Enterprise Institute's *Middle Eastern Outlook* series that laid the foundations for the book, are based on my research since the June 24, 2005, presidential election in Iran, which paved the path of Mahmoud Ahmadinejad, Iran's first soldier-president to the presidential palace in Tehran. I alone am responsible for the shortcomings of the book, but I am indebted to the many individuals and institutions that have helped my research. Birthe Hansen, professor in the Department of Political Science at the University of Copenhagen, urged me to embark on a comparative study of civil-military relations in the Middle East and North Africa, which helped me analyze the rise of the IRGC in theoretical perspective. Ole Kvaernoe, director of the Institute for Strategy at the Faculty of Strategy and Military Operations of the Royal Danish Defence College, most graciously hosted me, which among other things helped me witness civil-military relations in a democratic polity firsthand. The Danish Agency for Science, Technology and Innovation most generously provided financial support for my research while in Denmark. On the other side of the Atlantic, Danielle Pletka, American Enterprise Institute (AEI) vice president for foreign and defense policy studies, generously offered me a position at AEI, and the Smith Richardson Foundation equally generously provided financial support for my research and the publication of this book. My research has benefited from the advice and friendship of present and former colleagues at AEI, including Michael Rubin—without whose friendship this book would not have been possible—Frederick W. Kagan, Reuel Marc Gerecht, Gary J. Schmitt, Thomas Donnelly, Nicholas Eberstadt, Ahmad K. Majidyar, Maseh Zarif, and Will Fulton. While my assistant Daniel Vajdic organized the work of interns engaged in the research project with the zeal of Basij members in the field, AEI's editors and Karin Horler patiently made my English comprehensible. Outside of AEI I am indebted to a large group of individuals in the United States military and the Department of State who do not necessarily share my analysis, but have improved it by continuously inviting me to discuss my findings with them, and friends and colleagues in other think tanks: Patrick Clawson, who opened my eyes to the U.S. policy world by offering me an internship at the Washington Institute for Near East Policy in 1999, Mike Eisenstadt, Kenneth Pollack, Kenneth Katzman, Mehdi Khalaji, Karim Sadjadpour, Alex Vatanka, Afshin Molavi, Mohsen Sazegara, and other friends who prefer to remain anonymous.

1

Introduction

Iran is currently experiencing the most important change in its history since the revolution of 1979 and the establishment of the Islamic Republic: The regime in Tehran, traditionally ruled by the Shia clergy, is transforming into a military dictatorship dominated by the officers of the Islamic Revolutionary Guards Corps (IRGC; *Sepah-e Pasdaran-e Enqelab-e Eslami*). This transformation is changing not only the economy and society in Iran, but also the Islamic Republic's relations with the United States and its allies.

While the Iranian public is gradually coming to understand the scope of the IRGC's powers, policy makers in the United States with the notable exception of former Secretary of State Hillary Clinton, have largely ignored the transformative change in Iran and still consider the Islamic Republic a theocracy with Supreme Leader Ayatollah Ali Khamenei at its helm. This erroneous understanding of Iran has already led to failed U.S. policies. Extending hands of friendship to Khamenei; siding with the regime rather than with Iran's prodemocracy protest movement in the wake of the fraudulent presidential election of June 12, 2009; engaging in negotiations with representatives of the clerical class in Iran; holding a naïve belief in the possibility of a negotiated solution to the nuclear standoff with Iran; answering Iranian provocations with the statement that "all options are on the table" followed by various officials' statements stressing that the United States did not seek to use military power against the Islamic Republic; and instituting gradually tightening sanctions to which the regime in Tehran is adapting have all been counterproductive. The IRGC officers, the new rulers of the Islamic Republic, are likely to consider such initiatives as signs of weakness rather than strength and are therefore not likely to offer concessions in the areas of greatest importance to the United States.

This book aims at correcting the U.S. decision makers' understanding of the nature of the regime in Tehran by discussing how the IRGC is transforming the Islamic Republic into a military dictatorship. This introductory chapter presents the problem that an IRGC-dominated Islamic Republic poses to the West and includes a brief discussion of sources and prior studies. Chapter 2 traces the emergence of the IRGC as a military organization, which explains not only the nature of the IRGC but also the nature of the regime that this organization has managed to dominate. Chapter 3 discusses the IRGC's interventions in the domestic politics of the Islamic Republic. I argue that once the IRGC was invited to intervene in internal politics in order to ensure the survival of the regime, the IRGC took advantage of the disunited civilian politicians and began pursuing its own interests. Chapter 4 discusses the role of the IRGC as an internal security organization from the early years of the revolution until today. Chapters 5 and 6 discuss the IRGC's resiliency in the face of the civilian leadership's use of political/ideological indoctrination and political commissars to subject the IRGC to civilian control. Chapter 7 examines the economic role of the IRGC in the wake of the Iran-Iraq war. This chapter covers the presidencies of Akbar Hashemi Rafsanjani (1989–1997), Mohammad Khatami (1997–2005), and Mahmoud Ahmadinejad (2005–present) to demonstrate the increasing dominance of the IRGC in most fields, from the gradual involvement of the IRGC in the economy of Iran during the postwar reconstruction era to the business empire of the Guards during the Ahmadinejad presidency. Chapter 8 examines the confluence of the IRGC with terrorism under the banner of "exporting the revolution." It shows how the IRGC systematically uses the "export of the revolution" effort to destabilize Bosnia, Afghanistan, Iraq, and Lebanon. This chapter also discusses how external struggles allow the IRGC to strengthen its domestic power in Iran regardless of the catastrophic effects of such policies for the Iranian state as a whole. Finally, Chapter 9 presents the conclusions of the research and offers policy recommendations for the U.S. government.

Some comments on the sources: The erroneous understanding of the nature of the regime in Tehran in the United States may be due to the power of habit and established opinions, the stealthiness of the IRGC's coup d'état, and the limited literature available on the IRGC. Thirty years after the revolution in Iran and the establishment of the Revolutionary Guards, very few serious studies about the armed forces of the Islamic Republic of Iran have been conducted. This book is an attempt to contribute to that literature.

One of the earliest attempts at studying the IRGC still is among the best studies ever completed. Nikola B. Schahgaldian's 1987 book *The Iranian Military Under the Islamic Republic*,[1] prepared for the Office of the Under Secretary of Defense for Policy, remains one of the best studies of the Iranian military, including the IRGC. Systematic interviews with exiled Shah-era officers based in France and the United States, who at the time of the study still had connections with Iran, provided the author with opportunities to deliver a groundbreaking analysis of the IRGC at an early stage. Schahgaldian's study is an exemplary model of policy research, and this book updates the data and analysis provided by Schahgaldian's study beyond 1987. In addition to data provided in Schahgaldian's book, this book also benefits from access to the memoirs of principal actors in the Islamic Republic published in recent years, including the memoirs of Ayatollah Akbar Hashemi Rafsanjani, the late Grand Ayatollah Hossein-Ali Montazeri, and former IRGC commander Mohsen Rezaei.

In the spirit of Schahgaldian's book, Sepehr Zabih's 1988 book *The Iranian Military in Revolution and War*[2] provides some information about the IRGC's role in the immediate aftermath of the collapse of the imperial regime but focuses mostly on the Iran-Iraq war, thereby ignoring the role of the IRGC in internal politics of the Islamic Republic.

A third book, Kenneth Katzman's 1993 book *The Warriors of Islam: Iran's Revolutionary Guard*[3] is a true masterpiece, especially considering that the author wrote the book with no knowledge of the Persian language and only with information extracted from Western sources. Katzman's then controversial conclusion that the IRGC, as opposed to other revolutionary armies, has not become a professional army but still is an ideological force was as true in 1993 as it is today. This book shares this point of departure with Katzman's study.

A 2009 RAND study of the Revolutionary Guards, *The Rise of the Pasdaran: Assessing the Domestic Roles of Iran's Islamic Revolutionary Guards Corps* by Frederic Wehrey and colleagues,[4] does not live up to the standards of Schahgaldian's 1987 study.

The scarcity of literature on the rising power of the IRGC also reflects the fact that U.S. diplomats have had limited access to Iranian officials and the Iranian political process since the takeover of the American embassy in Tehran in 1979. Additionally, secret diplomacy between the United States and Iran, including information obtained through the Department of State's recently established Iran Regional Presence Offices, is restricted to official use, thereby excluding the wider policymaking community from access.

The limited access of the foreign press to Iran constitutes another problem in obtaining information about the Revolutionary Guards. Foreign journalists' and researchers' access to Iran is tightly controlled by the government, the foreign press is not permitted to interview the members of the Revolutionary Guards, and journalists and scholars visiting Iran doing research on far less sensitive issues are occasionally imprisoned on charges of espionage.

Outside the regime, a continuous stream of information is provided by Iranian exiles, including an aging population of civil servants of the prerevolutionary regime but also including an increasing number of revolutionary participants who supported the Islamic regime but have since broken with it and bombarded U.S. policy makers with information. Information provided by the exiles must be evaluated very carefully, but in specific cases, such as the secret correspondence between Bani-Sadr and Khomeini in 1980–1982 and memoirs of Ayatollah Ali-Akbar Hashemi Rafsanjani and Grand Ayatollah Hossein-Ali Montazeri, reveals important information about the Revolutionary Guards during the formative years of the Islamic Republic.

Yet another difficulty in gathering information about the Revolutionary Guards is that there are few former Guardsmen living in exile and available for systematic interviewing. This is primarily because most Guardsmen are heavily involved in shaping the politics of the regime and nurture great aspirations and career plans inside the Islamic Republic. Those Guardsmen who break with the regime may provide information to the secret agencies of Western countries, but such information is not publicly available and remains outside the realm of scholarly research.

This book rests on a systematic analysis of the Persian-language press, including the Revolutionary Guards' mouthpiece *Payam-e Enqelab*, *Sobh-e*

Sadeq, and current IRGC or security service outlets such as *Ansar News*. As the IRGC grows more influential in politics and, indeed, as IRGC service becomes a prerequisite for a political career, the book has also benefited from the wealth of information from various Iranian political factions' websites, which provide biographies and backgrounds of figures both well known in the West and marginal. Old revolutionary newspapers—many of which are available at Princeton University's library—enable documentation of the many parliamentarians, governors, and other bureaucrats who served in the IRGC. By determining which officials served together during the Iran-Iraq war, such analysis can provide insight into informal networks, which are as important as the formal diagrams of power.

Using these publicly available sources of information hitherto untapped, this book discusses how the IRGC officers have risen to power in Iran, and the conclusion discusses the impact of the Islamic Republic's transformation into a military dictatorship.

Notes

1. Nikola B. Schahgaldian, *The Iranian Military Under the Islamic Republic* (Santa Monica, CA: RAND, 1987).

2. Sepehr Zabih, *The Iranian Military in Revolution and War* (London: Routledge, 1988).

3. Kenneth Katzman, *The Warriors of Islam: Iran's Revolutionary Guard* (Boulder, CO: Westview, 1993).

4. Frederic Wehrey, Jerold D. Green, Brian Nichiaporuk, Alireza Nader, Lydia Hansell, Rasool Nafisi, and S. R. Bohandy, *The Rise of the Pasdaran: Assessing the Domestic Roles of Iran's Islamic Revolutionary Guards Corps* (Santa Monica, CA: RAND, 2009).

2

Emergence of the Guards

Each year the official calendar of the Islamic Republic of Iran celebrates Grand Ayatollah Rouhollah Khomeini's decree of April 22, 1979, establishing the Islamic Revolutionary Guards Corps (IRGC; *Sepah-e Pasdaran-e Enqelab-e Eslami*).[1] However, more often than not, the official calendars serve as instruments of historical revisionism depicting history as the Iranian officialdom desires it to have been. It is therefore important to discern between revolutionary mythology and the actual past in an attempt to understand the metamorphosis of the Guards from undisciplined armed groups emerging from the revolutionary chaos of 1979 to the omnipresent entity the IRGC has become.

Such an inquiry is not possible without investigating the formative phase of the IRGC in the year of the revolution. Specific historical circumstances such as the collapse of the Imperial Army intensified the struggle for power among revolutionary leaders after the revolutionary victory, and the threat of civil war in Iran to some degree determined the future role of the Guards in the politics of the Islamic Republic.

2.1. Not One, but Several Guards

On February 12, 1979, Iran descended into revolutionary chaos as the Imperial Army in a public statement declared its "neutrality"[2] in the revolution. Militias with conflicting political ideologies armed with weapons looted from the army and police garrisons emerged to fill the power vacuum in Iran.

The militias of the time can roughly be divided into leftist groups;[3] Islamist groups loyal to Khomeini and his clerical allies in the Council of the Revolution (*Showra-ye Enqelab*), the highest de facto governing body in revolutionary Iran; and opportunistic elements using the revolutionary chaos to enrich themselves. The Islamist groups gradually organized into four major groups: the National Guard (*Gard-e Melli*), the Islamic Revolutionary Guards Corps (*Sepah-e Pasdaran-e Enqelab-e Eslami*), Holy Warriors

TABLE 2-1

ISLAMIST KHOMEINI LOYALISTS AT THE EVE OF THE REVOLUTION

Name of Group	Leading Members
National Guard (*Gard-e Melli*), later called the Islamic Revolutionary Guards Corps (*Sepah-e Pasdaran-e Enqelab-e Eslami*)*	Hassan Abedi, Ali-Mohammad Besharati, Mohammad Gharazi, Danesh Monfared, Mohsen Rafiqdoust, Asghar Sabaghian, Mohsen Sazegara, Mohammad Tavassoli
Islamic Revolutionary Guards Corps (*Sepah-e Pasdaran-e Enqelab-e Eslami*)[1]	Abbas Aqa-Zamani (also known as Abou-Sharif), Abbas Douz-Douzani, Ebrahim Hajj-Mohammad-Zadeh, Yousef Kolahdouz, Javad Mansouri, Mohammad Montazeri
Holy Warriors of the Islamic Revolution (*Mojahedin-e Enqelab-e Eslami*)	Hossein Alam al-Hoda, Kazem Alam al-Hoda, Morteza Alviri, Mohammad Boroujerdi, Abbas Douz-Douzani, Hossein Fadayi, Yousef Foroutan, Ali Jahan-Ara, Behzad Nabavi, Ali-Akbar Parvaresh, Karim Rafii, Mohammad-Ali Rajaei, Mohsen Rezaei, Hossein Sadeqi, Gholam-Hossein Safati Dezfouli, Salman Safavi, Mohammad Salamati, Ali Shamkhani, Mostafa Taj-Zadeh, Mohammad Teyrani, Hassan Vaezi, Mohammad-Bagher Zolghadr
Guardians of the Islamic Revolution (*Gard-e Enqelab-e Eslami*)	Yousef Kolahdouz, Mohammad Montazeri, Mousa Namjou

* Despite having the same name, these groups were two separate organizations.
NOTE: Some individuals were active in several groups.
SOURCE: Rasoul Jafarian, *Jaryan-ha va Sazeman-ha-ye Mazhabi-Siyasi/ye Iran 1320–1357* [Politico-Religious Movements and Organizations in Iran 1941–1979], 5th ed (Tehran: Entesharat-e Markaz-e Asnad-e Enghelab-e Eslami-ye Iran, 2004), pp. 519–525.

of the Islamic Revolution (*Mojahedin-e Enqelab-e Eslami*), and Guardians of the Islamic Revolution (*Gard-e Enqelab-e Eslami*) (Table 2-1).

The National Guard, which gathered at the headquarters of the pre-revolutionary intelligence organization SAVAK (*Sazeman-e Ettelaat Va Amniyat-e Keshvar*) on Saltanat-Abad Avenue, was composed of individuals from the Iran Freedom Movement party led by Prime Minister Mehdi Bazargan and his top advisor and later foreign minister Ebrahim Yazdi. Already by 1953, following the 1953 coup d'état against the populist/nationalist prime minister Mohammad Mossadeq, the group had lost faith in the ability of the Shah's regime to reform itself and chose to prepare for armed struggle against the regime.[4] Besides radicalizing the Iranian political activists, the coup had probably also taught them that a revolutionary movement needed an armed wing to defend it against the army once the revolution had succeeded. Therefore, the Iran Freedom Movement dispatched many of its members to Algeria, Egypt (until 1966), Lebanon, Iraq, and the Palestinian terrorist camps of the Fatah movement[5] to receive military training. Those foreign-trained individuals composed the National Guard, the armed wing of the Iran Freedom Movement.[6] The National Guard later changed its name to the Islamic Revolutionary Guards Corps (*Sepah-e Pasdaran-e Enqelab-e Eslami*),[7] following Yazdi's suggestion.[8] By choosing a new name, the National Guard attempted to avoid linguistic connotations that would link it with the Shah's now-defunct Imperial Guard (*Gard-e Shahanshahi*)[9] and "incompatibility with Islamic culture and theories of Islamist ideology."[10]

The second group was incidentally also called the Islamic Revolutionary Guards Corps (*Sepah-e Pasdaran-e Enqelab-e Eslami*) but was formed by former political prisoners supporting the revolutionary leadership and was led by Ayatollah Abd al-Karim Mousavi Ardebili. On May 5, 1979, the Council of the Revolution issued a statement clarifying that this force was "created by the decree of the Grand Leader of the Islamic Revolution, Imam Khomeini" and functioned "under the supervision of the Council of the Revolution."[11]

Holy Warriors of the Islamic Revolution (*Mojahedin-e Enqelab-e Eslami*) was an umbrella organization encompassing seven armed groups: United Community of Believers (*Ommat-e Vahedeh*), Badr Divine [Organization] (*Towhidi-ye Badr*), Divine Enlistees' [Organization] (*Towhidi-ye*

Saf), Peasant (*Fallah*), Split [Organization] (*Falaq*), The Victorious (*Mansouroun*), and The United Ones (*Movahedin*) (Table 2-2).[12] These groups were prerevolutionary terrorist organizations whose leaders kept in close contact with Khomeini in the years before the revolution. Interestingly, most members of the seven groups were individuals who had left the Mojahedin-e Khalq organization after the Marxist orientation of the organization increased in prerevolutionary prisons.[13]

TABLE 2-2

COMPOSITION AND LEADING MEMBERS OF THE UMBRELLA ORGANIZATION
HOLY WARRIORS OF THE ISLAMIC REVOLUTION

Name of Group	Leading Members
United Community of Believers (*Ommat-e Vahedeh*)	Behzad Nabavi, Mohammad Salamati, Mohsen Makhmalbaf, Mohammad-Sadegh Nowrouzi, Ahmad Khatami, Ali Ghannad-ha, Feiz-Allah Arab-Sorkhi, Parviz Ghadyani, Mehdi Nikdel, Ali Shojai-Zand, Behnam Sharifi, Javad Sharifi, Ali Sakhy, Abbas Yazdan-Fam, Rahmani*
Badr Divine [Organization] (*Towhidi-ye Badr*)	Hossein Fadayi, Ali Asgari, Hossein Hashemi, Hassan Eslami-Mehr, Hamid Fatehi, Hassan Taher-Nezhad, Vahid Kalhor, Hossein Asef, Maddahi,* Mohammad-Ali Taghavi-Rad, Mohsen Okhovat, Abd al-Rasoul Sabzevari (Ramin), Hassan Abrisham-Chi, Reza Badeh-Peyma, Mohammad Fadayi, Safar Naimi, Hamid Ghalanbar, Masoumeh Jazayeri
Divine Enlistees' [Organization] (*Towhidi-ye Saf*)	Mohammad Boroujerdi, Hossein Sadeqi, Mostafa Tahayyori, Akbar Barati, Mohsen Armin, Salman Safavi, Hossein Shakouri, Hadi Bik-Zadeh, Ahmad Torshiji, Mojtaba Shakeri, Mohammad Shaghaghi, Amir Ostad-Ebrahim, Abbas-Ali Ahmadi, Davoud Ajab-Gol, Ali Tahayyori, Ali Nakhli, Naser Rahimi, Zohreh Bonyanian
Peasant (*Fallah*)	Morteza Alviri, Hassan Montazer-Ghaem, Mohammad Razavi, Mohsen Shariatmadari, Habib-Allah Dadashi, Masoumeh Khosh-Soulatan, Mahin Alviri, Hossein Sheikh-Attar, Nader Halimi, Hamid Maghfour Maghrebi, Esmail-Nezhad, Kalanki,* Yousef Foroutan, Haj-Ali-Beygi
Split [Organization] (*Falaq*)	Hassan Vaezi, Mostafa Tajzadeh, Javad Yasini, Mahmoud Yasini, Homayoun Khosravi, Ali Tabatabai, Behrouz Makouyi, Mohammad Teyrani, Hassan Poushnegar

The Victorious (*Mansouroun*)	Mohsen Rezaei, Mohammad-Bagher Zolghadr, Hossein Zibayi-Nezhad (Nejat), Hassan Hamid-Zadeh, Gholam-Reza Basir-Zadeh, Morteza Sarmast, Sarraf-Pour,* Abdollah-Zadeh, Ali Shamkhani, Gholam-Ali Rashid, Gholam-Hossein Safati Dezfouli, Karim Rafii, Ali Jahan-Ara, Nour al-Din Shah Safdari, Mehdi Honar-Dar, Esmail Daghayeghi, Aziz Safari, Hassan Hormozi
The United Ones (*Movahedin*)	Hossein Alam al-Hoda, Mahmoud Bakhshandeh, Mohammad-Ali Maleki

* First name unavailable.

SOURCE: Mohammad Saidi, *Sazeman-e Mojahedin-e Enghelab-e Eslami Az Tasis Ta Enhelal 1358–1365* [Mojahedin of the Islamic Revolution Organization from Establishment to Dissolution 1979–1986] (Tehran: Markaz-e Asnad-e Enghelab-e Eslami, 2006).

The fourth group, Guardians of the Islamic Revolution (*Gard-e Enqelab-e Eslami*), headed by Hojjat al-Eslam Mohammad Montazeri, son of Grand Ayatollah Hossein-Ali Montazeri, also functioned as the strong arm of Khomeini in the streets of Tehran. Mohammad Montazeri was also a former member of the Mojahedin-e Khalq organization.[14] Prior to the revolution, Mohammad Montazeri's group had its operational base and training facilities in Syria and Lebanon,[15] and Mohammad Montazeri's group also used "equipments of Palestinian fighters to train and organize it."[16]

Khomeini endorsed the four militias for several reasons. Despite the Imperial Army's declaration of neutrality, the revolutionary leadership did not trust it and feared a U.S.-backed military coup conducted by the remaining members of the Shah's army. Khomeini and his closest allies also distrusted leftist guerillas such as the Mojahedin-e Khalq organization, Fadayin, Tudeh, Peykar, Razmandegan, Rah-e Karegar, Shora-ye Mottahed-e Chap, Toufan, Sazeman-e Vahdat-e Komunisti, Ettehadiyeh-ye Komonist-ha, and the like.[17] Therefore, the revolutionary leadership felt the need for a trustworthy armed wing to protect Khomeini's regime against both the remnants of the Imperial Army and rival armed groups.

2.2. Unification of the Guards, Institutionalization of Factionalism

Khomeini instinctively knew that competition between the multiple guards loyal to him would weaken them and leave the revolutionary regime vulnerable to coup attempts. To solve the problem of competing guards, Khomeini, along with the revolutionary clergymen in the Council of the Revolution, suggested creation of a unified Revolutionary Guards Corps incorporating the four paramilitary forces. They tasked Mohsen Rafiqdoust, who served as Khomeini's chauffeur upon his return to Tehran, first to infiltrate the largest militia, the National Guard, and afterward to unify the National Guard with the other pro-Khomeini militias.[18]

According to Rafiqdoust's memoirs, he invited members of the various Guards "[Mohammad] Montazeri, [Mohammad] Boroujerdi, and [Abbas Aqa-Zamani, also known as] Abou-Sharif"[19] to his office and explained: "Your existence is not legally mandated. It is only the Guards [the militia of which Rafiqdoust was a member] which has been formed upon decree of the Imam [Khomeini]."[20] Rafiqdoust knew that one of the main reasons why the guards refused to unite was that they did not trust Bazargan's transitional government and preferred to be led by Khomeini. Therefore, Rafiqdoust added: "I too disagree with relationship of the Guards with the transitional government, but since it is the decree of the Imam [Khomeini] we must all obey. Now we are all neutralizing each other's efforts."[21] According to Rafiqdoust, the others protested against his proposal to unify the guards and centralize the revolutionary paramilitary organizations, but at some point Rafiqdoust allegedly took his Colt 45 and said: "If the problem is not solved here and now, I will first kill the three of you and then myself!"[22] If we believe Rafiqdoust's memoirs, his argument proved persuasive and the others agreed to appoint representatives to negotiate unification of the guards.[23]

Rafiqdoust's account leaves the impression of one man imposing his will upon four armed groups, which seems very unlikely. In reality, unification of the guards was subjected to a process of negotiation between the various armed militias (Table 2-3), and the result was a compromise between the different forces. Negotiations took place within the framework of the so-called IRGC Command Council, which was established with representatives present from all the groups constituting the new IRGC.

The IRGC Command Council, composed of the collective leadership of the IRGC, became the highest decision-making unit of the guards, but it was still unclear if it received its directions from the transitional government or from the Council of the Revolution. The IRGC weekly

TABLE 2-3

FACTIONS NEGOTIATING UNIFICATION OF THE GUARDS IN 1979

Militia Name	Members in the Command Council Preparing for Unification
National Guard	Mohammad Gharazi, Mohsen Rafiqdoust, Asghar Sabaghian, Mohsen Sazegara
Islamic Revolutionary Guards Corps	Abbas Aqa-Zamani, Abbas Douz-Douzani, Yousef Kolahdouz (representing Hojjat al-Eslam Mohammad Montazeri), Javad Mansouri
Holy Warriors of the Islamic Revolution	Morteza Alviri, Mohammad Boroujerdi, Yousef Foroutan, Mohsen Rezaei

SOURCES: Hadi Nokhi and Hossen Yekta (eds.), *Rouzshomar-e Jang-e Iran va Eragh* [Chronology of the Iran-Iraq War], vol. 1 (Tehran: Markaz-e Mottaleat va Tahghighat-e Jang-e Sepah-e Pasdaran-e Enghelab-e Eslami, 1996), p. 882. There is a slight difference in the names provided by Rafiqdoust. Mohsen Rafiqdoust, *Khaterat-e Mohsen Rafiqdoust* [Memoirs of Mohsen Rafiqdoust], edited by Davoud Ghasem-Pour (Tehran: Markaz-e Asnad-e Enqelab-e Eslami, 2004), pp. 180–181.

Payam-e Enqelab's retrospective article[24] and Abbas Douz-Douzani's memoirs[25] suggest the latter, pointing to Khomeini's decree of April 22, 1979,[26] while members of the transitional government and their supporters within the IRGC recall the former.[27]

Following the unification of the guards, with the notable exceptions of Rafiqdoust, the infiltrator, who was appointed logistics bureau chief, and intelligence and investigations bureau chief Ali-Mohammad Besharati, no other representatives of the pro–interim government National Guard militia were present in the IRGC Command Council. Financial and administration commander Esmail Davoudi Shamsi is believed to have been connected to several members of the Mojahedin-e Khalq organization through his company Cybernatics,[28] training bureau commander Captain Yousef Kolahdouz—a defector from the Imperial Army—was originally from Mohammad Montazeri's Guardians of the Islamic Revolution, operations bureau commander Abbas Aqa-Zamani was from Mousavi Ardebili's militia but was also an old ally of Mohammad Montazeri who facilitated his terrorist training in Lebanon in 1975,[29] and public relations bureau chief Morteza Alviri was originally from Holy

FIGURE 2-1

ATTEMPTED RECONSTRUCTION OF THE ORGANIZATIONAL CHART
OF THE IRGC AS OF APRIL 22, 1979

Armed forces commander in chief: Khomeini

Representative of Khomeini in
the IRGC: Lahouti Eshkevari

IRGC Coordination Council

Representatives of the Council of the Revolution Hashemi Rafsanjani and Khamenei; representative of the government Ebrahim Yazdi; representative of the IRGC Command Council Javad Mansouri

IRGC Command Council

IRGC commander in chief Javad Mansouri; training bureau commander Captain Yousef Kolahdouz; operations bureau commander Abbas Aqa-Zamani (Abou-Sharif); intelligence and investigations bureau commander Ali-Mohammad Besharati; financial and administration bureau commander Esmail Davoudi Shamsi; public relations bureau commander Morteza Alviri; deputy relations deputy Yousef Foroutan; logistics bureau commander Mohsen

| Logistics Bureau Commander: Mohsen Rafiqdoust | Financial and Administration Bureau Commander: Esmail Davoudi Shamsi | Training Bureau Commander: Captain Yousef Kolahdouz | Operations Bureau Commander: Abbas Aqa-Zamani (Abou-Sharif) | Intelligence and Investigations Bureau Commander: Ali-Mohammad Besharati | Public Relations Bureau Commander: Morteza Alviri |

Provincial IRGC Command Council

Unit chiefs at provincial level

Unit chiefs at subprovincial level

Individual IRGC members

SOURCES: "Zarourat-e Tashkil-e Sepah-e Pasdaran-e Enghelab-e Eslami" [The Necessity of Establishment of the Islamic Revolutionary Guards Corps], *Payam-e Enqelab* (Tehran), February 16, 1981, pp. 38–39; and Hadi Nokhi and Hossen Yekta (eds.), *Rouzshomar-e Jang-e Iran va Eragh* [Chronology of the Iran-Iraq War], vol. 1 (Tehran: Markaz-e Mottaleat va Tahghighat-e Jang-e Sepah-e Pasdaran-e Enghelab-e Eslami, 1996), p. 741.

Warriors of the Islamic Revolution. (See Figure 2-1.) Thereby the IRGC in reality institutionalized the factionalism that existed prior to unification of the guards, which as we shall see later created many crises within the guards, especially during the first decade of the Islamic Republic.

Notes

1. Asgar Abbas-Nezhad, "Ketab-Shenasi-ye Sepah-e Pasdaran-e Enqelab-e Eslami" [Bibliography of the Islamic Revolutionary Guards Corps], Iran Book News Agency (Tehran), April 21, 2009. Available in Persian at http://www.ibna.ir/vdcamane.49n0a15kk4.txt (accessed November 10, 2009).

2. Abbas Qarabaqi, *Haghayeghi Darbareh-ye Bohran-e Iran* [Facts about the Iranian Crisis] (Paris: Soheil, 1984), pp. 458–459.

3. Nikola B. Shahgaldian, *The Iranian Military under the Islamic Republic* (Santa Monica, CA: RAND, 1987), p. 65.

4. Nehzat-e Azadi-ye Iran, *Zendegi-Nameh-ye Sardar-e Rashid-e Eslam Shahid Doktor Mostafa Chamran* [Biography of the Great Commander of Islam, Martyr Dr. Mostafa Chamran] (N.p.: Iran Freedom Movement, November 1982), p. 19.

5. Ibid., pp. 21, 23, 27.

6. "Nahadi Movaghat Boud Ke Daemi Shod" [A Transitional Institution Made Permanent], Iran Freedom Movement website (Tehran), July 7, 2008. Available in Persian at http://www.nehzateazadi.net/bayanieh/87/87_n_0417_b.htm (accessed November 24, 2008).

7. "Mosahebeh-ye Matbouati-ye Masoulan-e Sepah-e Pasdaran-e Enqelab-e Eslami-ye Iran" [Press Interview of the Authorities of the Islamic Revolutionary Guards Corps of Iran], *Kayhan* (Tehran), June 13, 1979, p. 4, quoted in Hossein Yekta (ed.), *Rouzshomar-e Jang-e Iran va Eragh* [Chronology of the Iran-Iraq War], vol. 2, 2nd ed. (Tehran: Markaz-e Motaleat Va Tahghighat-e Jang, 2008), pp. 487–489.

8. "Tasis-e Sepah-e Pasdaran Be Revayat-e Ebrahim-e Yazdi" [Establishment of the Revolutionary Guards according to Ebrahim Yazdi], *Shahrvand-e Emrouz* (Tehran), September 16, 2007. Available in Persian at http://shahrvandemroz.blogfa.com/post-221.aspx (accessed December 6, 2008).

9. "Nahadi Movaghat Boud Ke Daemi Shod."

10. "Zarourat-e Tashkil-e Sepah-e Pasdaran-e Enqelab-e Eslami" [The Necessity of Establishment of the Islamic Revolutionary Guards Corps], *Payam-e Enqelab* (Tehran), February 16, 1981, p. 36.

11. "Bayaniyeh-ye Showra-ye Enqelab" [Statement of the Council of the Revolution], *Ettelaat* (Tehran), May 6, 1979, quoted in Akbar Hashemi Rafsanjani, *Enqelab Va Pirouzi* [Revolution and Victory], edited by Abbas Bashiri and Mohsen Hashemi (Tehran: Daftar-e Nashr-e Maaref-e Enqelab, 2004), pp. 283–284.

12. Mohammad Saidi, *Sazeman-e Mojahedin-e Enqelab-e Eslami Az Tasis Ta Enhelal 1358–1365* [Mojahedin of the Islamic Revolution Organization from

Establishment to Dissolution 1979–1986] (Tehran: Markaz-e Asnad-e Enqelab-e Eslami, 2006).

13. Ibid.

14. Shahrbanou Rajabi and Hojjat-Allah Taheri, *Shahid Mohammad Montazeri Be Revayat-e Asnad-e SAVAK* [Martyr Mohammad Montazeri according to the SAVAK Documents] (Tehran: Markaz-e Asnad-e Enqelab-e Eslami, 1999), p. 259.

15. Marziyeh Hadid-Chi Dabbagh, *Khaterat-e Marziyeh Hadid-Chi (Dabbagh)* [Memoirs of Marziyeh Hadid-Chi (Dabbagh)], 7th ed., edited by Mohsen Kazemi (Tehran: Daftar-e Adabyiat-e Enqelab-e Eslami, 2007), pp. 112–113.

16. Rajabi and Taheri, *Shahid Mohammad Montazeri Be Revayat-e Asnad-e SAVAK*, p. 60.

17. Shahgaldian, *The Iranian Military Under the Islamic Republic*, p. 65.

18. Ali Danesh-Monfared, *Khaterat-e Ali Danesh-Monfared* [Memoirs of Ali Danesh-Monfared], edited by Reza Bastami (Tehran: Markaz-e Asnad-e Enqelab-e Eslami, 2005), p. 89.

19. Mohsen Rafiqdoust, *Khaterat-e Mohsen Rafiqdoust* [Memoirs of Mohsen Rafiqdoust], edited by Davoud Ghasem-Pour (Tehran: Markaz-e Asnad-e Enqelab-e Eslami, 2004), p. 179.

20. Ibid.

21. Ibid.

22. Ibid.

23. Ibid., p. 180.

24. "Zarourat-e Tashkil-e Sepah-e Pasdaran-e Enqelab-e Eslami," p. 34.

25. "Tashkil-e Sepah Be Revayat-e Abbas-e Douz-Douzani" [Establishment of the Guards According to Abbas Douz-Douzani], Alef News (Tehran), April 21, 2008. Available in Persian at http://alef.ir/content/view/24972/ (accessed March 23, 2009).

26. "Zarourat-e Tashkil-e Sepah-e Pasdaran-e Enqelab-e Eslami," p. 36.

27. "Tasis-e Sepah-e Pasdaran Be Revayat-e Ebrahim-e Yazdi."

28. "Chegounegi-ye Nofouz-e Keshmiri" [Keshmiri's Infiltration], Mohammad-Mehdi Eslami's blog (Tehran), August 30, 2008. Available in Persian at http://taknevshteha.persianblog.ir/post/103 (accessed December 5, 2008).

29. Javad Mansouri, *Khaterat-e Javad-e Mansouri* [Memoirs of Javad Mansouri], 1st ed. (Tehran: Daftar-e Adabiyat-e Enqelab, 1997), p. 85.

3

The Revolutionary Guards' Role
in Domestic Politics

Ever since the emergence of the Revolutionary Guards from the revolutionary chaos of 1979, authority in the Islamic Republic has rested upon a fundamental alliance between the revolutionary Shia clergy and the Islamic Revolutionary Guards Corps (IRGC). Within the alliance there was a clear division of labor between the two institutions: While the revolutionary Shia clergy has ruled Iran since 1979, the IRGC was tasked with "safeguarding the revolution and its achievements,"[1] meaning the revolutionary and ideological nature of the regime, against internal and external enemies of the regime.[2] But today, as the IRGC is infiltrating all spheres of life in Iran, the Islamic Republic is increasingly being both ruled and guarded by the Guards. This development is in turn transforming Iran into a military dictatorship.

The rise of the Guards has been deliberate: As Grand Ayatollah Rouhollah Khomeini found his rule challenged by the domestic opposition, he systematically used the IRGC to suppress the challengers, which in turn made the IRGC a major player in the domestic politics of Iran during the first decade after the revolution. This trend accelerated under Ayatollah Ali Khamenei: Facing increasing internal pressures for political and economic liberalization, which the regime is either unwilling to deliver or incapable of delivering, and external pressures in the development of the Islamic Republic's nuclear program, Khamenei has instrumentally used the IRGC and its former officers, such as Mahmoud Ahmadinejad, in an attempt to suppress demands for reform. As Ahmadinejad grew too independent of Khamenei, the Supreme Leader has again used the IRGC to restrict the unruly president's powers, which further empowers the IRGC.

Just as they did under Khomeini, as former IRGC officers have seized positions of power, they have become indifferent to the preferences of the civilian leadership, and the IRGC uses disunity among the civilians to pursue its own corporate interests. The increasing rift between Khamenei and Ahmadinejad is a clear example of this phenomenon. This trend has made the Guards a state within the state, and civilian leaders, including Khamenei and anyone else who may succeed him, find themselves hostages in the hands of the regime's own praetorian guard.

3.1. Legal Framework

The IRGC's interventions in the domestic politics of the Islamic Republic can be traced back to the early days of the revolution and the extraordinary codified powers the civilian leadership gave to the Guards to protect the civilian leadership against internal enemies.

The official calendar of the Islamic Republic considers April 22, 1979, as the day the Leader of the Revolution, Khomeini, issued a decree formally recognizing the IRGC as a revolutionary institution.[3] The statute of the IRGC, which provided the earliest legal framework for the organization's operations, was, according to *Payam-e Enqelab*, the IRGC's official mouthpiece, prepared by "some brothers from the Guards" and was ratified on April 25, 1979,[4] by the Council of the Revolution,[5] the de facto highest governing body, in the months after Khomeini returned to Iran.[6]

The statute gave a very broad goal to the IRGC: "Article 1—The Goal: Guarding the Islamic revolution in Iran, expanding it [abroad] according to the pure Islamic ideology, and executing the will of the Islamic Republic is the goal of establishment of the Islamic Revolutionary Guards Corps."[7] In order to achieve this goal, the statute gave the IRGC both the role of an army in Article 2.1, "defending the country in the face of or during the presence of foreign occupiers inside of the country,"[8] and a police role in Article 2.2, "cooperating with the government in police and security affairs, pursuit and arrest of counterrevolutionary elements at the time of weakness of or lack of establishment of police forces to counter the armed counterrevolutionary currents."[9] The IRGC was also tasked with "intelligence collection" (Article 2.5), "assisting liberation justice seeking movements of the oppressed" (Article 2.10), and even relief and rescue missions in the case of natural disasters.[10]

The statute passed by parliament on September 6, 1982, made only slight changes in the original statute of the Guards and enshrined these principles in law.[11] However, the codified statute differentiated between individual and institutional activities. Most importantly, the statute prohibited individual Guardsmen from political activity and made "nonmembership in political parties, groupings, and institutions...[a] condition of being a member of the Revolutionary Guards"[12] but enabled ample avenues for the Guards to intervene as a whole. Indeed, the statute's first chapter charged the Guards, under the Supreme Leader's direction, to "realize the divine ideology and expand the rule of God through the legislation of the Islamic Republic of Iran," and in the second chapter the statute enabled the IRGC to "reinforce the defense body of the Islamic Republic through cooperation with other armed forces and military training and organization of popular forces."[13]

The Constitution of the Islamic Republic of Iran, which was adopted by referendum on October 24, 1979, and went into force on December 3, 1979, strengthened the politicized nature of the IRGC. Article 150 of the Constitution declared: "The Islamic Revolutionary Guards Corps...is to be maintained so that it may continue in its role of guarding the revolution and its achievements. The scope of the duties of this corps and its areas of responsibility, in relation to the duties and areas of responsibility of the other armed forces, are to be determined by law with emphasis on brotherly cooperation and harmony among them."[14]

A strict reading of Article 150 shows that the Guards' intervention in politics is not constitutionally mandated, yet at the same time such behavior is not legally prohibited. Nowhere does the Constitution define the "enemies" against whom the IRGC is obliged to guard the revolution. It is even unclear whether the IRGC's primary role would be defense against external threats, in which case it should act as an army, or internal threats, in which it might act as a police force, which maintained the dual ideological roles of the IRGC as army and police as defined in the first statute of the Guards.

Both the statute of the Guards and the Constitution gave the IRGC a distinctly politicized nature, which the IRGC leadership has since nurtured. The July 25, 1981, issue of *Payam-e Enqelab* defined "the two main tasks of the Guards" as "guarding the principle of government by the Guardian Jurist and the principle of *jihad* [holy struggle]." Therefore, the article concluded, "the Guards cannot be robbed of a political dimension or ideological beliefs."[15]

From its very start, therefore, Islamic Republic law made the Guards not only a military organization deterring foreign threats but also a political-military organization tasked with fighting domestic opposition. Today, the Guards defends its expansionist role by referring to the legal framework to justify IRGC interventions[16] and increasingly targets the very same civilian politicians who in the early years of the revolution gave those vast powers to the IRGC.

3.2. A History of Politicization

There is also another reason behind the transformation of the Islamic Republic into a military dictatorship: the Iranian leadership's continuous use of the Guards to suppress internal dissent. Khamenei and before him Khomeini actively employed the Revolutionary Guards to coerce and, when necessary, crush former political allies as they attempted to consolidate power among the revolutionary elites of the Islamic Republic. This policy not only paved the way for the IRGC to intervene in domestic politics of the Islamic Republic but also enabled the IRGC commanders to take advantage of the internal divisions among civilian politicians in order to keep the IRGC outside of civilian political control.

3.2.1. The IRGC against Mehdi Bazargan's Cabinet The first civilian government of the Islamic Republic was also the first victim of the predatory behavior of the IRGC. Prime Minister Mehdi Bazargan opposed the IRGC's existence outside of the control of the formal power centers,[17] called for incorporation of the IRGC into the police and regular army, and warned the Iranian public of the "imminent danger" of the Guards' intervention in politics. Bazargan begged Khomeini to enforce the principle of the military's nonintervention in political affairs, but to no avail.[18] Khomeini, on the other hand, issued the decree formally recognizing the IRGC, which demonstrates that Khomeini, from the outset, desired to marginalize Bazargan and the so-called "liberal" current by using the IRGC as an instrument to undermine Bazargan.

The IRGC willingly served as the strong arms of Khomeini against Bazargan and the interim government, which from the viewpoint of the IRGC were the main enemy. Former commander of the political bureau of the Guards Ebrahim Hajj-Mohammad-Zadeh in a later interview explained the conflict between the transitional government and the IRGC in detail: "The transitional government was of the belief that we have the Army, the Police and Gendarmerie. Therefore, the Guards and the [Revolutionary] Committees should only operate for a short period until those forces could reorganize and after that leave the arena in practical terms. This was the very root of the problem between the transitional government and the Guards."[19] Hajj-Mohammad-Zadeh also explains that the Guardsmen were of the belief that the revolutionary regime was in need of an ideological army: "The Islamic Revolutionary Guards Corps does not fulfill the mission of the Army, the Gendarmerie or the City Police and does not desire to become a rival to those forces. It is true that the Guards performs some of the obligations of those forces, but this is only temporary and the [real] mission of the Guards is to raise the Twenty Million Man Army."[20]

In later statements the IRGC complained of "uncooperativeness and even the transitional government ignoring the Guards,"[21] and *Payam-e Enqelab* went as far as calling the transitional government "groups opposed to Islam, the leadership and the Guardianship of the Jurist who in various ways opposed revolutionary institutions such as the Guards."[22]

The IRGC's machinations against Bazargan's government went far beyond slander and criticism in the IRGC media outlets. The November 4, 1979, seizure of the U.S. embassy in Tehran and hostage taking of American diplomats provided the IRGC with the opportunity to depose Bazargan's cabinet.

It is not difficult to establish the fact that the IRGC was tasked with guarding the U.S. embassy compound on November 4, 1979, on the day a group called Muslim Students Following the Line of the Imam[23] attacked the embassy in Tehran and took U.S. diplomats hostage for the following 444 days. According to the Revolutionary Guards themselves, the IRGC was tasked with guarding the U.S. embassy compound and indeed guarded it prior to and on the day of the takeover. On May 24, 1979, the public relations directorate of the Revolutionary Guards claimed responsibility in *Kayhan* for security of the U.S. embassy in the neighborhood in which the embassy is located. The statement was made prior to an announced anti-U.S. rally, and full cooperation of the public was required in order "not to provide the enemy with excuses."[24]

It is also possible to establish the fact that the IRGC was able to prevent the attack but chose not to. An *Ettelaat* report from the rally stressed that despite the ferocity of the demonstration, the U.S. embassy was guarded "severely" by the IRGC, which prevented the demonstrators from entering the premises of the embassy.[25] In other words, in May 1979 the Revolutionary Guards was fully capable of stopping the demonstrators from attacking the U.S. embassy. But why did the IRGC not intervene in November 1979 to prevent the seizure of the embassy?

The answer is that by at the very least failing to protect the U.S. embassy on November 4, 1979, or alternatively by using the anti-U.S. students as a cover to perpetrate the embassy takeover itself, the IRGC achieved several goals: First, the IRGC managed to remove the transitional government, which insisted that the IRGC should report to it[26] while the IRGC commanders desired to report to Khomeini.[27] Therefore, wishing to avoid subjugation of the IRGC to the transitional government, the IRGC had a strong motive to topple Bazargan. Second, by deliberately failing to defend the U.S. embassy or actively participating in the embassy takeover, the IRGC foiled the transitional government's dealings with U.S. representatives in Algiers on November 1, 1979. Third and most importantly, through the embassy takeover the IRGC obtained sensitive documents on secret negotiations between senior members of the transitional government, and clerical challengers to Khomeini such as Grand Ayatollah Mohammad-Kazem Shariatmadari, with American diplomats in Tehran, which the IRGC could use to discredit the challengers. Fourth, the IRGC, in a 1981 retrospective article, stressed that the seizure of the U.S. embassy and the hostage affair "showed the true nature of gangs and groups and deviant lines, whose positions had alienated them from the nation and [forced them to] oppose the line of the Imam [Khomeini]. ...Were it not for this affair, assessment of these intellectual and political movements would have taken years. ...The affair cleansed the revolution from impure elements."[28]

3.2.2. The IRGC against Bani-Sadr The Guards next set its sights on Abol-Hassan Bani-Sadr, first president of the Islamic Republic, and the Mojahedin-e Khalq organization, a one-time ally of Khomeini. Bani-Sadr's opposition to clerical rule and revolutionary excesses—such as the hostage taking of American diplomats in Tehran—put him in a permanent position of conflict with Grand Ayatollah Khomeini, large parts of the revolutionary clergy, and revolutionary institutions such as the IRGC.

Initially Khomeini appointed Bani-Sadr commander in chief of the armed forces,[29] in order to create a unified military command structure, but also to end ethnic uprisings in Iran's periphery regions. Bani-Sadr suggested a negotiated solution to end ethnic unrest. The IRGC, on the other hand, advocated a hardline policy and began scheming behind the back of the president and commander in chief.

In his first letter of complaint to Khomeini, dated May 22, 1980, Bani-Sadr raised the issue of the role of the Guards in suppression of "the unprivileged Arab people [in Southern Iran]." "I'm sure," wrote Bani-Sadr, "that their elements in the Guards will approach you and say things against the Army and the Gendarmerie and will once again do away with the cooperation between the two and will promote disorder and insecurity."[30] In another remarkable letter, dated June 15, 1980, Bani-Sadr warned Khomeini of further ethnic unrest in Iran as a result of the heavy-handed suppression of ethnic and religious minorities at the hands of the IRGC.[31] Bani-Sadr elaborated: "All in all, [the IRGC desires] to start an all-out general assault and subject the people to a series of great dangers, [and the IRGC desires] to arm the people under the auspices of an armed and ideological group—the sole incorruptible group—in order to cleanse Iran of the counterrevolution in a swift move and a general war."[32] Khomeini gravitated toward the IRGC's line, and Bani-Sadr lost his first battle to the IRGC.

Bani-Sadr also tried to use his powers to appoint his political allies as top IRGC commanders. On May 23, 1980, Bani-Sadr appointed Abbas Aqa-Zamani, also known as Abou-Sharif,[33] as IRGC commander, but Aqa-Zamani resigned shortly thereafter on June 17, 1980.[34] In a letter dated June 15, 1980, just two days prior to Aqa-Zamani's resignation, Bani-Sadr complained to Khomeini of "the trouble over leadership in the Revolutionary Guards."[35] As it appears from the text of the letter, the

Guards had directly challenged the president and the president's appointee to the IRGC: "Instead of proceeding with the plans they made it be known that one can't work with Abou-Sharif."[36] Bani-Sadr also faced a wave of resignations among the top IRGC leadership, personified by Abbas Douz-Douzani and Yousef Kolahdouz, in protest against the commander in chief's attempts at dominating the IRGC.[37] Bani-Sadr next turned to Mohammad-Kazem Mousavi Bojnourdi to head the IRGC, but after a few days of deliberation in which the most powerful elements within the IRGC expressed their opposition, he declined the appointment.[38] The IRGC lobbied for Morteza Rezaei, who was eventually appointed IRGC commander, demonstrating that the IRGC rather than the commander in chief had the real power to appoint the IRGC commander.

Once Bani-Sadr's attempt at subjecting the IRGC to command of his friends and allies failed, Bani-Sadr intensified his support of the regular army in order to counterbalance the power of the IRGC and the radical clerical faction allied with it. Ahmad Khomeini recalls: "Bani-Sadr did not like the Guards and it is obvious why. Bani-Sadr wanted to gain absolute power in Iran and considered the Guards the primary and most powerful group resisting him. When he was with the Imam [Khomeini] he would always oppose [positions of the] Guards, or badmouth pious and ideological elements of the Army."[39] Ahmad Khomeini also adds that Bani-Sadr would complain about the lack of discipline and the rebellious, antilegal nature of the Guards.[40] According to Ahmad Khomeini, Bani-Sadr saw to it that the Guardsmen were not allowed to have heavy arms and "hoped they would be killed in the hands of the Iraqis!"[41] Akbar Hashemi Rafsanjani's memoirs reveal the same story of Bani-Sadr ignoring the needs of the Guards, which naturally intensified the IRGC's machinations against him: "The revolutionary forces believed that one cannot deal lightly with Bani-Sadr ignoring the forces of the Guards, because it had locked all things in the front and there was no movement…they were denied arms."[42] These assessments in general reveal Bani-Sadr's preference for the regular military rather than the IRGC.

Bani-Sadr also received another blow from the hostile IRGC. Bani-Sadr was opposed to the prolongation of the hostage taking of the American diplomats in Tehran and argued: "It is such a great pity that we make an entire nation hostages of the United States in return for fifty individuals [the U.S. diplomats] and make the hostages a 'trump' against the president [a reference both to U.S. president Jimmy Carter and to Bani-Sadr himself]. ...Is it not a pity that we abandon our main job, which is the real independence of the country, and use the hostages in the internal power struggle?"[43] In later interviews, leading members of the Guards reveal Bani-Sadr's energetic attempts at freeing the hostages. Hajj-Mohammad-Zadeh recalls Bani-Sadr requesting a meeting with the IRGC leadership to discuss the hostage affair.[44] When Bani-Sadr showed up at the meeting he allegedly took a Quran out of his pocket, recited parts of it, and called for release of the hostages, only to be ignored by the IRGC commanders.[45]

Part of the reason why the IRGC leadership managed to neutralize Bani-Sadr's attempts at controlling the Guards was the IRGC's ability to use disunity among civilian politicians to their advantage. For example, the IRGC commanders would reach out to Grand Ayatollah Hossein-Ali Montazeri, convincing him that "Mr. Bani-Sadr takes the issue of the war very lightly, which will result in our defeat."[46] Grand Ayatollah Montazeri, who like the rest of the revolutionary clerical establishment considered Bani-Sadr a secularist, would use this information to reach out to Grand Ayatollah Khomeini to complain about Bani-Sadr.[47] Grand Ayatollah Montazeri also tried on several occasions to convince Khomeini that Bani-Sadr was sponsoring a "certain political movement in the Army,"[48] trying to scare Khomeini with the threat of Bani-Sadr planning a military coup against the clerics.

Increasingly isolated, Bani-Sadr tried to create an alliance with the Mojahedin-e Khalq organization leader Masoud Rajavi. When criticized for his contacts with the Mojahedin-e Khalq organization, Bani-Sadr allegedly responded:

> I need such groups. When we asked the [West] German govern-
> ment how come they have joined the sanctions regime against
> Iran, they told us that they had studied the medical records of
> the Imam [Khomeini] and concluded that he will not live for
> more than three months. Therefore, the Imam will pass away
> in three months and the clergy will become factionalized. This
> [the Mojahedin-e Khalq organization] is the only group which

will survive because of its organizational capabilities and they have takeover power. I need this group.[49]

Divisions between Bani-Sadr and the Khomeini loyalists became more manifest when he agreed to address the Mojahedin-e Khalq organization's March 5, 1981, rally, where the IRGC members, armed with sticks, attacked the rallying crowd.[50] By June 7, 1981, the Bani-Sadr mouthpiece *Jomhouri-e Eslami* was banned,[51] and Bani-Sadr fled to Kermanshah, after which Ayatollah Morteza Pasandideh, Grand Ayatollah Khomeini's brother, was the sole point of contact between the deposed president and the regime.[52] Bani-Sadr loyalist Ahmad Ghazanfar-Pour read aloud Bani-Sadr's final message to the people of Iran from the tribune of the parliament on June 14, 1981,[53] and according to Rafsanjani's memoirs Bani-Sadr, aided by the Air Force, fled Iran along with Rajavi on July 29, 1981.[54]

The IRGC, which had played an important role in destroying Bani-Sadr, arranged meetings with Rafsanjani and demanded authorization for the purge of Aqa-Zamani and his followers in the Guards.[55] By August 24, 1981, the purge of Aqa-Zamani supporters—who were considered also to be Bani-Sadr supporters—was a reality.[56]

3.2.3. The Khamenei and Rafsanjani Presidencies With Bani-Sadr's dismissal, and following the short tenure of Mohammad-Ali Rajaei as president, Ali Khamenei assumed the presidency (1981–1989). Both he and his successor, Akbar Hashemi Rafsanjani (1989–1997), benefited greatly from the Guards' purge of their enemies and competitors, but both feared the IRGC's inherent volatility. They sought to bureaucratize political decision making and professionalize and depoliticize the Guards, along with the rest of the bureaucracy of the Islamic Republic. Rafsanjani even tried unsuccessfully to merge the IRGC with the regular military.[57]

The IRGC's engagement in the war with Iraq during the Khamenei presidency greatly limited the Guards' involvement in domestic politics, but during Rafsanjani's tenure in office, which coincided with the era after the end of the war, Rafsanjani faced some difficulty keeping the IRGC out of politics. In public speeches Rafsanjani demanded discipline from the IRGC and urged the Guards to behave like a "serious military organization."[58] Khamenei too demanded that the IRGC should stay out of "petty politics" and professionalize.[59]

The IRGC leadership did not simply sustain the criticism, but retaliated. Despite being perfectly aware of the fact that Iran could not have continued the war against Iraq, the IRGC commanders blamed the civilian leadership, particularly Rafsanjani, of betraying the war effort and for accepting the ceasefire in 1988. In late September 1988, the IRGC convened a major meeting of its commanders in Tehran's Azadi Stadium to "survey their future plans for guarding the revolution."[60] The gathering was in reality a demonstration of force to Rafsanjani and the civilian leadership. Later, IRGC spokesman Ali-Reza Afshar stated that the failure of the clerics to preserve the ideology of the revolution would constitute a threat to the revolution itself.[61]

Following the IRGC's show of force, Rafsanjani abandoned the idea of merging the IRGC with the regular military, but tried to restrain its political interventions. Following Grand Ayatollah Khomeini's passing, Rafsanjani and Khamenei presented both the public and the Guards with Khomeini's "Political and Divine Testament," which reads:

> My emphatic counsel to the armed forces is to observe [and] abide by the military rule of noninvolvement in politics. Do not join any political party or faction. No military man, security policeman, no Revolutionary Guard, or Basij may enter into politics. Stay away from politics, and you'll be able to preserve and maintain your military prowess and be immune to internal division and dispute. Military commanders must forbid entrance into political ties by the men under their command. And, as the revolution belongs to all the nation, its preservation is also the duty of all. Therefore, the government, the nation, the Defense Council, and the Islamic Consultative Assembly are all charged with the religious and national responsibility to oppose, from the very beginning, any interference in politics or any action against the interests of Islam and the country by the armed forces, regardless of category, class, branch, and rank. Such involvement will surely corrupt and pervert them. It is incumbent on the leader and the Leadership

Council to prevent such involvement of the armed forces by decisive action so that no harm may beset the country.[62]

While Grand Ayatollah Khomeini was clear on the IRGC's noninvolvement in politics, some Guardsmen believed that the noninterference between the political and military spheres should be mutual. In 1991, as the Pentagon deployed tens of thousands of troops to Kuwait and Saudi Arabia in preparation for Kuwait's liberation, mutinous units of the Revolutionary Guards, allegedly with the blessing of Ahmad Khomeini, attempted to launch missile attacks against U.S.-led coalition forces in Saudi Arabia to trigger an armed conflict between Iran and the United States. Regular Iranian army forces and Guards members under the command of IRGC chief Mohsen Rezaei, then a Rafsanjani loyalist, rushed to the missile battery at Khorramshahr to prevent the missiles' firing.[63] After this incident, Ahmad Khomeini lived an isolated life until he died under mysterious circumstances in March 1995.

During his presidency, Rafsanjani continued his policy of depoliticizing the armed forces. But in so doing, he may have created new problems. To dissuade the IRGC from political involvement, he effectively bribed the Guards, funding a central role for the IRGC in postwar reconstruction schemes.[64] This placated many IRGC commanders, but not all of them. A year before Hojjat al-Eslam Mohammad Khatami's victory, for example, Rezaei warned an assembly of anti-riot force commanders in Tehran that "the cancerous tumor of liberalism is spreading in some corners of our country."[65] Throughout May 1996, IRGC commanders made public statements against "liberals," a reference to Rafsanjani and his technocratic elite. The IRGC and its allies—the paramilitary Basij and the vigilante group Ansar-e Hezbollah[66]—used force to back the commander's words, attacking cinemas and universities. Rezaei defended the actions of the Basij: "The duty of the Basij Force is not only security and protection, but ...challenging the counterrevolutionary forces."[67] As the civil-military tension continued, however, the civilians won another battle.

3.2.4. A Khatami Backlash On May 23, 1997, Khatami won a landslide election. On September 9, 1997, a month after Khatami's inauguration, Khamenei replaced IRGC chief Rezaei. The longtime commander of the

IRGC had paid for his opposition to "liberals" such as Rafsanjani and Khatami, but Khatami's success did not last. Khatami heralded a new era of political reforms in the Islamic Republic, but his landslide victory, demonstrating popular support for political and social reform, was also a source of great concern to Khamenei and many Revolutionary Guards-men, who feared that Khatami could be to Iran what Mikhail Gorbachev was to the Soviet Union: He might be sincere in his loyalty to regime ideology but might inadvertently unleash forces that would spin out of control and destroy the system.

Yahya Rahim Safavi, who owed his appointment as IRGC chief to his moderate and noninterventionist views, became a radical opponent of Khatami and the reform movement. Speaking to senior IRGC navy commanders on April 27, 1998, he asked, "Can we withstand American threats and [America's] domineering attitude with a policy of détente? Can we foil dangers coming from [America] through dialogue between civili-zations?" He then trained his sights on Ataollah Mohajerani, the reformist minister of Islamic guidance and culture: "I argued with Mr. Mohajerani for one hour and told him that his path threatened our national security and asked him if he knew where he was going," Safavi said. "Newspapers are published these days that threaten our national security. I am after uprooting antirevolutionaries everywhere. We must behead some and cut out the tongues of others." Then, turning on the universities, he com-plained, "Liberals have taken over our universities, and our youth are chanting 'Death to dictatorship' slogans."[68] Soon after, the IRGC's public relations bureau warned about "newspapers and poisoned and suspicious pens which have taken advantage of the free atmosphere in the country and the meekness and patience of revolutionary forces to inculcate sick ideas and debased thoughts in order to distract public opinion from the conspiracies and enmities of the sworn enemies of Islamic Iran."[69] Safavi continued attacking Khatami and mobilized the Basij to counter the student movement.[70]

Tensions erupted in July 1999 when paramilitary forces attacked a student dormitory after the students held a peaceful demonstration against the closure of a reformist daily. Within days, student protests spread nationwide and threatened to spin out of control. Khamenei and the IRGC commanders considered the protests a threat to the regime's foundations. On July 12, 1999, twenty-four top IRGC commanders sent Khatami a letter demanding immediate action, declaring, "Our patience has run out. We cannot tolerate this situation any longer."[71] Khatami stood aside as they suppressed the uprising.

Safavi continued his interventions after the restoration of calm. A constant theme of Safavi's justification was the need to defend against U.S. plots although these were more imaginary than real. In May 2002, he accused "uninformed people, traitors, and internal political factions" of aiding the United States by creating suspicion among the people; undermining the nation's resistance against America's domination; changing some articles if not the entire Constitution; attacking fundaments of revolution; separating the government from its religious and revolutionary aspect; and creating doubts and hesitation in the principles of the order of the Islamic Republic and the government's ability to overcome the country's difficulties.[72]

Speaking in Mashhad, Safavi warned against "the suspicious acts and behavior of some people siding with the U.S. policies and interests in the country," and added that some of these might even be working in governmental organizations.[73] He subsequently sent a letter to parliamentary speaker Mehdi Karrubi, asking him to control the "extreme behavior of some parliamentary deputies" and reminding him that taking legal action against elements and movements involved in sabotaging the Islamic Revolution remained a core IRGC mission.[74] Indeed, the IRGC soon began using special courts to harass and intimidate opponents. It lodged criminal complaints against dissenting clergy, such as Asadollah Bayat, who was summoned to a Special Clerical Court in Qom after he criticized Safavi's remarks in a press interview.[75]

The IRGC also used the courts to silence the media. On July 12, 2000, the IRGC filed a complaint against the weekly *Omid-e Zanjan* at Branch 1408 of Tehran's Public Court for insulting the IRGC and its commander in an article criticizing their interference in politics.[76] Safavi also condemned the student publication *Mowj* for "insulting the Lord of the Age," the so-called Hidden Imam.[77] *Mowj* was only one of several dozen newspapers and magazines banned during the Khatami presidency.[78] Despite his criticism and intimidation of the Khatami administration, Safavi drew a fine line between legal interference and treason.

Speaking at the Fadaiyan-e Emam combat camp, he said that the IRGC and Basij supported the Khatami government but hoped to strengthen it, though he added that "intellectuals and writers must respect the sanctity and honor of the forces which are defending the revolution, the system, the government, and the people."[79]

3.2.5. Rise of the Guards under Ahmadinejad On June 24, 2005, Mahmoud Ahmadinejad, the little-known mayor of Tehran, won a surprise victory in a runoff election to determine who would succeed Khatami. As president, Ahmadinejad differed from his predecessors in several regards. Unlike most previous presidents of the Islamic Republic, with the exception of the short presidencies of Bani-Sadr and Mohammad Rajaei, Ahmadinejad was not a cleric or even the son of a cleric. His humble provincial background, his family's migration to Tehran, and his admission to the Iran University of Science and Technology all personified the politicized, new middle class that emerged from the Shah's unbalanced modernization schemes.[80] But Ahmadinejad also distinguished himself from his fellow revolutionaries in another regard. Despite his participation in the revolution and some student activism after the revolution, it was Ahmadinejad's tenure as local governor in the northwestern provinces of Iran and his participation in a few operations during the war with Iraq that shaped his political fortunes. Not satisfied with Rafsanjani's attempts to bribe them out of politics and fearful of political oblivion, the generation that fought trench warfare initially used Ahmadinejad to demand its share of political influence.

IRGC intervention in internal Iranian politics has peaked under Ahmadinejad. As president, Ahmadinejad, himself a former officer of the Basij of the Guards,[81] presides over a cabinet where twelve out of eighteen ministers are former IRGC officers, a record number since 1979. The future of the Iranian presidency is also likely to be dominated by the IRGC. At the time of the writing of this book, three individuals seem to be competing for the 2013 presidential election: Ali Larijani, Mohammad-Baqer Qalibaf, and Qassem Suleimani, all of whom are former officers of the IRGC. So are an increasing number of members of the Islamic Consultative Assembly, the Iranian parliament. The Council of Guardians, which screens candidates before elections, has privileged IRGC veterans, who won the bulk of seats in the March 2008 parliamentary elections, and the 2012 parliamentary elections will most likely demonstrate a similar pattern. There is a similar statistical overrepresentation of IRGC veterans among general governors of the Islamic Republic.

The significance of such appointments is great. As journalist Kasra Naji's discussion of Ahmadinejad's tenure as governor of Ardebil demonstrates, governors exert considerable influence on presidential elections both by diverting public funds to candidates and by transferring income from transborder smuggling operations to campaigns. Naji writes that Ahmadinejad engaged in such activities to support parliamentary speaker Ali-Akbar Nateq Nouri, the hard-line front-runner in the 1997 campaign, which Khatami ultimately won.[82] By appointing his old comrades as governors of the thirty provinces of Iran, Ahmadinejad expected and received the same support in the 2009 presidential campaign. So should Ahmadinejad's successor, who is likely to be an IRGC veteran.

Not surprisingly, the IRGC commander in chief, Safavi, embraced the Ahmadinejad government in 2005. Speaking to trainees participating in the *Velayat* (Guardianship) Program of the Student Basij, Safavi defended the regime: "Some political groups are trying to weaken the new administration and pitch up the people's demands. …These groups are trying to obstruct the work of the new administration."[83] Several months later, as criticism of Ahmadinejad intensified, Safavi warned, "We know you, and we will sort you out in due course. The IRGC will stand against anyone who intends to confront the revolution."[84]

But Safavi's expression of loyalty toward Ahmadinejad was not enough to secure his position, and by September 1, 2007, Major General Mohammad Ali Jafari (also known as Aziz Jafari and Ali Jafari), the founder of the Revolutionary Guards Strategic Studies Center, which has been developing doctrines to suppress "velvet revolutions," succeeded Safavi as the commander in chief of the IRGC. Upon assuming the mantle of IRGC leadership, Jafari sought to implement the theories he had developed as head of the IRGC think tank. Believing the chief future threats to the regime were velvet revolutions and internal strife—perhaps supported by the hidden hands of outside powers—he argued that the IRGC needed to readjust to meet the challenge. The structure that had helped the Islamic Republic beat back Iraq needed reform. In a September 2007 speech, he confirmed the IRGC's new role: "The Revolutionary Guards are not a one-dimensional military organization. The mission of the Guards is guarding the revolution and its achievements against internal threats. ...The current strategy, which has been clarified by the leadership of the revolution, differs from the strategies of the [war] years. The main mission of the Guards today is countering internal threats."[85]

Jafari later affirmed the Guards' expanded role by describing the IRGC as not "solely a military organization" but also a "political and ideological organization."[86] On December 1, 2007, Masoud Jazayeri, deputy commander of the Culture and Propaganda Office of the Armed Forces Joint Command Council, elaborated upon Jafari's statement. Addressing IRGC commanders in Tehran, Jazayeri said: "The Basij is the strategic depth of the Islamic Revolution. ...We should take care that the rudder of legislation in the country does not fall into the hands of persons whose main concern is longing for personal power, or party political [aspirations], but rather [those who seek] advancement of the strength of the regime."

He then grew more specific. Referring to parliamentarians who, in the days of the Khatami administration, had used the bully pulpit of the parliament to protest hardline actions, he argued that those who contest elections "should not be people who use this stronghold to stage hunger strikes or 'political fasting,' stage provocations against the regime, or as a 'war room' against other parts of the regime."[87] There was little doubt among his audience that his speech was meant to encourage the IRGC and the Basij not only to enter overtly into politics but also to disenfranchise reformist elements and narrow even further the range of acceptable political debate within Iran's theocratic structure. The Supreme Leader endorsed Jafari's reform, an unsurprising move given that he does not generally appoint officials whose agenda he does not support. He was not alone in supporting this move. Mohammad Kowsari, another IRGC commander and current deputy head of the parliamentary National Security and Foreign Policy Committee, said the Guards' intervention in politics had been "successful" since those who left school to fight in the Iran-Iraq war could now enter "a new scene" to preserve the "Islamic nature of the regime."[88] Indeed, the Supreme Leader's representative to the organization urged the officer corps to take an active role in parliamentary politics.[89]

In the run-up to the 2008 parliamentary elections, the IRGC went further in advancing its involvement from advocacy and participation into intimidation. Major General Hassan Firouzabadi, chief of the Armed Forces General Command Headquarters, condemned Iranian politicians close to Khatami who had allegedly written letters seeking cooperation with Washington in the wake of the 2003 U.S. invasion of Iraq, those who had written to the Supreme Leader asking him to consider détente with Washington, and students who voiced tolerance toward the United States at Iranian universities. "The people of Iran should know these elements," he declared. "Don't let the U.S. control the seats of the parliament through them."[90]

Ebrahim Jabari, the IRGC commander in Qazvin, used public speeches to intimidate the local reformist candidate: "The person who questions eight years of sacred defense on BBC radio...wants to run for parliament. ...We should do our utmost so we do not experience the sixth parliament [dominated by the reformists] again. ...We should not allow dirty people to enter the parliament to fill the parliament with dirt. Those whose presence is religiously not permissible in the parliament should not enter it."[91]

The 2008 parliamentary elections solidified the IRGC's political infiltration and demonstrated that the Supreme Leader supports the IRGC's growing role. According to the minister of interior, 7,168 candidates registered for the elections,[92] of whom 31.5 percent were veterans of the Iran-Iraq war. By January 22, 2008, the Council of Guardians had approved the candidacy of about five thousand candidates, or 69 percent of the registrants. Of the 31 percent whose candidacy was not approved, two-thirds were simply disqualified, and the remaining one-third were members of the outgoing parliament who had approval of their credentials revoked.[93] The Ministry of Interior provided a number of excuses to those who failed to qualify: 69 candidates had missed the deadline to file paperwork; 131 had a record of treason, fraud, or embezzlement; and 329 had a bad reputation in their neighborhood. In addition, 188 individuals were deemed to have a deficient educational background or lacked five years of senior professional experience.[94] The bulk of those disqualified, the ministry explained, had lost their right to candidacy for narcotics addiction or involvement in drug smuggling, connections to the Shah's prerevolutionary government, lack of belief in or insufficient practice of Islam, being "against" the Islamic Republic, or having connections to foreign intelligence services.[95] If such measures were not enough to bar undesired candidates from winning the parliamentary elections, Khamenei also appointed former IRGC commander Ali-Reza Afshar to oversee the elections. In this role, he has the power to appoint and manage seven hundred thousand officials to run the elections and will adjudicate any disputes.[96] Another IRGC veteran, Ezzatollah Zarghami, who now heads Islamic Republic of Iran Broadcasting (IRIB), refused to air remarks by reformist candidates.

After the March 14, 2008, elections, the Islamic Republic's reformist faction complained that the Ministry of Interior, the election's organizer, had been transformed into a "military base."[97] Mehdi Karrubi, a former parliamentary speaker, an unsuccessful presidential candidate in 2005 as well as in 2009, and one of the leaders of the Green Movement, was more refined, asking rhetorically, "Does it mean that if two individuals are engaged in a rivalry during elections, this force [the IRGC] should engage in supporting one of the two?"[98] Karrubi may have meant his question to be rhetorical, but within the Islamic Republic today, it has no easy answer.

Ahmadinejad and Khamenei do not intend the IRGC's and the Basij's insertion into politics to be temporary. The weekly *Sobh-e Sadeq*, successor to *Payam-e Enqelab* as mouthpiece of the IRGC, addressed the apprehension of civilian politicians in a long piece meant to assuage those worried by the Guards' new role. But far from choosing a conciliatory tone toward the critics of the Guards, Yadollah Javani, head of the political bureau of the IRGC's Joint Command Council, explained: "In case a movement, or a party, or a group has the political or cultural potential to topple [the regime], one can't expect the Guards to deal with it militarily. Under such circumstances, the duty of the Guards is political and cultural resistance. Therefore, and because the Guards is needed to get involved in political or cultural work, one can't restrict the nature of the Guards to the military sphere alone."[99]

The IRGC intervened again in the 2009 presidential election. The IRGC responded swiftly to Khamenei's green light to attack Ahmadinejad's opponents. Not all IRGC commanders' speeches to the men under their command have been published, but it appears that after Khamenei's speech likening Khatami to Shah Soltan Hossein, IRGC chiefs in all thirty-one regional command centers started or strengthened efforts to mobilize support for Ahmadinejad. In the Greater Tehran district, for example, IRGC chief Colonel Abdollah Eraqi's speech beseeched his men to support the incumbent.[100]

The second phase of the IRGC's operation against Ahmadinejad's critics began with a speech by Major General Hassan Firouzabadi, chief of the General Staff, in which he not only openly endorsed Ahmadinejad, but also labeled his rivals as "too old and frail" to be president.[101] The attacks against Ahmadinejad's rivals continued as Safavi, former IRGC chief and current senior security adviser to the Supreme Leader, praised Ahmadinejad as a role model for members of the Basij[102] and attacked "the liberals" who "have dealt the greatest blows to the Islamic Republic."[103] Such an open and direct assault against Ahmadinejad's rivals was a significant shift from earlier elections in which the IRGC engineered attacks indirectly, using proxies such as Ansar-e Hezbollah.

The third phase in the IRGC's operation also signifies a major shift. It began with the speech of current IRGC chief Mohammad Ali Jafari to the Basij in which he urged Basij members to intervene in politics in order to defend the Principalist camp, the faction with which Ahmadinejad identifies that seeks to return to the "principles" of the early revolutionary years.[104] The IRGC's subsequent blatant mobilization of voters raised a storm of criticism among Ahmadinejad's critics and opponents of armed forces intervention in politics. Tabnak News, close to Mohsen Rezaei, one of the four candidates in this election, disclosed that the lower ranks of the Basij are deeply engaged in a campaign on behalf of Ahmadinejad,[105] and even parliamentary speaker Ali Larijani, who is generally in line with the Supreme Leader, called for the security services to withdraw from politics.[106] Unsurprisingly, these protests had absolutely no effect on the Guards, based on their new doctrine enabling if not encouraging such political activity.

Popular uprisings in the wake of the fraudulent June 12, 2009, presidential election forced the IRGC and the Basij militia to directly engage in suppression of the opposition and arrest of opposition leaders and mid-level managers, which has been politically costly for the IRGC. However, the IRGC has been rewarded for its support of Ahmadinejad.

While the presence of former IRGC officers in the cabinet is not a new phenomenon, their numbers under Ahmadinejad—they occupied twelve of the eighteen ministry positions as of January 2012—are unprecedented, and the IRGC has been rewarded with economic benefits and monopolies during the Ahmadinejad presidency. However, the IRGC has generally supported the line of the Supreme Leader against Ahmadinejad in the conflict between the civilian leaders.

One example is the position of the IRGC in the row over the Intelligence Ministry. On April 17, 2011, Ahmadinejad dismissed Hojjat al-Eslam Heydar Moslehi, the influential minister of intelligence and a close ally of Supreme Leader Khamenei.[107] Less than an hour after Ahmadinejad's decree appeared in the media, Fars News Agency reported that Khamenei had reinstated Moslehi,[108] a move that infuriated Ahmadinejad, who refused to attend cabinet meetings for two weeks. Khamenei's unconstitutional overruling of the president in the fight over the strategically important ministry was meant to reassert his authority in the struggle for power with Ahmadinejad.

The IRGC responded with attacks on Ahmadinejad. On April 20, 2011, *Javan*, one of several IRGC mouthpieces, accused "a deviant current" of trying to "fabricate files" and "abusing the Intelligence Ministry" for political purposes.[109] The same day, Basij chief Mohammad-Reza Naqdi warned the public against "those with apparent interest in Messianism [*Mahdaviat*] who may fight against the Guardianship [of the Jurist]."[110] On April 22, the Day of the Guards, IRGC chief Jafari criticized Ahmadinejad indirectly by stressing that the greatest worry of the late Ayatollah Khomeini, founder of the Islamic Republic, was "internal enemies," and that "the sedition of 2009" was founded on the green prodemocracy movement's "opposition to the issue of the Guardianship of the Jurist."[111] The same criticism could, of course, be directed against Ahmadinejad. In the second part of the interview, Jafari warned against "a deviant current" that has "infiltrated the regime," but also said that the deviant current was "hiding behind a popular figure [Ahmadinejad]."[112] On April 24, Jafari used equally nuanced tactics, praising Ahmadinejad and his cabinet's performance while simultaneously attacking "a deviant current" within the government.[113]

Within the IRGC, the harshest attacks against Ahmadinejad were launched by the political/ideological commissars: Hojjat al-Eslam Ali Saidi, the Supreme Leader's representative to the IRGC, and his deputy, Hojjat al-Eslam Mojtaba Zolnour. "Disobeying the command of the Guardian Jurist equals disobeying the commandment of God and the Imam of the Era," charged Saidi.[114] His deputy went so far as to claim that Esfandiar Rahim-Mashaei, a close confidante of Ahmadinejad, was the real president[115] and warned that a president who does not seek legitimacy from the Guardian Jurist is *Taqout* (one who revolts against God), a Koranic reference to Satan.[116]

Remarkably, as Ahmadinejad capitulated to Khamenei and acquiesced to Moslehi's presence in the cabinet, *Javan* and other IRGC mouthpieces continued to attack Ahmadinejad, insisting that "the new sedition" would raise fresh challenges to the Guardian Jurist.[117] This indicates the opportunism of the IRGC: the IRGC initially managed to use the conflict between the president and the Supreme Leader to partially take over the Intelligence Ministry, but as soon as this goal was achieved it decided to intervene on Khamenei's behalf to preserve the balance between the president and the leader. In other words, the IRGC has emerged as the final arbiter of power in the Islamic Republic. Although the IRGC sided with Khamenei against Ahmadinejad, the Supreme Leader is at the mercy of former and current members of the IRGC and the Basij, who in turn have become power brokers in their own right and no longer consider themselves subservient to Khamenei. He is aware of the problems he faces, and most of his moves betray his anxiety to restore the balance within the regime. While remaining silent himself, Khamenei has systematically supported the parliament and the judiciary—headed by brothers Ali and Sadegh Larijani—in their attacks against the Ahmadinejad government. Parliamentary resistance to Ahmadinejad's economic reform scheme— manifested in a prolonged approval process for the national budget—as well as criticism by parliament of the Ahmadinejad government's haphazard law enforcement, notably its refusal to allow judicial investigation into alleged governmental mismanagement, led to the establishment of a working group for conflict resolution between the parliament and the government. However, on the whole, Khamenei's balancing act does not seem to work as Ahmadinejad's civilian critics are disunited and weak, and the Revolutionary Guards, which are handsomely rewarded for their support of the regime in general and Ahmadinejad in particular, have little incentive to oppose the president.[118]

3.3. Conclusion

While democracies fear external enemies, undemocratic regimes fear their own populations, whose choices and aspirations they suppress by military means. In the short term, Khamenei's tactic might work. A unified and consolidated elite composed of the IRGC officer corps enables the Islamic Republic to maintain a tough international stance while repressing unrest at home. But the price for such a policy will prove high. Not only will it politicize civil society and radicalize university students, labor activists, women in urban centers, and civil rights activists against the regime, but it will also alienate traditional regime supporters such as the bazaar merchant class, Rafsanjani-era technocratic and economic elites, and Khatami-era reformers whose hopes are already frustrated. More dangerously, the Supreme Leader's sole reliance on the Revolutionary Guards— should the IRGC manage to preserve its cohesion as a social group in Iranian politics—will make Khamenei a prisoner of his own praetorian guard, paving the way for a military dictatorship.

Notes

1. "Ghanoun-e Asasi-ye Jomhouri-ye Eslami-ye Iran" [Constitution of the Islamic Republic of Iran], Article 150. Darbareh-ye Majles-e Showra-ye Eslami website (Tehran), n.d. Available in Persian at http://www.majlis.ir/majles/index. php?option=com_content&task=view&id=12&Itemid=88 (accessed February 28, 2010).

2. "Asas-Nameh-ye Sepah-e Pasdaran-e Enqelab-e Eslami" [Statute of the Army of the Guardians of the Islamic Revolution], Hafezeh-ye Ghavanin website (Tehran), n.d. Available in Persian at http://tarh.majlis.ir/?ShowRule&Rid=1D49 73FB-9551-4F8D-AEB3-DAEFD52791F1 (accessed February 28, 2010).

3. "Salrouz-e Tasis-e Sepah" [Anniversary of the Establishment of the Guards], Tebyan (Tehran), April 21, 2007. Available in Persian at http://www.tebyan.net/ Politics_Social/News/Military_Defence/2007/4/21/40529.html (accessed April 16, 2012).

4. "Avalin Asasnameh-ye Sepah" [First Statute of the Guards], Fars News (Tehran), October 14, 2008. Available in Persian at http://www.farsnews.com/newstext.php?nn=8707220459 (accessed April 16, 2012).

5. "Asasnameh-ye Sepah" [Statute of the Guards], *Payam-e Enqelab* (Tehran), February 16, 1981.

6. Majid Saeli Kordeh-Deh, *Showra-ye Enqelab-e Eslami-ye Iran* (Tehran: Markaz-e Asnad-e Enqelab-e Eslami, 2005), pp. 20–40.

7. "Avalin Asasnameh-ye Sepah."

8. Ibid.

9. Ibid.

10. Ibid.

11. "Asasnameh-ye Sepah-e Pasdaran-e Enqelab-e Eslami" [Statute of the Islamic Revolutionary Guards Corps], Paygah-e Ettelae-Resani-ye Qavanin va Moqararat-e Keshvar (Tehran), n.d. Available in Persian at http://www.dastour.ir/brows/?lid=112374 (accessed April 16, 2012).

12. Ibid.

13. Ibid.

14. "Ghanoun-e Asasi-ye Jomhouri-ye Eslami-ye Iran."

15. "Asasnameh-ye Sepah-e Pasdaran-e Enqelab-e Eslami" [The Statute of the Islamic Revolutionary Guards Corps], *Payam-e Enqelab* (Tehran), no. 37, July 25, 1981.

16. "Nirou-ha-ye Mossalah; Voroud ya Adam-e Voroud–Barresi-ye Mabani-ye Jorm-Engari-ye Faaliyat-e Siyasi-ye Nirou-ha-ye Mossalah" [The Armed Forces: Intervention or Nonintervention: Research into Definitions of Crime Concerning the Political Activities of the Armed Forces], *Sobh-e Sadeq* (Tehran), December 31, 2006.

17. Kenneth Katzman, *The Warriors of Islam: Iran's Revolutionary Guard* (Boulder, CO: Westview, 1993), pp. 51–52.

18. Nehzat-e Azadi-ye Iran (Iran Freedom Movement), June 14, 1981.

19. "Sepah: Bazou-ye Velayat-e Faqih" [The Guards: The Arms of the Guardian Jurist], *Payam-e Enqelab* (Tehran), July 11, 1981, p. 45.

20. Ibid.

21. "Zarourat-e Tashkil-e Sepah-e Pasdaran-e Enqelab-e Eslami" [The Necessity of Establishment of the Islamic Revolutionary Guards Corps], *Payam-e Enqelab* (Tehran), February 16, 1981, p. 41.

22. Ibid.

23. In Persian: *Daneshjou-yan-e Mosalman-e Peyrov-e Khat-e Emam.*

24. "Ettelaiyeh-ye Sepah-e Pasdaran" [Announcement of the Revolutionary Guards], *Kayhan* (Tehran), May 24, 1979, p. 1, quoted in Hossein Yekta (ed.), *Rouzshomar-e Jang-e Iran Va Eragh* [Chronology of the Iran-Iraq War], 2nd ed. (Tehran: Markaz-e Motaleat Va Tahghighat-e Jang, 2008), p. 278.

25. *Ettelaat* (Tehran), May 26, 1979, pp. 4–5, quoted in Yekta (ed.), *Rouzshomar-e Jang-e Iran Va Eragh*, p. 278.

26. "Tasis-e Sepah-e Pasdaran Be Revayat-e Ebrahim-e Yazdi" [Establishment of the Revolutionary Guards According to Ebrahim Yazdi], *Shahrvand-e Emrouz* (Tehran), September 16, 2007. Available in Persian at http://shahrvandemroz. blogfa.com/post-221.aspx (accessed December 6, 2008).

27. Mohsen Rafiqdoust, *Khaterat-e Mohsen Rafiqdoust* [Memoirs of Mohsen Rafiqdoust], edited by Davoud Ghasem-Pour (Tehran: Markaz-e Asnad-e Enqelab-e Eslami, 2004), p. 191. See also Hadi Nokhi and Hossen Yekta (eds.), *Rouzshomar-e Jang-e Iran va Eragh* [Chronology of the Iran-Iraq War], vol. 1 (Tehran: Markaz-e Mottaleat va Tahghighat-e Jang-e Sepah-e Pasdaran-e Enqelab-e Eslami, 1996), p. 882. Douz-Douzani claims to have sought the council of Khomeini in Qom on April 20, 1979, along with Mohsen Rezaei and Mohsen Rafiqdoust. Speaking about the exact circumstances, Douz-Douzani recalls: "During that audience the blessed Imam [Khomeini] uttered: 'What about the issue you were working on?' I said, 'We [the unified IRGC Command Council] have almost reached the conclusion but the transitional government, especially Mr. Yazdi, is of the belief that the government must establish the Guards.' The blessed Imam [Khomeini] opposed this and said go and establish the Guards, and we considered the words of the Imam [Khomeini] as a decree." See "Tashkil-e Sepah Be Revayat-e Abbas-e Douz-Douzani" [Establishment of the Guards According to Abbas Douz-Douzani], Alef News (Tehran), April 21, 2008. Available in Persian at http://alef.ir/content/view/24972/ (accessed March 23, 2009).

28. "Amrika taslim-e eradeh-ye ommat-e eslam shod" [The United States Capitulated to the Will of the *Umma* of Islam (the community of believers)], *Payam-e Enqelab* (Tehran), no. 25, January 31, 1981, p. 2.

29. Katzman, *Warriors of Islam*, pp. 53–57.

30. Abol-Hassan Bani-Sadr, *Nameh-ha Az Agha-ye Bani-Sadr Be Agha-ye Khomeini Va Digaran...*[Letters from Mr. Bani-Sadr to Mr. Khomeini and Others], edited by Firouzeh Bani-Sadr (Frankfurt, Germany: Entesharat-e Enqelab-e Eslami, 2006), p. 47.

31. Ibid., p. 56.

32. Ibid.

33. "Aks-ha-ye Montasher-Nashodeh Az Nokhostin Farmandeh-ye Sepah" [Unpublished Photos of the First Commander of the Guards], Jam News (Tehran), July 13, 2011. Available in Persian at http://jamnews.ir/NSite/FullStory/News/?Id=8143&Serv=10 (accessed April 16, 2012).

34. "Zendegi-Nameh-ye Abbas-e Aqa-Zamani" [Biography of Abbas Aqa-Zamani], *Iran* (Tehran), September 13, 2010. Available in Persian at http://www.iran-newspaper.com/1389/6/22/Iran/4/Page/50/Index.htm (accessed April 16, 2012). See also "Showra-ye Enqelab-e Eslami" [The Council of the Islamic Revolution], *Iran* (Tehran), September 13, 2010. Available in Persian at http://www.iran-newspaper.com/1389/6/22/Iran/4/Page/49/Index.htm (accessed April 16, 2012).

35. Bani-Sadr, *Nameh-ha Az Agha-ye Bani-Sadr Be Agha-ye Khomeini Va Digaran* ..., p. 55.

36. Ibid.

37. "Tashkil-e Sepah Be Revayat-e Abbas-e Douz-Douzani."

38. Katzman, *Warriors of Islam*, p. 54.

39. "Emam Va Sepah Az Badv-e Tashkil Ta Hal. Mosahebeh Ba Seyyed Ahmad Khomeini" [The Imam and the Guards from Establishment to Now: Interview with Seyyed Ahmad Khomeini], *Payam-e Enqelab* (Tehran), May 29, 1982, p. 10.

40. Ibid.

41. Ibid., p. 11.

42. Akbar Hashemi Rafsanjani, *Enqelab Dar Bohran. Karnameh Va Khaterat-e Sal-e 1359* [Revolution in Crisis: Memoirs of the Year 1979–1980], edited by Abbas Bashiri (Tehran: Daftar-e Nashr-e Maaref-e Enqelab, 2005), p. 325.

43. Bani-Sadr, *Nameh-ha Az Agha-ye Bani-Sadr Be Agha-ye Khomeini Va Digaran* ..., p. 46.

44. "Sepah: Bazou-ye Velayat-e Faqih," p. 48.

45. Ibid.

46. Ayatollah Hossein-Ali Montazeri, *Khaterat-e Ayatollah Hossein-Ali Montazeri* [Memoirs of Ayatollah Hossein-Ali Montazeri] (Los Angeles: Ketab, 2001), p. 318.

47. Ibid.

48. Bani-Sadr, *Nameh-ha Az Agha-ye Bani-Sadr Be Agha-ye Khomeini Va Digaran...*, p. 258.

49. "Bayaniyeh-ye Shomareh-ye 21 Daftar-e Siyasi-ye Sepah-e Pasdaran" [Statement Number 21 of the Political Directorate of the Revolutionary Guards], Tehran, Political Directorate of the Revolutionary Guards, September 12, 1981, quoted in Rahim Safavi, *Az Jonoub-e Lobnan Ta Jonoub-e Iran–Khaterat-e Sardar Seyyed Rahim-e Safavi* [From Southern Lebanon to Southern Iran: Memoirs of Commander Seyyed Rahim Safavi], 2nd ed., edited by Majid Najaf-Pour (Tehran: Markaz-e Asnad-e Enqelab-e Eslami, 2006), p. 274.

50. Ibid.

51. Bani-Sadr, *Nameh-ha Az Agha-ye Bani-Sadr Be Agha-ye Khomeini Va Digaran...*, p. 447.

52. Ibid., p. 451.

53. Ibid., p. 463.

54. Akbar Hashemi Rafsanjani, *Obour Az Bohran. Karnameh Va Khaterat-e Hashemi Rafsanjani* [Through Crisis: Deeds and Memoirs of Hashemi Rafsanjani], edited by Yaser Hashemi (Daftar-e Nashr-e Maaref-e Enqelab, 1999), p. 219.

55. Ibid.

56. Ibid., p. 254.

57. Katzman, *Warriors of Islam*, p. 59.

58. Ibid., p. 60.

59. Ibid.

60. Ibid., p. 59.

61. Ibid.

62. For an official English translation, see Ruhullah al-Musawi al-Khomeini, "The Last Message: The Political and Divine Will of His Holiness Imam Khomeini," Islamic Republic News Agency (IRNA, Tehran), February 15, 1983. Available at http://www.irna.ir/occasion/ertehal/english/will/lmnew1.htm (accessed February 12, 2008).

63. John Bulloch, Ahmad Vahdatkhah, and Safa Haeri, "Crisis in the Gulf: Iran Foils Pro-Saddam Mutiny," *The Independent* (London), February 3, 1991, p. 2.

64. Ali Alfoneh, "How Intertwined Are the Revolutionary Guards in Iran's Economy?" *Middle Eastern Outlook*, no. 3, American Enterprise Institute, Washington, DC, October 2007.

65. *The Iran Brief*, Middle East Data Project, Bethesda, MD, June 3, 1996.

66. Michael Rubin, *Into the Shadows: Radical Vigilantes in Khatami's Iran* (Washington, DC: Washington Institute for Near East Policy, 2001), pp. 44–88.

67. *The Iran Brief*, June 3, 1996.

68. *The Iran Brief*, Middle East Data Project, Bethesda, MD, May 4, 1998.

69. IRNA, May 3, 1998, in *BBC Monitoring Middle East: Political*, May 4, 1998.

70. IRNA, June 2, 1998, in *BBC Monitoring Middle East: Political*, June 3, 1998.

71. Jomhuri-ye Eslami (Tehran), July 19, 1999.

72. Iranian Students' News Agency (ISNA, Tehran), May 21, 2002, in *BBC Monitoring Middle East: Political*, May 21, 2002.

73 IRNA, May 23, 2003, in *BBC Monitoring Middle East: Political*, May 23, 2003.

74. IRNA, November 12, 2003, in *BBC Monitoring International Reports*, November 12, 2003.

75. *Aftab-e Yazd* (Tehran), December 3, 2000, in *BBC Summary of World Broadcasts*, December 5, 2000.

76. IRNA, July 12, 2000, in *BBC Summary of World Broadcasts*, July 14, 2000.

77. Voice of the Islamic Republic of Iran (Tehran), September 27, 1999, in *BBC Summary of World Broadcasts*, September 29, 1999; for an annotated version of *Mowj*, see Michael Rubin, "Iran's 'Blasphemous' Play," *Middle East Quarterly*, December 1999, pp. 83–86.

78. *Iran Report*, Radio Free Europe/Radio Liberty Newsline, May 1, 2000.

79. Vision of the Islamic Republic of Iran, Network 1 (Tehran), July 31, 1999.

80. For biographical information on Ahmadinejad's social background, see Yossi Melman and Meir Javedanfar, *The Nuclear Sphinx of Tehran: Mahmoud Ahmadinejad and the State of Iran* (New York: Carroll & Graf, 2007), pp. 1–20; Kasra Naji, *Ahmadinejad: The Secret History of Iran's Radical Leader* (Berkeley: University of California Press, 2008), pp. 1–57.

81. "Zendeginameh" [Biography], Riasat-e Jomhouri-e Eslami-ye Iran Website (Tehran), n.d. Available in Persian at http://www.president.ir/fa/ (accessed March 2, 2010).

82. Naji, *Ahmadinejad*, pp. 36–40.

83. *Siyasat-e Rouz* (Tehran), August 13, 2005, in BBC *Monitoring Middle East: Political,* August 27, 2005.

84. Fars News Agency (Tehran), January 16, 2006, in BBC *Monitoring Middle East: Political,* January 16, 2006.

85. "Sardar Jafari: Mamouriat-e asli-ye sepah-e pasdaran moghabeleh ba tahdid-ha-ye dakheli ast" [Commander Jafari: The Main Responsibility of the Revolutionary Guards Is to Counter Internal Threats], *Hamshahri* (Tehran), September 29, 2007. Available in Persian at http://www.hamshahrionline.ir/News/?id=33971 (accessed April 16, 2012).

86. "Mardom-e Iran dar sarasar-e keshvar aks-e gofteh-ye nezamiyan amal konand" [The People of Iran Should Do the Opposite of What the Military Commands], Agahsazi (Tehran), March 7, 2008. Available in Persian at http://www. agahsazi.com/News.asp?NewsID=4065 (accessed April 16, 2012).

87. "Basij omgh-e estratezhik-e padideh-ye enqelab-e eslami ast" [The Basij Is the Strategic Depth of the Phenomenon of the Islamic Revolution], *Basij* (Tehran), December 1, 2007. Available in Persian at http://www.basijnews.com/ Ndetail.asp?NewsID=13448 (accessed February 12, 2008); and "Sardar Jazayeri: Jang-e narm-e amrika entekhabat-e hashtom-e majles ra neshan gerefteh ast" [Commander Jazayeri: Soft Warfare of the United States Has Targeted the Eighth Round of Parliamentary Elections], Islamic Republic News Agency, November 28, 2007. Available in Persian at http://www2.irna.ir/fa/news/view/ line-2/8609078015232946.htm (accessed February 12, 2008). For reference to protests occurring during the sixth parliament (2000–2004), see "Q & A: Iranian Election Row," BBC News, February 10, 2004. Available at http://news.bbc. co.uk/1/hi/world/middle_east/3452839.stm (accessed February 12, 2008).

88. "Goft-e gou-ye tafsili-ye Raja News ba sardar Mohammad Kowsari" [The Lengthy Discussion of Raja News with Commander Mohammad Kowsari], Agahsazi (Tehran), March 9, 2008. Available in Persian at http://www.agahsazi. com/News.asp?NewsID=4082 (accessed April 16, 2012).

89. "Namayandeh-ye Vali-ye Faqih dar Sepah dar gofte-gou-ye ekhtesasi ba Sobh-e Sadeq: Majlesi ke poshtiban-e Velayat bashad khast-e doshman nist" [Representative of the Jurist of Law in Exclusive Interview with *Sobh-e Sadeq*: A Parliament That Supports the Velayat Is Not Wanted by the Enemy], *Sobh-e Sadeq* (Tehran), March 3, 2008. Available in Persian at http://www.sobhesadegh. ir/1386/0342/M08.HTM (accessed April 16, 2012).

90. "Hoshdar-e entekhabati-ye reis-e setad-e koll-e nirou-ha-ye mossallah" [Election Warnings of the Chief of the General Command Headquarters], *Etemad* (Tehran), February 3, 2008. Available in Persian at http://www.etemaad. com/Released/86-11-14/103.htm (accessed February 12, 2008).

91. "Farmandeh-ye sepah-e Qazvin: Deghat konid majles-e sheshom tekrar nashavad" [Revolutionary Guards Commander of Qazvin: Pay Attention So the Sixth Parliament Is Not Repeated], *Noandish* (Tehran), January 3, 2008. Available

in Persian at http://www.noandish.com/com.php?id=13287 (accessed February 12, 2008).

92. Islamic Republic of Iran Ministry of Interior, "Ettelaiyeh shomareh-ye 8 setad-e entekhabat-e keshvar adar khosous-e amar-e qati-ye sabt-e-nam-shodeh-gan-e entekhabat-e majles-e hashtom" [Bulletin Number VIII of the Headquarters for Elections on the Final Statistics of Registered Candidates for the Eighth Parliamentary Elections]. http://www.moi.ir/Portal/Home/Show-Page.aspx?Object=Standard&CategoryID=da3dfedf-2133-461e-8f0b-90dd22bf1 8a3&LayoutID=52012b04-039d-4115-8d1b-3562c062764c&ID=085f2469-1e2a-4e35-b122-a1cea2b49175 (accessed February 12, 2008).

93. Islamic Republic of Iran Ministry of Interior, "Ettelaiyeh shomareh-ye 10 Setad-e Entekhabat-e Keshvar" [Information Bulletin Number 10 of the Country's Election Headquarters]. http://www.moi.ir/Portal/Home/ShowPage. aspx?Object=Standard&CategoryID=da3dfedf-2133-461e-8f0b-90dd22bf18a3 &LayoutID=52012b04-039d-4115-8d1b-3562c062764c&ID=cae2e7f9-6070-40d6-a7d8-113f7eb31b12 (accessed February 12, 2008).

94. "Ettelaiyeh Vezarat-e Keshvar dar-bareh-ye bargozari-ye entekhabat-e hashto-min dowreh-ye Majles-e Showra-ye Eslami" [The Information Bulletin of the Ministry of Interior about the Elections to the Eighth Congregation of the Islamic Consulta-tive Assembly]. Available in Persian at http://www.moi.ir/Portal/Home/ShowPage. aspx?Object=Standard&CategoryID=da3dfedf-2133-461e-8f0b-90dd22bf18a3 &LayoutID=52012b04-039d-4115-8d1b-3562c062764c&ID=a01d5747-c7d0-4b68-8e23-5795de4d98ba (accessed February 12, 2008).

95. Islamic Republic of Iran Ministry of Interior, "Ettelaiyeh shomareh-ye 10 Setad-e Entekhabat-e Keshvar."

96. Arash Sigarchi, "Nezamiyan bara-ye entekhabat be saf shodand" [Military Men in Line for the Elections], Rooz (Amsterdam), February 7, 2007; and "Iran Appoints Former Revolutionary Guard Commander to Oversee Parliamentary Elections," Associated Press, November 24, 2007.

97. "Rad-de salahiyat-e namzadan-e eslah-talab dar heyat-ha-ye nezarat (ba akha-rin taghirat)" [Disqualification of Reformist Candidates by the Supervisory Commit-tees (with the Latest Changes)], Baharestan-e Iran (Tehran), February 5, 2008.

98. "Dabir koll-e hezb-e Etemad-e Melli: Farmandeh-ye Koll-e Sepah towzih dahad" [General Secretary of the Etemad-e Melli Party: Commander in Chief of the Guards Should Explain], Agahsazi (Tehran), May 10, 2008. Available in Persian at http://www.agahsazi.com/News.asp?NewsID=4678 (accessed April 16, 2012).

99. "Negaran-e tajdid-e nazar dar sakhtar-e sepah nabashid" [Don't Worry about Reconsiderations in the Structure of the Guards], Sobh-e Sadeq (Tehran), May 19, 2008. Available in Persian at http://www.sobhesadegh.ir/1387/0350/ M02.HTM (accessed April 16, 2012).

100. "Farmandeh-ye Sepah-e Tehran-e Bozorg: Bayad Az Dowlat-e Ahmadineajd Hemayat Konim" [Greater Tehran IRGC Chief: We Must Support the Ahmadinejad

Government], *Aftab-e Yazd* (Tehran), January 20, 2009. Available in Persian at http://www.aftab-yazd.com/pdf/2549/2.pdf (accessed May 18, 2009).

101. "Dar Mored-e Ahmadinejad Baz-ham Mortakeb-e Eshtebah-e Entekhabat-e Nohom Shodand" [With Regard to Ahmadinejad They Have Again Committed the Same Mistake as the Ninth Election], Raja News Agency (Tehran), January 27, 2009. Available in Persian at http://www.rajanews.com/detail.asp?id=23887 (accessed May 18, 2009).

102. "Eteghad Be Basij Ra Dar Modiriat-ha Ba Barnameh-Rizi-ha Piadeh Konim" [We Should Realize Our Belief in the Basij by Engaging It in Executive and Planning Affairs], Agahsazi, (Tehran), February 1, 2009. Available in Persian at http://www.agahsazi.com/article.asp?id=2459&cat=7 (accessed May 18, 2009).

103. "Sardar Safavi: Liberal-ha Bozorgtarin Zarbe Ra Be Keshvar Zadand" [Commander Safavi: The Liberals Dealt the Greatest Blows to the Country], Alef News Agency (Tehran), February 4, 2009. Available in Persian at http://alef.ir/content/view/40400 (accessed May 18, 2009).

104. "Farmandeh-ye Sepah: Basij Bayad Az Osoul-garayan Moraghebat Konad" [The Guards' Commander: Basij Must Protect the Principalists], Shahab News (Tehran), February 7, 2008. Available in Persian at http://shahabnews.ir/vdce.n8zbjh87f9bij.html (accessed May 10, 2009).

105. "Estafadeh-ye Entekhabati Az Basij Bar Khalaf-e Nazar-e Sarih-e Rahbar-e Enqelab" [Election Utilization of the Basij in Opposition to the Frank Statement of the Leader of the Revolution], Tabnak News (Tehran), May 7, 2009. Available in Persian at http://www.tabnak.ir/ fa/pages/?cid=46762 (accessed May 17, 2009).

106. "Ba Tavvahom Nabayad Harf Zad" [One Must Not Speak with Delusional Fear], *Abrar* (Tehran), May 5, 2009. Available in Persian at http://abrarnews.com/politic/1388/880215/html/rooydad.htm#s356799 (accessed May 17, 2009).

107. Presidency of the Islamic Republic of Iran, "Doktor Ahmadinejad ba Qaboul-e Estefa-ye Vazir-e Ettelaat Vey ra be Onvan-e Moshaver-e Reis-Jomhour Dar Omour-e Ettelaati Mansoub Kard" [By Accepting the Intelligence Minister's Resignation, Dr. Ahmadinejad Appoints Him Presidential Intelligence Adviser], news release, April 17, 2011. Available in Persian at http://www.president.ir/fa/?ArtID=27843 (accessed April 28, 2011).

108. "Moslehi Dar Vezarat-e Ettelaat Mandani Shod" [Moslehi Remains at the Intelligence Ministry], Fars News Agency (Tehran), April 18, 2011. Available in Persian at http://www.farsnews.net/newstext.php?nn=9001290001 (accessed April 28, 2011).

109. "Jaryan-e Enherafi Be Donbal-e Parvandeh-Sazi-ye Amniati" [The Deviant Current Tries to Fabricate Security Files], Javan Online (Tehran), April 20, 2011. Available in Persian at http://www.javanonline.ir/Nsite/FullStory/?Id=351123 (accessed May 10, 2011).

110. "Hoshdar-e Naqdi Be Fetneh-ye Badi" [Naqdi's Warning to the Next Sedition], Shafaf News (Tehran), April 20, 2011. Available in Persian at http://www.shafaf.ir/fa/pages/?cid=53096 (accessed May 10, 2011).

111. "Sepah-e Pasdaran Javab-e Eqdam-e Doshman Dar Elayh-e Iran Ra Dar Abha-ye Dourdast Khahad Dad" [The Revolutionary Guards Will Retaliate Enemy Actions against Iran in Distant Waters], Fars News Agency (Tehran), April 22, 2011. Available in Persian at http://www.farsnews.net/newstext.php?nn= 9001312352 (accessed May 10, 2011).

112. Ibid.

113. "Tamam-e Dashteh-ha-ye Sepah Az Enqelab-e Eslami Ast Na Az Iran va Maktab-e Iran" [Everything the Guards Has Is Derived from Islam and Not from the School of Iran], Ammariyon News (Tehran), April 24, 2011. Available in Persian at http://www.ammariyon.ir/fa/pages/?cid=9617 (accessed May 10, 2011).

114. "Takhalof Az Farman-e Vali-ye Faqih Dar Hokm-e Mokhalefat Ba Farman-e Khoda va Emam-e Zaman Ast" [Disobeying the Command of the Guardian Jurist Equals Disobeying the Commandment of God and the Imam of the Era], Fars News Agency (Tehran), April 27, 2011. Available in Persian at http://www.farsnews.net/newstext.php?nn=9002060712 (accessed May 10, 2011).

115. "Zolnour: Mashaei Dar Sadad-e List-e Entekhabat Ast" [Zolnour: Mashaei Is Preparing for Elections], Asr-e Iran News (Tehran), April 30, 2011. Available in Persian at http://www.asriran.com/fa/news/164063/%D8%B0%D9%88%D8% A7%D9%84%D9%86%D9%88%D8%B1-%D9%85%D8%B4%D8%A7%DB% 8C%DB%8C-%D8%AF%D8%B1-%D8%B5%D8%AF%D8%AF-%D9%84%DB% 8C%D8%B3%D8%AA-%D8%A7%D9%86%D8%AA%D8%AE%D8%A7%D8 %A8%D8%A7%D8%AA-%D8%A7%D8%B3%D8%AA-%D8%8C-%D9%85% D8%B5%D9%84%D8%AD%DB%8C-%D9%88%D8%A7%D9%82%D8%B9% DB%8C%D8%AA-%D9%87%D8%A7-%D8%B1%D8%A7-%D9%85%D9%86 D8%AA%D9%82%D9%84-%D9%85%DB%8C-%DA%A9%D9%86%D8%AF- %D9%88-%D8%A7%D8%B2-%D9%86%D8%B8%D8%B1-%D9%85%D8% B4%D8%A7%DB%8C%DB%8C-%D8%A8%D8%A7%DB%8C%D8%AF-%D8% A8%D8%B1%D9%88%D8%AF (accessed May 10, 2011). Clerics attack associates of the president to send a message to the president without tarnishing the presidency as an institution.

116. "Bakhsh-e Payani-ye Sokhanrani-ye Hojjat al-Eslam Mojtaba Zolnour" [Final Part of Hojjat al-Eslam Mojtaba Zolnour's Speech], Khabar Online (Tehran), May 3, 2011. Available in Persian at http://khabaronline.ir/news-148453.aspx (accessed May 10, 2011).

117. "Chalesh-e Mostamar" [Continual Challenge], Javan Online (Tehran), May 9, 2011. Available in Persian at http://www.javanonline.ir/Nsite/FullStory/ ?Id=352434 (accessed May 10, 2011).

118. Ali Alfoneh, "The Revolutionary Guards' Looting of Iran's Economy," *Middle East Outlook*, no. 3, June 2010.

4

The IRGC as an Internal Security Organization in Contemporary Iran

On September 1, 2007, Supreme Leader Ayatollah Ali Khamenei appointed Brigadier General Mohammad Ali Jafari—also known as Aziz Jafari and Ali Jafari—to be the seventh commander in chief of the Islamic Revolutionary Guards Corps (IRGC).[1] Two days later, he promoted him to major general.[2] Jafari immediately announced fundamental structural reform in the security apparatus of the Islamic Republic, moving the IRGC's primary focus from external defense to internal security. Jafari's announcement in reality reflected a reorganization that already had taken place over a longer period of time, but it did signal a renewed crackdown on reformism and civil society.

Jafari's career success has been intertwined with growing regime acceptance of his once controversial threat assessment. Jafari earned his stripes during the Iran-Iraq war, in which he was chief of the IRGC's Najaf base.[3] Against the backdrop of the grueling war, the Iranian defense doctrine focused on countering external threats. Conscripts were the frontline grunts, and the IRGC became the elite units. After the war, Jafari served as commander of the IRGC Ground Forces for more than a decade (1994–2005). He then became chief of the newly established IRGC Strategic Studies Center.[4] Under his supervision, the center began to conduct research into "velvet revolutions" and alleged U.S. "soft regime change policies."[5] He argued that the IRGC should focus on future internal threats to the Islamic Republic's stability, a push that led the IRGC to establish the Al-Zahra and Ashoura Brigades to serve as anti-riot forces within the organizational framework of the paramilitary Basij resistance force,[6] long the subordinate of the IRGC.

Upon assuming the mantle of IRGC leadership, Jafari sought to implement the theories he had developed as head of the IRGC think tank. If the chief future threats were velvet revolutions and internal strife—perhaps supported by the hidden hands of outside powers—then the IRGC needed to readjust to meet the challenge. The structure that had helped the Islamic Republic beat back Iraq needed reform.

Jafari's reorganization had two major components: merging the Basij into the IRGC and restructuring the IRGC itself to become less centralized and more focused on the provinces. Jafari justified merging the paramilitary Basij with the elite IRGC because both organizations shared the same goal of "guarding achievements of the Revolution."[7] On September 28, 2007, at the farewell ceremony for Basij chief Brigadier General Mohammad Hejazi, Jafari explained that the IRGC was a "military-political-cultural organization sharing the same organizational goals as the Basij" and that "half of the Revolutionary Guards' mission is placed on the shoulders of the Basij."[8] Then, on October 25, 2007, Jafari assured Basij members that their organization would not be merged into the IRGC Ground Forces, but would remain as a distinct unit within the IRGC[9]—a promise Jafari did not keep.

The Supreme Leader endorsed Jafari's reorganization, an unsurprising move given that he does not generally appoint officials whose agenda he does not support. Indeed, when he appointed Hejazi as deputy chief of the IRGC on May 22, 2008,[10] he demonstrated his full support for formally folding the Basij into the IRGC. After all, such an appointment involved displacing IRGC graybeards such as former IRGC chief and counterintelligence director Brigadier General Morteza Rezaei.[11] Khamenei also preserved the special status of the Basij when, on July 13, 2008, he appointed Hojjat al-Eslam Hossein Taeb to be "IRGC Basij chief."[12]

4.1. Formal Merger of the IRGC with the Basij

Jafari initiated a process in which he was likely to encounter resistance: incorporation of the Basij, an organization whose independence is more form than substance. The Basij and the IRGC both arose out of the chaos and upheaval that led to the Islamic Revolution. The leader of the Islamic

Revolution, Grand Ayatollah Rouhollah Khomeini, established the paramilitary Basij by a November 26, 1979, decree,[13] but the Basij was already a fact on the ground before Khomeini formalized its existence.

Initially, Khomeini supervised the Basij, but in August 1980, President Abol-Hassan Bani-Sadr laid claim to the Basij in his capacity as commander in chief. The IRGC opposed Bani-Sadr's claim, which they saw as a power grab,[14] and legally the control of the Basij remained disputed. After Bani-Sadr fell from favor and fled into exile in June 1981, the Basij theoretically fell under the control of the Ministry of Interior, but in reality, the IRGC never lost control from the very beginning of the Basij.

The March 19, 1980, issue of the IRGC mouthpiece *Payam-e Enqelab*, a weekly newspaper, explained that the IRGC had formed the Basij as a specialized unit within its own organizational structure to "answer the call of the Leader of the Revolution Imam Khomeini to expand military training all over the country, especially among the youth." It was composed of "representatives of different units of the Guards."[15] The IRGC was further responsible for "registration, screening, training and organizing,"[16] hardly a factor that would suggest the Basij to be an organization independent of the IRGC. Any remaining doubt should have been put to rest when, on February 17, 1981, the Iranian parliament formally incorporated the Basij into the IRGC's organizational structure.[17] In subsequent years, the IRGC focused on primary security threats—largely external—while the Basij filled secondary gaps. The statute of the Revolutionary Guards, passed by parliament on July 6, 1982, listed the obligations of the Basij as defense of the country and the regime and response to natural disasters (earthquakes are quite common in Iran). With the IRGC taking command of the front with Iraq, the Basij focused on internal security to ensure discipline and loyalty to the regime, even as privations increased. The Basij divided Iranian cities into large resistance areas that were divided into zones and smaller bases, basically at the neighborhood level, at which local clergy and "trusted citizens" aided recruitment.[18] Tehran, for example, was divided into eight Basij areas with three hundred IRGC members serving as instructors.[19] Weekly IRGC reports show that the Basij initially fulfilled its role enforcing internal security, but as the Iran-Iraq war progressed, they also became more active as soldiers on the front lines.[20] Thus, while the IRGC may have been the varsity team and the Basij junior varsity, they played the same game. Bifurcation was more theoretical than real.

Underlying this point was the fact that, while the IRGC took predominant responsibility for operations beyond Iran's borders, the Basij also played a role. In 1982, for example, the IRGC established a Basij unit in Lebanon to "counter Zionist Israel's expansive and multidimensional invasion of Lebanon."[21]

Since the end of the Iran-Iraq war, IRGC members were largely recruited from the ranks of the Basij. But the Basij also assumed a role in defense, especially in nonurban areas.[22] The Iranian leadership may bill Jafari's changes as pathbreaking and radical, but a close examination shows more continuity than change.

4.2. The Mosaic Doctrine

The second major reform Jafari introduced was his "Mosaic Doctrine," which involved dividing the IRGC into thirty-one commands—one for each province and two for Tehran (see Table 4-1). The IRGC has, from its beginning, been a centralized entity. Throughout summer 2008, Jafari and Hejazi named the thirty-one units and appointed their chiefs and deputies. The Office of the Supreme Leader has appointed representatives in each unit to be the eyes and ears of the Supreme Leader. The provincial basis of IRGC units is meant to better local commanders' control over recruitment,[23] but it also restructures IRGC capabilities as an anti-riot force and guards the organization against any attempts to decapitate it, such as might occur should U.S. or Israeli military forces strike the Islamic Republic.

However, the reform seems to have formalized a structure that existed de facto prior to the reform. Many of the commanders and deputies resumed service in the same province in which they had already been based and in units that had been little more than renamed. For example, the Hazrat-e Abbas Brigade was based in the northwestern province of Ardebil both before and after implementation of the Mosaic Doctrine. The same holds true for the Ashoura Brigade in East Azerbaijan, the Shohada Brigade in West Azerbaijan, the Imam Sadeq Brigade in Bushehr, the Ansar al-Hossein Brigade in Hamedan, the Neynava Brigade in

TABLE 4-1

IRGC ORGANIZATIONAL STRUCTURE AT GENERAL GOVERNORATE LEVEL AS OF JULY 2008

Province	IRGC Unit	Current IRGC Commander	IRGC Commander in 2008	Previous Position of the IRG Commander in 2008	Current IRGC Deputy	IRGC Deputy in 2008	Previous Position of the Deputy in 2008
Ardebil	Hazrat-e Abbas[1]	Colonel Jalil Baba-Zadeh	Colonel Jalil Baba-Zadeh[2]	Ardebil Hazrat-e Abbas Brigade chief[3]	Colonel Qanbar Karimnejad[4]	Colonel Qanbar Karimnejad[5]	Ardebil Basij chief[6]
Azerbaijan, East	Ashoura[7]	Brigadier General Ali-Akbar Pourjamshidian[8]	Commander Mohammad-Taghi Ossanlou[9]	31st Armored Ashoura Division chief[10]	Colonel Mohammad-Esmail Saidi[11]	Not known	Not known
Azerbaijan, West	Shohada[12]	Commander Yousef Shakeri[13]	Brigadier General Mehdi Moini[14]	West Azerbaijan Shohada IRGC Force chief[15]	Colonel Abedin Khorram[16]	Commander Said Qorbannejad[17]	West Azerbaijan Basij chief[18]
Bushehr	Imam Sadeq[19]	Commander Fath-Allah Jamiri[20]	Colonel Fath-Allah Jamiri[21]	Bushehr Basij chief[22]	Commander Alireza Gharibi[23]	Colonel Abdol-Reza Matal[24]	Bushehr Basij deputy[25]
Chahar-Mahal and Bakhtiari	Ghamar Bani-Hashem[26]	Brigadier General Reza-Mohammad Suleimani[27]	Brigadier General Reza-Mohammad Suleimani[28]	Fars senior IRGC commander[29]	Commander Yazdan Jalali[30]	Commander Mehdi Jamshidi[31]	Not known
Fars	Fajr[32]	Brigadier General Gholam-Hossein Gheibparvar[33]	Brigadier General Gholam-Hossein Gheibparvar[34]	25th Karbala Division chief[35]	Commander Abolfazl Gazami[36]	Commander Mohammad-Reza Mehdianfar[37]	Fars Basij chief[38]
Gilan	Qods[39]	Commander Hamoun Mohammadi[40]	Commander Hamoun Mohammadi[41]	Iran-Iraq war veteran[42]	Brigadier General Nazar-Ali Alizadeh[43]	Commander Nazar-Ali Alizadeh[44]	Gilan Basij chief[45]

Golestan	Neynava[46]	Commander Mohammad-Hossein Babyi[47]	Commander Brigadier General Naser Razaghian[48]	Gorgan-based First Brigade of Twenty-fifth Karbala Division chief[49]	Colonel Hossein Karimi Aval[50]	Daryoush Alazmani[51]	Golestan Basij chief[52]
Hamedan	Ansar al-Hossein[53]	Commander Abd al-Reza Azadi[54]	Commander Abd al-Reza Azadi[55]	Hamedan IRGC chief[56]	Commander Mehdi Sediq[57]	Commander Mehdi Sediq[58]	Ansar Brigade deputy, Qods training camp chief, Mottahari training camp chief, Ansar al-Hossein Division deputy[59]
Hormozgan	Imam Sajjad[60]	Commander Mohammad Marani[61]	Commander Khalil Rastegar[62]	Not known	Colonel Mohammad-Mehdi Zarei[63]	Colonel Mousa Mowlaparast[64]	Not known
Ilam	Amir al-Momenin[65]	Commander Jamal Shakarami[66]	Brigadier General Sadeq Kaki[67]	Hamedan IRGC senior commander,[68] Third Ansar al-Hossein Brigade of the Fourth Besat Division chief[69]	Commander Mohammad-Taqi Qassemi[70]	Not known	Not known
Isfahan	Saheb al-Zaman[71]	Commander Gholam-Reza Suleimani[72]	Brigadier General Gholam-Reza Suleimani[73]	Senior Isfahan IRGC commander, Fourteenth Imam Hossein Division chief[74]	Commander Mojtaba Fada[75]	Not known	Not known

Province	IRGC Unit	Current IRGC Commander	IRGC Commander in 2008	Previous Position of the IRG Commander in 2008	Current IRGC Deputy	IRGC Deputy in 2008	Previous Position of the Deputy in 2008
Kerman	Sar-Allah[76]	Commander Rouhollah Nouri[77]	Commander Rouhollah Nouri[78]	Hamzeh Seyyed al-Shohada base chief[79]	Commander Morteza Mousavi[80]	Commander Gholam-Ali Abou-Hamzeh[81]	Kerman Basij chief[82]
Kermanshah	Kermanshah IRGC	Commander Mohammad-Nazar Azimi[83]	Commander Mohammad-Nazar Azimi[84]	Fourth Besat Infantry Division chief[85]	Commander Bahman Reyhani[86]	Commander Bahman Reyhani[87]	Not known
Khorasan, North	Javad al-Aemeh[88]	Commander Hossein-Ali Yousef-Ali-Zadeh[89]	Commander Ali Mirza-Pour[90]	Not known	Commander Rashid Mohammadi[91]	Hossein-Ali Yousef-Ali-Zadeh[92]	Khorasan North Basij chief[93]
Khorasan, Razavi	Imam Reza[94]	Gholam-Reza Ahmadi[95]	Commander Ghodrat-Allah Mansouri[96]	Fifth Nasr Division chief[97]	Commander Hashem Ghiasi[98]	Commander Hashem Ghiasi[99]	Khorasan Razavi Basij chief[100]
Khorasan, South	Ansar al-Reza[101]	Commander Yaqoub-Ali Nazari[102]	Brigadier General Commander Gholam-Reza Ahmadi[103]	Khorasan South Basij chief[104]	Gholam-Reza Mohammadpour[105]	Not known	Not known
Khuzestan	Vali-ye Asr[106]	Brigadier General Hassan Shahvarpour[107]	Commander Mohammad Kazemeini[108]	Seventh Vali Asr Division chief[109]	Commander Mahmoud Moinpour[110]	Commander Mehdi Saadati[111]	Khuzestan Basij chief[112]
Kohkilou-yeh and Boyer-Ahmad	Fath[113]	Commander Younes Amiri[114]	Commander Avaz Shahabi-Far[115]	Forty-eighth Independent Brigade chief[116]	Commander Ali-Asghar Habibi[117]	Colonel Ali-Asghar Habibi[118]	Not known

Kordestan	Beit al-Moghaddas[119]	Mohammad-Hassan Rajabi[120]	Allah-Nour Nour-Allahi[121]	Kordestan Basij chief[122]	Colonel Hamzeh-Ali Alikhani[123]	Not known	Not known
Lorestan	Abol-Fazl al-Abbas[124]	Mohammad Shahrokhi[125]	Commander Shahrokhi[126]	Independent Fifty-seventh Hazrat-e Abolfazl Brigade chief[127]	Commander Yadollah Bouali[128]	Colonel Teymour Sepahvand[129]	Lorestan Basij chief
Markazi	Rouh-Allah[130]	Commander Gholam-Ali Abou-Hamzeh[131]	Commander Mohammad-Taghi Shah-Cheraghi[132]	Golestan Basij chief[133]	Commander Nour-Khoda Qassemi[134]	Commander Nour-Khoda Qassemi[135]	Chief of First Routhollah Infantry Brigade of Arak Seventeenth Ali Ibn Abi-Taleb Division[136]
Mazandaran	Karbala[137]	Commander Mohammad Shah-e-Cheraqi[138]	Brigadier General Ali Shalikar[139]	Twenty-fifth Karbala Division chief[140]	Colonel Rahmatollah Sadeqi[141]	Commander Ali Garmeh-i[142]	Mazandaran Basij chief[143]
Qazvin	Saheb al-Amr[144]	Commander Mehdi Taherkhani[145]	Brigadier General Salar Abnoush[146]	Twelfth Hazrat-e Qaem Brigade chief[147]	Colonel Habibollah Vafapour[148]	Not known	Not known
Qom	Ali Ibn-e Abi-Taleb[149]	Commander Mehdi Mahdavinejad[150]	Brigadier General Akbar Nouri[151]	Seventeenth Qom Ali-Ibn-e Abi-Taleb Infantry Division chief[152]	Commander Reza Hafezi[153]	Not known	Not known
Semnan	Hazrat-e Ghaem al-Mohammad[154]	Commander Ali-Naqi Hemmati[155]	Colonel Mohammad-Hossein Babayi[156]	Kerman Basij chief[157]	Colonel Abd al-Rahim Fereydoun	Not known	Not known

Province	IRGC Unit	Current IRGC Commander	IRGC Commander in 2008	Previous Position of the IRG Commander in 2008	Current IRGC Deputy	IRGC Deputy in 2008	Previous Position of the Deputy in 2008
Sistan and Baluchestan	Salman[158]	Commander Ali-Reza Azimi Jahed[159]	Brigadier General Rajab-Ali Mohammad-Zadeh[160]	Not known	Colonel Habibollah Lakzaei[161]	Colonel Habib Lak-Zayi[162]	Sistan and Baluchestan Basij deputy[163]
Tehran	Seyyed al-Shohada[164]	Commander Bahram Hosseini[165]	Commander Ali Fazli[166]	Deputy operations chief of IRGC Central Command[167]	Commander Ali Nasiri[168]	Commander Morteza Shaneh-Saz[169]	Tehran Basij chief[170]
Tehran, Greater	Mohammad Rasoul-Allah[171]	Commander Mohsen Kazemeini[172]	Brigadier General Abdollah Eraqi;[173] followed by Brigadier General Hossein Hamadani[174]	Greater Tehran Basij chief[175]	Commander Ahmad Zolqadr[176]	Commander Ebrahim Jabari[177]	Qazvin Basij commander[178]
Yazd	Al-Ghadir[179]	Commander Akbar Fotouhi[180]	Brigadier General Mohammad-Ali Allah-Dadi[181]	Independent Al-Ghadir Brigade chief[182]	Colonel Mohammad-Hossein Fayazipour[183]	Not known	Not known
Zanjan	Not known	Commander Jahanbakhsh Karami[184]	Commander Mehdi Mousavi[185]	Not known	Commander Mohammad Esmaili[186]	Not known	Not known

NOTE: *Commander* is used when the exact rank is unknown.
NOTE: Table notes can be found at the end of the chapter

Golestan, the Ali Ibn-e Abi-Taleb Brigade in Qom, the Hazrat-e Ghaem al-Mohammad Brigade in Semnan, and the Al-Ghadir Brigade in Yazd. The only significant change in the structure of personnel appears to be the promotion of former Basij provincial chiefs to be IRGC deputy chiefs—the continuation of the pattern set by the promotion of former national Basij chief Hejazi to deputy IRGC chief. The Tehran appointments deviated slightly from the pattern since the top commanders were recruited from among central cadres of the IRGC.

The IRGC is the main pillar of defense for the Islamic Republic. Originally envisioned to counter both internal and external threats, the IRGC was forced to focus on external defense after Iraq's 1980 invasion of Iran. Since the war's end more than twenty years ago, the IRGC has been looking for a clear role and purpose. Jafari appears to have found it. "For the time being the main responsibility of the Revolutionary Guards is to counter internal threats, and [only] aid the Army in case of external military threat," he clarified.[24] Indeed, internal threats dominated Jafari's speeches.[25] At a press conference, he explained that the IRGC's responsibilities necessitated a "special and flexible force able to counter different types of threats."[26]

4.3. Conclusion

While democracies fear external enemies, undemocratic regimes fear their own people. The paranoid dynamics of politics in the Islamic Republic make authorities look for—and find—internal enemies, saboteurs, and, more recently, "velvet revolutionaries."[27] The imagined state of emergency and fantastic claims of U.S. plots against the Islamic Republic serve the regime well. Any sign of dissent or the slightest opposition to the Islamic Republic is depicted as involvement in a foreign conspiracy. The paranoia also legitimizes IRGC intervention in domestic politics.

Jafari's restructuring is an acknowledgment of the regime's weakness, but its actual impact is slight, more smoke and mirrors than a real change in command. In practice, the Basij has always been subordinate to the IRGC. Its independence was more form than substance. Likewise, the IRGC's new provincial structure simply legalizes what had become informal reality. The IRGC has long acted as a parallel bureaucracy in the provinces. Whether Jafari truly wants reform is impossible to tell. What is clear is that reform is difficult for the Islamic Republic. Still, sometimes even cosmetic reform can be telling. Whenever the Islamic Republic looks for internal enemies, it finds them. Indeed, having made defense against velvet revolutions his defining issue, Jafari must now prove that he will succeed. The Basij-IRGC merger and the Mosaic Doctrine may not do much for national defense, but they certainly suggest strengthening of the IRGC in internal politics of the Islamic Republic—a power that is more than likely to be used, not only against dissidents, but also against loyal elements of the Islamic Republic who challenge the creeping coup d'état of the Revolutionary Guards.

Notes

1. "Sarlashgar Jafari farmandeh-ye koll-e Sepah-e Pasdaran shod" [Major General Jafari Appointed Commander in Chief of the Revolutionary Guards], Mehr News Agency (Tehran), September 1, 2007. Available in Persian at http://www.mehrnews.com/fa/NewsDetail.aspx?NewsID=544358 (accessed July 29, 2008).

2. "Rahbar-e mozzam-e enqelab be farmandeh-ye jadid-e Sepah darajeh-ye sarlashkari eta kardand" [Supreme Leader of the Revolution Promotes Commander in Chief of the Guards to Major General], *Hamshahri* (Tehran), September 3, 2007. Available in Persian at http://www.hamshahrionline.ir/News/?id=31692 (accessed August 4, 2008).

3. "Farmandeh-ye jadid-e Sepah-e Pasdaran kist?" [Who Is the New Chief of the Guards Corps?], Baztab (Tehran), September 1, 2007. Available in Persian at http://www.baztab.com/news/74278.php (accessed August 4, 2008).

4. "Entesabat-e jadid dar Sepah-e Pasdaran-e Enqelab-e Eslami" [New Appointments in Islamic Revolutionary Guards Corps], Aftab News (Tehran), August 20, 2005. Available in Persian at http://www.aftabnews.ir/vdcb9a8brhb9.html (accessed August 4, 2008).

5. Mohsen Sazegara, "Iran in Three Dimensions" (speech, AEI, Washington, DC, May 19, 2008). Available at http://www.aei.org/event/1726.

6. "Dovvomin marhaleh-ye razm-ayesh-e bozorg-e payambar-e azam aghaz shod" [Second Phase of the Great Prophet War Game Begins], Mehr News Agency, November 1, 2006. Available in Persian at http://www.mehrnews.com/fa/NewsDetail.aspx?NewsID=400882 (accessed August 4, 2008).

7. Ibid.

8. "Sardar Jafari: Mamouriat-e asli-ye Sepah moghabeleh ba tahdid-ha-ye dakheli ast" [Commander Jafari: The Main Mission of the Guards Is to Counter

Internal Threats], *Hamshahri* (Tehran), September 29, 2007. Available in Persian at http://www.hamshahrionline.ir/News/?id=33971 (accessed August 4, 2008).

9. "Basij dar nirou-ye zamini-ye Sepah edgham nemishavad" [Basij Will Not Be Dissolved in the Ground Forces of the Guards], *Hamshahri* (Tehran), October 26, 2007. Available in Persian at http://www.hamshahrionline.ir/News/?id=36411 (accessed August 4, 2008).

10. "Sardar Hejazi janeshin-e farmandeh-ye koll-e Sepah shod" [Commander Hejazi Appointed Deputy Commander in Chief of the IRGC], Fars News Agency (Tehran), May 23, 2008. Available in Persian at http://www.farsnews.net/newstext.php?nn=8703030441 (accessed August 4, 2008).

11. "Tashkil-e Sepah-e Pasdaran-e Enqelab-e Eslami be Revayat-e Mohsen Rafiqdoust" [Establishment of the Islamic Revolutionary Guards Corps According to Mohsen Rafiqdoust], Iranian Students News Agency (ISNA) (Tehran), April 22, 2007. Available in Persian at http://iranianuk.com/article.php?id=10554 (accessed August 4, 2008); and "Moarefeh va towdie chahar farmandeh-ye arshad-e Sepah" [Presentation and Farewells of Four Senior Guards Commanders], *Kayhan* (Tehran), May 7, 2006.

12. "Marasem-e moarefeh-ye farmandehan-e nirou-ye zamini-ye Sepah, nirou-ye moghavemat-e Basij va Gharar-Gah-e Sar-Allah" [Presentation Ceremonies of the Guards Ground Forces, the Basij Resistance Force, and Sar-Allah Base Chief], ISNA (Tehran), July 13, 2008. Available in Persian at http://isna.ir/ISNA/NewsView.aspx?ID=News-1163318&Lang=P (accessed August 4, 2008).

13. "Artesh-e bist milyouni" [Twenty-Million-Men-Strong Army], *Payam-e Enqelab* (Tehran), November 28, 1981.

14. "Sepah, bazou-ye Velayat-e Faqih" [The Guards, Arms of the Supreme Jurist], *Payam-e Enqelab* (Tehran), July 11, 1981.

15. "Gousheh-i az karnameh-ye Sepah dar sali ke gozasht" [Activities of the Guards in the Last Year at a Glance], *Payam-e Enqelab* (Tehran), March 19, 1980.

16. Ibid.

17. "Ghanoun-e edgham-e Sazeman-e Basij-e Melli (Mostazafin) dar Sepah-e Pasdaran-e Enqelab-e Eslami" [Law on Incorporation of the National Mobilization Organization of the Oppressed into the Islamic Revolutionary Guards Corps], *Rouznameh-ye Rasmi* (Tehran), March 7, 1981.

18. "Fasl-e chaharom-e asasnameh-ye Sepah-e Pasdaran-e Enqelab-e Eslami dar khosous-e asasnameh-ye vahed-e Basi-e Mostazafin" [Fourth Chapter of the Statute of the Islamic Revolutionary Guards Corps Regarding the Statute of the Basij of the Oppressed], *Rouznameh-ye Rasmi*, October 3, 1982.

19. "Morouri bar faaliyat-ha-ye 'Basij'-e Sepah" [A Survey of Activities of the "Basij" of the Guards], *Payam-e Enqelab* (Tehran), February 16, 1981.

20. "Sepah va Basij-e Sepah" [The Guards and the Basij of the Guards], *Payam-e Enqelab* (Tehran), May 29, 1982.

21. "Gozareshi az tashkil-e Basij-e Sepah-e Pasdaran dar Lobnan" [A Report on Establishment of the Basij of the Revolutionary Guards in Lebanon], *Payam-e Enqelab* (Tehran), October 22, 1982.

22. "Mosahebeh-ye matbouati" [Press Interview], *Payam-e Enqelab* (Tehran), January 27, 1990.

23. "Farmandeh-ye nirou-ye zamini-ye Sepah: Tarh-e mozaik-ha-ye defai sorat-e amal-e Sepah va Basij ra bala mibarad" [IRGC Ground Forces Chief: Realization of the Mosaic Defensive Doctrine Increases Operational Speed of the Guards and the Basij], *Mardomsalari* (Tehran), July 27, 2008.

24. "Sardar Jafari: Mamouriat-e asli-ye Sepah moghabeleh ba tahdid-ha-ye dakheli ast."

25. "Sardar Jafari: Ghenaat be vaz-e mowjoud khata-ye rahbordi ast" [Commander Jafari: Being Satisfied with Status Quo Would Be a Strategic Mistake], *Hamshahri* (Tehran), September 4, 2007. Available in Persian at http://www.hamshahrionline.ir/News/?id=31793 (accessed August 4, 2008); and "Taghir-e rahbord-e Sepah-e Pasdaran" [Change of the Revolutionary Guards' Strategy], *Hamshahri* (Tehran), September 25, 2007. Available in Persian at http://www.hamshahrionline.ir/News/?id=31729 (accessed August 4, 2008).

26. "Marasem-e moarefeh-ye farmandeh-ye jadid-e Sepah" [Presentation Ceremony of New Commander in Chief of the Guards], *Hamshahri* (Tehran), September 3, 2007. Available in Persian at http://www.hamshahrionline.ir/News/?id=31729 (accessed August 4, 2008).

27. Middle East Media Research Institute, TV Monitor Project, "Iranian Intelligence Ministry Broadcast Encouraging People to Snitch on Spies Features 'John McCain' Masterminding a Velvet Revolution in Iran from the White House," February 5, 2007. Available through http://www.memritv.org/clip/en/1678.htm (accessed August 11, 2008).

Notes for Table 4-1

1. "Farmandeh-ye Sepah-e Hazrat-e Abbas-e (A) ostan-e Ardebil moarrefi shod" [Chief of the Hazrat-e Abbas (Peace Be upon Him) Army of Ardebil Province Appointed], Islamic Republic News Agency (IRNA) (Tehran), July 17, 2008. Available in Persian at http://www.irna.ir/View/FullStory/?NewsId=105653 (accessed July 21, 2008).

2. Ibid.

3. "Mohajeman-e mossallah dar marz-e Iran va Torkiyeh koshteh shodand" [Armed Assailants Killed in Iranian-Turkish Border], BBC Persian (London), March 1, 2007. Available in Persian at http://www.bbc.co.uk/persian/iran/story/2007/03/070301_he-insurgents.shtml (accessed July 22, 2008).

4. "Janeshin-e Farmandeh-ye Sepah-e Ardebil: 16 Karevan Az Ardebil Rahi-ye Manateq-e Amaliati-ye Jonoub Mishavad" [Ardebil Guards Deputy: 16 Caravans Will Be on Their Way to the Southern Operational Zones], Arya News (Tehran),

March 14, 2011. Available in Persian at http://www.aryanews.com/lct/fa-ir/News/
20110314/20110314172727908.htm (accessed April 11, 2012).
    5. "Farmandeh-ye Sepah-e Hazrat-e Abbas-e (A) ostan-e Ardebil moarrefi shod."
    6. Ibid.
    7. "Farmandeh-ye Sepah-e Ashoura-ye Azarbaijan-e Sharghi moarrefi shod"
[Chief of Ashoura Army of East Azerbaijan Appointed], IRNA, June 28, 2008.
Available in Persian at http://www2.irna.ir/05/news/view/line-156/870408660
9163547.htm (accessed July 21, 2008). The Ashoura Army is a merger of the
Thirty-first Ashoura Army, the Regional Basij Resistance Force, IRGC in the prov-
ince, and other command layers of East Azerbaijan.
    8. "Farmandeh-ye Sepah-e Ashoura: Azarbaijan-e Sharghi az Amn-Tarin-e
Ostanhast" [Ashoura Guards Commander: East Azerbaijan Province is among the
Safest Provinces]," IRNA (Tehran), December 1, 2011. Available in Persian at http://
irna.ir/News/30692031/%D9%81%D8%B1%D9%85%D8%A7%D9%86%D8%AF%D9%87-
%D8%B3%D9%BE%D8%A7%D9%87-%D8%B9%D8%A7%D8%B4%D9%88%D8%B1
%D8%A7,-%D8%A2%D8%B0%D8%B1%D8%A8%D8%A7%DB%8C%D8%AC
%D8%A7%D9%86-%D8%B4%D8%B1%D9%82%DB%8C-%D8%A7%D8%B2-
%D8%A7%D9%85%D9%86-%D8%AA%D8%B1%DB%8C%D9%86-%D8%A7
%D8%B3%D8%AA%D8%A7%D9%86-%D9%87%D8%A7%D8%B3%D8%AA/
%D8%B3%D9%8A%D8%A7%D8%B3%D9%8A/ (accessed April 11, 2012).
    9. Ibid. Ossanlou's predecessor as IRGC chief in East Azerbaijan was Com-
mander Mohammad-Yousef Shakeri.
    10. "Farmandeh-ye Lashkar-e mekanizeh-ye 31 Ashoura: Razmandegan-e in
lashkar hamchoun defae moghaddas az arman-e Emam-e rahel va nezam-e eslami
defae khahand kard" [Thirty-first Mechanized Ashoura Lashkar Chief: Fighters of
This Army Will Defend the Ideals of the Blessed Imam and the Islamic Regime
Like the Sacred Defense], ISNA (Tehran), June 15, 2008. Available in Persian at
http://isna.ir/ISNA/NewsView.aspx?ID=News-1147721 (accessed July 22, 2008).
    11. "Janeshin-e Sepah-e Ashoura-ye Azarbaijan-e Sharghi: Fath-e Khorram-
shahr Jahan Ra Dar Boht Forou Bord" [East Azerbaijan Ashoura Guards Deputy:
Liberation of Khorramshahr Stupified the Entire World], Arya News (Tehran),
n.d. Available in Persian at http://www.aryanews.com/Lct/fa-ir/News/20110525/
20110525101258265.htm (accessed April 11, 2012).
    12. "Farmandeh-ye koll-e Sepah: Doshmanan jorat-e tahdid-e mostaghim-e
keshvar-e ma ra nadarand" [IRGC Commander in Chief: The Enemies Do Not
Dare Pose a Direct Threat against Our Country], IRNA (Tehran), July 16, 2008.
Available in Persian at http://www2.irna.ir/fa/news/view/menu-151/870426846
1073447.htm (accessed July 21, 2008).
    13. "Sardar Mohammad-Yousef shakeri Farmandeh-ye Jadid-e Sepah-e Shohada-
ye Azarbaijan-e Gharbi" [Commander Mohammad-Yousef Shakeri, New West
Azerbaijan Shohada Guards Commander], Khoy Online (Khoy), January 6, 2009.
Available in Persian at http://www.khoyonline.com/index.php?option=com_con-

tent&view=article&id=1308:1389-10-16-10-48-28&catid=59:1389-03-19-14-43-48&Itemid=101 (accessed April 11, 2012).

14. Ibid.

15. "Farmandeh-ye Sepah-e Shohada-ye Azerbaijan-e Gharbi" [Chief of West Azerbaijan IRGC Force], Alborz News (Tehran), July 20, 2008. Available in Persian at http://www.alborznews.net/pages/?cid=6051 (accessed July 22, 2008).

16. "Janeshin-e Sepah-e Shohada-ye Azerbaijan-e Gharbi: Ettehad Va Hamdeli-ye Mellat Zamen-e Eghtedar-e Enqelab-e Eslami va Nirou-ha-ye Mossallah-e Keshvar Ast" [West Azerbaijan Shohada Guards Commander: Unity and Solidarity of the Nation Is the Guarantor of the Greatness of the Islamic Revolution and the Armed Forces of the Country], Arya News (Tehran), February 11, 2011. Available in Persian at http://www.aryanews.com/Lct/fa-ir/News/20110211/2011021 1121758392.htm (accessed April 11, 2012).

17. "Farmandeh-ye koll-e Seah-e Pasdaran-e Enqelab-e Eslami: Niro-ha-ye mardomi bayad be badaneh-ye sepah ettesal yabad" [IRGC Commander in Chief: Popular Forces Must Be Attached to the Body of the Guards], ISNA (Tehran), July 16, 2008. Available in Persian at http://isna.ir/Isna/NewsView.aspx?ID=News-1164863 (accessed July 21, 2008).

18. "Razmayesh-e bozorg-e ettehad-e melli va ensejam-e eslami-ye basijian dar Mahabad payan yaft" [Great War Game of National Unity and Islamic Harmony of the Basij Members in Mahabad Ends], IRNA (Tehran), October 23, 2007. Available in Persian at http://www2.irna.ir/en/news/view/line-7/8608013761132845. htm (accessed July 21, 2008).

19. "Farmandeh-ye Sepah-e ostan-e Bushehr: Jang-e resaneh-I az khatarnak-tarin hajmeh-ha-ye doshmanan ast" [IRGC Bushehr Provincial Chief: Media Warfare Is the Most Dangerous of the Enemy's Assaults], IRNA (Tehran), July 8, 2008. Available in Persian at http://www.khabarfarsi.com/news-162363.htm (accessed July 21, 2008).

20. "Farmandeh-ye Sepah-e Bushehr: Taffakor-e Basij Tamam-e Donya Ra That-e Tasir-e Khod Gharar Dadeh" [Bushehr Guards Commander: The Mentality of the Basij Has Impacted the Entire World], IRNA (Tehran), December 3, 2011. Available in Persian at http://irna.ir/News/30695656/%D9%81%D8% B3%D9%85%D8%A7%D9%86%D8%AF%D9%87-%D8%B3%D9%BE%D8% A7%D9%87-%D8%A8%D9%88%D8%B4%D9%87%D8%B1,%D8%AA%D9 %81%D9%83%D8%B1-%D8%A8%D8%B3%DB%8C%D8%AC%D8%AA %D9%85%D8%A7%D9%85-%D8%AF%D9%86%DB%8C%D8%A7-%D8%B1 %D8%A7-%D8%AA%D8%AD%D8%AA-%D8%AA%D8%A7%D8%AB%DB% 8C%D8%B1-%D8%AE%D9%88%D8%AF-%D9%82%D8%B1%D8%A7%D8% B1%D8%AF%D8%A7%D8%AF%D9%87-%D8%A7%D8%B3%D8%AA/%D8% B3%D9%8A%D8%A7%D8%B3%D9%8A/ (accessed April 11, 2012).

21. Ibid.

22. "Vaziran-e kar va sanaye dar ordou-ye sarasari-ye modiran-e Basij-e Karegari dar Bushehr" [Ministers of Labor and Industry at the Labor Basij Camp

Hosting Basij Executives in Bushehr], Namayan News (Bushehr), April 27, 2008. Available in Persian at http://www.namayannews.com/module-pagesetter-viewpub-tid-1-pid-44.html (accessed July 21, 2008).

23. "Ezzat-e Donya-ye Eslam Az Vojoud-e Velayat-e Faqih Ast" [The Dignity of the World of Islam Is Due to the Guardianship of the Jurist], Ghatreh News (Tehran), October 24, 2011. Available in Persian at http://www.ghatreh.com/news/nn8515234/%D8%AC%D8%A7%D9%86%D8%B4%DB%8C%D9%86-%D9%81%D8%B1%D9%85%D8%A7%D9%86%D8%AF%D9%87-%D8%B3%D9%BE%D8%A7%D9%87-%D8%A8%D9%88%D8%B4%D9%87%D8%B1-%D8%B9%D8%B2%D8%AA-%D8%AF%D9%86%DB%8C%D8%A7%DB%8C-%D8%A7%D8%B3%D9%84%D8%A7%D9%85-%D9%88%D8%AC%D9%88%D8%AF-%D9%88%D9%84%D8%A7%DB%8C%D8%AA-%D9%81%D9%82%DB%8C%D9%87 (accessed April 2012).

24. "Aghaz-e ordou-ha-ye Hejrat-e Basij-e Jame-ye Pezeshki-ye Bushehr" [Beginning of Hejrat Camps of Bushehr Physician's Association], Ebtekar (Tehran), July 6, 2008. Available in Persian at http://www.ebtekarnews.com/Ebtekar/Article.aspx?AID=7158 (accessed July 23, 2008).

25. "Aghaz-e marhaleh-ye ostani-ye tour-e emdadi-ye docharkheh-savari-ye sabz-e Shohada" [Shohada Green Relief Cycling Tour Begins Its Provincial Level], Nasim-e Jonoub (Bushehr), n.d. Available in Persian at http://nasimjonoub.com/articles/article.asp?id=2847 (accessed July 23, 2008).

26. "Farmandeh-ye Sepah-e Ghamar-e Bani-Hashem Chahar-Mahal va Bakhtiari moarrefi shod" [Ghamar-e Bani-Hashem IRGC Army of Chahar-Mahal and Bakhtiari Appointed], IRNA (Tehran), July 2, 2008. Available in Persian at http://www2.irna.ir/fa/news/view/menu-155/8704121672123456.htm (accessed July 21, 2008).

27. "Farmandeh-ye Sepah-e Chahar-Mahal va Bakhtiari Khabar Dad..." [Chahar-Mahal va Bakhtiari Guards Commander Informed...], Ghatreh News (Tehran), December 10, 2011. Avaiable in Persian at http://www.ghatreh.com news/nn8822554/%D9%81%D8%B1%D9%85%D8%A7%D9%86%D8%AF%D9%87-%D8%B3%D9%BE%D8%A7%D9%87-%DA%86%D9%87%D8%A7%D8%B1%D9%85%D8%AD%D8%A7%D9%84-%D8%A8%D8%AE%D8%AA%D9%8A%D8%A7%D8%B1%D9%8A-%D8%AE%D8%A8%D8%B1-%D8%AF%D8%A7%D8%AF-%D8%A7%D8%B9%D8%B2%D8%A7%D9%85-%D8%AF%D8%A7%D9%86%D8%B4-%D8%A2%D9%85%D9%88%D8%B2%D8%A7%D7%D9%86-%D8%AF%D8%AE%D8%AA%D8%B1 (accessed April 11, 2012).

28. Ibid.

29. "Akhbar-e Koutah" [Brief News], Sobh-e Sadeq (Tehran), October 20, 2003. Available in Persian at http://sobhesadegh.ofogh.net/1382/0123/matn/04.htm (accessed July 23, 2008).

30. "Janeshin-e Farmandeh-ye Sepah-e Chahar-Mahal va Bakhtiari..." [Chahar-Mahal va Bakhtiari Guards Deputy...], Fars News (Tehran), April 13, 2010.

Available in Persian at http://www.farsnews.com/newstext.php?nn=8901231330 (accessed April 11, 2012).

31. "Farmandeh-ye Sepah-e Ghamar-e Bani-Hashem Chahar-Mahal va Bakhtiari moarrefi shod."

32. "Sepah-e Fajr-e ostan-e Fars, goshayesh-e fasl-e jadid-e eftekhar-afarini-ye salahshouran-e sarzamin-e Fars" [Fajr Army of Fars Province, Beginning of a New Chapter of Valorous Deeds of the Land of Fars], IRNA (Tehran), June 28, 2008. Available in Persian at http://www2.irna.ir/fa/news/view/menu-155/8704080334124146.htm (accessed July 21, 2008).

33. "Amniat-e Melli-ye Keshvar Bedoun-e Basij Moyassar Nist" [The National Security of the Country Is Not Possible Without the Basij], Fars News (Tehran), November 21, 2011. Available in Persian at http://www.farsnews.com/newstext. php?nn=13900830001662 (accessed April 11, 2012).

34. Ibid.

35. "Roydad-ha-ye Sepah" [News from the Guards], *Sobh-e Sadeq* (Tehran), January 9, 2006. Available in Persian at http://www.sobhesadegh.ir/1384/0235/p04.pdf (accessed July 22, 2008).

36. "Janeshin-e Farmandeh-ye Sepah-e Fajr-e Fars…" [Fars Fajr Guards Deputy…], IRNA (Tehran), June 21, 2011. Available in Persian at http://shiraz.irna. ir/News/30441142/%D8%AC%D8%A7%D9%86%D8%B4%D9%8A%D9%86-%D9%81%D8%B1%D9%85%D8%A7%D9%86%D8%AF%D9%87-%D8%B3 D9%BE%D8%A7%D9%87-%D9%81%D8%AC%D8%B1-%D9%81%D8% A7%D8%B1%D8%B3,-%D8%A7%D8%B2-%D9%83%D9%85-%D8%B1%D9% 86%DA%AF-%D8%B4%D8%AF%D9%86-%D8%A7%D8%B1%D8%B2% D8%B4-%D9%87%D8%A7-%D8%AC%D9%84%D9%88%DA%AF%D9%8A% D8%B1%D9%8A-%D9%83%D9%86%D9%8A%D9%85/%D8%A7%D8%AC% D8%AA%D9%85%D8%A7%D8%B9%D9%8A/ (accessed April 11, 2012).

37. "Sepah-e Fajr-e ostan-e Fars, goshayesh-e fasl-e jadid-e eftekhar-afarini-ye salahshouran-e sarzamin-e Fars."

38. "Tarh-e 'Neshat va taali' dar Fars ejra mishavad" ["Happiness and Exaltation" Scheme to Be Conducted in Fars], *Ebtekar* (Tehran), June 18, 2008. Available in Persian at http://www.ebtekarnews.com/ebtekar/News.aspx?NID=33199 (accessed July 22, 2008).

39. "Yek magham-e Sepah: Masouliat-e Sepah dar in borhe az zaman besyar bozorg ast" [An IRGC Authority: Responsibility of the Guards in This Era Is Very Great], IRNA (Tehran), June 28, 2008. Available in Persian at http://www. khabarfarsi.com/news-140184.htm (accessed July 21, 2008).

40. "Basij Tanha Dar Sayeh-ye Velayat Harekat Mikonad" [The Basij Only Moves in the Shadow of the Guardianship], Ghatreh (Tehran), November 22, 2011. Available in Persian at http://www.ghatreh.com/news/nn8688767/%D9% 81%D8%B1%D9%85%D8%A7%D9%86%D8%AF%D9%87-%D8%B3%D9% BE%D8%A7%D9%87-%D9%82%D8%AF%D8%B3-%DA%AF%DB%8C% D9%84%D8%A7%D9%86-%D8%A8%D8%B3%DB%8C%D8%AC-%D8%AA%

D9%86%D9%87%D8%A7-%D8%B3%D8%A7%DB%8C%D9%87-%D9%88%
D9%84%D8%A7%DB%8C%D8%AA-%D8%AD%D8%B1%DA%A9%D8%AA-
%DA%A9%D9%86%D8%AF (accessed April 11, 2012).

41. Ibid.

42. "Shahid Torab Pour-Gholi, avvalin shahid-e ostan-e Gilan dar defae moghaddas" [Martyr Torab Pour-Gholi, the First Martyr of Gilan in the Sacred Defense], Gilan News (Gilan), April 8, 2008. Available in Persian at http://www.gilannews.ir/841.html (accessed July 22, 2008).

43. "Janeshin-e Farmandeh-ye Sepah-e Quds-e Gilan..." [Gilan Quds Force Deputy...], Fars News (Tehran), May 23, 2011. Available in Persian at http://www.farsnews.com/newstext.php?nn=9003022500 (accessed April 11, 2012).

44. "Yek magham-e Sepah: Masouliat-e Sepah dar in borhe az zaman besyar bozorg ast."

45. "Farmandeh-ye Sepah-e Quds-e Gilan moarrefi shod" [IRGC Quds Force Appointed], Gilan News (Rasht), June 29, 2008. Available in Persian at http://www.gilannews.ir/1088.html (accessed July 22, 2008).

46. "Farmandeh-ye Basij-e keshvar: Sepah va Basij do now-avari-ye Emam va Enqelab-e Eslami boud" [Basij Chief of the Country: The Guards and Basij Were Two Innovations of the Imam and the Islamic Revolution], IRNA (Tehran), July 8, 2008. Available in Persian at http://www1.irna.ir/fa/news/view/menu-149/8704181849214607.htm (accessed July 21, 2008).

47. "570 Barnameh Dar Rabeteh Ba Hafteh-ye Basij Dar Golestan Bargozar Mishavad" [570 Programs Will Take Place in Golestan (Province) on the Occasion of the Basij Week], Qatreh News (Tehran), October 25, 2011. Available in Persian at http://www.ghatreh.com/news/nn8682613/%D9%81%D8%B1%
D9%85%D8%A7%D9%86%D8%AF%D9%87-%D8%B3%D9%BE%D8%A7%
D9%87-%D9%86%DB%8C%D9%86%D9%88%D8%A7-%DA%AF%D9%
84%D8%B3%D8%AA%D8%A7%D9%86-%D8%A8%D8%B1%D9%86%D8%
A7%D9%85%D9%87-%D8%B1%D8%A7%D8%A8%D8%B7%D9%87-
%D9%87%D9%81%D8%AA%D9%87-%D8%A8%D8%B3%DB%8C%D8%AC-
%DA%AF%D9%84%D8%B3%D8%AA%D8%A7%D9%86-%D8%A8%D8%B1
%DA%AF%D8%B2%D8%A7%D8%B1 (accessed April 13, 2012).

48. Ibid.

49. Ibid.

50. "Mehvar-e Faaliat-e Basij Tashkil-e Halgeh-ha-ye Tarh-e Salehin Ast" [The Activities of the Basij Revolve around the Salehin Rings Scheme], Qatreh News (Tehran), July 30, 2011. Available in Persian at http://www.ghatreh.com/news/
nn8055447/%D8%AC%D8%A7%D9%86%D8%B4%DB%8C%D9%86-%D9%
81%D8%B1%D9%85%D8%A7%D9%86%D8%AF%D9%87-%D8%B3%D9%
BE%D8%A7%D9%87-%D9%86%DB%8C%D9%86%D9%88%D8%A7-%DA%
AF%D9%84%D8%B3%D8%AA%D8%A7%D9%86-%D9%85%D8%AD%D9
%88%D8%B1-%D9%81%D8%B9%D8%A7%D9%84%DB%8C%D8%AA-%D

8%A8%D8%B3%DB%8C%D8%AC-%D8%AA%D8%B4%DA%A9%DB%8C%
D9%84-%D8%AD%D9%84%D9%82%D9%87 (accessed April 13, 2012).

51. "Ejra-ye Qanoun-e Hadafmandsazi-ye Yaraneh-ha Nezam va Enqelab Ra
Taqviat Mikonad" [Execution of the Bill Reforming the Subsidies Strengthens the
Regime and the Revolution], Shaba (Tehran), December 1, 2012. Available in
Persian at http://www.shabanews.ir/ViewDetail/Print/82cab264-fd17-11df-9157-
005056a97b93 (accessed April 13, 2012).

52. Ibid.

53. "Farmandeh-ye Sepah-e Ansar al-Hossein-e ostan-e Hamedan mansoub
shod" [IRGC Chief of Ansar al-Hossein Army of Hamedan Appointed], Tebyan-e
Hamedan (Hamedan), July 3, 2008. Available in Persian at http://www.tebyan-
hamedan.ir/mehr/archives/post_268.php (accessed July 21, 2008).

54. "Bidari-ye Eslami Nashat-Gerefteh Az Defae-e Moqaddas Ast" [The Islamic
Awakening Is Inspired by the Sacred Defense], IRNA (Tehran), September 22,
2011. Available in Persian at http://www.irna.ir/News/30576260/%D9%81%
D8%B1%D9%85%D8%A7%D9%86%D8%AF%D9%87-%D8%B3%D9%BE%
D8%A7%D9%87-%D9%87%D9%85%D8%AF%D8%A7%D9%86,%D8%A8%
DB%8C%D8%AF%D8%A7%D8%B1%DB%8C-%D8%A7%D8%B3%D9%
84%D8%A7%D9%85%DB%8C-%D9%86%D8%B4%D8%A7%D8%AA-%DA
%AF%D8%B1%D9%81%D8%AA%D9%87-%D8%A7%D8%B2-%D8%AF%
D9%81%D8%A7%D8%B9-%D9%85%D9%82%D8%AF%D8%B3-%D8%A7%
D8%B3%D8%AA%D8%A7%D8%B3%D8%AA%D8%A7%D9%86%D9%87%
D8%A7/ (accessed April 13, 2012).

55. Ibid.

56. "Sardar Ayoub Soleymani: Nirou-ye Moghavemat-e Basij dar sal-e 85
amalkard-e derakhshani dasht" [Commander Ayoub Soleymani: Basij Resistance
Force Has a Shining Record for the Year 2007], Hegmataneh (Hamedan), February 7, 2008. Available in Persian at http://www.hegmataneh.org/1386/03/05/_
85_1.php (accessed July 22, 2008).

57. "Begou-Magou-ha-ye Barkhi Masoulan Risheh-ye Moezelat-e Emrouz-e
Jameeh Ast" [Verbal Fights among the Authorities Is the Root of the Problems
of Today's Society], Fars News (Tehran), November 27, 2011. Available in
Persian at http://www.ghatreh.com/news/nn8737558/%D8%AC%D8%A7%
D9%86%D8%B4%DB%8C%D9%86-%D9%81%D8%B1%D9%85%D8%A7%D
9%86%D8%AF%D9%87-%D8%B3%D9%BE%D8%A7%D9%87-%D8%A7%D
9%86%D8%B5%D8%A7%D8%B1%D8%A7%D9%84%D8%AD%D8%B3%DB
%8C%D9%86%28%D8%B9%29-%D9%87%D9%85%D8%AF%D8%A7%D9%
86-%D8%A8%DA%AF%D9%88%D9%85%DA%AF%D9%88%D9%87%D8%
A7%DB%8C-%D8%A8%D8%B1%D8%AE%DB%8C-%D9%85%D8%B3%D8%
A6%D9%88%D9%84%D8%A7%D9%86-%D8%B1%DB%8C%D8%B4%
D9%87-%D9%85%D8%B9%D8%B6%D9%84%D8%A7%D8%AA (accessed
April 13, 2012).

58. "Ghabeliat-ha va zarfiat-ha-ye Sepah ra dar anjam-e mamouriat-ha afza-yesh dahim" [Let's Increase Capacities and Capabilities of the Guards While Attending to Duties], Shabestan (Hamedan), July 20, 2008. Available in Persian at http://www.shabestan.ir/newsdetail.asp?newsid=87043012353825&code=76 (accessed July 21, 2008).

59. Ibid.

60. "Dar pey-e taghirat-e sakhtari-ye Sepah dar ostan-ha, Sepah-e Emam Sajjad-e Hormozgan tashkil shod" [Following IRGC's Provincial Structural Changes, Imam Sajjad IRGC Army of Hormozgan Was Formed], ISNA (Tehran), July 14, 2008. Available in Persian at http://branch.isna.ir/Mainoffices/NewsView. aspx?ID=News-79462 (accessed July 21, 2008).

61. "Ba Hozour-e Sardar Salami, Farmandeh-ye Jadid-e Sepah-e Hormozgan Moarrefi Shod" [The New Commander of the Guards in Hormozgan Was Presented in Commander Salami's Presence], Hormozgan News (Hormozgan), May 18, 2011. Available in Persian at http://hormozgan.basij.ir/?q=node/10410 (accessed April 13, 2012).

62. Ibid.

63. "Zarei Janeshin-e Mowlaparast Dar Sepah-e Emam Sajjad Shod" [Zarei Was Appointed Mowlaparast's Deputy in Imam Sajjad Guards], Hormozgan News (Hormozgan), September 29, 2011. Available in Persian at http://www. hormozgannews.com/Pages/News-1652.html (accessed April 13, 2012).

64. Ibid.

65. "Reis-polis-e Ilam: Tahajom-e farhangi shiveh-ye doshmanan bara-ye moghabeleh ba nezam ast" [Ilam Police Chief: Cultural Invasion Is the Method of the Enemy to Counter the Regime], IRNA (Tehran), July 5, 2008. Available in Persian at http://www2.irna.com/fa/news/view/menu-269/8704150068132503. htm (accessed July 22, 2008).

66. "Besyari Az Khavas Emtehan-e Khoubi Pas Nadadand" [Many Elites Did Not Pass the Exam], Fars News (Tehran), n.d. Available in Persian at http://www.ghatreh.com/ news/nn8801206/%D9%81%D8%B1%D9%85%D8%A7%D9%86%D8%AF% D9%87-%D8%B3%D9%BE%D8%A7%D9%87-%D8%A7%DB%8C%D9%84 %D8%A7%D9%85-%D8%A8%D8%B3%DB%8C%D8%A7%D8%B1%DB% 8C-%D8%AE%D9%88%D8%A7%D8%B5-%D8%A7%D9%85%D8%AA%D8 %AD%D8%A7%D9%86-%D8%AE%D9%88%D8%A8%DB%8C-%D9%86% D8%AF%D8%A7%D8%AF%D9%86%D8%AF (accessed April 13, 2012).

67. "Farmandeh-ye gharar-gah-e Najaf: Sepah-e Pasdaran dar behtarin sharayet gharar darad" [Najaf Base Chief: The Revolutionary Guards Are in the Best Position], IRNA (Tehran), June 24, 2008. Available in Persian at http://www2.irna. ir/fa/news/view/menu-155/8704049728142655.htm (accessed July 22, 2008).

68. "Enteghad-e shadid al-lahn-e sardar Kaki farmandeh-ye arshad-e Sepah-e Hamedan az masoulin-e nakaramad-e ostan-e Ilam" [Harsh Criticism of Senior Hamedan IRGC Commander Kaki of Incompetent Authorities in Hamedan],

Ilam News (Ilam), January 26, 2008. Available in Persian at http://ilam-new.blogfa.com/post-171.aspx (accessed July 22, 2008).

69. "Rouy-dad-ha-ye Sepah" [News from the Guards], *Sobh-e Sadeq* (Tehran), February 19, 2007. Available in Persian at http://www.sobhesadegh.ir/1385/0291/p04.pdf (accessed July 22, 2008).

70. "Razmayesh-e Tamrinat-e Taktiki-ye Basijian-e Dehloran Bargozar Shod" [Tactical War Game of the Basij Members of Dehloran Took Place], Fars News (Tehran), February 20, 2010. Available in Persian at http://www.farsnews.com/newstext.php?nn=8812010287 (accessed April 13, 2012).

71. "Farmandeh-ye Sepah-e Saheb al-Zaman-e ostan-e Esfahan moarrefi shod" [Commander of the Saheb al-Zaman (Peace Be upon Him) Army of Isfahan Appointed], IRNA (Tehran), June 30, 2008. Available in Persian at http://www2.irna.com/03/news/view/menu-626/8704106269131923.htm (accessed July 21, 2008).

72. "Bayad Dar Ghozat va Vokala Tafakor-e Basiji Vojoud Dashteh Bashad" [Basij Mentality Must Be Present among Lawyers and Judges], ISNA (Tehran), December 2, 2011. Available in Persian at http://isfahan.isna.ir/Default.aspx?NSID=5&SSLID=46&NID=6606 (accessed April 13, 2012).

73. Ibid.

74. Ibid.

75. "5 Prozheh-ye Omrani-ye Basij Dar Nain Eftetah va be Bahrebardari Resid" [Five Developmental Projects of the Basij in Nain Were Inaugurated], IMNA (Tehran), November 24, 2011. Available in Persian at http://www.imna.ir/vdcjvoex.uqeohzsffu.txt (accessed April 13, 2012).

76. "Sepah-e ostan-e Kerman ba onvan-e 'Sepah-e Sarallah' tashkil shod" [IRGC Army of Kerman Formed under the Name of "Sarallah Army"], Fars News Agency (Tehran), June 30, 2008. Available in Persian at http://www.farsnews.com/newstext.php?nn=8704101150 (accessed July 21, 2008).

77. "Ostan-e Kerman 900,000 Basiji Darad" [Kerman Province Has 900,000 Basij Members], IRNA (Tehran), November 24, 2011.Available in Persian at http://irna.ir/News/30680180/%D9%81%D8%B1%D9%85%D8%A7%D9%86%D8%AF%D9%87%20%D8%B3%D9%BE%D8%A7%D9%87%20%D8%AB%D8%A7%D8%B1%D8%A7%D9%84%D9%84%D9%87,%20%D8%A7%D8%B3%D8%AA%D8%A7%D9%86%20%D9%83%D8%B1%D9%85%D8%A7%D%86%20900%20%D9%87%D8%B2%D8%A7%D8%B1%20%D8%A8%D8%B3%DB%8C%D8%AC%DB%8C%20%D8%AF%D8%A7%D8%B1%D8%AF/%D8%B3%D9%8A%D8%A7%D8%B3%D9%8A/ (accessed April 13, 2012).

78. Ibid.

79. "Sharh-e majara" [The Course of Events], Shahid Hajj-Ahmad Kazemi blog (Iran), April 13, 2007. Available in Persian at http://ahmad-kazemi.blogfa.com/post-34.aspx (accessed July 22, 2008).

80. "Baznamayi-ye Amaliat-e Valfajr-e 8 Dar Mouzeh-ye Defaei-e Moghaddas-e Kerman" [Inauguration of the Valfajr 8 Operation at Kerman's Sacred Defense

Museum], Fars News (Tehran), September 23, 2010. Available in Persian at http://www.farsnews.com/newstext.php?nn=8907010115 (accessed April 13, 2012).

81. "Sepah-e ostan-e Kerman ba onvan-e 'Sepah-e Sarallah' tashkil shod."

82. "Ahdaf-e tarh-e misagh-e Basij elam shod: Jazb-e gorouh-ha-ye bishtar, ensejam-e nirou-ha-ye sazemandehi-shodeh-ye Basij" [Goals of the Misagh Scheme of the Basij Announced: More Recruitment, Harmonization of the Organized Basij Forces], Kerman-e Ma (Kerman), June 10, 2007. Available in Persian at http://www.kermanema.com/module-pagesetter-viewpub-tid-1-pid-1308.html (accessed July 22, 2008).

83. "Farmandeh-ye Sepah-e Nabi-ye Akram-e Ostan-e Kermanshah..." [Kermanshah Province Nabi-ye Akram Guards Commander...], Kermanshah Basij (Kermanshah), n.d. Available in Persian at http://kermanshah.basij.ir/?q=node/20721 (accessed April 13, 2012).

84. "Farmandeh-ye Sepah-e ostan-e Kermanshah moarrefi shod" [IRGC Chief of Kermanshah Province Appointed], ISNA (Tehran), July 2, 2008. Available in Persian at http://kermanshah.isna.ir/mainnews.php?ID=News-17896 (accessed July 21, 2008).

85. "Farmandeh-ye arshad-e Sepah dar gharb-e keshvar" [Senior IRGC Commander in Western Iran], ISNA (Tehran), March 5, 2008. Available in Persian at http://kermanshah.isna.ir/mainnews.php?ID=News-16240 (accessed July 21, 2008).

86. "Tafakor-e Basiji Monjar be Sarafrazi-ye Iran dar Donya Shodeh Ast" [Basij Mentality Has Led to Pride of Iran Internationally], Fars News (Tehran), November 23, 2010. Available in Persian at http://www.farsnews.com/newstext.php?nn=8909020767 (accessed April 13, 2012).

87. "Farmandeh-ye Sepah-e ostan-e Kermanshah moarrefi shod."

88. "Farmandeh-ye Sepah-e Khorasan-e Shomali moarrefi shod" [North Khorasan IRGC Chief Appointed], Farda News (Tehran), June 28, 2008. Available in Persian at http://www.fardanews.com/fa/pages/?cid=54797 (accessed July 21, 2008).

89. "Bidari-ye Eslami Hasel-e Khoun-e Shohada va Basijian Ast" [The Islamic Awakening Is the Result of the Blood of the Martyrs and the Basij Members], IRNA (Tehran), November 23, 2011.Available in Persian at http://irna.ir/News/30677886/%D9%81%D8%B1%D9%85%D8%A7%D9%86%D8%AF%D9%87%20%D8%B3%D9%BE%D8%A7%D9%87%20%D8%AE%D8%B1%D8%A7%D8%B3%D8%A7%D9%86%20%D8%B4%D9%85%D8%A7%D9%84%DB%8C,%20%D8%A8%DB%8C%D8%AF%D8%A7%D8%B1%DB%8C%20%D8%A7%D8%B3%D9%84%D8%A7%D9%85%DB%8C%20%D8%AD%D8%A7%D8%B5%D9%84%20%D8%AE%D9%88%D9%86%20%D8%B4%D9%87%D%AF%D8%A7%20%D9%88%20%D8%A8%D8%B3%DB%8C%D8%AC%DB8C%D8%A7%D9%86%20%D8%A7%D8%B3%D8%AA/%D8%A7%D8%AC%D8%AA%D9%85%D8%A7%D8%B9%D9%8A/ (accessed April 13, 2012).

90. Ibid.

91. "Roshd-e 176 Darsadi-ye Faaliatha-ye Basij-e Sazandegi Dar Khorasan-e Shomali" [176 Percent Growth in Basij Activities in North Khorasan (Province)], Khorasan-e Shomali (North Khorasan), January 3, 2011. Available in Persian at http://khshomali.sbs.gov.ir/sites/index.php?Page=definition&UID=216827 (accessed April 13, 2012).

92. Ibid.

93. "Akhbar-e Koutah" [Brief News], *Quds* (Mashhad), November 14, 2006. Available in Persian at http://www.qudsdaily.com/archive/1385/html/8/1385-08-23/page3.html (accessed July 23, 2008).

94. Sepah-e Emam Reza dar Khorasan-e Razavi tashkil shod" [Emam Reza Guards (Unit) Was Established in Khorasan-e Razavi], Shabestan News (Mashhad), July 2, 2008. Available in Persian at http://www.shabestannews.com/newsdetail.asp?newsid=87041213080934&code=58 (accessed July 21, 2008).

95. "Bargozari-ye Yadvareh-ye Shohada Dar Moghabeleh Ba Fetneh Zarouri Ast" [Commemoration of the Martyrs of the Sedition Is Necessary], Fars News (Tehran), May 23, 2011. Available in Persian at http://www.farsnews.com/news text.php?nn=9003022677 (accessed April 13, 2012).

96. Ibid.

97. Ibid.

98. "Basijian-e Sazeman-yafteh-ye Khorasan-e Razavi Az Marz-e Yek Mellion Nafar Gozasht" [The Number of Organized Basij Members in Khorasan Surpasses One Million], Fars News (Tehran), November 17, 2011. Available in Persian at http://www.farsnews.com/printable.php?nn=13900826000438 (accessed April 13, 2012).

99. Ibid.

100. Ibid.

101 "203 paygah-e Basij dar ostan-e Khorasan-e Jonoubi mojri-ye tarh-e neshat va taali hastand" [203 Basij Bases in South Khorasan Province Engaged in the Happiness and Exaltation Scheme], Basij News (Tehran), June 26, 2008. Available in Persian at http://www.basijnews.com/Ndetail.asp?NewsID=19344 (accessed July 21, 2008).

102. Vazheh-ha-ye Eslami Dar Defae-e Moghaddas Einiat Peyda Kard" [Islamic Concepts Became Visible During the Sacred Defense], Arya News (Tehran), November 8, 2011. Available in Persian at http://www.aryanews.com/Lct/fa-ir/News/20111108/20111108164424194.htm (accessed April 13, 2012).

103. Ibid.

104. "Taghdir-e farmandeh-ye mantaghe-ye moghavemat-e Basij-e Sepah-e Khorasan-e Jonoubi sartip-dovvom-e pasdar Gholam-Reza Ahmadi az basijian-e ostan" [Brigadier General Reza Ahmadi Praises Members of the Guard's Basij in Southern Khorasan Operational Area], South Khorasan Portal (Khorasan), November 27, 2007. Available in Persian at http://www.sk-portal.ir/index.php?option=com_content&task=view&id=291&Itemid=1 (accessed July 22, 2008).

105. "Doshman Ba Tahrim-ha Mikhahad Iran Az Amadegi Ghafel Shavad" [The Enemy Intends to Dilute Iran's Attention through Sanctions], Fars News (Tehran), November 28, 2011. Available in Persian at http://www.ghatreh.com/news/nn8753805/%D8%AC%D8%A7%D9%86%D8%B4%DB%8C%D9%86-%D9%81%D8%B1%D9%85%D8%A7%D9%86%D8%AF%D9%87-%D8%B3%D9%BE%D8%A7%D9%87-%D8%AE%D8%B1%D8%A7%D8%B3%D8%A7%D9%86-%D8%AC%D9%86%D9%88%D8%A8%DB%8C-%D8%AF%D8%B4%D9%85%D9%86-%D8%AA%D8%AD%D8%B1%DB%8C%D9%85-%D8%AE%D9%88%D8%A7%D9%87%D8%AF-%D8%A7%DB%8C%D8%B1%D8%A7%D9%86-%D8%A2%D9%85%D8%A7%D8%AF%DA%AF%DB%8C (accessed April 13, 2012).
106. "Namayandeh-ye vizheh-ye farmandeh-ye koll-e Sepah: Gharn-e bist va yekom gharn-e Eslam ast" [Special Representative of Commander in Chief of the Guards: The Twenty-first Century Is the Century of Islam], IRNA (Tehran), July 1, 2008. Available in Persian at http://www.khabarfarsi.com/news-148398.htm (accessed July 21, 2008).
107. "Meydan-e Mobarezeh Ba Tahajom-e Farhangi Ra Khali Nemikonim" [We Will Not Retreat from the Arena of Cultural Struggle], Fars News (Tehran), November 28, 2011. Available in Persian at http://www.ghatreh.com/news/nn8754001/%D9%81%D8%B1%D9%85%D8%A7%D9%86%D8%AF%D9%87-%D8%B3%D9%BE%D8%A7%D9%87-%D9%88%D9%84%DB%8C-%D8%B9%D8%B5%D8%B1%28%D8%B9%D8%AC%29-%D8%AE%D9%88%D8%B2%D8%B3%D8%AA%D8%A7%D9%86-%D9%85%DB%8C%D8%AF%D8%A7%D9%86-%D9%85%D8%A8%D8%A7%D8%B1%D8%B2%D9%87-%D8%AA%D9%87%D8%A7%D8%AC%D9%85-%D9%81%D8%B1%D9%87%D9%86%DA%AF%DB%8C-%D8%AE%D8%A7%D9%84%DB%8C (accessed April 13, 2012).
108. Ibid.
109. "Towdie va moarefeh-ye masoul-e namayandegi-ye Vali-ye Faqih dar Lashkar-e 7 Vali Asr" [Farewell and Presentation Ceremony of the Supreme Leader's Representatives in the Seventh Vali Asr Lashkar], Nour-e Khouzestan (Khouzestan), n.d. Available in Persian at http://www.ahwazstudies.org/main/index.php?option=com_content&task=view&id=2297&Itemid=48&lang=PR (accessed July 23, 2008).
110. "Hamayesh-e Ostani-ye Pishgiri Az Voghou-e Jorm Dar Nirou-ha-ye Mossallah" [Provincial Level Crime Prevention in the Armed Forces Seminar], Qatreh (Tehran), December 26, 2010. Available in Persian at http://www.ghatreh.com/news/nn6665786/%D9%87%D9%85%D8%A7%DB%8C%D8%B4-%D8%A7%D8%B3%D8%AA%D8%A7%D9%86%DB%8C%D9%BE%DB%8C%D8%B4%DA%AF%DB%8C%D8%B1%DB%8C-%D9%88%D9%82%D9%88%D8%B9-%D8%AC%D8%B1%D9%85-%D9%86%DB%8C%D8%B1%D9%88%D9%87%D8%A7%DB%8C-%D9%85%D8%B3%D9%84%D8%AD-%D8%AC%D8%A7%D9%86%D8%B4%DB%8C%D9%86-%D9%81%D8%B1%

D9%85%D8%A7%D9%86%D8%AF%D9%87-%D8%B3%D9%BE%D8%A7%
D9%87 (accessed April 13, 2012).

111. "Namayandeh-ye vizheh-ye farmandeh-ye koll-e Sepah: Gharn-e bist va
yekom gharn-e Eslam ast."

112. "Howeizeh yek ghate-ye ashoura-yi va mandegar ast" [Howeizeh Is
an Ashurayean Piece and Therefore Eternal], Shahid Hossein Alam al-Hoda
(Mashhad), n.d. Available in Persian at http://www.alamalhoda.com/index.php?
option=com_content&task=view&id=164&Itemid=1 (accessed July 21, 2008).

113. "Hamdeli va ekhlas-e Pasdaran ramz-e tahhavol-e Sepah ast" [Unity of Heart
and Sincerity of the Guardsmen Is the Secret of Transformation of the Guards],
Basij News (Tehran), July 21, 2008. Available in Persian at http://www.basijnews.
com/Ndetail.asp?NewsID=20303 (accessed July 21, 2008).

114. "Khoun-e Shohada Va Amal-e Basijian Amniat-e Keshvar Ra Bimeh Kard"
[The Blood of the Martyrs and Deeds of the Basij Members Ensured the Security
of the Country], Qatreh (Tehran), November 24, 2011. Available in Persian at
http://www.ghatreh.com/news/nn8702528%D9%81%D8%B1%D9%85%D8
%A7%D9%86%D8%AF%D9%87-%D8%B3%D9%BE%D8%A7%D9%87%
DA%A9%D9%87%DA%AF%DB%8C%D9%84%D9%88%DB%8C%D9%87
%D8%A8%D9%88%DB%8C%D8%B1%D8%A7%D8%AD%D9%85%D8%
AF-%D8%AE%D9%88%D9%86-%D8%B4%D9%87%D8%AF%D8%A7-
%D8%B9%D9%85%D9%84-%D8%A8%D8%B3%DB%8C%D8%AC%DB%8C
%D8%A7%D9%86-%D8%A7%D9%85%D9%86%DB%8C%D8%AA%DA%A9
%D8%B4%D9%88%D8%B1 (accessed April 13, 2012).

115. "Farmandeh-ye Sepah-e ostan-e Kohkilouyeh va Boyer-Ahmad moarrefi
shod" [IRGC Chief of Kohkilouyeh and Boyer-Ahmad Appointed], ISNA (Tehran), July 2, 2008. Available in Persian at http://isna.ir/Isna/NewsView.aspx?ID=
News-1157123 (accessed July 21, 2008).

116. "Dast-yabi be fan-avari-ye soukht-e hasteh-I jahan ra mottehayyer kard"
[Access to Nuclear Fuel Technology Has Stupified the World], Fars News (Tehran),
April 13, 2006. Available in Persian at http://www.farsnews.com/newstext.
php?nn=8501240129 (accessed July 21, 2008).

117. "Amaliat-e Beit al-Moghaddas Neshaneh-ye Eghtedar-e Razmandegan-e
Eslam Boud" [The Beit al-Moghadddas Operation Was a Sign of the Might of the
Warriors of Islam], Fars News (Tehran), May 23, 2009. Available in Persian at http://
www.farsnews.com/newstext.php?nn=8803020964 (accessed April 13, 2012).

118. "Gheflat az rah-e shohada bozorgtarin tahdid bara-ye keshvar ast" [Ignorance
on the Path of the Martyrs Is the Greatest Threat to the Country], Basij Students'
News Network (Tehran), July 15, 2008. Available in Persian at http://snn.ir/
NewsContent.aspx?NewsID=74190 (accessed July 23, 2008).

119. "Farmandeh-ye Sepah-e Beit al-Moghaddas-e Kordestan moarrefi shod"
[Commander of Beit al-Moghaddas IRGC Army of Kordestan Appointed], Basij
News (Tehran), July 5, 2008. Available in Persian at http://www.basijnews.ir/
Ndetail.asp?NewsID=19725 (accessed July 21, 2008).

120. "Nirou-ha-ye Nezami-ye Kordestani Goush Be Farman-e Vali-ye Faqih-And" [Kurdish Military Forces Abide the Orders of the Guardian Jurist], Fars News (Tehran), September 27, 2011. Available in Persian at http://www.farsnews.com/newstext.php?nn=13900705000646 (accessed April 13, 2012).
121. Ibid.
122. Ibid.
123. "Janeshin-e Sepah-e Beit al-Moghaddas-e Kordestan..." [Kurdistan Beit al-Moghaddas Guards Deputy...], Qatreh (Tehran), October 28, 2011. Available in Persian at http://www.ghatreh.com/news/nn8540887/%D8 AC%D8%A7% D9%86%D8%B4%DB%8C%D9%86%D8%B3%D9%BE%D8%A7%D9%87- %D8%A8%DB%8C%D8%AA-%D8%A7%D9%84%D9%85%D9%82%D8%A F%D8%B3-%DA%A9%D8%B1%D8%AF%D8%B3%D8%AA%D8%A7%D9% 86-%D9%81%D8%B1%D9%87%D9%86%DA%AF-%D8%A8%D8%B3% DB%8C%D8%AC%DB%8C-%D8%AA%D9%84%D8%A7%D8%B4-%D9%87 %D8%A7%DB%8C-%D8%AF%D8%B4%D9%85%D9%86%D8%A7%D9%86 (accessed April 13, 2012).
124. "Farmandeh-ye Sepah-e Lorestan moarrefi shod" [IRGC Chief of Lorestan Appointed], ISNA (Tehran), July 5, 2008. Available in Persian at http://isna.ir/Isna/NewsView.aspx?ID=News-1159191 (accessed July 21, 2008).
125. "Roshd va Taali-ye Keshvar Mostalzem-e Paybandi Be Osoul-e Basij Ast" [Loyalty toward the Foundations of the Basij Is the Precondition for the Growth and Exaltation of the Country], IRNA (Tehran), November 23, 2011. Available in Persian at http://irna.ir/News/30677660/%D8%B1%D8%B4%D8%AF-%D9% 88-%D8%AA%D8%B9%D8%A7%D9%84%DB%8C-%D9%83%D8%B4% D9%88%D8%B1-%D9%85%D8%B3%D8%AA%D9%84%D8%B2%D9%85-% D9%BE%D8%A7%DB%8C%D8%A8%D9%86%D8%AF%DB%8C-%D8%A8% D9%87-%D8%A7%D8%B5%D9%88%D9%84-%D8%A8%D8%B3%DB%8C% D8%AC-%D8%A7%D8%B3%D8%AA/%D8%B3%D9%8A%D8%A7%D8%B3% D9%8A/ (accessed April 13, 2012).
126. Ibid.
127. "Dovvomin jashnvareh-ye nava-ha-ye hemasi-e Rahmat" [Second Rahmat Military March Festival], Soureh-ye Mehr (Khorram Abad), n.d. Available in Persian at http://www.iricap.com/magentry.asp?id=5219 (accessed July 23, 2008).
128. "Tedad-e Shohada-ye Enfejar-e Mohemmat-e Padegan-e Emam Ali-ye Lorestan Farda Elam Mishavad" [The Number of the Martyrs of the Imam Ali Garrison Explosion Will Be Announced Tomorrow], Fars News (Tehran), October 12, 2010. Available in Persian at http://www.farsnews.com/newstext. php?nn=8907201746 (accessed April 13, 2012).
129. "Farmandeh-ye Sepah-e Lorestan moarrefi shod."
130. "Farmandeh-ye Sepah-e Rouhollah-e ostan-e Markazi moarrefi shod" [IRGC Rouhollah Army Chief of Markazi Province Appointed], IRNA (Tehran), July 1, 2008. Available in Persian at http://www2.irna.com/fa/news/view/menu-273/8704114113182024.htm (accessed July 21, 2008).

131. "Ezharat-e Farmandeh-ye Sepah-e Rouhollah-e Ostan…" [Statements of the Commander of the Rouhollah Guards (unit)], Markazi Daily (Markazi), November 23, 2011. Available in Persian at http://markazidaily.ir/?p=34616 (accessed April 13, 2012).

132. Ibid. Prior to this appointment, Brigadier General Ahmad Salim-Abadi was the IRGC chief in Markazi province.

133. "Farmandeh-ye Basij-e Golestan: Gharb dar moghabeleh ba keshvar-ha-ye eslami be amaliyat-e ravani rouy-avard" [The West Uses Psychological Operations against Islamic Countries], IRNA (Tehran), November 27, 2007. Available in Persian at http://www1.irna.com/ar/news/view/line-9/8609065179155929.htm (accessed July 23, 2008).

134. "Ezharat-e Janeshin-e Farmandeh-ye Sepah-e Rouhollah…" [Statements of the Rouhollah Guards (Unit) Deputy…], Markazi Daily (Markazi), October 14, 2011. Available in Persian at http://markazidaily.ir/?p=32243 (accessed April 13, 2012).

135. "Janeshin-e farmandehi-ye Sepah-e Rouhollah-e ostan-e Markazi moarrefi shod." [Deputy Chief of Rouhollah IRGC Army of Markazi Province Appointed], IRNA (Tehran), July 21, 2008. Available in Persian at http://www2.irna.ir/fa/news/view/menu-155/8704315420095631.htm (accessed July 21, 2008).

136. Ibid.

137. "Farmandeh-ye Sepah-e Karbala-ye Mazandaran: Sepah bazou-ye tavanmand-e nezam-e eslami ast" [Karbala IRGC Army Chief in Mazandaran: The Guards Is the Powerful Arm of the Islamic Regime], IRNA (Tehran), June 29, 2008. Available in Persian at http://www2.irna.ir/fa/news/view/menu-155/8704092756145855.htm (accessed July 21, 2008).

138. "Farmandeh-ye Sepah-e Karbala-ye Mazandaran…" [Mazandaran Guards (unit) Commander…], Qatreh (Tehran), November 9, 2011. Available in Persian at http://www.ghatreh.com/news/nn8612679%D9%81%D8%B1%D9%85%D%A7%D9%86%D8%AF%D9%87-%D8%B3%D9%BE%D8%A7%D9%7-%DA%A9%D8%B1%D8%A8%D9%84%D8%A7%DB%8C-%D9%85%D8%A7%D8%B2%D9%86%D8%AF%D8%B1%D8%A7%D9%86-%D8%A7%D9%87%D8%AF%D8%A7%D9%81-%D9%85%D8%AE%D8%B1%D8%A8-%D8%BA%D8%B1%D8%A8-%D8%AC%D9%86%DA%AF-%D8%B1%D8%B3%D8%A7%D9%86%D9%87-%D8%A8%D8%B1%D8%A7%DB%8C (accessed April 13, 2012).

139 Ibid.

140 "Akhbar-e tarh-e takrim" [News from the Takrim Scheme], Governorate of Mazandaran (Mazandaran), July 2, 2008. Available in Persian at http://64.233.183.104/search?q=cache:_7zINgSo6PMJ:prinfo-mz.ir/News Reports/70231111348.htm+%D8%B9%D9%84%D9%8A+%D8%B4%D8%A7%D9%84%D9%8A%D9%83%D8%A7%D8%B1&hl=en&ct=clnk&cd=6&gl=ru (accessed July 23, 2008).

141 "Janeshin-e Farmandehi-ye Sepah-e Karbala…" [Karbala Guards (unit) Deputy…],Qatreh (Tehran), August 1, 2011. Available in Persian at http://www.ghatreh.com/news/nn7993958/%D8%AC%D8%A7%D9%86%D8%B4%DB%

8C%D9%86-%D9%81%D8%B1%D9%85%D8%A7%D9%86%D8%AF%D9%
87%DB%8C-%D8%B3%D9%BE%D8%A7%D9%87-%DA%A9%D8%B1%D8%
A8%D9%84%D8%A7-%D8%B4%D8%AC%D8%B1%D9%87-%D8%B7%DB%
8C%D8%A8%D9%87-%D8%A8%D8%B3%DB%8C%D8%AC-%D8%B3%D9%
BE%D8%A7%D9%87-%D8%B1%DB%8C%D8%B4%D9%87-%D8%B9%D8%
A7%D8%B4%D9%88%D8%B1%D8%A7 (accessed April 13, 2012).

142. "Farhang-e defae moghaddas va isar dar jameeh gostaresh yabad" [The Culture of the Sacred Defense and Self-Sacrifice Should Proliferate in the Society], Shabestan (Mazandaran), July 9, 2008. Available in Persian at http://www.shabestan.ir/newsdetail.asp?newsid=87041911070440 (accessed July 23, 2008).

143. "Mohandes Shaffeghat dar jalaseh-ye showra-ye edari-ye ostan-e Mazandaran elam kard" [Engineer Shaffeghat Announces at the Administrative Council of the Mazandaran Province], Public Relations Office of Mazandaran Province (Mazandaran), March 13, 2007. Available in Persian at http://prinfo-mz.ir/News/Ostandari/851222105934-311.html (accessed July 23, 2008).

144. "Sardar Hejazi: Sakhtar-e jadid, amadegi-ye Sepah dar barabar-e tahdidat afzayesh midahad" [Commander Hejazi: The New Structure Increases the Preparedness of the Guards toward Threats], IRNA (Tehran), June 29, 2008. Available in Persian at http://www2.irna.ir/fa/news/view/menu-155/8704092720122557.htm (accessed July 21, 2008).

145. "Farmandeh-ye Sepah-e Nahiyeh-ye Qazvin…" [Qazvin Zone Guards Commander…], Qatreh (Tehran), November 21, 2011. Available in Persian at http://www.ghatreh.com/news/nn8678125/%D9%81%D8%B1%D9%85%D8%A7%D9%86%D8%AF%D9%87-%D8%B3%D9%BE%D8%A7%D9%87-%D9%82%D8%B2%D9%88%DB%8C%D9%86-%D8%AA%D8%A7%D8%B3%DB%8C-%D9%85%D9%82%D8%A7%D9%85-%D9%85%D8%B9%D8%B8%D9%85-%D8%B1%D9%87%D8%A8%D8%B1%DB%8C-%D9%85%D9%82%D8%AA%D8%AF%D8%B1%D8%A7%D9%86%D9%87-%D8%A7%DB%8C%D8%B3%D8%AA%D8%A7%D8%AF%D9%87-%D8%A7%DB%8C%D9%85 (accessed April 13, 2012).

146. Ibid.

147. Ibid.

148. "Janeshin-e Farmandeh-ye Tip-e Saheb al-Amr-e Sepah-e Ostan-e Qazvin…" [Qazvin Province Saheb al-Amr Guards Deputy…], *Resalat* (Tehran), April 22, 2009. Available in Persian at http://www.basijnews.com/Ndetail.asp?NewsID=100475 (accessed April 15, 2012).

149. Bizhan Yeganeh, "Taghir-e sakhtar va barkenari-ye gostardeh farmandehan-e miani-ye Sepah" [Structural Change and Widespread Dismissal of Midlevel Commanders of the Guards], Radio Farda (Prague), June 30, 2008. Available in Persian at http://www.radiofarda.com/Article/2008/06/30/f4_Revolutiaonary_Guard_changes_Iran.html (accessed July 21, 2008).

150. "Aghaz-e Amaliat-e Toseeh…" [The Beginning of the Expansion Activity…], Qatreh (Tehran), November 16, 2011. Available in Persian at http://www.

ghatreh.com/news/nn8652181/%D8%AD%D8%B6%D9%88%D8%B1-%
D9%81%D8%B1%D9%85%D8%A7%D9%86%D8%AF%D9%87-%D8%B3%
|D9%BE%D8%A7%D9%87-%D8%B9%D9%84%DB%8C-%D8%A7%D8%
A8%DB%8C-%D8%B7%D8%A7%D9%84%D8%A8%28%D8%B9%29%
D8%B5%D9%88%D8%B1%D8%AA-%DA%AF%D8%B1%D9%81%D8%
AA-%D8%A2%D8%BA%D8%A7%D8%B2-%D8%B9%D9%85%D9%84%
DB%8C%D8%A7%D8%AA-%D8%AA%D9%88%D8%B3%D8%B9%D9%87
(accessed April 15, 2012).

151. Ibid.

152. "Dar marasem-e todie va moarefeh-e farmandeh-ye Lashkar-e 17 onvan
shod" [Said at the Presentation of Seventeenth 'Lashkar'], *Shakhe-ye Sabz* (Qom),
January 4, 2008. Available in Persian at http://shsabznews.blogfa.com/post-231.
aspx (accessed July 23, 2008).

153. "Sakhteman-e Paygah-e Shahid Hasheminezhad-e Qom Eftetah Shod"
[Martyr Hasheminejad Base Building in Qom Was Inaugurated], Fars News
(Tehran), November 27, 2011. Available in Persian at http://www.ghatreh.com/
news/nn8734391/%D8%AD%D8%B6%D9%88%D8%B1-%D8%AC%D8%A7%
D9%86%D8%B4%DB%8C%D9%86-%D9%81%D8%B1%D9%85%D8%A7%
D9%86%D8%AF%D9%87-%D8%B3%D9%BE%D8%A7%D9%87-%D8%B9%
D9%84%DB%8C-%D8%A7%D8%A8%DB%8C%D8%B7%D8%A7%D9%84%
D8%A8%28%D8%B9%29-%D8%B3%D8%A7%D8%AE%D8%AA%D9%85%
D8%A7%D9%86-%D9%BE%D8%A7%DB%8C%DA%AF%D8%A7%D9%87-
%D8%B4%D9%87%DB%8C%D8%AF-%D9%87%D8%A7%D8%B4%D9%85%
DB%8C (accessed April 15, 2012).

154. "Moarrefi-ye farmandeh-ye Sepah-e Hazrat-e Ghaem-e ostan-e Semanan"
[Appointment of Chief of Hazrat-e Ghaem IRGC Army of Semnan Province],
Islamic Republic of Iran Broadcasting (Tehran), June 30, 2008. Available in Persian
at http://www.iribnews.ir/VmkNews.aspx?ID=V303012 (accessed July 21, 2008).

155. "Sepah Dar Kenar-e Masajed Paygah-e Moghavemat Misazad" [The Guards
Builds Resistance Bases Next to Mosques], Fars News (Tehran), November
13, 2011. Available in Persian at http://www.farsnews.com/newstext.php?nn=
13900822001426 (accessed April 15, 2012).

156. Ibid. Prior to this appointment, Commander Abnoush was the IRGC chief
of Semnan province.

157. "Entesabat-e jadid-e shahrestan-ha…" [Appointments at Provincial Levels…],
Kayhan (Tehran), April 28, 2008. Available in Persian at http://www.kayhannews.
ir/870209/11.htm (accessed July 21, 2008).

158. "Sepah-e pasdaran-e enqelab-e eslami-ye Sistan va Baluchestan ba tarkib-e
jadid tashkil shod" [Sistan and Baluchestan Province IRGC Formed with New
Structure], IRNA (Tehran), July 2, 2008. Available in Persian at http://www.
khabarfarsi.com/news-150396.htm (accessed July 21, 2008).

159. "Farmandeh-ye Sepah-e Salman…" [Salman Guards' Commander…], IRNA
(Tehran), December 8, 2011. Available in Persian at http://irna.ir/News/30701

921/%D9%81%D8%B1%D9%85%D8%A7%D9%86%D8%AF%D9%87-%
D8%B3%D9%BE%D8%A7%D9%87-%D8%B3%D9%84%D9%85%D8%A7%
D9%86,%D8%B1%D8%B2%D9%85%D8%A7%DB%8C%D8%B4-%D8%B9
%D8%A7%D8%B4%D9%88%D8%B1%D8%A7%D8%A6%DB%8C%D8%A7%
D9%86-%D8%AF%D8%B1%D8%AA%D8%A7%D9%85%DB%8C%D9%86-%
D8%A7%D9%85%D9%86%DB%8C%D8%AA-%D8%B3%DB%8C%D8%B3%
D8%AA%D8%A7%D9%86-%D9%88%D8%A8%D9%84%D9%88%DA%86%D
8%B3%D8%AA%D8%A7%D9%86-%D8%AE%D9%88%D8%A8-%D8%A8
%D9%88%D8%AF/%D8%A7%D8%B3%D8%AA%D8%A7%D9%86%D9%87%
D8%A7/ (accessed April 15, 2012).

160. "Farmandeh-ye Sepah-e ostan-e Sistan va Baluchestan moarrefi shod" [Sistan
and Baluchestan Province IRGC Chief Appointed], ISNA (Tehran), July 2, 2008.
Available in Persian at http://sb.isna.ir/mainnews.php?ID=News-14388 (accessed
July 21, 2008).

161. "Azadi va Amniat-e Ma Natijeh-ye Khoun-e Pak-e Shohada-ye Enqelab-e
Eslami Ast" [Our Freedom and Security Is the Result of the Pure Blood of the
Martyrs of the Islamic Revolution], Qatreh (Tehran), October 18, 2011. Available in Persian at http://www.ghatreh.com/news/nn8480746/%D8%AC%D8%
A7%D9%86%D8%B4%DB%8C%D9%86-%D9%81%D8%B1%D9%85%D8%A
7%D9%86%D8%AF%D9%87-%D8%B3%D9%BE%D8%A7%D9%87-%D8%B3
%D9%84%D9%85%D8%A7%D9%86-%D8%B3%DB%8C%D8%B3%D8%AA%
D8%A7%D9%86-%D8%A8%D9%84%D9%88%DA%86%D8%B3%D8%AA%D
8%A7%D9%86-%D8%A2%D8%B2%D8%A7%D8%AF%DB%8C-%D8%A7%D
9%85%D9%86%DB%8C%D8%AA-%D9%86%D8%AA%DB%8C%D8%AC%D
9%87-%D8%AE%D9%88%D9%86 (accessed April 15, 2012).

162. "Mosahebe ba janeshin-e farmandeh-ye Sepah-e Salman-e ostan-e Sistan va
Balouchestan" [Interview with Deputy Chief of Salman IRGC of Sistan and Baluchestan Province], Basij News Agency (Tehran), July 17, 2008. Available in Persian at
http://www.basijnews.com/Ndetail.asp?NewsID=20067 (accessed July 23, 2008).

163. "Eraeh-ye gozaresh-e kolli az amal-kard-e tarh-e Hejrat-e 3 dar Tabestan-e
86 dar ostan-e Sistan va Balouchestan" [Presentation of General Report Evaluating the Hejrat 3 Scheme of Summer of 2007], Hemaseh-ye Javidan dar Sistan
va Baluchestan (Zahedan), n.d. Available in Persian at http://hemasebasij.blogfa.
com/post-63.aspx (accessed July 23, 2008).

164. "Ali-ye Fazli farmandeh-ye Sepah-e ostan-e Tehran shod" [Ali Fazli
Appointed IRGC Chief of Tehran Province], Borna News (Tehran), June 30, 2008.
Available in Persian at http://www.bornanews.com/Nsite/FullStory/?Id=163439
(accessed July 21, 2008).

165. "Basijian-e Varamin Hamvareh be Tehran Komak Kardehand" [The Basij
Members of Varamin Have Always Helped Tehran], Aftab News (Tehran), April 9,
2010. Available in Persian at http://www.aftabnews.ir/vdccsiqo.2bqm08laa2.html
(accessed April 15, 2012).

166. Ibid.

167. "Sardar Ali Fazli farmandeh-ye Sepah-e Seyyed al-Shohada-ye ostan-e Tehran shod" [Commander Ali Fazli Appointed Seyyed al-Shohada IRGC of Tehran Province], Fars News (Tehran), June 29, 2008. Available in Persian at http://www.farsnews.com/newstext.php?nn=8704091090 (accessed July 23, 2008).

168. "Sardar Nasiri Farmandeh-ye Sepah-e Seyyed al-Shohada Shod" [Commander Nasiri Was Appointed Seyyed al-Shohada Chief], Mashregh News (Tehran), November 8, 2011. Available in Persian at http://www.mashreghnews.ir/fa/news/78023/%D8%B3%D8%B1%D8%AF%D8%A7%D8%B1-%D9%86%D8%B5%DB%8C%D8%B1%DB%8C-%D9%81%D8%B1%D9%85%D8%A7%D9%86%D8%AF%D9%87-%D8%B3%D9%BE%D8%A7%D9%87-%D8%B3%DB%8C%D8%AF%D8%A7%D9%84%D8%B4%D9%87%D8%AF%D8%A7-%D8%B4%D8%AF (accessed April 15, 2012).

169. "Ali-ye Fazli farmandeh-ye Sepah-e ostan-e Tehran shod."

170. Ibid.

171. "Sardar Eraghi farmandeh-ye Sepah-e Mohammad Rasoul-allah-e Tehran-e bozorg" [Commander Eraghi Appointed Mohammad Rasoul-Allah IRGC Army of Greater Tehran], Fars News (Tehran), July 1, 2008. Available in Persian at http://www.farsnews.com/newstext.php?nn=8704110628 (accessed July 21, 2008).

172. "Farmandeh-ye Jadid-e Sepah-e Tehran Kist?" [Who Is the New Tehran Guards Commander?], Khabar Online (Tehran), December 24, 2011.Available in Persian at http://www.khabaronline.ir/detail/190855/%D8%B3%D9%BE%D8%A7%D9%87-%D9%BE%D8%A7%D8%B3%D8%AF%D8%A7%D8%B1%D8%A7%D9%86-%D8%AD%D8%B3%DB%8C%D9%86-%D9%87%D9%85%D8%AF%D8%A7%D9%86%DB%8C--/%D9%86%D8%B8%D8%A7%D9%85%DB%8C/%D8%B3%DB%8C%D8%A7%D8%B3%D8%AA (April 15, 2012).

173. Ibid. Prior to this appointment, Brigadier General Javad Khezrayi was the chief of the Twenty-seventh Mechanized Lashkar Mohammad Rasoul-Allah.

174. "Hoshdar-e Farmandeh-ye Sepah-e Tehran Nesbat Be Edameh-ye Fetneh dar Sal-e 90" [Tehran Guards Commander's Warning against Continuity of the 2009 Sedition], Khabar Online (Tehran), May 13, 2011. Available in Persian at http://www.khabaronline.ir/news-150461.aspx (accessed April 15, 2012).

175. "Sardar Eraghi be onvan-e farmandeh-ye jadid-e Mantagheh-ye Basij-e Tehran-e Bozorg Moarrefi shod" [Commander Eraghi Appointed Chief of Greater Tehran Basij Area], IRNA (Tehran), May 4, 2008. Available in Persian at http://www2.irna.ir/fa/news/view/line-9/8702152498140818.htm (accessed July 21, 2008).

176. "Ahmad-e Zolqadr Janeshin-e Farmandeh-ye Sepah-e Mohammad Rasoulollah Shod" [Ahmad Zolqadr Appointed Mohammad Rasoul-Allah Guards Deputy], Asr-e Iran (Tehran), June 1, 2009. Available in Persian at http://www.asriran.com/fa/news/73987/%D8%A7%D8%AD%D9%85%D8%AF-%D8%B0%D9%88%D8%A7%D9%84%D9%82%D8%AF%D8%B1-%D8%AC%D8%A7%D9%86%D8%B4%D9%8A%D9%86-%D9%81%D8%B1%D9%85%D8%A7%D9%86%D8%AF%D9%87-%D8%B3%D9%BE%D8%A7%D9%87-%D9%85%D8%AD%D9%85%D8%AF-%D8%B1%D8%B3%D9%88%D9%84%E2%80%8

C%D8%A7%D9%84%D9%84%D9%87%D8%B5-%D8%B4%D8%AF (accessed April 15, 2012).

177. "Janeshin-e Farmandeh-ye Sepah-e Tehran-e Bozorg" [Greater Tehran Guards Deputy], Raja News (Tehran), June 1, 2009. Available in Persian at http://www.rajanews.com/detail.asp?id=30268 (accessed April 15, 2012).

178. Ibid.

179. "Moarrefi-ye farmandeh-ye jadid-e 'tip-e' mostaghel-e 18 Al-Ghadir ba hozour-e farmandeh-ye nirou-ye zamini-ye Sepah-e Pasdaran-e Enqelab-e Eslami" [Presentation of the New Chief of Eighteenth Al-Ghadir Independent 'Tip' in the Presence of IRGC Ground Forces Chief], General Government of Yazd (Yazd), January 13, 2007. Available in Persian at http://www.ostan-yz.ir/modules.php?name=News&file=article&sid=826 (accessed July 23, 2008).

180. "Todie va Moarefeh-ye Farmandeh-ye Sepah-e Al-Ghadir-e Ostan-e Yazd" [Farewell and Appointment Ceremonies of the Yazd Province Guards Commander], Al-Ghadir-e Yazd (Yazd), June 20, 2011. Available in Persian at http://alghadiryazd.blogfa.com/post-1502.aspx (accessed April 15, 2012).

181. "Farmandeh-ye arshad-e Sepah-e Yazd: Moghabeleh ba doshman niazmand be farhang-e isar va shahadat ast" [Countering the Enemy Necessitates a Culture of Self-Sacrifice and Martyrdom], IRNA (Tehran), June 22, 2008. Available in Persian at http://www2.irna.ir/fa/news/view/menu-155/8704028507111909.htm (accessed July 21, 2008).

182. "Moarrefi-ye farmandeh-ye jadid-e tip-e mostaghel-e 18 Al-Ghadir..." [Appointment of the New Commander of the Independent Eighteenth Al-Ghadir Brigade...], Yazd-e Farda (Yazd), January 14, 2007. Available in Persian at http://yazdfarda.com/news/1391/01/4476.html (accessed April 15, 2012).

183. "Janeshin-e Farmandehi-ye Tip-e Al-Ghadir-e Ostan-e Yazd..." [Yazd Province Al-Ghadir Brigade Deputy...], Mehriz (Yazd), October 11, 2009. Available in Persian at http://www.mehriz.gov.ir/c/portal/layout?p_l_id=PUB.1266.1&p_p_id=62_INSTANCE_e4fn&p_p_action=0&p_p_state=maximized&p_p_mode=view&struts_action=%2Fjournal_articles%2Fview&andOperator=true&groupId=1266&searchArticleId=&version=1.0&name=&description=&content=&type=&structureId=&templateId=&status=approved&articleId=3409 (accessed April 15, 2012).

184. Ibid.

185. "Farmandeh-ye Sepah-e mantaghe-ye Zanjan: Hich selahi borrandeh-tar az selah-e ma'naviat nist" [Zanjan Area IRGC Commander: No Weapon Is Sharper Than Spirituality], IRNA (Tehran), June 16, 2008. Available in Persian at http://www1.irna.ir/fa/news/view/menu-155/8703276005122125.htm (accessed July 21, 2008).

186. "Sepah Tavanayi-ye Moqabeleh Ba Teoteeh-ha-ye Doshman Ra Daarad" [The Guards Has the Ability to Counter the Conspiracies of the Enemies], Fars News (Tehran), April 21, 2010. Available in Persian at http://www.farsnews.com/newstext.php?nn=8902011029 (accessed April 15, 2012).

5

Collapse of the Commissariat

Since the revolution of 1979, the civilian leadership in Iran has used political/ideological commissars to act as its eyes and ears within the ranks of the Islamic Revolutionary Guards Corps (IRGC). Ideally, the commissars should subject the IRGC to civilian control, but the Guards have demonstrated great resilience in the face of such attempts.

Hojjat al-Eslam Ali Saidi is the latest Representative of the Guardian Jurist (*Namayandeh-ye Vali-ye Faghih*) to the IRGC who acts as the head of the ideological/political commissariat in the Guards. However, despite the expansive formal power Saidi's commissariat commands, he increasingly acts like a spokesman for the IRGC's interests rather than a political commissar enforcing civilian control within the Guards.[1]

Such behavior is far from unprecedented, and a survey of the performance of the political commissariat of the Guards shows that the IRGC leadership has systematically conspired against the commissars, killing a few while isolating and intimidating the rest. In later periods the political commissars have de facto become the IRGC's extended arms to control the civilian leadership rather than serving as the civilian leadership's eyes and ears in the Guards. This in turn is another indication of the Guards' being outside the control of the civilian leadership of the Islamic Republic.

5.1. Legal Framework

Representatives of the Grand Ayatollah Rouhollah Khomeini and Ayatollah Ali Khamenei to the IRGC work within the organizational framework of the Office of the Representative of the Imam to the Guards (*Daftar-e Namayandeh-ye Emam Dar Sepah*), which following Khomeini's death in

1989 was called the Office of the Representative of the Guardian Jurist to the Guards (*Daftar-e Namayandegi-ye Vali-ye Faghih Dar Sepah*).

Ever since its de facto establishment in 1979, the office has functioned as the eyes and ears of Khomeini and subsequently Khamenei in the Guards, its main task being to secure ideological and political conformity of the Guards with the dominant ideology among Iran's civilian leadership and IRGC obedience toward the Leader of the Revolution (*Rahbar-e Enqelab*), who according to Article 110 of the March 1979 constitution is also the armed forces commander in chief.[2]

The legal framework and powers of the commissariat in the Guards is partially based on the Statute of the Guards, which was passed by parliament on September 6, 1982, codifying the role of the representative,[3] and partially based on individual decrees Khomeini and Khamenei issued to the representatives, which will be dealt with in the sections of this chapter relating to each of the representatives. (See Table 5-1 for a chronological list of the representatives.)

Article 1 of the Statute of the Guards formally subordinates the IRGC to the authority of the Leader of the Revolution.[4] But since the Leader of the Revolution is not personally involved in daily affairs of the IRGC, the Guards must refer to the representative of the leader to the Guards. The representative is not alone in this task but heads a commissariat. According to clauses A and B of Article 27 of the statute, the commissariat is divided into a Supervisory Bureau (*Daftar-e Nezarat*) and a Political Bureau (*Daftar-e Siyasi*).[5] The Supervisory Bureau is "responsible to supervise all affairs of the Guards and prepare reports to the Representative of the Supreme Leader."[6] The Political Bureau, on the other hand, is "responsible to collect and compile daily reports on the news and political events."[7] But as we shall see, in practice there is no clear division of labor, and various offices have in reality many overlapping fields of responsibility, which has been a permanent source of conflict between competing commissariats in the IRGC.

Section K of Article 18 of the Statute of the Guards clarifies that the "Representative of the Leader (in case there is one)" is a member of the Guards Supreme Council (*Showra-ye Ali-ye Sepah*),[8] which refers to the period until mid-1980s in which the IRGC had such a council. Article 20 stresses that the "meetings of the Supreme Council of the Guards are

TABLE 5-1

REPRESENTATIVES OF GRAND AYATOLLAH KHOMEINI AND
AYATOLLAH KHAMENEI TO THE IRGC, 1979–2011

Title and Name	Year of Birth	Place of Birth	Educational Background	Career Prior to Appointment	Functioning Period
Ayatollah Hassan Lahouti Eshkevari	ca. 1927	Roudsar	Elmiyyeh Theological Seminary in Qom	Prerevolution: Revolutionary preacher supporting Grand Ayatollah Khomeini. Postrevolution: Member of the first parliament from Rasht, representative of Grand Ayatollah Khomeini in Gilan province, head of local branch of the Revolutionary Committee.	September 16, 1979[1] – November 25, 1979[2]
Ayatollah Akbar Hashemi Rafsanjani	1934	Rafsanjan	Elmiyyeh Theological Seminary in Qom	Prerevolution: Revolutionary activist, interned on several occasions. Postrevolution: Member of the Council of the Revolution, speaker of the parliament.	1980 (no decree)
Ayatollah Ali Khamenei	1939	Mashhad	Theological Seminaries in Mashhad and Qom	Prerevolution: Revolutionary activist, interned on several occasions. Postrevolution: Representative of Grand Ayatollah Khomeini to the Defense Ministry.	1980 (no decree)
Hojjat al-Eslam Fazl-Allah Mehdi-Zadeh Mahallati[3]	ca. 1930[4]	Mahallat[5]	Elmiyyeh Theological Seminary in Qom[6]	Prerevolution: Revolutionary activity since 1947, imprisonment in 1953 and internal exile. Postrevolution: Member of the committee welcoming Grand Ayatollah Khomeini back to Iran in 1979, deputy chief of the Revolutionary Committee, elected parliamentarian from Mahallat and Delijan, member of the Defense Committtee.[7]	June 18, 1980[8] – February 20, 1986[9]
Hojjat al-Eslam Hassan Taheri Khorram-Abadi[10]	May 22, 1938[11]	Khorram Abad[12]	Haghani School of the Elmiyyeh Theological Seminary in Qom[13]	Prerevolution: Scholarly activity Postrevolution: Member of the first Assembly of Experts of the Constitution,[14] Representative of Grand Ayatollah Khomeini in Hajj and Pilgrim Affairs.[15]	December 14, 1981[16] – August 25, 1982; June 29, 1983[17] – December 17, 1983[18]

Title and Name	Year of Birth	Place of Birth	Educational Background	Career Prior to Appointment	Functioning Period
Hojjat al-Eslam Moham-mad-Reza Faker[19]	ca. 1945[20]	Mashhad[21]	Mashhad Theological Seminary[22]	Prerevolution: Theology teacher, interned three times for revolutionary activity. Postrevolution: Established the Islamic Publishing House of the Teachers' Association of Qom Theological Seminary, representative of Grand Ayatollah Khomeini on the Supreme Council of Propaganda.	August 25, 1982[23] – June 29, 1983[24]
No Representative	–	–	–	–	February 20, 1986–March 9, 1989
Hojjat al-Eslam Abdollah Nouri	1949	Isfahan	Theological Seminary	Prerevolution: Student at a theological seminary. Postrevolution: Director General of the Islamic Republic of Iran Broadcasting, deputy foreign minister, representative of Grand Ayatollah Khomeini in Supreme Council of Justice, Construction Jihad, and IRGC.	March 9, 1989[25] – ca. March 1990[26]
Hojjat al-Eslam Mahmoud Mohammadi Eraqi (Earlier) Representative of the Supreme Leader in an acting capacity)[27]	ca. 1952	Kang-Avar	Haghani School of the Elmiyyeh Theological Seminary in Qom	Posrerevolution: Locum tenens for representative of Ayatollah Khamenei in the IRGC.	June 26, 1990[28] – unknown
Ayatollah Moham-mad-Ali Movahedi Kermani[29]	ca. 1931[30]	Kerman	Theological Seminary in Qom	Prerevolution: Friday prayer imam at the Moslem Ibn al-Aqil Mosque in Tehran. Postrevolution: Member of Tehran Combatant Clergy Association, parliamentarian and deputy speaker of the Iranian parliament.[31]	February 17, 1992[32] – December 16, 2005[33]
Hokjkjat al-Eslam Ali Saidi[34]	ca. 1950[35]	Semnan[36]	Theological Seminary[37]	Postrevolution: Member of the Combatant Clergy Association[38] and head of its political bureau.[39]	December 24, 2005–present[40]

TABLE 5-2

REPRESENTATIVES OF THE SUPREME LEADER IN THE IRGC

Position	Individual
Representative to the IRGC	Hojjat al-Eslam Ali Saidi[1]
Deputy Representative to the IRGC	Hojjat al-Eslam Mojtaba Zolnour (until summer of 2011)[2]
Representative to Quds Force	Hojjat al-Eslam Ali Shirazi[3]
Representative to IRGC Navy	Hojjat al-Eslam Abd al-Nabi Sedaqat[4]
Representative to IRGC Ground Force	Hojjat al-Eslam Mohammad-Hadi Rezaei[5]
Representative to IRGC Air Force	Hojjat al-Eslam Ayoub Hassan-Zadeh[6]
Representative to Basij Force	Hojjat al-Eslam Ali Mohammadi[7]

NOTE: See end of chapter for table notes.

not authoritative in absence of the Representative of the Leader (or his Deputy)."[9] Article 21 also specifies that the Representative of the Leader has the authority to summon the Supreme Council to convene at extraordinary sessions besides the weekly sessions of the Guards.[10]

There is also a further sign of the power of the Office of the Representative. According to Article 31, "IRGC Deputy Commander in Chief, IRGC Central Command Council Chief, and the unit chiefs at the IRGC Central Command Council can be appointed or dismissed by approval of the Leader or his Representative in the Guards."[11] Section 1 of Article 31 also points out that the chiefs of ideological/political indoctrination bureaus and censors of IRGC publications must be "approved by the Leader or his Representative in the Guards."[12] Also, clauses A and B of Article 33 empower the representative by charging him with "securing congruity between decisions taken by the Guards commanders and Islamic Law [*Sharia*]," by authorizing the representative to appoint a deputy to each unit at all levels of the Guards, and by authorizing the representative to communicate with the leader's representatives to other branches of the armed forces in order to "enhance brotherly cooperation between the IRGC and other branches of the armed forces."[13] (See Tables 5-2 and 5-3.)

The statute may leave an impression of the representative to the Guards as being the head of a strong commissariat with formidable powers resembling the powers of the political commissars in the Red Army in the Soviet Union, but a survey of the establishment, evolution, and current state of the actual powers of the representative shows that those powers have been more formal than real. In practice, Guards commanders have systematically opposed and restricted the power of the commissars and managed to play the commissars against each other, and today the representative is in reality the spokesman of the Guards in the political life of the Islamic Republic rather than the civilian leadership's political commissar within the body of the IRGC.

5.2. Early History and Establishment

Establishment of a commissariat in the Revolutionary Guards predates the Statute of the Guards and can be traced back to the revolutionary chaos of 1979 and Khomeini's attempt at controlling the armed militias that emerged in the aftermath of the collapse of the Shah's regime. The multitude of the armed revolutionary groups and the ideological rivalries between them—as discussed in earlier chapters—was a major source of concern among the leadership of the revolution, and Khomeini was concerned that he was unaware of their number, leadership, and allegiances. Hojjat al-Eslam Ahmad Khomeini, son of the founder of the Islamic Republic, in an early interview with the IRGC weekly *Payam-e Enqelab*, recalled his father asking: "What is this Guard? How many chiefs does it have? Every day a group approaches me and wants to meet us presenting themselves as senior commanders of the Guards!"[14]

Besides the issues of who represented the Guards and who was in command of the armed militias, there were also issues of ideological factionalism and conflicting tactical and strategic approaches within the competing militias all purporting to be guardians of the revolution. For example, Grand Ayatollah Hossein-Ali Montazeri recalls in his memoirs disputes among the various guards: "[Hojjat al-Eslam] Mohammad [Montazeri, son of Grand Ayatollah Montazeri and chief of one Revolutionary Guards faction] had a revolutionary way of thinking and believed that with regard to the matters of the revolution one must act in a revolutionary manner."[15] The National Guard faction, on the other hand, which

TABLE 5-3

REPRESENTATIVES OF THE SUPREME LEADER TO THE IRGC
AT THE PROVINCIAL LEVEL

Province	IRGC Unit	Representative
Ardebil	Hazrat-e Abbas	Hojjat al-Eslam Asadollah Rezvani[1]
Azerbaijan, East	Ashoura	Hojjat al-Eslam Hassan Kameli-Far[2]
Azerbaijan, West	Shohada	Hojjat al-Eslam Mohammad-Mehdi Mahdavi[3]
Bushehr	Imam Sadeq	Hojjat al-Eslam Mohammad Hajizadeh[4]
Chahar Mahal Va Bakhtiari	Ghamar Bani-Hashem	Hojjat al-Eslam Hassan-Ali Moazzeni[5]
Esfahan	Saheb al-Zaman	Hojjat al-Eslam Hossein Teyyebi-Far[6]
Fars	Fajr	Hojjat al-Eslam Abol-Ghasem Alizadeh[7]
Gilan	Qods	Hojjat al-Eslam Gholam-Reza Shafi-Pour[8]
Golestan	Neynava	Hojjat al-Eslam Yadollah Gholami[9]
Hamedan	Ansar al-Hossein	Hojjat al-Eslam Mohammad-Vali Razavi-Rad[10]
Hormozgan	Imam Sajjad	Hojjat al-Eslam Abd al-Nabi Sedaqat[11]
Ilam	Amir al-Momenin	Hojjat al-Eslam Qasem Khaziravi[12]
Kerman	Sar-Allah	Hojjat al-Eslam Ali Arabpour[13]
Kermanshah	Kermanshah IRGC	Hojjat al-Eslam Mahmoud Goudarzi[14]
Khorasan, North	Javad al-Aemeh	Hojjat al-Eslam Ahmad Khorram[15]
Khorasan, Razavi	Imam Reza	Hojjat al-Eslam Mehdi Abedi[16]
Khorasan, South	Ansar al-Reza	Hojjat al-Eslam Gholam-Hossein Nofarasti[17]
Khuzestan	Vali-ye Asr	Hojjat al-Eslam Mohammad Mousavi[18]
Kohkilou-ye Va Boyer-Ahmad	Beit al-Moghaddas	Hojjat al-Eslam Mohsen Heydarian[19]
Lorestan	Abol-Fazl al-Abbas	Hojjat al-Eslam Ali-Reza Karami[20]
Markazi	Rouh-Allah	Hojjat al-Eslam Reza Nour-Allahi[21]
Mazandaran	Karbala	Hojjat al-Eslam Mokhtar Nazari[22]

Province	IRGC Unit	Representative
Qazvin	Saheb al-Amr	Hojjat al-Eslam Morteza Hosseini[23]
Qom	Ali Ibn-e Abi-Taleb	Hojjat al-Eslam Hassan Akbari[24]
Semnan	Hazrat-e Ghaem al-Mohammad	Hojjat al-Eslam Jafar Roayati[25]
Sistan Va Baluchestan	Salman	Hojjat al-Eslam Javad Alavi[26]
Tehran	Seyyed al-Shohada	Hojjat al-Eslam Nemat Fakhri[27]
Tehran, Greater	Mohammad Rasoul-Allah	Hojjat al-Eslam Abd al-Ali Govahi[28]
Yazd	Al-Ghadir	Hojjat al-Eslam Abbas Sobhanian[29]
Zanjan	Zanjan IRGC	Hojjat al-Eslam Ali Maboudi[30]

NOTE: See end of chapter for table notes.

was ideologically and politically closer to Prime Minister Mehdi Bazargan's transitional government, "concentrated," according to Grand Ayatollah Montazeri, "[its efforts] more on internal and international order and [establishing correct] relations with the governments and that the regime should be stabilized."[16] Montazeri also recalls a certain "enmity" between the Islamic Republican Party (*Hezb-e Jomhouri-ye Eslami*) founder Ayatollah Mohammad Beheshti and his son Mohammad Montazeri.[17]

Ahmad Khomeini also recalls conflicting political and ideological currents among the different militias purporting to guard the revolution:

> Whenever they wanted to prepare future planning for the Guards they would come and make proposals based upon their [ideological] values. For example, the martyr Sheikh Mohammad Montazeri believed that we should raise a revolutionary mayhem in the [Middle East and North Africa] region, which would also clarify the role of the Guards in export of the revolution. ...Mr. [Ebrahim] Yazdi [transitional government foreign minister, who was close to the National Guard faction], who is a disciplined type, would argue: "We should not intervene in affairs of the others and we should think of Iran and develop this country, and preserve order. What happens in

Kuwait, Bahrain, Pakistan, and Afghanistan has nothing to do with us." Well, both of them were on top of the Guards, two lines with one hundred eighty degrees difference.[18]

But the real conflict between the various guards, including the one between Mohammad Montazeri and the Guards loyal to Bazargan's interim government, along with at least two other groups each purporting to be the authentic guardians of the revolution, seems to have been the issue of who should be in charge of the Guards. One of the cofounders of the Guards and later the Revolutionary Guards minister, Mohsen Rafiqdoust, correctly sums up Mohammad Montazeri's viewpoint: "He believed that the Guards should not be subjected to the control of the interim government, and should be independent."[19] This must also have been the major source of concern of other groups competing for Khomeini's support and fearing a monopoly of power by the interim government.

5.3. Khomeini's Commissars

Well aware that survival of the revolutionary regime was dependent on effective coordination between the political leadership of the revolution and its strong arms at street level, Khomeini and the Council of the Revolution (*Showra-ye Enqelab*), the shadow government and de facto highest governing body in revolutionary Iran, appointed several personal representatives to the four leading armed groups loyal to Khomeini in order to coordinate their efforts and assert a degree of civilian control over his armed loyalist groups.[20]

Thus, Khomeini appointed the veteran political dissident, firebrand preacher, and former political prisoner Ayatollah Hassan Lahouti Eshkevari, seconded by Yazdi, as his personal representative to the nascent National Guard. On September 16, 1979, Lahouti Eshkevari's appointment became formal as he received Khomeini's signed decree authorizing him to participate in "all the meetings of the Supreme Council for Coordination and Decision Making of the Guard Corps and supervise the proceedings directly," and tasking Lahouti Eshkevari with "send[ing] the undersigned weekly reports of the workings of the Guard Corps."[21]

Khomeini also appointed representatives to other precursors of the IRGC for whom he did not issue formal decrees. Mousavi Ardebili, an old student of Khomeini and member of the Council of the Revolution, along with Ayatollah Akbar Hashemi Rafsanjani, also a veteran revolutionary and member of the Council of the Revolution, de facto represented Khomeini in the IRGC unit based at the Jamshidiyeh Garrison.[22] Revolutionary theoretician Ayatollah Morteza Mottahari served as Khomeini's representative to the armed wing of the Holy Warriors of the Islamic Revolution based at the Towhid Building on Shariati Avenue; and Mohammad Montazeri was both representative of Khomeini to and chief of a group of guardsmen composed of Palestinian guerillas and a few defectors from the Shah's army based at a building on Sattar-Khan Avenue.[23]

Thus, appointment of representatives to the precursors of the IRGC became the first attempt of the civilian leadership to subordinate the armed revolutionary forces to civilian control. This was also the first serious attempt at establishing a political commissariat to control the Guards like the ones in the Red Army of the Soviet Union and in present-day China's People's Liberation Army. However, a review of the performance of the commissars demonstrates that the guardsmen managed to exploit divisions among the civilian leadership to minimize civilian control of the competing guards. The conspiracy of some of the leading commanders of the Guards along with certain clerical elements against Lahouti Eshkevari, the mysterious martyrdom of another of Khomeini's representatives, and isolation of the other commissars in the IRGC provide interesting cases.

5.3.1. Lahouti Eshkevari's Brief Tenure As noted above, among all the commissars appointed to the precursors of the IRGC, Lahouti Eshkevari was the only individual formally appointed by Khomeini's decree of September 16, 1979.[24] Ahmad Khomeini in an interview recalled the process leading to his father's official appointment of Lahouti Eshkevari. Allegedly, Lahouti Eshkevari—who was already involved in the National Guards and was ideologically close to Prime Minister Bazargan's interim government—sought out Khomeini and said: "I am working in the Guards, but as long as I don't have a decree from you I can't do any work and you really must give me the decree. If you don't give me the decree as head man [*sarparast*] of the Guards I can't work there."[25] According to Ahmad

Khomeini, his father accepted Lahouti Eshkevari's wish "because of his affection towards Mr. Lahouti [Eshkevari]."[26] Yazdi's account differs from Ahmad Khomeini's. According to Yazdi, it was not at the request of Lahouti Eshkevari but due to the intervention of Yazdi and the interim government that Khomeini issued the decree.[27] Yazdi's claim is not necessarily contrary to Ahmad Khomeini's account since ideologically Lahouti Eshkevari was closer to the interim government practically run by Bazargan and Yazdi than to the Council of the Revolution. More importantly, as we shall see, Lahouti Eshkevari, according to many sources, desired to subordinate the Guards to the authority of the interim government rather than the authority of the Council of the Revolution. Both factors explain Yazdi's motives for persuading Khomeini to issue a decree to Lahouti Eshkevari.

In any case, members of the other political factions among the civilian leadership, especially the members of the Islamic Republican Party, perceived Khomeini's decree to Lahouti Eshkevari as an existential threat, and feared a military coup led not by the monarchist officers and the remnants of the Imperial Army but by the interim government, with the help of the Guards unit controlled by commissar Lahouti Eshkevari. They began therefore to conspire against Lahouti Eshkevari along with a number of central IRGC personalities.

Hojjat al-Eslam Mohammad-Reza Mahdavi Kani, a leading Islamic Republican Party member of the period, reveals in his memoirs the general mood upon Lahouti Eshkevari's appointment: "On March 1, or 2, 1979," Mahdavi Kani began—the date provided by Mahdavi Kani is in conflict with the date of Khomeini's decree, which is September 16, 1979—continuing,

> We were assembled at the Refah School. I remember that the blessed Martyr Beheshti, Martyr [Hojjat al-Eslam Mohammad-Javad] Bahonar, Mr. Hashemi [Rafsanjani], Ayatollah [Ali] Khamenei, Ayatollah [Mohammad] Moffateh, Ayatollah [Fazl-Allah] Mahallati, Ayatollah [Mohammad-Ali] Shah-Abadi and Mr. [Hojjat al-Eslam Ali-Akbar] Nateq Nouri were present in that meeting. In the room we were discussing the affairs of the state and around half past eleven the blessed Martyr Mottahari

in a state of agitation entered the room and said: "Now the [Iran Freedom] Movement people and some of the cabinet ministers of the [Iran Freedom] Movement are in the company of the Imam [Grand Ayatollah Khomeini] and the Imam has issued a decree appointing Mr. Lahouti [Eshkevari as Representative of the Leader to the Guards] and the news will be broadcasted from the radio at twelve o'clock. This is a disaster, not because of Mr. Lahouti [Eshkevari] who himself is not a bad man. But he is an emotional and simple individual. He is surrounded by them [Bazargan, Yazdi, and the first president of the Islamic Republic, Abol-Hassan Bani-Sadr]."[28]

Ahmad Khomeini, who by then was still a leading Islamic Republican Party member, also reveals in a later interview that the Islamic Republican Party faction was worried about Lahouti Eshkevari not so much as an individual but as an instrument in the hands of the Bazargan-led interim government, which the Islamic Republican Party members distrusted: "People of the interim government did whatever they could to organize the Guards in such way so they could be its masters,"[29] Ahmad Khomeini complained.

Concern and apprehension also appeared upon Lahouti Eshkevari's appointment among some leading members of the Guards factions other than the one ideologically close to the interim government. Also in this camp Lahouti Eshkevari's appointment was interpreted as the interim government's attempt to control the various guards politically and outcompete other factions. Ebrahim Hajj-Mohammad-Zadeh, later head of the political bureau of the IRGC, explained in an interview in *Payam-e Enqelab*: "They wanted to follow a line desirable to the [interim] government."[30]

There is indeed some evidence that the Islamic Republican Party and anti–interim government factions within the IRGC were right to be concerned about Lahouti Eshkevari. Rather than the simpleton Mahdavi Kani depicts in his memoirs, or the political pawn described by Ahmad Khomeini or Hajj-Mohammad-Zadeh, an early report on Lahouti Eshkevari's activities leaves the impression of an effective ideological/political commissar in the National Guard who energetically attempted to secure interim government control over the Guards. Lahouti Eshkevari personally presided over the ideological/political indoctrination program of the

National Guard prior to the unification of the Guards and had managed to establish an "investigations group" researching the background of applicants to the Guard.[31] Guardsmen under his command went through a ten-day period of ideological/political indoctrination and military training.[32] Lahouti Eshkevari's program consisted of four to five hours of ideological/political indoctrination and ten hours of military training each day.[33] Only when the "ethical and religious dimensions of the personality of the recruits along with their mental and physical health" were approved were they provided with a Guards ID.[34]

Therefore, Lahouti Eshkevari must have been considered a deadly enemy of the Islamic Republican Party and several factions within the IRGC leadership: as a charismatic leader and an efficient political commissar appointed by Khomeini, Lahouti Eshkevari could shift the balance of power within the Guards to the benefit of the interim government.

The Islamic Republican Party and the Guards commanders opposed to the interim government took elaborate countermeasures. They first formalized establishment of the Revolutionary Committee (*Komiteh-ha-ye Enqelab-e Eslami*), a revolutionary body created as much to counterbalance what remained of the Shah's police as to counterbalance the Guards led by Lahouti Eshkevari.[35] Next they infiltrated the ranks of Lahouti Eshkevari's Guards militia, incorporated Lahouti Eshkevari's militia into a larger body of the Guards, and finally marginalized and destroyed the very person of Lahouti Eshkevari.

To return to Mahdavi Kani's tale of the conspiracy meeting against Lahouti Eshkevari, Mottahari left the circle of conspirators upon hearing rumors of the appointment of Lahouti Eshkevari as representative to the Guards, and rushed to Khomeini's office in Qom to persuade him to revoke the decree to Lahouti Eshkevari.[36] Failing to do so, Mottahari, according to Mahdavi Kani's memoirs, explained to Khomeini the necessity of formalizing the Revolutionary Committee and the need to have two different authorities commanding the Guards and the Revolutionary Committee rather than concentrating command over both revolutionary organizations in the same entity.[37]

Next the Islamic Republican Party began infiltrating the ring of U.S. and Canadian university graduates composing the core of the National Guard, which was close to the interim government, with uneducated

elements such as Mohsen Rafiqdoust. Rafiqdoust, a young revolutionary activist, served as Khomeini's chauffeur upon his return to Tehran
from Paris and was a member of the Committee Welcoming the Imam
(*Komiteh-ye Esteghbal Az Emam*), which in reality functioned as Khomeini's
bodyguards.[38] According to Rafiqdoust, he was originally a member of
the Revolutionary Committee led by Mahdavi Kani.[39] On September 16,
1979, the same day that Khomeini issued the decree to Lahouti Eshkevari,
Mohammad Montazeri, the radical leader of Guardians of the Islamic Revolution, along with Mottahari and Beheshti—who according to Mahdavi
Kani's memoirs had just held the meeting conspiring against Lahouti Eshkevari—ordered Rafiqdoust to participate in the formal founding convention
of the National Guard at the logistics headquarters of the army on Abbas
Abad Avenue.[40] According to his own memoirs, Rafiqdoust gate-crashed
the founding convention armed and while the intellectuals "[Asghar]
Sabaghian, [Masoud] Tehranchi, [Gholam-Reza] Danesh Ashtiani, Lahouti
[Eshkevari], Mohsen Sazegara and Gholam-Ali Afrouz"[41] were engaged in
discussions about formation of a popular army, Rafiqdoust allegedly took
a piece of paper and wrote, "The Revolutionary Guards Corps is formed.
[Member number] 1. Mohsen Rafiqdoust,"[42] after which he passed the
paper to the next person. The names Rafiqdoust provides in an interview
on April 22, 2007, are slightly different from the names presented in his
memoirs: "Engineer [Asghar] Sabaghian, [Masoud] Tehranchi, the blessed Ali
Farzin, [Mohammad-Ali?] Jafari, Mohsen Sazegara, [Mohammad-Ebrahim]
Sanjaghi, and…"[43] but the story is otherwise the same.

Rafiqdoust's personal relationship with Lahouti Eshkevari deteriorated
rapidly. Recalling his conflicts with Lahouti Eshkevari, Rafiqdoust discloses his personal conflict with the political commissar:

> One day he [Lahouti Eshkevari] called upon me and said,
> "[R]esign from the Guards and get lost." When I asked why, he
> said that some of the educated members say the Guard is either
> for us or for Rafiqdoust and he mentioned the name of some
> of those with foreign [university] education. I told him that I
> had no trouble with their presence, but regarding my staying or
> leaving, the Guards is the most important thing of all to me and
> therefore I'll not go. Mr. Lahouti [Eshkevari] said, "I'll throw

you out," and I answered, "You can't do so. I'll throw you out of the Guards."[44]

This incident reveals not only the personal conflict between Rafiqdoust and Lahouti Eshkevari but also the deeper conflict between the Western-educated members of the IRGC and the uneducated infiltrators originating from the radical elements incorporated into the growing body of the Guards.

Rafiqdoust also confesses breaching the chain of command of the IRGC and badmouthing the political commissar by personally seeking Grand Ayatollah Khomeini: "In order to end the conflict I sought the Imam [Khomeini] and spoke of all the problems that Mr. Lahouti [Eshkevari] had made for the Guards, including [his] unauthorized and unmeasured decrees."[45] Rafiqdoust repeated such breaches in the chain of command and aligned himself with fellow Guards members Mohammad Gharazi and Mrs. Marziyeh Hadid-Chi Dabbagh—whose memoirs contain no reference to Grand Ayatollah Khomeini's character assassination of Lahouti Eshkevari but an account of Dabbagh badmouthing another moderate element, foreign minister Sadegh Ghotbzadeh, in Khomeini's presence.[46] According to Rafiqdoust, the three of them bypassed the chain of command in the Guards, reached out to Khomeini, and convinced him of subjecting the IRGC to direct control by the Council of the Revolution rather than the transitional government: "The Imam [Khomeini] said '[T]he Guards must be supervised by the Council of the Revolution.'…Later that day we [Rafiqdoust and his allies] informed the Council of the Revolution of the news which led to Mr. Lahouti [Eshkevari's] leaving the Guards."[47] According to a separate account, it was the triumvirate of Rafiqdoust, later IRGC chief Mohsen Rezaei, and another IRGC chief, Abbas Douz-Douzani, who persuaded Khomeini to subject the IRGC to control by the Council of the Revolution.[48]

At any rate, the conspiracies of the IRGC commanders and the Islamic Republican Party had an effect on Grand Ayatollah Khomeini, who changed his mind with regard to the IRGC reporting to the Council of the Revolution rather than to the interim government. Ahmad Khomeini also backs up this account in a retrospective interview: "I remember that the Imam would say: 'The Guards must be separated from the governmental people.

The Guards must still be independent because the circumstances are still revolutionary and the Guards must preserve these circumstances for us. If they want to subject the Guards to governmental supervision—with the way it is—there would be nothing left of the Guards.'"[49]

Rafiqdoust and other members of the Guards could not have breached the chain of command and conspired against Lahouti Eshkevari alone. It is therefore most probable that the leading Islamic Republican Party members who formalized the existence of the Revolutionary Committees in the first place and tasked Rafiqdoust with the job of infiltrating the National Guards were also actively engaged in directing Rafiqdoust's meetings with Grand Ayatollah Khomeini. In this context the roles of Rafsanjani and Ahmad Khomeini, the gatekeeper to the Leader of the Revolution without whose permission Rafiqdoust could not have met the Grand Ayatollah, are of particular interest.

Rafsanjani was an old prisonmate of Lahouti Eshkevari from Evin Prison,[50] and two of Rafsanjani's daughters, Faezeh[51] and Fatemeh,[52] are to this day married to sons of Lahouti Eshkevari: Hamid and Said Lahouti Eshkevari. The marital bond between the families was to foster a lasting political alliance boosting the political careers of both clerical clans, but the affair proved to be one of Rafsanjani's greatest miscalculations when Lahouti Eshkevari directly criticized Grand Ayatollah Khomeini and the revolutionary regime. Lahouti Eshkevari's actions may have rested upon two main reasons. Dissatisfaction with the fact that he was not included in the narrow circle around Khomeini in the Council of the Revolution made Lahouti Eshkevari voice his dissatisfaction on several occasions to Rafsanjani,[53] but Lahouti Eshkevari also seems to have been an independent man of honor with great personal integrity. As the totalitarian dynamics of the Islamic Republic evolved, Lahouti Eshkevari backed off from the regime. Still worse, from Grand Ayatollah Khomeini's perspective, Lahouti Eshkevari also had sympathies with the Mojahedin-e Khalq organization via one of his sons, Vahid, who was a member of the organization.[54]

As the conspiracy of the radical elements in the Guards and among the Islamic Republican Party elites against the commissar Lahouti Eshkevari developed, even Ahmad Khomeini and Rafsanjani joined their ranks. At this point Rafsanjani probably considered his family ties with Lahouti

Eshkevari a terrible liability harming his future ambitions rather than the asset he believed it to be when he arranged the marriage of his daughters with Lahouti Eshkevari's sons.

Aside from the machinations of the Islamic Republican Party and concerns about the growing power of the interim government, Ahmad Khomeini must also have had personal grudges against Lahouti Eshkevari, who had disclosed that Ahmad Khomeini had ordered setting a cinema showing Western movies ablaze, killing many civilians in Qom prior to the revolution.[55]

In a later interview with *Payam-e Enqelab*, Ahmad Khomeini disclosed that he had a conversation with Rafsanjani in which he explained to Rafsanjani that despite Grand Ayatollah Khomeini's decree to Lahouti Eshkevari,

> there are many people in the Guards who do not respect the authority of Lahouti [Eshkevari]. The guardsmen need some-one with characteristics of a leader. He [Rafsanjani] told me it is your responsibility to discuss this matter with the Imam [Grand Ayatollah Khomeini]. I told the Imam that he [Lahouti Eshkevari] commands no authority. The Imam said: "I did not know this and my benevolent assessment of Mr. Lahouti [Eshkevari] was based upon his record of struggle [against the Shah's regime.]" After that I shared this matter with Mr. Lahouti [Eshkevari], of course not directly, he resigned and the Imam accepted.[56]

Ahmad Khomeini's recollection of this conversation may be true, but it may also reflect his attempt to implicate Rafsanjani in Lahouti Eshkevari's downfall. Regardless of the authenticity of Ahmad Khomeini's recollections, Rafsanjani and Ahmad Khomeini probably both had conversations with Khomeini to demand Lahouti Eshkevari's dismissal.

The conspiracy of leading IRGC commanders, Islamic Republican Party officials, Ahmad Khomeini, and possibly Rafsanjani against Lahouti Eshkevari proved effective. Grand Ayatollah Khomeini's informal dismissal of Lahouti Eshkevari was expressed in his public speech on November 25, 1979. Addressing the IRGC personnel, Grand Ayatollah Khomeini said: "Your country is in a state of turmoil. If we are not alert enough, we

will be done for. We should stay united. ...Now, our only concern should
be confronting the United States."[57] Khomeini continued:

> You are aware that I like him [Lahouti Eshkevari]. He wrote
> to me that he was sick and that he has a heart condition, and
> he asked me to appoint somebody else for his position. So far,
> I have not replied to him, but we cannot risk having a sick
> person stay in a position while he is not physically ready for it.
> I want him to go abroad and have his heart treated. You should
> help him with this trip too. If there is any other problem, it is
> proper for him to come over and discuss it with me. He could
> send somebody else to discuss his problem with me.[58]

Khomeini then warned: "However, I would not support chaos and con-
vulsion..."[59] and also warned: "Such problems should not be discussed
in commotions. Rather, their representatives should come and discuss the
problems with us."[60] But he also complained: "He has not come to me,
either, to discuss his problem with me."[61]

Grand Ayatollah Khomeini's de facto dismissal of Lahouti Eshkevari as
his representative to the Guards was also a last warning to the independent-
minded Lahouti Eshkevari. Lahouti Eshkevari not only ignored this
warning but intensified his criticism of Khomeini and the revolutionary
leadership. To Rafsanjani's dismay, Lahouti Eshkevari also systematically
communicated his dissatisfaction to the Iranian public. According to a
Fars News Agency report of November 26, 1980, Lahouti Eshkevari and
Ahmad Salamatian, parliamentarian and supporter of President Abol-
Hassan Bani-Sadr, arranged rallies in Mashhad in which the demonstrators
shouted "Death to Beheshti" and "Our Voice and Vision [of the Islamic
Republic] must be freed from the claws of the ruling party," referring to
increasing control of the media in the hands of the Islamic Republican
Party.[62] In the November 29, 1980, issue of Bani-Sadr's mouthpiece
Enqelab-e Eslami, Lahouti Eshkevari challenged Khomeini's authority
directly: "The people did not revolt so people like you and me could rule
them. If bullying and the logic of the club is your [preferred] method of
government, before you there was the *Aryamehr* [Light of the Aryans, one
of the titles of the Shah]. The ruling system is [in effect functions as] a

single-party system and one hears the footsteps of Fascism. Pity a revolution where eight percent rule over eighty percent. If might could repress people, there were people before you who were even mightier. You don't do anything but repressing and bringing hardships upon the people."[63]

Despite Lahouti Eshkevari's being dismissed as Khomeini's representative to the Guards, the IRGC never forgave him, closely monitoring his movements and reporting them in its classified internal bulletin, which warned the members of the Guards against the counterrevolution of the so-called "scientific Islam" of Bani-Sadr and Lahouti Eshkevari.[64] The entry in Rafsanjani's memoirs for April 19, 1981, mentions a private conversation between the two men during which Lahouti Eshkevari protests against the "Kouchesfehan [Gilan province] affair."[65] The affair refers to an incident in which members of the "Hezbollah faction," which in reality means local branches of the Revolutionary Committee and the Revolutionary Guards, armed with clubs attacked Lahouti Eshkevari, who had arranged a rally declaring his support for Bani-Sadr. One of Lahouti Eshkevari's bodyguards was killed in the clashes.[66] Also, the June 12, 1981, entry in Rafsanjani's memoirs notes the growing gap between Lahouti Eshkevari's position and the Khomeini loyalists in the Islamic Republican Party: "At night, Mr. Lahouti [Eshkevari] came and we had a long discussion about him. He criticized positions of the Imam [Khomeini], us, the people, [the Islamic Republic] Voice and Vision and the parliament."[67]

The Revolutionary Guards and the Islamic Republican Party finally revenged Lahouti Eshkevari's attempt at subjecting the IRGC to political control, and control by the moderate transitional government at that. According to the October 28, 1981, entry in Rafsanjani's memoirs, agents of Supreme Public Prosecutor and IRGC cofounder Mousavi Ardebili raided the home of Lahouti Eshkevari "to search for documents on Vahid [Lahouti Eshkevari's son]. ...In the evening, news came that Mr. Lahouti [Eshkevari] was imprisoned."[68] Vahid was executed ten days prior to his father's arrest because of his membership in the Mojahedin-e Khalq organization. On October 29, 1981, Rafsanjani was told that Lahouti Eshkevari had died of a heart attack.[69] The news of Lahouti Eshkevari's death was conveyed to Rafsanjani while he, in his position as speaker of the parliament, was presiding over a parliamentary session, and Rafsanjani wept while the proceedings were broadcasted on live television.[70]

Twenty-seven years later, his daughters disclosed in an interview that while imprisoned in Evin, Lahouti Eshkevari was poisoned with strychnine by prison warden Assadollah Lajevardi.[71] *Shahrvand-e Emrouz*, which had published the Rafsanjani family's disclosures, was banned in November 2008.

Such was the destiny of the first commissar supposed to act as the eyes and ears of the country's leader in the Guards. And such was the power of the IRGC, which managed to exploit divisions among the civilian leadership to eliminate the very individual tasked with the job of subjecting the Guards to civilian control. With unchecked power the IRGC managed to pursue its predatory interests with little regard to the civilian leadership of the Islamic Republic.

5.3.2. Brief tenures of Rafsanjani and Khamenei With the Lahouti Eshkevari incident in mind, Grand Ayatollah Khomeini must have realized that he needed to control the Revolutionary Guards by not one but several personal representatives. By having one representative in the now-unified IRGC, Khomeini risked another Lahouti Eshkevari: a charismatic leader who in the worst-case scenario could end up commanding control over the IRGC and challenge Khomeini's authority. Several representatives, on the other hand, would compete against each other, which reduced the risk of one of them taking over the entire IRGC. The shortcoming of this strategy was a weak civilian oversight apparatus due to interagency rivalry and double administration. The civilian leadership's solution was to establish functionally specialized ideological/political commissariats with slightly overlapping fields of competence, each reporting to Khomeini separately, but as we shall see, such functional specialization never materialized and the commissars expended more effort fighting each other than subjecting the IRGC to civilian control.

The first person to replace the deposed Lahouti Eshkevari as representative of Khomeini in the IRGC was Rafsanjani himself.[72] Ebrahim Hajj-Mohammad-Zadeh recalls in an early interview: "The Imam [Grand Ayatollah Khomeini] appointed Mr. Hashemi Rafsanjani as the contact person between the Guards and the Council of the Revolution. After this, the Imam stressed that the Guards [units] should not be controlled by the [interim] government and should be unified."[73] Prior to this informal appointment Rafsanjani had been formally appointed deputy interior minister responsible for internal security and the IRGC in early July 1979,[74] but Rafsanjani resigned on February 26, 1980, in order to run for parliament.[75] After a short period Khamenei had a short-lived role as Khomeini's representative in the Guards.[76] Also prior to his appointment Khamenei had some contact with the IRGC in his capacity as deputy defense minister appointed in early July 1979,[77] but he resigned on February 24, 1980.[78]

There is little record of Rafsanjani's and Khamenei's activities as Khomeini's representatives to the Guards. They were both destined for higher offices, and competing factions among the revolutionary elites probably pressured Khomeini not to concentrate so much power in the hands of these two individuals.

5.3.3. Quadrant of Chaos: Mahallati, Taheri Khorram-Abadi, Faker, and Eraqi
Following the exit of Rafsanjani and Khamenei, Khomeini was once again forced to appoint a new representative to the Guards. The representative had to be strong enough to command some authority among IRGC members and capable of establishing the infrastructure of the commissariat in the Guards but not so strong as to outcompete the revolutionary leadership in Tehran. The commissars also needed to be capable organizers who could establish an ideological/political indoctrination infrastructure and a civilian oversight apparatus in the IRGC, but not strong enough to provoke a hostile counterreaction from the commanders of the Guards.

Initially Khomeini chose to replace Rafsanjani and Khamenei with Hojjat al-Eslam Fazl-Allah Mahallati, appointed on June 18, 1980,[79] but with the Islamic Republic being a highly factionalized regime, Khomeini was forced—both by civilian factions and by their followers within the Guards—to appoint three other commissars: Ayatollah Hassan Taheri Khorram-Abadi, appointed on December 14, 1981;[80] Hojjat al-Eslam Mohammad-Reza Faker, appointed on August 25, 1982;[81] and Hojjat al-Eslam Mahmoud Mohammadi Eraqi, who was appointed deputy representative to the IRGC and never received an official decree from Khomeini.

Mahallati, Khomeini's initial choice as replacement commissar, was a graduate of the Elmiyyeh Theological Seminary in Qom,[82] and more importantly a childhood friend of Mostafa Khomeini, the late son of Grand Ayatollah Khomeini, whom Mahallati befriended during the Khomeini family's vacation excursions to Mahallat. In the 1950s, Mahallati, who in the meantime had married, purchased a house in front of the Khomeini residence in the Yakhchal-e Qazi neighborhood in Qom.[83] Besides the prerevolutionary ties between Mahallati and the Khomeinis, Mahallati also proved his worth after the revolution as a member of the Committee Welcoming the Imam upon Grand Ayatollah Khomeini's return to Iran from exile, which practically guaranteed Khomeini's safety in the midst of the revolutionary chaos of 1979.[84] The choice of Mahallati probably also rested upon the fact that Mahallati's unprivileged rural background denied him a commanding position among peer clerics, who most probably looked down upon the little-known and mysterious follower of Khomeini. This background may have been a qualifying factor after all the trouble with the popular and charismatic Lahouti Eshkevari. Two other very important factors qualifying Mahallati for the post must have been his active role in the ratification of the Statute of the Revolutionary Guards in the parliament[85] and, even more importantly, Mahallati's membership in the Islamic Republican Party and the backing he must have received from the party leadership.[86]

The text of Khomeini's decree ordered Mahallati "in cooperation with the gentlemen representing me [Khomeini] in the Army, Gendarmerie and the Police and an assembly of Muslim and committed law enforcement forces approved by most of the honorable gentlemen to establish an organization studying affairs of the armed forces. This organization is obliged to report on a weekly basis to me upon what happens in the Army, the Police, Gendarmerie and the Revolutionary Guards in detail and with great care."[87] The decree concluded: "The armed forces personnel are obliged to cooperated with you."[88] In practical terms, Mahallati was to realize Khomeini's declared policy of controlling the unruly Guards from his office physically located in the central headquarters of the IRGC.

Mahallati proved an energetic commissar, and according to one source, soon after his appointment Mahallati managed to establish an expansive ideological/political commissariat with "more than seventy offices" in various regions of Iran and all levels of the Guards in order to secure supervision on coordination and "cooperation of this institution [the IRGC] with the line of the *Vali-ye Faqih* [Guardian Jurist, referring to Grand Ayatollah Khomeini]."[89] A survey of the *Payam-e Enqelab* weekly, mouthpiece of the IRGC, also shows that Mahallati was an important speaker at the assemblies of the IRGC commanders, such as the gathering of April 15, 1981, at the Ghadir IRGC garrison in Isfahan.[90] Mahallati's speeches revolved around disciplinary issues, and in most of his speeches he warned IRGC members against membership in political parties,[91] a theme Mahallati would frequently return to.[92]

Mahallati also faced serious challenges. Although organizationally unified within the structural frameworks of the IRGC, many guardsmen preserved their loyalties to the groups and factions they belonged to prior to the unification of the Guards. Factional disputes came to the surface on occasions such as Khomeini's July 19, 1980, appointment of Morteza Rezaei as IRGC chief,[93] which proved highly controversial among other factions of the Guards. Thus, only a month into his appointment Mahallati found himself in a leadership crisis in the IRGC in which many commanders bypassed him and directly sought the council of Khomeini in order to dismiss Morteza Rezaei. Mahallati must have witnessed firsthand IRGC commanders' reaching out to the highest political positions in the Islamic Republic with no reverence for Khomeini's representative to the Guards.

Mahallati probably also complained to Khomeini, who in a later speech to IRGC commanders felt compelled to stress the importance of his representative: "I cannot intervene in every issue [of the Guards] directly," said Khomeini, adding: "That is why I appoint representatives and, for example, approve of you [Mahallati] to be in the Guards, and to direct the affairs. My representatives are the ones responsible to be directly in contact with the issues. This is how I can act and so whatever you do there [in your area of duty] means that I have done it. Those who like to take orders from me must obey you [in order to obey me]."[94]

The Iraqi invasion of Iran on September 22, 1980, made Mahallati's task vital for the clerical establishment, and by May 10, 1981, Mahallati tried to calm the internal struggle within the Guards between Morteza Rezaei and factions opposing the chief. In a secret conversation with Rafsanjani, Mahallati reported a permanent state of conflict between the IRGC Command Council and IRGC chief Morteza Rezaei.[95] But it must have been the dominant faction within the IRGC, and not Mahallati, that

persuaded Khomeini to appoint Mohsen Rezaei as IRGC chief and transferred Morteza Rezaei to the Intelligence Directorate of the Guards. In this
issue Mahallati seems to have played a minimal role, which shows that
the influence of Khomeini's representative was very limited with regard to
factional dynamics within the IRGC.

As the war was being fought, Mahallati also found himself involved in
purging the Guards of the network of the first and deposed IRGC chief
Abbas Aqa-Zamani (also known as Abou-Sharif), which Mahallati considered a risky affair.[96] Aqa-Zamani was loyal to the interim government and
thus was considered an undesirable and untrustworthy element by leading
Islamic Republican Party members and many IRGC commanders. Despite
the interim government's already having been deposed in the wake of
the seizure of the U.S. embassy in Tehran, Mahallati feared its influence
among revolutionary elites of the Islamic Republic. On September 12,
1982, the problem seemed still unsolved, and Mahallati in conversations
with Rafsanjani expressed concern about the IRGC's being infiltrated by
Iran Freedom Movement supporters.[97]

While it is impossible to obtain exact information about the degree of
internal factional disputes in the Guards, Khomeini's speeches stressing
the necessity of unity in the IRGC may indicate the degree of the problem. Thus, in his speech of May 16, 1983, Khomeini urged the Guards
to be "united...and not have specific inclinations towards this group or
that group."[98] Khomeini's speeches also indicate that Mahallati's attempt
at suppressing factional disputes had not proved effective and that the
first attempt at purging the IRGC could only be done with cooperation of
IRGC chief Mohsen Rezaei.

The greatest challenge to Mahallati's authority was from supporters of
Grand Ayatollah Montazeri, Khomeini's successor designate. Opposition
to Mahallati was especially felt in the Isfahan branch of the IRGC, as the
entire city of Isfahan became the battleground for the struggle for power
between clergymen close to the Islamic Republican Party, who were close
to Rafsanjani, Ahmad Khomeini, Khamenei, and Montazeri's supporters
(as a native of Najaf-Abad of Isfahan, Grand Ayatollah Montazeri commanded great local influence). On November 19, 1981, for example,
Rafsanjani reports Mahallati's complaints of being totally ignored by the
Isfahan branch of the IRGC, which was close to Montazeri.[99]

As the challenge to Mahallati's authority grew, Khomeini on December 14, 1981, appointed Taheri Khorram-Abadi as Mahallati's fellow representative to the Guards.[100] Taheri Khorram-Abadi was a graduate of the Haghani School of the Elmiyyeh Theological Seminary, also in Qom, and a former student of Khomeini, but was recommended as Khomeini's representative in the Guards by Montazeri.[101] By appointing Taheri Khorram-Abadi as a corepresentative, Khomeini hoped to accommodate the wishes of the Montazeri faction within the Guards, but the appointment created bigger problems.

Khomeini's decree of December 14, 1981, to Taheri Khorram-Abadi, for example, had a slightly different text from Mahallati's decree: "You are hereby notified that Hojjat al-Eslam…Haj Sheikh Hossein-Ali Montazeri—may his graces last—recommended you look into the affairs of the IRGC, and therefore I appoint you to this post to ensure that the rules and decisions of the IRGC Council comply with the Islamic standards. You are also required to keenly track the ideological leanings of the IRGC throughout the country and firmly stem any deviation or violation."[102] Thus, the decree does not provide any specific description of Taheri Khorram-Abadi's tasks in the IRGC. Explaining the decree, *Payam-e Enqelab* described Taheri Khorram-Abadi's obligations as follows:

> [Preserving] the bond between the Guards and the clergy…by:
> 1. Direct presence of clerics in different cadres of the Guards and their membership and fields of responsibilities in this institution. 2. Continuous meetings of the Guard members with senior members of the clergy and professors at the Elmiyyeh Theological Seminary in Qom [back then directed by Grand Ayatollah Montazeri]. 3. Direct presence of the representative of Ayatollah Montazeri in the Guards and his supervision in the affairs of the Guards. 4. Direct connection with the Supreme Leader who is the highest authority of the clergy.[103]

In another interview Taheri Khorram-Abadi explained his tasks as "control[ing] conformity of the decisions of the Council of the Guards with Sharia principles,"[104] supervision of decisions of the Guards' Council, and further development of the internal ideological/political indoctrination of the Guards, while Mahallati was responsible for internal disciplinary committees of the IRGC.[105] Such division of labor is also apparent in *Payam-e Enqelab*'s report from the Third Seminar of the Guard Commander. Both Mahallati and Taheri Khorram-Abadi delivered speeches, the former on the importance of discipline and the latter on the importance of ideological purity.[106]

With no clear distinctions between their spheres of competence and because of their factional differences, Mahallati and Taheri Khorram-Abadi were bound to collide. For example, Taheri Khorram-Abadi in his January 14, 1982, meeting with Rafsanjani accused many individuals close to Mahallati and the Islamic Republican Party of being former members of the illegal Hojjatiyyeh secret society who were trying to infiltrate the IRGC.[107] Lack of available material restricts our attempt at reconstructing the rivalry between Mahallati and Taheri Khorram-Abadi, but their relationship must have been so poor that Khomeini appointed Taheri Khorram-Abadi head of a mission to Pakistan sometime prior to August 25, 1982.[108]

But Taheri Khorram-Abadi's exile was far from a clear victory for Mahallati. With Taheri Khorram-Abadi abroad, Khomeini issued a decree to Hojjat al-Eslam Mohammad-Reza Faker, a graduate of the theological seminary in Mashhad, on August 25, 1982.[109] As apparent in the text of the decree, the appointment was due to Taheri Khorram-Abadi's "overseas mission,"[110] referring to his temporary removal because of the conflict with Mahallati. The decree also specified that Faker was authorized "to take charge of his [Taheri Khorram-Abadi's] responsibility in his absence in the Islamic Revolutionary Guards Corps and follow up on the cultural and Islamic issues seriously."[111] Faker was an early pro-Khomeini activist who was radicalized in the beginning of the 1960s and was imprisoned in the second half of the 1970s.[112]

The appointment of Faker did not solve any of the IRGC's problems and created new ones. Faker's relationship with Mahallati must have been so poor that on January 23, 1983, Rafsanjani had to summon Mahallati, Mohi al-Din Anvari, Hojjat al-Eslam Gholam-Hossein Haghani, Ayatollah Mohammad-Ali Movahedi Kermani, and Hojjat al-Eslam Ali-Akbar Nateq Nouri to discuss creation of a council coordinating the work of Khomeini's representatives to the armed forces.[113]

In the meantime, the IRGC commanders exploited the conflict between the commissars, bypassed the chain of command, and badmouthed the commissars among the civilian leadership such as Rafsanjani. For example, on February 19, 1983, Rafiqdoust protested against Faker's veto right at IRGC Command Council meetings, especially with regard to operational issues.[114] Faker, in return, in his April 12, 1983, meeting with Rafsanjani retaliated by complaining about "lack of discipline" in the Guards.[115] By April 15, 1983, Rafsanjani and Ahmad Khomeini were discussing how to divide the spheres of competence of the commissars to solve the crisis between the IRGC commanders and the commissars. But regardless of their efforts, Faker's destiny in the IRGC followed a pattern well known from other ideological/political commissars: the IRGC commander in chief threatened to resign in protest against Faker's interventions in affairs of the Guards.[116]

It may also have been due to Mahallati's permanent state of conflict with the IRGC commanders—not to mention his conflict with Faker—that on April 15, 1983, Rafsanjani and Ahmad Khomeini discussed how to divide Mahallati's sphere of competence with Faker.[117] On April 19, 1983, Rafsanjani embarrassed Mahallati in front of other representatives of Khomeini to the armed forces by criticizing Mahallati's inability to establish a unitary organization to supervise the entire body of the armed forces.[118] But the effort failed to stabilize the commissariat, and the political commissar Faker, not the IRGC chief Rezaei, was dismissed from the Guards on July 21, 1983.[119] In other words, the Guards managed to impose its will upon the clerical oversight apparatus that was meant to subject it to civilian control.

After Faker's disastrous interlude, Khomeini reinstated Taheri Khorram-Abadi as representative to the Guards on June 29, 1983, and urged him in a decree: "Please take action with care and detail with regard to the duties of my representatives stated in the memorandum of association of the Revolutionary Guards Corps of the Islamic Republic [the Statute of the Guards]. I am optimistic that with the help and sincerity of Hojjat al-Eslam Fakir [Faker] and Hojjat al-Eslam Mahallati and His Excellency the Minister of the Guards Corps [Rafiqdoust] and Mr. Muhsin Ridai [Mohsen Rezaei], whom I respect and whom I approve, you shall attend to the condition of the Guards Corps in a better way. It is necessary that the Minister of Guards Corps [Rafiqdoust], the commander of the Guards Corps [Rezaei], other commanders and those that occupy senior positions in the Guards Corps endorse my representative Mr. Tahiri [Taheri]. In matters related to him, they should follow his advice according to the religious and legal regulations and in keeping with the lofty interests of the country and the Islamic Republic. It is necessary to remind that obeying Mr. Muhsin Ridai [Mohsen Rezaei], the commander-in-chief of the Guards Corps and other commanders based on the chain of command and regulations of the Guards Corps is a divine religious duty in the Islamic Republic of Iran and that to infringe upon them has religious responsibility in addition to legal prosecution."[120]

As Rafsanjani's and the Islamic Republican Party's relations with Khomeini's successor designate, Grand Ayatollah Montazeri, deteriorated, Rafsanjani also began to worry about Montazeri's influence in the Guards. On June 13, 1983—even before Khomeini's reinstatement of Taheri Khorram-Abadi—Rafsanjani discussed the role of Taheri Khorram-Abadi with then prosecutor general Hojjat al-Eslam Mohammad-Mehdi Rabbani Omleshi, who died under mysterious circumstances on July 8, 1985, and whose daughter Zahra to this day is married to Hojjat al-Eslam Ahmad Montazeri, son of Grand Ayatollah Montazeri.[121]

By August 5, 1983, Mahallati could no longer hide his contempt for Taheri Khorram-Abadi and at a secret meeting with Rafsanjani demanded a clear division of labor between the political commissars.[122] Mahallati seems to have won this battle, as on August 30, 1983, Taheri Khorram-Abadi expressed his desire to return to Pakistan to continue his missionary work.[123] It may also be about this time that Taheri Khorram-Abadi betrayed his old master, Grand Ayatollah Montazeri, and aligned himself with Rafsanjani and Ahmad Khomeini, as it is not imaginable that Montazeri had approved of Taheri Khorram-Abadi's leaving such a sensitive position in the Guards. It is also remarkable that a few months before the suspicious death of Grand Ayatollah Montazeri's student Rabbani Omleshi, Rabbani Omleshi was invited by Taheri Khorram-Abadi to travel to the front,[124] after which Rabbani Omleshi fell ill and died. Was this another act of treason against Grand Ayatollah Montazeri and another attempt of Taheri Khorram-Abadi to prove his loyalty to the Rafsanjani camp? Was this the price Taheri Khorram-Abadi had to pay in order to convince Rafsanjani and the Islamic Republican Party faction of his defection from Montazeri's camp? Taheri Khorram-Abadi was most certainly promoted and was elected member of the Board of Directors of the Parliament on July 13, 1985.[125] And in a final display of distancing himself from Montazeri, Taheri Khorram-Abadi claimed that Hojjat al-Eslam Mehdi Hashemi, brother of Montazeri's son-in-law Hadi Hashemi, tried to poison him,[126] or in other words the exact same deed Taheri Khorram-Abadi may have committed against Rabbani Omleshi. It is clear that under such circumstances the commissar Taheri Khorram-Abadi could not have concentrated his efforts on subjecting the Guards to civilian control but fought for his own survival in the midst of the battle between Montazeri's network and the Islamic Republican Party.

Conspiracies of the Isfahan branch of the IRGC against Mahallati must have worked, since in their August 5, 1983, meeting Rafsanjani, Ahmad Khomeini, and Mahallati vehemently protested Grand Ayatollah Khomeini's decree to Taheri Khorram-Abadi and demanded a clear division of labor with him in the IRGC.[127] On August 31, 1983, the humiliated Mahallati demanded restoration of his honor after Grand Ayatollah Khomeini's decree to Taheri Khorram-Abadi and asked Rafsanjani to consult with Mahdavi Kani.[128] Mahallati's protests produced some results, and on December 17, 1983, Grand Ayatollah Khomeini, who in the meantime had sent Taheri Khorram-Abadi on a mission to Pakistan—probably to boost Mahallati's prestige—in a new decree increased the scope of Mahallati's responsibilities in the absence of Taheri Khorram-Abadi: "Since Hojjat al-Eslam Taheri [Khorram-Abadi] is going to travel, you are required to undertake all his responsibilities in *Sepah-e Pasdaran* [Revolutionary Guards] in addition to your own responsibilities in *Sepah-e Pasdaran*."[129] This incident shows that the personal prestige of Grand Ayatollah Khomeini, along with the brinkmanship of Ahmad Khomeini and Rafsanjani, was needed to restore balance within the IRGC and empower Mahallati.

But the conflicts between the followers of Montazeri and the Islamic Republican Party continued in the IRGC, and by January 2, 1984, Khomeini had to summon Mahallati, Hojjat al-Eslam Mostafa Mohaghegh Damad, Khomeini's representative to the Isfahan IRGC, and Reza Seyf-Allahi, Isfahan IRGC chief: "The gentlemen going there [Isfahan] should be careful not [to] tilt toward anyone and try to keep *Sepah* [the Guards] independent. Of course, treat all with sincerity. Try not to transmit the difference of opinion that exists everywhere to *Sepah* [the Guards]. Your main concern should be the war. Try to hearten the people."[130] In a much later interview Mohaghegh stressed that Grand Ayatollah Khomeini was concerned about Montazeri's supporters in Isfahan who refused to subject themselves to the authority of the IRGC leadership,[131] but back then even Khomeini did not move directly against Montazeri's supporters. However, Khomeini's mediation was to no avail, and on June 16, 1985, a parliamentary faction close to Montazeri tried to exploit the weak performance of the IRGC on the front to oust Mohsen Rezaei as IRGC commander in chief.[132] According to Rafsanjani's memoirs, the parliamentarians demanding the ouster of Mohsen Rezaei belonged to the "Isfahan faction," which is a clear reference to Grand Ayatollah Montazeri and his supporters.[133]

Another issue constantly weakening Mahallati's prestige within the IRGC was his involvement in tactical and operational issues of the IRGC on the front. The IRGC commanders considered the issue outside the sphere of competence of the clerical commissars, and they were also concerned about the nature of the reports Mahallati sent to the civilian leadership in Tehran. For example, on March 22 and March 27, 1982, Mahallati was back in Tehran to evaluate the advances of the Fath al-Mobin operation with Rafsanjani.[134] The IRGC leadership expected a favorable report, but Mahallati's comments to Rafsanjani were critical of the role of the IRGC. But more important was the strategic question of the continuation of the war after the liberation of Khorramshahr on May 24, 1982. While Khomeini and his representative to the IRGC were inclined toward ceasefire with Iraq and against continuation of the war on Iraqi soil,[135] the IRGC leadership demanded war until achievement of a military victory, since a swift end to the war would endanger the IRGC's ambitions to expand its organization and influence. With this aim in mind, Mahallati's badmouthing of IRGC commanders was not left unanswered by IRGC commanders, and Rezaei and IRGC minister Rafiqdoust intensified their secret warfare against Mahallati the commissar.

Failed military operations of the Guards proved even more difficult for the IRGC and Mahallati to handle. On February 12, 1983, Rafsanjani, Rafiqdoust, and Mahallati had a stormy meeting evaluating unsuccessful military operations of the Guards,[136] and on March 7, 1983,

Rafiqdoust began seeking Rafsanjani's company to badmouth Mahallati and complain about his meddling in tactical issues.[137] By mid-1983 the IRGC resistance toward Mahallati had reached such a degree that at a meeting prior to the Supreme Defense Council (*Showra-ye Ali-ye Defae*) session Rafsanjani and Khamenei were discussing how to solve the state of permanent crisis between the representative and the IRGC leadership.[138] Rafsanjani continued the discussion with Ahmad Khomeini, presumably in order to indirectly inform Grand Ayatollah Khomeini, on June 20, 1983.[139]

The conflict between Mahallati and leading members of the IRGC deteriorated, and on June 24, 1985, Grand Ayatollah Khomeini wrote to Mahallati to mediate between him and the commanders of the Guards, specially Ali Shamkhani, who seems to have written a letter of complaint to Khomeini: "Mr. [Ali] Shamkhani is a righteous and committed person; in a letter he has written of what has happened, he has expressed regret and apology. God willing, you will ignore what has been passed by and treat him and other *Sepahi* [Guardsmen] brothers as brotherly as before. Dear *Sepah* brothers should note that Mr. Mahallati, my representative, is struggling, upright and battle-tested, and observing his respect and attention to his guidelines is necessary."[140]

Even Grand Ayatollah Khomeini's letter did not help, and in a letter to the Grand Ayatollah, Mahallati demanded answers to the following questions as a way of obtaining increased authority within the IRGC: "1. Is my previous decree representing my appointment as the Imam's representative in *Sepah* [Guards] still effective?"[141] Grand Ayatollah Khomeini responded: "It is still effective."[142] Mahallati also asked: "2. Who is responsible for following up and attending to the question of grouping [political factionalism] in *Sepah* in Your Excellency's order issued to the armed forces?"[143] Grand Ayatollah Khomeini responded: "One is you and the other the Council of *Sepah* with discretion of majority. As regards this subject that is concerned with the fate of *Sepah* it is necessary to deal with it decisively and without consideration for anyone."[144]

Shamkhani continued his campaign against Mahallati, and on July 5, 1984, at a secret meeting with Rafsanjani, he demanded restriction of Mahallati's sphere of influence.[145] Yet another meeting, this time with Rafsanjani, Rafiqdoust, Rezaei, and Yahya Rahim Safavi present, took place at Rafsanjani's office; at this meeting the IRGC commanders complained against Mahallati's intervention in the affairs of the IRGC and informed Rafsanjani of a letter they had sent to Grand Ayatollah Khomeini.[146] In his September 21, 1984, memoirs, Rafsanjani notes that Ahmad Khomeini disclosed to him that the writer of the letter to Grand Ayatollah Khomeini was Mohsen Rezaei and that the letter protested against Mahallati's intervention in tactical issues of the war.[147] On September 24, 1984, Mohsen Rezaei sought the assistance of Rafsanjani to reduce Mahallati's intervention in the affairs of the Guards,[148] a request Rezaei also made to Rafsanjani on September 30, 1984.[149] Rezaei's requests made an impression on Rafsanjani, who discussed the issue with Ahmad Khomeini on October 4, 1984.[150] Following a subsequent meeting between Rafsanjani and Rezaei on October 8, 1984,[151] Rafsanjani, Ahmad Khomeini, Khamenei, and a triumphant Rezaei informed Mahallati of restrictions on his mandate.[152]

Even restrictions on Mahallati's mandate failed to improve relations between the commissar and the Guardsmen because Mahallati started a counteroffensive against Rezaei. On November 18, 1984, Mahallati reported to Rafsanjani that there was a "wave of opposition" against the leadership of the Guards within the ranks, and he warned against the danger and complaints being ignored by IRGC commanders.[153] Mahallati continued his venomous attacks against Rezaei and also reported critical operational circumstances on the front on March 16, 1985,[154] and complained about poor IRGC leadership in Operation Badr at a meeting with Rafsanjani on March 21, 1985,[155] and again on April 10, 1985.[156] Rafsanjani's memoirs also reveal that on March 21, 1985, Mahallati renewed his complaints about Rezaei's management of the Badr operation. Badr was indeed a serious setback for the Guards: commander Mehdi Bakeri, Thirty-first Ashoura IRGC unit chief, and commander Abbas Karimi, Twenty-seventh Hazrat-e Rasoul unit chief, were killed, along with at least two thousand others.[157] Mahallati knew how to scandalize Rezaei and capitalized on the weakening of Rezaei's position within the Guards and Rafsanjani's criticism of his leadership.[158] Rezaei's star was declining, and Rafsanjani noted in his April 3, 1985, memoirs: "Mr. Mohsen Rezaei came and gave an incomplete report of the Badr Operation. He did not provide any acceptable information and it seems that he has not even any remarkable plans for the future. Apart from this, he does not agree with the plans of [Regular Army Chief] Mr.

Sayyad [Shirazi] and says the precondition of future operations is transfer of the Army's armaments [to the Guards]."[159]

At this time, Mahallati's interventions against Mohsen Rezaei must have been considered with the greatest concern by the IRGC leadership, and the IRGC leadership must have been busy with countermeasures against Mahallati's interventions. Mahallati, on the other hand, ignoring concerns of the IRGC leadership, could hardly hide his joy at an April 19, 1985, meeting with Rafsanjani when reporting on cancellation of the IRGC/regular army offensive due to unwillingness of the IRGC leadership.[160] Mahallati continued his criticism of the IRGC leadership in the presence of Rafsanjani on May 18, 1985.[161] At the meeting of Rafsanjani and Mahallati on June 7, 1985, the two gentlemen discussed the death of one of Mahallati's deputies at the front.[162] Was this the IRGC's warning to Mahallati of what he could expect from the Guards should he continue his interference in the affairs of the Guards?

Warning or not, Mahallati seems to have ignored it, and on July 6, 1985, the IRGC commanders once again sought Rafsanjani to complain of the problems Mahallati had created for them in the Guards.[163] On August 16, 1985, Mahallati complained to Rafsanjani about his reduced powers in the IRGC,[164] and more dramatically, on October 13, 1985, Mahallati shared with Rafsanjani his concern about the character assassination of him in the IRGC, where he was depicted as "an opponent of Grand Ayatollah Khomeini," and his concern that "the Guards no longer will guard" him physically.[165] Rafsanjani's memoirs also note two meetings, the first with the other commissar, Eraqi, on January 2, 1986,[166] and the other with Fakhr al-Din Hejazi on January 28, 1986, in which Hejazi complained about Mahallati's role in the Guards.[167]

On February 20, 1986, Mahallati's function as an ideological/political commissar came to an abrupt end as Mahan Air's Friendship plane carrying him and a group of parliamentarians from Tehran to Ahwaz was allegedly shot down at Wein, 25 kilometers north of Ahwaz, by Iraqi fighters.[168] There were no survivors; Mahallati died along with the forty other passengers, including many members of the National Security Committee of the parliament.[169] Rafsanjani quotes Revolutionary Guard minister Rafiqdoust as saying that the bodies "could not be identified…because of fire,"[170] but later official historiography of the Islamic Republic claims that there was "no fire and that the bodies of the martyrs remained intact."[171] The official report also clarifies that Mahallati's team was on the way to inspect the latest Iranian offensives in Faw Peninsula, the very scene of one of the greatest military defeats of the IRGC during the Iran-Iraq war.[172]

Rafsanjani was informed of Mahallati's death in a "plane crash"[173] the very day of the accident, but remarkably, at a secret meeting on February 21, 1986, the day after Mahallati's death, Rafsanjani urged Ahmad Khomeini to behave in such a way that the IRGC commanders would be "not harmed."[174] Did Rafsanjani consider Mahallati's death suspicious? This must have been the case; otherwise, there would have been no reason to caution Ahmad Khomeini. After all, Rafsanjani had sensed the deterioration of Mahallati's relations with the IRGC leadership from firsthand experience and was afraid that public accusations against the IRGC could lead to further deterioration of the IRGC's relationship with the civilian leadership.

In another sign of the civilian leadership's interpretation of Mahallati's death, Grand Ayatollah Khomeini did not appoint a new representative to the IRGC until the end of the war with Iraq, which indicates that the civilian leadership of the Islamic Republic suspected the Guards' leadership of having murdered Mahallati. The Mahallati affair clearly demonstrates that the IRGC managed to take advantage of Khomeini's several representatives in the Guards in order to advance its policies.

The affair also demonstrates that the Revolutionary Guards managed to exploit the factionalism within the civilian leadership, specially the issue of succession in the Islamic Republic, to make the commissars Mahallati, Taheri Khorram-Abadi, and Faker fight among themselves rather than efficiently control the IRGC. As in the case of Lahouti Eshkevari, the IRGC started its campaign against Mahallati by playing him against the other commissars, advanced to character assassination of him among the top civilian leadership, then isolated him within the IRGC, and finally exterminated him physically.

Hojjat al-Eslam Mahmoud Mohammadi Eraqi—also from the Haghani School of the Elmiyyeh Theological Seminary in Qom—is son of the late Ayatollah Baha al-Din Mohammadi Eraqi,[175] a veteran political dissident against the Shah's regime and a good friend of Khomeini. Incidentally, Mohammadi Eraqi is also the son-in-law of Ayatollah Mohammad-Taqi

Mesbah Yazdi.[176] Interestingly, Grand Ayatollah Khomeini's relations with Mesbah Yazdi are reported to have been particularly bad at the time of the revolution. According to some sources, Mesbah Yazdi was a central member of the Hojjatiyyeh secret society, which actively opposed the revolution and the establishment of an Islamic government prior to the emergence of the Mahdi, the Imam of the Era,[177] and cooperated with the prerevolutionary national intelligence and security organization SAVAK (*Sazeman-e Ettelaat Va Amniyat-e Keshvar*).[178] But after the revolution, which materialized prior to the emergence of the Imam of the Era, members of the Hojjatiyyeh secret society were allegedly encouraged to infiltrate the security agencies of the Islamic Republic to destroy evidence of their prerevolutionary cooperation with SAVAK.[179] Grand Ayatollah Khomeini, who feared Hojjatiyyeh, found it expedient to place an individual who may have been a former collaborator with SAVAK in the IRGC just to avoid a greater evil: dominance of one of his other representatives in the Guards.[180] But unlike the other commissars, Mohammadi Eraqi never received an official decree from Grand Ayatollah Khomeini.

Rather than being a formal representative, Eraqi, deputy representative of Grand Ayatollah Khomeini to the IRGC, served in an acting capacity until the end of the war. Eraqi did his best to get a formal decree from Grand Ayatollah Khomeini, and in his letter of February 8, 1988, to Grand Ayatollah Khomeini, Eraqi wrote:

> With the approach of parliamentary elections and Your Emi-
> nence's emphatic order to the armed forces not to interfere in
> the political contest, kindly express in writing your answer to
> the following questions to help remove doubts some of the
> brothers have entertained in their minds: 1. The responsibility
> of attending to the issue of noninterference of the IRGC and
> volunteer forces in the political contest as per Your Eminence's
> decree has been shouldered by your Eminence's representative
> and the Supreme Council of the IRGC. As your Eminence's
> deputy representative, do I have the responsibility with respect
> to investigation of election-related violations, which are clear
> manifestations of noninterference in the political contest, or

not? 2. Is this decree applicable to the IRGC or does it also cover the three forces of the IRGC, which have been formed on your Eminence's order?[181]

Grand Ayatollah Khomeini answered: "With respect to the first issue, you are responsible. Concerning the second case, the decree includes all the former IRGC and the three forces of the IRGC."[182] But still, Grand Ayatollah Khomeini did not appoint Eraqi his representative to the IRGC, but made a point of praising the late Mahallati in his February 22, 1986, official declaration about the "martyrdom of Mahallati."[183] The lack of a decree from Grand Ayatollah Khomeini, and the civilian leadership's abstaining from appointing a formal representative to the Guards—maybe out of fear that the representative would suffer the fate of Mahallati—show that the IRGC was outside of civilian control for the last two years of the war with Iraq.

On April 9, 1986, Eraqi sought Rafsanjani's help to receive a formal decree from Grand Ayatollah Khomeini to make him the official representative to the Guards.[184] In his journal Rafsanjani wrote that the civilian leadership had chosen to delay the appointment in order to open the hands of the Guards commanders, but he also remarks: "There has usually been conflict between the Representative of the Imam [Khomeini] and the commanders of the Guards."[185] Eraqi reiterated his demand to Rafsanjani on June 25, 1986.[186] On yet another occasion, on July 6, 1986, Eraqi and other clerical commissars in the Guards sought the counsel of Rafsanjani, complained of the lack of coordination of the Guards' leadership's activities with clerical representatives, and again stressed the necessity of Khomeini's appointing a formal representative in the Guards.[187] Eraqi also complained about the allegedly weak performance of the Guards' leadership during the Karbala II operation.[188] Khomeini did not appoint any representative to the Guards until after the end of the war with Iraq.

5.3.4. Nouri the Commissar As discussed above, following Mahallati's mysterious death Khomeini refused to appoint a formal representative to the Guards, which is a clear indication that the civilian leadership suspected the Guards of engineering Mahallati's death. It was indeed not until March 9, 1989, after Iran accepted United Nations Security Council Resolution 598 declaring ceasefire between Iran and Iraq, that Grand Ayatollah Khomeini appointed Hojjat al-Eslam Abdollah Nouri as his representative to the IRGC.[189]

The decree issued for Nouri praises Mahallati in exalted words: "In the memory of the self-sacrifice of one of the commanders of the Islamic movement of Iran, the blessed martyr Hojjat al-Eslam Mr. Hajj Sheikh Fazl-Allah Mahallati, one of the loyal supporters of this writer who suffered great hardships during the struggle of the Islamic Revolution of Iran and also a truthful and self-sacrificing man and a caring brother for the dear members of the Guards, I pray that God blesses him and accepts him in his bosom."[190] After this introduction comes a surprisingly short description of the duties of Nouri: "I find it fit to remind you and my dear children in the Guards of a few matters: Your legal obligations must be attended to very precisely and you must not violate them. My dear children in the Guards must also not break the law in even the slightest way."[191] Khomeini also praised the efforts of Eraqi, the deputy representative: "I would like to express my gratitude to the efforts of his deputy, his eminence Hojjat al-Eslam Iraqi [Eraqi]. He was a religious and righteous person who has rendered praiseworthy services during the war and, God willing, from now on he will be at the service of Islam, Iran and the Islamic Revolution." Addressing Nouri, the decree reads:

I designate you; I believe that you are an erudite, combatant, and pious person with unique political acumen, not to mention being among the honorable families of the martyrs, and honor by itself as my representative in the Islamic Revolutionary Guards Corps. It is necessary to remind you as well as my dear children in the IRGC of the following points: 1. The duties legally entrusted to you must be carefully observed; you should never disregard them. My children in the IRGC should not commit the least violation of the law. 2. Your being my representative encompasses the military, administrative, and ministerial affairs of the IRGC. Thus, all the cultural, political-ideological, and intellectual issues, propagation and press activities, preservation of information, and other legal issues are under your supervision, and you must be the guide in all the mentioned cases. 3. All my children in the IRGC including the commanders and others should always make necessary coordination with my honorable representative; violation of this order will be dealt with accordingly.[192]

The appointment of Nouri is somewhat puzzling since Nouri was a lifelong student and follower of Grand Ayatollah Montazeri, who in the meantime had fallen from grace, was removed as Grand Ayatollah Khomeini's successor designate, and lost the power struggle to Rafsanjani, Khamenei, Ahmad Khomeini, and the Mohsen Rezaei faction within the Revolutionary Guards. It is plausible that the appointment of Nouri was due to Nouri's betrayal of his old master Grand Ayatollah Montazeri. According to Montazeri's memoirs, in the final phase of execution of the conspiracy against him Nouri tried hard to persuade him to write a letter to Grand Ayatollah Khomeini admitting that the "Montazeri household has been infiltrated by the Mojahedin-e Khalq organization,"[193] which would explain why Montazeri took a position in defense of all political prisoners in the Islamic Republic, including members of the Mojahedin-e Khalq organization. Montazeri, on the other hand, knew that Rafsanjani, Khamenei, Ahmad Khomeini, and the IRGC leadership opposed to him would not allow Grand Ayatollah Khomeini to pardon him and would only exploit such a confession against him. Therefore, Montazeri refused Nouri's suggestion.[194]

But after Grand Ayatollah Montazeri was deposed, Nouri's defection was rewarded with the appointment as Grand Ayatollah Khomeini's representative to the IRGC. Apart from this, Khomeini's appointment of Nouri probably also aimed at pacifying elements of the Guards still loyal to Montazeri. Nouri indeed managed to purge the IRGC of Montazeri's followers.

Nouri served as representative to the IRGC and interior minister simultaneously.[195] But Nouri's tenure proved short because of Khomeini's death on June 3, 1989. Right after the transfer of power from Khomeini to Khamenei, Khamenei appointed Hojjat al-Eslam Ebrahim Razini as deputy of the Guardian Jurist's Office in the IRGC, Hojjat al-Eslam Abd al-Nabi Namazi as IRGC ideological/political indoctrination chief, and Hojjat al-Eslam Abol-Hassan Navab as deputy representative to the

IRGC.[196] In other words, some evidence suggests that Khamenei, much more aggressively than Khomeini, attempted to place his people in the IRGC to subject it to civilian control.

Payam-e Enqelab's report on the seminar of the representatives of the Supreme Leader on January 27–28, 1990, leaves an interesting impression of the political dynamics prevalent among clerical commissars employed in the Guards.[197] Attempting to repair the deeply troubled relationship between the IRGC and the clerical commissars after the mysterious death of Mahallati, Khamenei urged his representatives to engage in a "hearty relationship with commanders of the Guards" and "not to intervene in each others' work."[198] The very same problem led to the endless conflict between Mahallati and the Guards' leadership. Interestingly, as a sign of unity of the civilian leadership, Ahmad Khomeini spoke at the seminar in order to legitimize Khamenei's power. It is unclear if Ahmad Khomeini spoke under duress, but the very same man who energetically resisted Khamenei's takeover of power after the death of Grand Ayatollah Khomeini urges the Guardsmen to "obey the Supreme Leader His Holiness Ayatollah Khamenei."[199]

5.4. Khamenei's Commissars

After the end of the war with Iraq and especially after Grand Ayatollah Khomeini's death in 1989, the Iranian political elite feared resurgent IRGC political intervention. Therefore, Rafsanjani and Khamenei presented both the public and the Guards with the late Grand Ayatollah Khomeini's *Political and Divine Testament*, which read:

> My emphatic counsel to the armed forces is to observe [and] abide by the military rule of noninvolvement in politics. Do not join any political party or faction. No military man, security policeman, Revolutionary Guard, or Basij may enter into politics. Stay away from politics, and you'll be able to preserve and maintain your military prowess and be immune to internal division and dispute. Military commanders must forbid entrance into political ties by the men under their command.

And, as the revolution belongs to all the nation, its preservation is also the duty of all. Therefore, the government, the nation, the Defense Council, and the Islamic Consultative Assembly are all charged with the religious and national responsibility to oppose, from the very beginning, any interference in politics or any action against the interests of Islam and the country by the armed forces, regardless of category, class, branch, and rank. Such involvement will surely corrupt and pervert them. It is incumbent on the leader and the Leadership Council to prevent such involvement of the armed forces by decisive action so that no harm may beset the country.[200]

Addressing the Sixth and Seventh Command and Headquarters Courses at the Imam Hossein University, Khamenei explained the importance of "abstention of the armed forces from involvement and participation in political groupings"[201] and stressed the importance of the role of the representatives of the leader to the Revolutionary Guards and the Army.[202] Also, in later speeches at assemblies of the representatives to the Guards, Khamenei recited the political and spiritual will of Khomeini in order to stress the importance of the nonintervention of the armed forces in politics.[203]

The Khamenei presidency indeed proved an era of very tight control of the IRGC, and the Guards experienced an ideological/political control much stronger than ever before. It is not possible to reconstruct the clerical oversight structure, but according to *Payam-e Enqelab*, by December 30, 1989, Hojjat al-Eslam Majid-Khani[204] was the head of the office of propaganda and the publication directorate of the Guards, Hojjat al-Eslam Abdollah Nouri was the representative of the leader to the Guards, Hojjat al-Eslam Ebrahim Razini was deputy coordination chief of the office of the representative, Hojjat al-Eslam Abd al-Nabi Namazi was head of the ideological/political indoctrination education for the Guards, and Hojjat al-Eslam Navab was deputy representative of the leader in the IRGC.[205]

5.4.1. Eraqi the Commissar On June 26, 1990, Khamenei appointed Eraqi his representative in the Guards.[206] Eraqi recalls: "His Holiness

Ayatollah Khamenei said: 'the main responsibility of my representative in the Guards is continuous supervision in preservation of consolidation of this fundamental foundation…and dealing with disciplinary issues and preventing them.'"[207] Eraqi also added that the priority for the 1990s was "expansion of the Imam Hossein University…and training of more ideological/political indoctrination instructors."[208] Eraqi thanked Mahallati and also Nouri, "whose responsibilities in the Interior Ministry did not allow the IRGC to utilize his insight as much as the IRGC should."[209]

Eraqi announced an eleven-point program for his tenure as the leader's representative in the IRGC:

> 1. Strengthening of the ideological/political units, 2. Establishment and expansion of offices of the representatives of the Supreme Leader, especially in combat units, 3. Strengthening and establishment of clearance offices at all levels necessary, 4. Establishment of office of the representative of the Supreme Leader in the IRGC Intelligence Directorate, 5. Active presence in educational facilities, especially the Imam Hossein University, 6. Greater attention towards propaganda and artistic issues and changing the public relations programs of the IRGC, 7. Strengthening of contacts with the committed clergy and theological seminaries, 8. Expansion and spread of the political guidance apparatus, 9. Strengthening and follow-up of the late Imam's [Grand Ayatollah Khomeini's] decree on prevention of spread of party politics and infiltration of political groupings of the IRGC, 10. Establishment of Islamic verification mechanisms for rules and regulations of the IRGC so they are in accordance with Islamic values, and 11. Coordination of the efforts between the commander in chief, the representative and the logistics.[210]

The appointment of Eraqi shows Khamenei's early alliance with the Mesbah Yazdi circle in Qom, whose totalitarian interpretation of the concept of the Guardianship of the Jurist was to the liking of Khamenei. Unlike Grand Ayatollah Khomeini, Khamenei was not a Shia source of emulation, and upon Grand Ayatollah Khomeini's death on June

3, 1989, Khamenei's title was not even Ayatollah but Hojjat al-Eslam, which is a midlevel theological rank. Mesbah Yazdi produced a theological foundation for Khamenei that not only recognized Khamenei as an ayatollah but also provided the institution of Guardianship with religious legitimacy and theoretical power greater than the formal power of Khomeini.[211] With the son-in-law of Mesbah Yazdi producing and providing all the political/ideological indoctrination materials taught among the armed forces, including the Revolutionary Guards, Khamenei the Supreme Leader was able to control the indoctrination and thereby also the loyalty of the Guards.

5.4.2. Movahedi Kermani the Commissar On February 17, 1992, Khamenei appointed Hojjat al-Eslam Mohammad-Ali Movahedi Kermani as his representative to the Guards.[212] In the text of the decree Khamenei clarified that the appointment took place because of the "resignation of Mr. Mohammad Eraqi,"[213] and he assured Movahedi Kermani of "maximum cooperation and coordination of all commanders and authorities of that institution to perform all duties and missions"[214] and that he would experience the cooperation of "all clerics, authorities and employees of the circle of the Representative."[215]

Movahedi Kermani is perhaps the most serious religious scholar to have held the position of the representative of the leader to the Guards. Born in a clerical family in Kerman, Movahedi Kermani started his theological studies in Kerman, but the pursuit of knowledge soon led the bright student to the theological seminaries of Qom and Najaf in Iraq. In Qom, Movahedi Kermani was a student of Mohaghegh Damad and Grand Ayatollah Khomeini, and in Najaf he was a student of Grand Ayatollah Abu al-Qasim Khoei, Grand Ayatollah Mahmoud Shahroudi, and Grand Ayatollah Mirza-Bagher Zanjani. For a shorter period of time, Movahedi Kermani studied in Mashhad under the supervision of Ayatollah Mohammad-Hadi Milani.[216] It was probably also in Mashhad that he befriended a young Khamenei.[217] Movahedi Kermani's other classmates were prominent theologians and later personalities of the Islamic Republic such as Rafsanjani, Rabbani Omleshi, Mottahari, Mohammad Beheshti, Mohammad Momen, Ahmad Jannati, Taheri Khorram-Abadi, and Mahdavi Kani.[218]

After the revolution Movahedi Kermani was one of the founding fathers of the Tehran Combatant Clergy Association; was elected parliamentarian in the first, second, third, fourth, and fifth parliaments; served as Kermanshah Friday prayer leader during the Iran-Iraq war; and was a member of the Assembly of Experts since the revolution.[219] On October 4, 1988, Khamenei appointed Movahedi Kermani to the Expediency Council,[220] and he was reappointed on November 14, 1992.[221] Prior to his appointment as the leader's representative to the IRGC, Movahedi Kermani served as head of the ideological/political indoctrination bureau (appointed November 29, 1989),[222] and he is also considered one of the several "spiritual guides of the [early] Basij."[223]

Khamenei's decree appointing Movahedi Kermani as representative to the Guards is hardly informative, but in Movahedi Kermani's own words, he was tasked with "informing the Guardsmen of the issues and politics of the day so they know the conspiracies and schemes of the enemy against the revolution, but also their duties [to protect the revolution]."[224] Explaining his work, Movahedi Kermani continued: "The Representative of the Guardian Jurist must also totally supervise the entire body of this institution so there is no deviation in it."[225] Among other duties, Movahedi Kermani mentioned supervision of all the regulations of the Guards in order to preserve their Islamic character.[226]

In practice, preservation of the "Islamic character of the Guards" meant continued purging of the IRGC of elements believed to be loyal to Grand Ayatollah Montazeri. In his January 14, 1995, letter to Khamenei, Montazeri complained of the arrest and imprisonment of clerics Hojjat al-Eslam Ahmad Zamanian, a member of the Basij; war veterans Hojjat al-Eslam Hassan-Ali Nouri-ha, Hojjat al-Eslam Hajj-Seyyed Naser Mousavi, and Hojjat al-Eslam Abrahim Hejazi; and many other Montazeri supporters who were purged during Movahedi Kermani's tenure.[227] Toward the end of his tenure Movahedi Kermani became one of the first ideological/political commissars to crush a serious mutiny within the ranks of the Guards. The mutiny was led by Mehdi Kazemi Douz-Douzani, deputy financial officer of the IRGC Ground Forces and a former commander in the independent Al-Ghadir Brigade during the Iran-Iraq war. In protest against economic corruption in the Guards, especially in the IRGC Ground Forces, which he accused of running

147 economic enterprises in Iran, Dubai, and Europe and making "illicit money," Douz-Douzani established a group called the United Movement of Self-Sacrificers[228] in 2001.[229] Douz-Douzani's group arranged a sit-in at the IRGC Joint Forces Command Council in Ghasr-e Firouzeh Garrison and declared: "If the Guards is only meant to let blood for existence of the [clerical] gentlemen and their sons, we kiss this uniform goodbye."[230] At this point Movahedi Kermani intervened and threatened to inform the Supreme Leader of their actions, and after Movahedi Kermani's intervention, Hossein Allah-Karam of the Ansar-e Hezbollah vigilante organization closely linked with the Guards beat up and arrested the mutineers.[231] Commander Douz-Douzani was convicted of treason and of "disturbing the economy of the country" and was executed at Heshmatiyyeh Prison on January 14, 2004.[232]

It was during the tenure of Movahedi Kermani that the representative of the Imam was systematically used not only to enforce the will of the Supreme Leader within the ranks of the Revolutionary Guards but also to engage in broader political issues. It is also interesting that Movahedi Kermani's engagement in the political debate became more energized during the presidency of Hojjat al-Eslam Mohammad Khatami (1997–2005).

For example, Movahedi Kermani not only publicly defended the Revolutionary Guards' intervention to crush the student uprisings of 1999 but also encouraged the IRGC to engage in "fighting the devil."[233] Movahedi Kermani also began mobilizing the Basij of Theological Students to defend the ideological purity of the Islamic Republic. In a speech to members of the Basij of Theological Students in Kermanshah, Movahedi Kermani said: "Now, in the Islamic Revolution, a political movement has taken shape which attempts to spread cynicism towards the Revolution and the Guardian Jurist. The task of the Basij of Theological Students is to combat such deviations and discover such conspiracies in society and the Basij."[234] Responding to the September 11, 2001, terrorist attacks against the United States, Movahedi Kermani, addressing the Besat Fourth Infantry Division, warned against the "fifth columnists of the United States in this country," and said: "We believe that U.S. mercenaries were behind the September 11th events."[235]

In 2003 Movahedi Kermani urged members of the Guards to actively "scrutinize the work of the parliament and see where it is leading to.

What is the mentality of each parliamentarian and what is he following? Is he supporting the Guardian Jurist or not?"[236] While claiming the Guards should abstain from intervention in politics, Movahedi Kermani demanded that the Guards ensure that the president "executes the orders of the Supreme Leader."[237]

At the 2005 presidential election, Movahedi Kermani stressed that since Mohammad-Baqer Qalibaf had presented his letter of resignation to the Supreme Leader there was no legal obstacle to his running for presidency.[238] But Movahedi Kermani urged the IRGC to reach out to the members of the Basij to vote.[239] Movahedi Kermani's resignation has since been attributed to disagreements with the policies and style of Mahmoud Ahmadinejad and his overt use of the Guards and the Basij for political purposes, but the official reason given was old age.[240]

5.4.3. Saidi the Commissar On December 24, 2005, Khamenei appointed Saidi as his representative to the Guards due to the "resignation" of Mova-hedi Kermani, tasking him with the job of "increasing spirituality among the Guards."[241] Not much is known about Saidi besides his own claim that he is a graduate of the Haghani School of the Theological Seminary of Qom and a former student of Mesbah Yazdi.[242] Prior to his appoint-ment as representative, he served as the IRGC counterespionage chief, appointed on November 20, 1984.[243] To judge by Rafsanjani's memoirs, the position could not have been a very successful experience for Saidi: in every single volume of the memoirs, Saidi complains of being completely ignored by the Guardsmen.[244] Saidi's term as IRGC counterespionage chief ended on March 7, 1994, when Khamenei replaced Saidi with Morteza Rezaei.[245]

Saidi continuously stresses the importance of religious propagation as "the most important field of activities of the Representative of the Supreme Leader in the Guards" and notes that the representative "must act in such a way that the atmosphere of the Guards remains a divine and spiritual one."[246] But the spiritual atmosphere Saidi is trying to establish is dominated by the intellectual line of Mesbah Yazdi and continues the trend of the IRGC under Mohammadi Eraqi, the first representative of Khamenei in the Guards. Indeed, Saidi has openly said that in his opinion, "among the viewpoints of all holy warriors [*Mojahedin*], the viewpoints of Mesbah Yazdi are the closest ones to the viewpoints of Grand Ayatollah Khomeini."[247]

Saidi appointed Hojjat al-Eslam Mojtaba Zolnour as deputy representative of the Supreme Leader in the Guards (see Table 5-2),[248] who in turn used his entire inaugural speech to defend the intellectual line of Mesbah Yazdi.[249] Saidi has also claimed that Mesbah Yazdi is "one of the holy warriors closest to the mentality and thought of the Imam [Grand Ayatollah Khomeini]."[250] With the vast powers provided to Khamenei under Mesbah Yazdi's theory of state and interpretation of Guardianship of the Jurist, it is hardly surprising that Khamenei desires to see the Guards indoctrinated according to the ideas of Mesbah Yazdi.

A dominant theme in Saidi's speeches is the issue of "soft warfare of the enemy" and the threat of a "velvet revolution." Saidi used this rhetoric to launch an attack against well-known elites of the Islamic Republic, and in the aftermath of the June 12, 2009, presidential election, Saidi said: "During the hard war—the Iran-Iraq war—the people passed the exam, but during the soft war—the postelection events—some elites did not pass the exam."[251] Saidi also accused them of being misled by "Western political thought such as [that of] Max Weber."[252]

Strategic issues such as the Palestine centrism of the Islamic Republic's foreign policy also enjoy the interest of Saidi, who in a speech delivered in Qazvin said that "the Palestine issue has become the centerpiece of world affairs."[253]

The very issue of how the Islamic Republic should be ruled is also a subject of Saidi's discussions. Addressing the Saheb al-Amr Revolutionary Guards unit of Qazvin, he stated:

> There were some elements and movements who without paying attention to the consequences of their statements and with certain motives discussed this issue [of collective leadership]. In reality, however, this is not appropriate and does not solve any problem in our country. We have witnessed determination, strength, intelligence and managerial skills in the leadership both during the era of the blessed Imam [Khomeini] and during the leadership of Grand Ayatollah Khamenei. ...The leadership council is not in line with the national interest

and the interests of the revolution and this issue has been formulated for certain political and personal motives. ...The Revolutionary Guards, which has solid presence at the village level, has 45,000 resistance bases, 4,500 resistance districts and this provides a suitable basis to deal with the widespread movement of the enemy.[254]

He also stated: "The revolution is going through the phase of minor emergence [of the Imam of the Era]."[255]

The principle of nonintervention of the IRGC in politics is discussed by Saidi, who explains why it is not valid:

This issue must be totally revealed, and the circumstances and the time during which the decree was issued must be taken into consideration. It is quite possible that a certain issue is bound to time and space, necessitating special conditions which may not be present in other circumstances. ...In the beginning of the revolution there were political parties and groupings which asked their members to become members of the Revolutionary Guards. For example, Mr. [Mohsen] Rezaei entered the Guards from the Mojahedin [Holy Warriors] of the Islamic Revolution organization, and some other faces entered the Guards from other parties. In other words, it was possible that the Guards could have become an arena for interparty rivalry. When the Imam [Khomeini] was informed of this, he said that the Guardsmen had to choose between member-ship in the parties or in the Guards and that the armed forces should not be active in the parties. ...The institution of the Islamic Revolutionary Guards Corps belongs to the foundation of the regime and must be a consolidated and uniform orga-nization which obeys the orders of the Guardian Jurist of the era. ...Therefore, what is discussed as nonintervention of the Guards in elections is, first, not using the money and materials of the Guards for elections and, secondly, not supporting a certain candidate.[256]

On a separate occasion Saidi explained that the IRGC is not a classical army and should therefore be free to intervene in politics.[257]

Saidi also engages in political debates on the nature of the regime, such as the role of the people in the Islamic Republic.[258] According to this theory, anyone who "resists the Guardian Jurist is resisting the Imam of the Era."[259]

Unlike his predecessors, Saidi also engages actively in political issues of the day, including the June 12, 2009, presidential election. Thus, addressing the IRGC Zanjan unit, Saidi urged the public to vote for a candidate who works in the path and line of Khomeini, and warned the Guardsmen against "deception of some candidates."[260] In later speeches, Saidi mentioned whom he meant by this "deception," and addressing the Sixth Grand Assembly of Representatives of the Supreme Leader to the Basij, he condemned the "lax attitude" that allegedly began during "the era of the reformists...especially under Ayatollah Mohajerani, President Khatami's minister of Islamic Guidance and Culture."[261]

Saidi's attacks against Mohammad Khatami may have been motivated by rumors of a meeting that allegedly took place between the former president and some IRGC commanders. Commenting on the rumors about the meeting, Saidi said:

> I know neither what meeting it was nor who the Guardsmen present were. ...But the path is very transparent since we have declared what is prohibited and we do not under any circumstances allow any Guardsman to intervene in elections. ...The opportunities of the Guards should not be abused, the Guards must not be the arena of parties and groups, and on the other hand the parties and groups must not have such expectations from the Guards because that would be outside its legal obligations. ...What the Guards want is active presence in the realm of elections, and what we tell the Guards complex reflects the values and indicators, as the late Imam [Khomeini] and the Supreme Leader have said.[262]

On another occasion, addressing some 700 guardsmen, Saidi urged them to vote for Ahmadinejad, doing everything but mentioning Ahmadinejad's name.[263] Saidi has in general been very positive toward the performance of the Ahmadinejad government, and he continues his attacks against Ahmadinejad's rivals:

> The Imam [Khomeini's] statement "Don't let the Revolution to get into the hands of the uninitiated ones" has made the duty of revolutionary forces and revolutionary institutions clear. ...The Revolutionary Guards supports the movement which defends the ideals of the revolution and Islamic values...the Supreme Leader supports the government. The government may have weaknesses, but compared with its strength the weaknesses are few...but there are those who magnify the slightest mistakes of the government and reflect it. Earlier no one would have done such a thing. ...Why are we being criticized for our offensive foreign policy? Why is the offensive policy under attack? Today, Iran has internationally reached a position of honor and power.[264]

However, as Ahmadinejad's relations with Khamenei became strained during Ahmadinejad's second term in office, Saidi has followed the dominant political line in the IRGC and increasingly criticizes Ahmadinejad, whom he has accused of being a backer of the "current of deviation,"[265] and "unpredictable."[266] Saidi also increasingly serves the interests of the IRGC rather than fulfilling his mission as the eyes and ears of the Supreme Leader in the Guards, and openly advocates further IRGC involvement in politics. Commenting on the role of the IRGC in the 2012 parliamentary election, Saidi said:

> The role of the Guards is above supporting political groups or raising the flag of this party, group or individual. We will not allow the Guards to be the standard-bearer of the parties and political groups. ...But if individuals or political groups announced positions which are similar to the standards of the Guards, it is not a problem; indeed, we would like such a thing. ...The Guards are loyal to the principles and slogans and are in the path of the Imam and the Leader. ...The parliament must be in the hands of principled and pious persons, and the statesmen must have these qualifications.[267]

5.5. Conclusion

As this survey of the performance of the political/ideological commissariat of the IRGC shows, the Guardsmen have managed to escape control of the commissars by various means, destroying a few while making the latest commissar, Saidi, the infiltrator of the Guards within the civilian structure rather than the eyes and ears of the civilian leadership within the Guards.

Notes

1. For a recent example, see "Hojjat al-Eslam Ali Saidi Dar Nameh-i Khatab Be Mohammad-Ali Ansari: Che Kasi Bayad Pasokhgou Bashad?" [Hojjat al-Eslam Ali Saidi in a Letter Addressed to Mohammad-Ali Ansari: Who Is Responsible?], *Sobh-e Sadeq* (Tehran), March 1, 2010. Available in Persian at http://www.sobhesadegh.ir/1388/0440/M09.HTM (accessed March 1, 2010).

2. "Constitution of the Islamic Republic of Iran, Chapter VIII, The Leader or Leadership Council," Iran Chamber Society website (Tehran), n.d. Available at http://www.iranchamber.com/government/laws/constitution_ch08.php (accessed December 25, 2009).

3. "Asasnameh-ye Sepah-e Pasdaran-e Enqelab-e Eslami" [Statute of the Islamic Revolutionary Guards Corps], Majles-e Showra-ye Eslami website (Tehran), n.d. Available in Persian at http://tarh.majlis.ir/?ShowRule&Rid=1D4973FB-9551-4F8D-AEB3-DAEFD52791F1 (accessed October 30, 2009).

4. Ibid.

5. Ibid.

6. Ibid.

7. Ibid.

8. Ibid.

9. Ibid.

10. Ibid.

11. Ibid.

12. Ibid.

13. Ibid.

14. "Emam Va Sepah Az Badv-e Tashkil Ta Hal. Mosahebeh Ba Hojjat al-Eslam Seyyed Ahmad Khomeini" [The Imam and the Guards from Establishment until Now: Interview with Hojjat al-Eslam Seyyed Ahmad Khomeini], *Payam-e Enqelab* (Tehran), May 29, 1982, p. 9.

15. Ayatollah Hossein-Ali Montazeri, *Khaterat-e Ayatollah Hossein-Ali Montazeri* [Memoirs of Ayatollah Hossein-Ali Montazeri] (Los Angeles: Ketab, 2001), p. 249.

16. Ibid.

17. Ibid.

18. "Emam Va Sepah Az Badv-e Tashkil Ta Hal," p. 10.

19. Mohsen Rafiqdoust, *Khaterat-e Mohsen Rafiqdoust* [Memoirs of Mohsen Rafiqdoust], edited by Davoud Ghasem-Pour (Tehran: Markaz-e Asnad-e Enqelab-e Eslami, 2004), p. 176.

20. Hadi Nokhi and Hossein Yekta (eds.), *Rouzshomar-e Jang-e Iran va Eragh* [Chronology of the Iran-Iraq War], vol. 1 (Tehran: Markaz-e Mottaleat va Tahghighat-e Jang-e Sepah-e Pasdaran-e Enqelab-e Eslami, 1996), p. 882.

21. Moassesseh-ye Tanzim Va Nashr-e Asar-e Emam Khomeini, *Sahifeh-ye Hazrat-e Emam Khomeini* [Pages of His Holiness Imam Khomeini] (Tehran: Moassesseh-ye Tanzim Va Nashr-e Asar-e Emam Khomeini, n.d.), vol. 9, p. 493.

22. Nokhi and Yekta, *Rouzshomar-e Jang-e Iran va Eragh*, vol. 1, p. 882.

23. Ibid.

24. Khomeini, *Sahifeh-ye Hazrat-e Emam Khomeini*, vol. 9, p. 493.

25. "Emam Va Sepah Az Badv-e Tashkil Ta Hal."

26. Ibid.

27. "Tasis-e Sepah-e Pasdaran Be Revayat-e Ebrahim-e Yazdi" [Establishment of the Revolutionary Guards according to Ebrahim Yazdi], *Shahrvand-e Emrouz* (Tehran), September 16, 2007. Available in Persian at http://shahrvandemroz.blogfa.com/post-221.aspx (accessed December 6, 2008).

28. Ayatollah Mohammad-Reza Mahdavi Kani, *Khaterat-e Ayatollah Mahdavi Kani* [Memoirs of Ayatollah Mahdavi Kani], edited by Gholam-Reza Khajeh-Sarvi (Tehran: Markaz-e Asnad-e Enqelab-e Eslami, 2007), p. 227.

29. "Emam Va Sepah Az Badv-e Tashkil Ta Hal," p. 9.

30. "Sepah: Bazou-ye Velayat-e Faqih" [The Guards: The Arms of the Guardian Jurist], *Payam-e Enqelab* (Tehran), July 11, 1981, pp. 45–46.

31. "Mosahebeh-ye Matbouati-ye Masoulan-e Sepah-e Pasdaran-e Enqelab-e Eslami-ye Iran" [Press Interview of the Authorities of the Islamic Revolutionary Guards Corps], *Kayhan* (Tehran), June 13, 1979, p. 4, quoted in Hossein Yekta (ed.), *Rouz Shomar-e Jang-e Iran Va Eragh–Zamineh-Sazi. Ketab-e Dovvom. Bohran Dar Khouzestan* [Chronology of the Iran-Iraq War–Background: The Second Book: Crisis in Khouzestan], 2nd ed. (Tehran: Markaz-e Mottaleat va Tahghighat-e Jang, 2008), pp. 487–489.

32. Ibid.

33. Ibid.

34. Ibid.

35. For an overview of the Revolutionary Committee, see Ali Hashemi and Mehdi Ranjbar Azarbayejan, *Tarikh-e Shafahi-ye Komiteh-ha-ye Enqelab-e Eslami* [Oral History of the Committees of the Islamic Revolution] (Tehran: Markaz-e Asnad-e Enqelab-e Eslami, 2008).

36. Mahdavi Kani, *Khaterat-e Ayatollah Mahdavi Kani*, pp. 227–228.

37. Ibid.

38. Rafiqdoust, *Khaterat-e Mohsen Rafiqdoust*, pp. 138–139.

39. Ibid., p. 174.

40. Ibid., pp. 138–139.

41. Ibid.

42. Ibid.

43. "Mohsen Rafiqdoust Dar Goft-Va-Goud Ba Khabargozari-ye ISNA" [Mohsen Rafiqdoust in a Conversation with ISNA News Agency], ISNA (Tehran), April 22, 2007. Available in Persian at http://www.roshangari.net/as/ds.cgi?art=200708170 84317.html (accessed July 7, 2009).

44. Rafiqdoust, Khaterat-e Mohsen Rafiqdoust, p. 190.

45. Ibid.

46. Marziyeh Hadid-Chi Dabbagh, Khaterat-e Marziyeh Hadid-Chi (Dabbagh) [Memoirs of Marziyeh Hadid-Chi (Dabbagh)], 7th ed., edited by Mohsen Kazemi (Tehran: Daftar-e Adabyiat-e Enqelab-e Eslami, 2007), pp. 225–226.

47. Rafiqdoust, Khaterat-e Mohsen Rafiqdoust, p. 191.

48. Nokhi and Yekta, Rouzshomar-e Jang-e Iran va Eragh.

49. "Emam Va Sepah Az Badv-e Tashkil Ta Hal," p. 10.

50. Akbar Hashemi Rafsanjani, Dowran-e Mobarezeh [Era of Struggle], vol. 1, edited by Mohsen Hashemi (Tehran: Daftar-e Nashr-e Maaref-e Enqelab-e Eslami, 1997), pp. 96, 294–295.

51. "Pasokh-e Faezeh be Shaeat" [Faezeh Answers the Rumors], Shahrvand-e Emrouz (Tehran), November 2, 2008. Available in Persian at http://www.shahrvandemrouz.com/70/default.aspx (accessed November 26, 2008).

52. "Baba Goft Be Khater-e Enqelab Sokout Konid" [Daddy Said Be Silent for the Sake of the Revolution], Shahrvand-e Emrouz (Tehran), November 2, 2008. Available in Persian at http://www.shahrvandemrouz.com/content/3672/default.aspx (accessed November 26, 2008).

53. Rafsanjani, Dowran-e Mobarezeh, vol. 1, p. 336.

54. "Lahouti, Soqout az Nour-Cheshm-e Emam ta Amel-e Monafeqin" [Lahouti, the Fall from Being the Favorite of the Imam to the Agent of the Hypocrites], Iran (Tehran), December 8, 2010. Available in Persian at http://www.magiran.com/npview.asp?ID=2202867 (accessed July 9, 2011).

55. "Ayatollah Lahouti Dar Mosahebeh-ye Ekhtesasi Ba Kayhan: Dar Zaman-e Taghout Sinama-ye Qom Be Dastour-e Seyyed Ahmad Khomeini Monfajer Shod" [Ayatollah Lahouti in an Exclusive Interview with Kayhan: During the Era of the Shah, Seyyed Ahmad Khomeini Ordered Setting a Cinema in Qom Ablaze], Kayhan (Tehran), December 13, 1979. Available in Persian at http://enghelab-57.blogfa.com/post-46.aspx (accessed November 26, 2008).

56. "Emam Va Sepah Az Badv-e Tashkil Ta Hal," p. 10.

57. Khomeini, Sahifeh-ye Hazrat-e Emam Khomeini, vol. 11, p. 98.

58. Ibid., pp. 98–99.

59. Ibid., p. 99.

60. Ibid.

61. Ibid.

62. "Gozaresh-ha-ye Vizheh" [Special Reports], Fars News Agency (Tehran), November 26, 1980, quoted in Ali-Reza Lotf-Allah-Zadegan (ed.), *Rouzshomar-e Jang-e Iran Va Eragh. Ketab-e Yazdahom. Hoveyzeh, Akharin Gamha-ye Eshghalgar* [Chronology of the Iran-Iraq War: Eleventh Book: Hoveyzeh, the Last Steps of the Occupier], 3rd ed. (Tehran: Markaz-e Tahghighat-e Jang, 2008), p. 446.

63. "Ayatollah Lahouti: Seda-ye Pa-ye Fashism" [Ayatollah Lahouti: Sound of the Footsteps of Fascism], *Enqelab-e Eslami* (Tehran), November 29, 1980. Available in Persian at http://enghelab-57.blogfa.com/post-8.aspx (accessed November 26, 2008).

64. "Rouydad-ha Va Tahlil" [Events and Analyses], no. 6, December 16, 1980, quoted in Lotf-Allah-Zadegan, *Rouzshomar-e Jang-e Iran Va Eragh. Ketab-e Yazdahom. Hoveyzeh, Akharin Gamha-ye Eshghalgar*, pp. 446–448.

65. Akbar Hashemi Rafsanjani, *Obour Az Bohran. Karnameh Va Khaterat-e Hashemi Rafsanjani.* [Through Crisis: Deeds and Memoirs of Hashemi Rafsanjani], edited by Yaser Hashemi (Tehran: Daftar-e Nashr-e Maaref-e Enqelab, 1999), p. 74.

66. "Yadnameh-ye Ayatollah Lahouti" [In Memoriam: Ayatollah Lahouti], *Shahrvand-e Emrouz* (Tehran), November 2, 2008. Available in Persian at http://www.shahrvandemrouz.com/content/3669/default.aspx (accessed November 26, 2008).

67. Rafsanjani, *Obour Az Bohran*, p. 151.

68. Ibid., p. 348.

69. Ibid., p. 349.

70. Ibid.

71. "Baba Goft Be Khater-e Enqelab Sokout Konid."

72. "Sepah: Bazou-ye Velayat-e Faqih" [The Guards: The Arms of the Guardian Jurist], *Payam-e Enqelab* (Tehran), July 11, 1981, p. 46.

73. Ibid., pp. 45–46.

74. Akbar Hashemi Rafsanjani, *Enqelab Va Pirouzi: Karnameh Va Khaterat-e Salha-ye 1357–1358* [Revolution and Victory: Deeds and Memoirs of the Years 1979–1980], edited by Abbas Bashiri and Mohsen Hashemi (Tehran: Daftar-e Nashr-e Maaref-e Enqelab, 2004), p. 334.

75. Ibid., p. 449.

76. Rafiqdoust, *Khaterat-e Mohsen Rafiqdoust*, p. 191.

77. Rafsanjani, *Enqelab Va Pirouzi*, p. 334.

78. Ibid., p. 449.

79. Khomeini, *Sahifeh-ye Hazrat-e Emam Khomeini*, vol. 12, p. 383.

80. Ibid., vol, 15, p. 369.

81. Ibid., vol, 16, p. 379.

82. Soheila Tayee, "Be Monasebat-e Salrouz-e Shahadat-e Hojjat al-Eslam Mahallati Va 50 Nafar Az Hamrahanash: Ou Ashegh-e Haghighi-ye Rah-e Emam Boud" [On the Occasion of Commemoration of the Martyrdom of Hojjat al-Eslam Mahallati and His 50 Followers: He Was Devoted to the Path of the Imam], *Iran* (Tehran), February 21, 2008. Available in Persian at http://www.magiran.com/npview.asp?ID=1577497 (accessed December 2, 2008).

83. "Namayandeh-ye Hazrat-e Emam Dar Sepah-e Pasdaran-e Enqelab-e Eslami" [Representative of His Holiness the Imam in the Islamic Revolutionary Guards Corps], Sajed website (Tehran), December 21, 2006. Available in Persian at http://www.sajed.ir/pe/content/view/3234/193/ (accessed January 5, 2009).

84. "Shahadat-e Ayatollah Mahallati" [Martyrdom of Ayatollah Mahallati], Islamic Revolution Documentation Center website (Tehran), n.d. Available in Persian at http://www.irdc.ir/event.asp?id=106 (accessed January 5, 2009).

85. "Nim Qarn Mobarezeh va Jahad" [Half a Century of Struggle and Jihad], Pegah-e Howzeh (Qom), February 2004. Available in Persian at http://www.hawzah.net/en/MagArt.html?MagazineArticleID=85998&MagazineNumberID=7084&SubjectID=82114 (accessed November 3, 2011).

86. "Negahi be Aghaz Ta Enhelal-e Hezb-e Jomhouri-ye Eslami" [A Look from the Beginning to the Dissolution of the Islamic Republican Party], Raja News (Tehran), n.d. Available in Persian at http://www.rajanews.com/detail.asp?id=66908 (accessed November 3, 2011).

87. Khomeini, Sahifeh-ye Hazrat-e Emam Khomeini, vol. 12, p. 383.

88. Ibid.

89. "Shahid Mahallati dar Sepah," [Martyr Mahallati in the Guards], Payegah-e Ettelae-Resani-ye Jang-e Iran va Eragh [Information Website of the Iran-Iraq War] (Tehran), n.d. http://www.ciw8.ir/commanders.asp?show=text&ID=13177&Pa=1 (accessed November 10, 2008).

90. "Gozareshi Kotah Az Seminar Farmandehan-e Sepah Dar Esfahan" [Short Report from the Seminar of the Guards Commanders in Isfahan], Payam-e Enqelab (Tehran), May 2, 1981, pp. 58–63.

91. "Seminar-e Farmandehan-e Sepah Dar Tehran" [Seminar of Commanders of the Guards in Tehran], Payam-e Enqelab (Tehran), July 10, 1982, pp. 62–63.

92. "Seminar-e Sarasari-ye Farmandehan-e Sepah" [Countrywide Seminar of the Commanders of the Guards], Payam-e Enqelab (Tehran), January 22, 1983, pp. 31–32.

93. Khomeini, Sahifeh-ye Hazrat-e Emam Khomeini, vol. 13, p. 36.

94. Ibid., p. 40.

95. Rafsanjani, Obour Az Bohran, p. 104.

96. Ibid., p. 208.

97. Akbar Hashemi Rafsanjani, Pas Az Bohran. Karnameh Va Khaterat-e Hashemi Rafsanjani [After the Crisis: Deeds and Memoirs of Hashemi Rafsanjani], 2nd ed. (Tehran: Daftar-e Nashr-e Maaref-e Enqelab, 2001), p. 247.

98. Khomeini, Sahifeh-ye Hazrat-e Emam Khomeini, vol. 17, p. 408.

99. Rafsanjani, Obour Az Bohran, p. 373.

100. Khomeini, Sahifeh-ye Hazrat-e Emam Khomeini, vol 15, p. 369.

101. Hassan Taheri Khorram-Abadi, Khaterat-e Ayatollah Taheri Khorram-Abadi [Memoirs of Ayatollah Taheri Khorram-Abadi] (Tehran: Markaz-e Asnad-e Enqelab-e Eslami, 2005). Available in Persian at http://www.shora-gc.ir/portal/siteold/ketabkhaneh/TAHERI/01.htm (accessed December 2, 2008). For the

relationship between Taheri Khorram-Abadi and Grand Ayatollah Montazeri, see "Goftegou Ba Masoulin-e Sepah. In Hafteh: Hojjat al-Eslam Taheri Khorram-Abadi Namayandeh-ye Emam Dar Sepah-e Pasdaran-e Enqelab-e Eslami" [Conversation with Authorities of the Guards. This Week: Hojjat al-Eslam Taheri Khorram-Abadi, Representative of the Imam in the Islamic Revolutionary Guards Corps], *Payam-e Enqelab* (Tehran), January 23, 1982, pp. 46–49.

102. Khomeini, *Sahifeh-ye Hazrat-e Emam Khomeini*, vol. 15, p. 369.

103. "Rowhaniyat Va Sepah" [The Clergy and the Guards], *Payam-e Enqelab* (Tehran), May 29, 1982, p. 82.

104. "Goftegou Ba Masoulin-e Sepah. In Hafteh: Hojjat al-Eslam Taheri Khorram-Abadi Namayandeh-ye Emam Dar Sepah-e Pasdaran-e Enqelab-e Eslami," p. 46.

105. Ibid., p. 47.

106. "Sevvomin Seminar-e Sarasari-ye Farmandehan-e Sepah-e Pasdaran-e Enqelab-e Eslami" [Third Countrywide Seminar of the Commanders of the Islamic Revolutionary Guards Corps], *Payam-e Enqelab* (Tehran), February 20, 1982, pp. 38–39.

107. Rafsanjani, *Obour Az Bohran*, p. 440.

108. Rafsanjani, *Pas Az Bohran*, p. 264.

109. Khomeini, *Sahifeh-ye Hazrat-e Emam Khomeini*, vol. 16, p. 379.

110. Ibid.

111. Ibid.

112. "Zendegi-Nameh-ye Hazrat-e Hojjat al-Eslam Va Al-Moslemin Mohammad-Reza Faker" [Biography of His Holliness Hojjat al-Eslam Mohammad-Reza Faker], Jameyeh Modarresin-e Howzeh-ye Elmiyyeh-ye Qom [Association of the Professors at the Theological Seminary of Qom] website (Qom), n.d. Available in Persian at http://www.jameehmodarresin.org/index.php?Itemid=36&id=49&option=com_content&task=view (accessed December 2, 2008).

113. Akbar Hashemi Rafsanjani, *Aramesh Va Chalesh. Karnameh Va Khaterat-e Sal-e 1362 Hashemi Rafsanjani* [Calm and Challenge: Deeds and Memoirs of Hashemi Rafsanjani of the Year 1983/1984], 2nd ed., edited by Mehdi Hashemi (Tehran: Daftar e Nashr-e Maaref-e Enqelab, 2003), p. 368.

114. Rafsanjani, *Pas Az Bohran*, pp. 394–395.

115. Rafsanjani, *Aramesh Va Chalesh*, p. 34.

116. Ibid., p. 157.

117. Ibid., p. 38

118. Ibid., p. 42.

119. Ibid., p. 192.

120. Khomeini, *Sahifeh-ye Hazrat-e Emam Khomeini*, vol. 17, pp. 471–472, and vol. 18, section 2.

121. Rafsanjani, *Aramesh Va Chalesh*, p. 138.

122. Ibid., p. 221.

123. Ibid., p. 256.

124. Akbar Hashemi Rafsanjani, *Be Sou-ye Sarnevesht. Karnameh Va Khaterat-e Sal-e 1363 Hashemi Rafsanjani* [Towards Destiny: Deeds and Memoirs of Hashemi Rafsanjani of the Year 1984/1985], edited by Mohsen Hashemi (Tehran: Nashr-e Maaref-e Enqelab, 2006), p. 525.

125. Akbar Hashemi Rafsanjani, *Omid Va Delvapasi. Karnameh Va Khaterat-e Sal-e 1364* [Hope and Concern: Deeds and Memoirs of the Year 1985/1986], 3rd ed., edited by Sarah Lahouti (Tehran: Daftar-e Nashr-e Maaref-e Enqelab, 2008), p. 187.

126. Hassan Taheri Khorram-Abadi, "Khaterat-e Ayatollah Taheri Khorram-Abadi–Fasl-e Dovvom" [Memoirs of Ayatollah Taheri Khorram-Abadi–Chapter Two], Ketabkhaneh-ye Showra-ye Negahban (Tehran), n.d. Available in Persian at http://www.shora-gc.ir/portal/siteold/ketabkhaneh/TAHERI/02.htm (accessed November 10, 2008).

127. Rafsanjani, *Aramesh Va Chalesh*, p. 221.

128. Ibid., p. 257.

129. Khomeini, *Sahifeh-ye Hazrat-e Emam Khomeini*, vol. 18, p. 203.

130. Ibid., p. 229.

131. "Mosahebeh Ba Hojjat al-Eslam Va Al-Moslemin Mohaghegh, Ostad-e Daneshgah-e Emam Hossein–Allayh-e Al-Salam" [Interview with Hojjat al-Eslam Mohaghegh, Professor at Imam Hossein University, Peace Be Upon Him], Setad-e Kongereh-ye Shohada-ye Rowhani-ye Sarasar-e Keshvar [Website of the Head-quarters for the Congress of Clerical Martyrs of the Country] (Qom), n.d. Available in Persian at http://shohadayeroohani.com/Portal/Cultcure/Persian/CaseID/40432/71243.aspx (accessed November 1, 2011).

132. Rafsanjani, *Omid Va Delvapasi*, p. 130.

133. Ibid., p. 131.

134. Rafsanjani, *Pas Az Bohran*, pp. 34, 40.

135. Montazeri, *Khaterat-e Ayatollah Hossein-Ali Montazeri*, pp. 330, 332. See also "Sokhanan-e Ahmad Khomeini" [Words of Ahmad Khomeini], *Jomhouri-ye Eslami* (Tehran), April 3, 1995, p. 14. Available in Persian at http://enghelab-57.blogfa.com/8703.aspx (accessed July 7, 2009).

136. Montazeri, *Khaterat-e Ayatollah Hossein-Ali Montazeri*, p. 389.

137. Rafsanjani, *Pas Az Bohran*, p. 414.

138. Rafsanjani, *Aramesh Va Chalesh*, p. 135.

139. Ibid, p. 143.

140. Khomeini, *Sahifeh-ye Hazrat-e Emam Khomeini*, vol. 19, p. 268.

141. Ibid., p. 269.

142. Ibid.

143. Ibid.

144. Ibid.

145. Rafsanjani, *Be Sou-ye Sarnevesht*, p. 173.

146. Ibid., p. 293.

147. Ibid., p. 298.

148. Ibid., p. 304.

149. Ibid., p. 315.

150. Ibid., p. 319.

151. Ibid., p. 322.

152. Ibid., p. 324.

153. Ibid., p. 386.

154. Ibid., p. 546.

155. Rafsanjani, *Omid Va Delvapasi*, p. 39.

156. Ibid., p. 63.

157. Ibid., pp. 39, 63.

158. Ibid., p. 65.

159. Ibid., p. 53.

160. Ibid., p. 69.

161. Ibid., p. 100.

162. Ibid., p. 122.

163. Ibid., p. 179.

164. Ibid., p. 222.

165. Ibid., p. 283.

166. Ibid., pp. 368–369.

167. Ibid., p. 394.

168. Ibid., p. 423.

169. Ibid.

170. Ibid.

171. "Sheikh Fazl-Allah Mehdi-Zadeh Mahallati" [Sheikh Fazl-Allah Mehdi-Zadeh Mahallati], Navid-e Shahed Website (Tehran), July 15, 2008. Available in Persian at http://www.navideshahed.com/fa/index.php?Page=definition&UID=1 18496 (accessed November 10, 2008).

172. Rafsanjani, *Omid Va Delvapasi*, p. 423.

173. Ibid.

174. Ibid., p. 427.

175. "Shahadat-e Ayatollah Baha al-Din Mohammadi-Eraqi," Fanous, the religio-scientific website of the Student Basij at the Payam-e Nour University of Kangavar (Kangavar), n.d. Available in Persian at http://basijpnukangavar1378.blogfa.com/post-34.aspx (accessed December 5, 2008).

176. Gholam-Ali Rajai, "Akharin Khatereh-ye Ayatollah Tavassoli Che Boud?" [What Was the Last Memoir of Ayatollah Tavassoli?], Tabnak News (Tehran), April 19, 2008. Available in Persian at http://www.tabnak.ir/pages/?cid=9276 (accessed December 2, 2008).

177. "Doktor Soroush: Jaryan-e Mesbah Yani Fashism" [Dr. Soroush: The Movement of Mesbah Is Fascism], Advar News (n.p.), January 30, 2006. Available in Persian at http://www.advarnews.us/idea/909.aspx (accessed December 2, 2008).

178. Emad al-Din Baghi, *Dar Shenakht-e Hezb-e Ghaedin-e Zaman (Mowsoum Be Anjoman-e Hojjatiyyeh)* [Study of the Party of the Leaders of the Era (Also

Known as the Hojjatiyyeh Society)] (N.p.: Nashr-e Danesh-e Eslami, 1984), pp. 333–340.

179. According to Ayatollah Ahmad Jannati, the Hojjatiyyeh Secret Society had infiltrated all the security organizations after the revolution of 1979 and systematically cleansed archives of the prerevolutionary secret agencies of all files documenting Hojjatiyyeh's cooperation with SAVAK. See Jannati's Friday prayer sermon of October 1, 1982, quoted in Mohammad-Reza Akhgari, *Velayati-ha-ye Bi-Velayat* [Followers of the Guardianship without Guardian] (Tehran: Mohammad-Reza Akhgari, 1988), p. 62.

180. Rajai, "Akharin Khatereh-ye Ayatollah Tavassoli Che Boud?"

181. Khomeini, *Sahifeh-ye Hazrat-e Emam Khomeini*, vol. 20, p. 444.

182. Ibid., p. 445.

183. Ibid., vol 19, pp. 447–448.

184. Akbar Hashemi Rafsanjani, *Owj-e Defae* [The Apex of Defense], edited by Emad Hashemi (Tehran: Daftar-e Nashr-e Maaref-e Enqelab, 2010), p. 53.

185. Ibid.

186. Ibid., p. 146.

187. Ibid., pp. 162, 164.

188. Ibid., p. 261.

189. Khomeini, *Sahifeh-ye Hazrat-e Emam Khomeini*, vol. 21, section 3.

190. Ibid.

191. Ibid.

192. Ibid., vol. 21, p. 314.

193. Montazeri, *Khaterat-e Ayatollah Hossein-Ali Montazeri*, p. 377.

194. Ibid., p. 414.

195. "Ahkam-e Rahbar-e Enqelab-e Eslami Be Se Tan Az Masoulan-e Howzeh-ye Namayandegi-ye Vali-ye Faqih Dar Sepah" [Decrees of the Leader of the Islamic Revolution to Three Authorities from the Representation of the Guardian Jurist in the Guards], *Payam-e Enqelab* (Tehran), December 30, 1989, p. 5.

196. "Ahkam-e Rahbar-e Enqelab-e Eslami Be Se Tan Az Masoulan-e Howzeh-ye Namayandegi-ye Vali-ye Faqih Dar Sepah," p. 5.

197. "Seminar-e Do-Rouzeh-ye Masoulin-e Dafater-e Namayandegi-ye Vali-ye Faqih Dar Sepah" [Two-Day Seminar of Representatives of the Offices of the Guardian Jurist in the Guards], *Payam-e Enqelab* (Tehran), February 10, 1990, pp. 6–7.

198. Ibid., p. 6.

199. Ibid.

200. Ruhullah al-Musawi al-Khomeini, "The Last Message: The Political and Divine Will of His Holiness Imam Khomeini," Islamic Republic News Agency (IRNA, Tehran), February 15, 1983.

201. "Gozaresh-e Didar-e Rahbar-e Enqelab Az Sepah" [Report on Visit of the Leader of the Revolution to the Guards], *Payam-e Enqelab* (Tehran), December 2, 1989, p. 20.

202. Ibid.
203. "Ahkam-e Rahbar-e Enqelab-e Eslami Be Se Tan Az Masoulan-e Howzeh-ye Namayandegi-ye Vali-ye Faqih Dar Sepah," p. 5.
204. First name unavailable.
205. "Ahkam-e Rahbar-e Enqelab-e Eslami Be Se Tan Az Masoulan-e Howzeh-ye Namayandegi-ye Vali-ye Faqih Dar Sepah."
206. "Hokm-e Entesab-e Namayandeh-ye Vali-ye Faghih Dar Sepah-e Pasdaran" [The Supreme Leader's Decree Appointing the Supreme Leader's Representative in the Revolutionary Guards], News Site of the Institute for Preserving and Publishing Works by Ayatollah Seyyed Ali Khamenei (Tehran), n.d. Available in Persian at http://farsi.khamenei.ir/FA/News/detail.jsp?id=690405A (accessed December 2, 2008).
207. "Goftegou-ye Ekhtesasi-ye Khabarnegar-e Payam-e Enqelab Ba Hojjat al-Eslam Mohammadi Eraqi Namayandeh-ye Mohtaram-e Magham-e Moazzam-e Rahbari Dar Sepah" [Exclusive Interview of Payam-e Enqelab's Journalist with Hojjat al-Eslam Mohammadi Eraqi, the Honorable Representative of the Supreme Leader in the Guards], Payam-e Enqelab (Tehran), September 1990, p. 10.
208. Ibid.
209. Ibid, pp. 10–11.
210. "Gozareshi Koutah Az Marasem-e Moarefeh-ye Namayandeh-ye Mohtaram-e Magham-e Rahbari Dar Sepah" [Short Report on the Presentation Ceremony of the Honorable Representative of the Supreme Leader in the Guards], Payam-e Enqelab (Tehran), September 1990, p. 31.
211. Ayatollah Mohammad-Taqi Mesbah Yazdi, Dar Partov-e Velayat [In the Halo of Guardianship], (Qom: Markaz-e Entesharat-e Moassesseh-ye Amouzeshi Va Pazhouheshi-ye Emam Khomeini, 2004).
212. "Entesab-e Agha-ye Mohammad-Ali Movahedi Kermani Be Semat-e Namayandegi-ye Vali-ye Faghih Dar Sepah" [Appointment of Mr. Mohammad-Ali Movahedi Kermani as Representative of the Guardian Jurist to the Guards], The Office of the Supreme Leader website (Tehran), n.d. Available in Persian at http://www.leader.ir/langs/fa/?p=contentShow&id=639 (accessed January 18, 2010).
213. Ibid.
214. Ibid.
215. Ibid.
216. "Hemayat-ha-ye Ayatollah Movahedi Kermani Az Doktor Mohsen Rezaei" [Support of Ayatollah Movahedi Kermani to Dr. Mohsen Rezaei], IFNA News (Tehran), June 3, 2009. Available in Persian at http://www.ifnanews.comvdcbu0b0prhb0.iur.html (accessed January 18, 2010).
217. "Ramz-e Movaffaghiyat-e Rahbar-e Enqelab" [The Secret Behind Success of the Supreme Leader of the Revolution], Zekr (Tehran), June 2008. Available in Persian at http://www.zekr.ir/article.asp?lng=&aid=696 (accessed January 9, 2009).
218. "Hemayat-ha-ye Ayatollah Movahedi Kermani Az Doktor Mohsen Rezaei."
219. Ibid.

220. "Entesab-e Aza-ye Majma-e Tashkhis-e Maslehat-e Nezam Be Moddat-e Se Sal" [Appointment of Members of the Expediency Council for Three Years], The Office of the Supreme Leader website (Tehran), n.d. Available in Persian at http://www.leader.ir/langs/fa/?p=contentShow&id=172 (accessed January 18, 2010).

221. "Hokm-e Entesab-e Aza-ye Majma-e Tashkhis-e Maslehat-e Nezam" [Decree Appointing Members of the Expediency Council], The Office of the Supreme Leader website (Tehran), n.d. Available in Persian at http://www.leader.ir/langs/fa/?p=bayanat&id=764 (accessed January 18, 2010).

222. "Entesab-e Hojjat al-Eslam Movahedi Kermani Be Riasat-e Daftar-e Aghidati/Siyasi-ye Setad-e Farmandehi-ye Koll-e Ghova" [Appointment of Hojjat al-Eslam Movahedi Kermani as Head of the Ideological/Political Indoctrination Bureau of the General Staff], The Office of the Supreme Leader website (Tehran), n.d. Available in Persian at http://www.leader.ir/langs/fa/?p=contentShow&id=217 (accessed January 18, 2010).

223. Hassan Sherafati, "Negahi Be Basij Az Ebteda Ta Konoun" [A Look at the Basij from the Beginning until Now], Kerman News (Kerman), November 26, 2009. Available in Persian at http://kermannews.blogsky.com/1388/09/05/post-3385/ (accessed January 18, 2010).

224. "Namayandegi-ye Vali-ye Faghih Bayad Sepahian Ra Az Masael-e Va Siasat-e Rouz Agah Konad" [Representative of the Guardian Jurist Must Inform the Guardsmen of the Issues and Politics of the Day], Sobh-e Sadeq (Tehran), February 25, 2002. Available in Persian at http://www.sobhesadegh.ir/1380/0042/pdf/p14.pdf (accessed January 18, 2010).

225. Ibid.

226. Ibid.

227. Montazeri, Khaterat-e Ayatollah Hossein-Ali Montazeri, pp. 766–777.

228. In Persian: Jonbesh-e Mottahed-e Isargaran.

229. "Edam-e Sardar Douz-Douzani" [Execution of Commander Douz-Douzani], Iran Va Jahan website (Paris), January 27, 2002. Available in Persian at http://www.iranvajahan.net/cgi-bin/news.pl?l=fa&y=1382&m=11&d=08&a=1 (accessed January 9, 2009).

230. Ibid.

231. Ibid.

232. Ibid.

233. "Havades-e Akhir Hameh-ye Zarfiyat-e Mokhalefan-e Nezam Ra Neshan Dad" [The Recent Events Showed the Entire Capacity of the Opponents of the Regime], Sobh-e Sadeq (Tehran), July 7, 2003. Available in Persian at http://www.sobhesadegh.ir/1382/0108/pdf/p04.pdf (accessed November 1, 2011).

234. "Vazifeh-ye Basij-e Tollab Moghabeleh Ba Enherafat-e Jaryan-ha-ye Siyasi Ast" [The Duty of the Basij of Theological Students Is to Combat Deviations of Political Movements], Sobh-e Sadeq (Tehran), August 26, 2002. Available in Persian at http://www.sobhesadegh.ir/1381/0065/pdf/p15.pdf (accessed January 20, 2010).

235. "Tarahan-e Hadeseh-ye 11 Septambr Mikhastand Saran-e Amrika Ra Motie Khod Sazand" [Planners of the September 11th Events Wanted to Make the U.S. Authorities Subservient to Them], *Sobh-e Sadeq* (Tehran), September 30, 2002. Available in Persian at http://www.sobhesadegh.ir/1381/0070/pdf/p14.pdf (accessed January 20, 2010).
236. Sadegh-e Saba, "Sepah Bayad Tafakor-e Namayandegan Ra Kontrol Konad" [The Guards Must Control the Mentality of the Parliamentarians], BBC Persian (London), April 29, 2003. Available in Persian at http://www.bbc.co.uk/persian/iran/030429_v-sepah.shtml (accessed January 9, 2009).
237. "Movahedi-ye Kermani: Nirouha-ye Mossallah Az Voroud Be Jaryan-ha-ye Siyasi Nahy Shodeh-And" [Movahedi Kermani: The Armed Forces Have Been Prohibited from Entering the Political Groups], ILNA (Tehran), February 5, 2005. Available in Persian at http://www.didgah.net/print_Maghaleh.php?id=2189 (accessed January 9, 2009).
238. "Movahedi Kermani: Omidvarim Kandidaha-ye Osoulgara Be Vahdat Beresand" [Movahedi Kermani: We Hope Principled Candidates Reach Unity], Fars News Agency (Tehran), April 22, 2005. Available in Persian at http://www.farsnews.net/newstext.php?nn=8402020019 (accessed February 25, 2010).
239. "Namayandeh-ye Vali-ye Faghih Dar Sepah: Hadian-e Siyasi-e Sepah Bayad Basijian Ra Bara-ye Sherkat-e Gostardeh Dar Entekhabat Targhib Konand" [Representative of the Guardian Jurist to the Guards: Political Guides of the Guards Must Urge the Basij Members to Participate in Election], Fars News Agency (Tehran), December 22, 2004. Available in Persian at http://www.farsnews.net/newstext.php?nn=8310020245 (accessed February 25, 2010).
240. "Movahedi Kermani Dalil-e Estefa-ye Khod Ra Kohoulat-e Sen Onvan Kard" [Movahedi Kermani Says Old Age Is Reason Behind Resignation], Aftab News (Tehran), December 20, 2005. Available in Persian at http://www.aftabnews.ir/vdcjy8euqiett.html (accessed January 9, 2009).
241. "Entesab-e Namayandeh-ye Rahbari Dar Sepah-e Pasdaran-e Enqelab-e Eslami" [Appointment of the Representative of the Leader to the Islamic Revolutionary Guards Corps], The Office of the Supreme Leader website (Tehran), n.d. Available in Persian at http://www.leader.ir/langs/fa/?p=contentShow&id=2837 (accessed February 25, 2010).
242. "Namayandeh-ye Vali-ye Faqih Dar Sepah Ba Rad-e Edea-ye Yek Sayt-e Interneti" [Representative of the Supreme Leader in the Guards Refutes a Claim Made by a Website], *Kayhan* (Tehran), April 28, 2008. Available in Persian at http://www.kayhannews.ir/870209/3.htm#other303 (accessed January 9, 2009)
243. Khomeini, *Sahifeh-ye Hazrat-e Emam Khomeini*, vol. 19, p. 94.
244. Rafsanjani, *Owj-e Defae*, pp. 91–92.
245. "Hokm-e Entesab-e Agha-ye Morteza Rezaei be Semat-e Hefazat-e Ettelaat-e Sepah" [Decree Appointing Mr. Morteza Rezaei the Guards' Counterintelligence Commander], Paygah-e Ettela-Resani-ye Daftar-e Maqam-e Moazzam-e Rahbari

(Tehran), March 7, 1994. Available in Persian at http://www.leader.ir/langs/fa/?p=bayanat&id=975 (accessed November 1, 2011).

246. "Tablighat Faragir-tarin Arseh-ye Faaliyat-e Howzeh-ye Namayandegi Ast" [Propagation Is the Most Comprehensive Field of Activity of the Represenative], *Sobh-e Sadeq* (Tehran), October 13, 2008. Available in Persian at http://www.sobhesadegh.ir/1387/0371/p04.pdf (accessed January 9, 2009).

247. Arash Sigarchi, "Showra-ye Howzeh-ye Elmiyyeh-ye Qom Bedoun-e Mesbah-e Yazdi" [Council of the Theological Seminary of Qom without Mesbah-Yazdi], Rooz (Amsterdam), April 28, 2008. Available in Persian at http://www.roozonline.com/persian/archive/news/news/article/2008/april/28//-29b5644c1e.html (accessed March 15, 2010).

248. "Janeshin-e Namayandeh-ye Vali-ye Faqih Dar Sepah Moarrefi Shod" [Deputy Representative of the Supreme Leader in the Guards Appointed], *Sobh-e Sadeq* (Tehran), July 7, 2008. Available in Persian at http://www.sobhesadegh.ir/1387/0357/p01.pdf (accessed January 9, 2009).

249. "Eddeh-I Be Nam-e Emam Sahm-Khahi Mikonand" [There Are Some Who Demand a Share in the Name of the Imam], *Sobh-e Sadeq* (Tehran), July 7, 2008. Available in Persian at http://www.sobhesadegh.ir/1387/0357/p01.pdf (accessed January 9, 2009).

250. "Namayandeh-ye Vali-ye Faqih Dar Sepah Ba Rad-e Edea-ye Yek Sayt-e Interneti."

251. "Namayandeh-ye Vali-ye Faqih Dar Sepah: Jang-e Narm Dar Charkheh-ye Demokrasi Ast" [Representative of the Guardian Jurist to the Guards: Soft Warfare Is among the Methods of Democracy], Aftab News (Tehran), September 29, 2009. Available in Persian at http://aftabnews.ir/vdcb80b9.rhb5apiuur.html (accessed February 25, 2010).

252. "Tashakkor Az Sepah Bara-ye Raftar-e Ensani Ke Dar Koutah Moddat Baes-e Eteraf Va Hedayat-e Bazdashti-ha Shod" [Thanking the Guard for the Humane Behavior That during a Short Time Led to Confession and Guiding of the Interned], Asr-e Iran (Tehran), September 1, 2009. Available in Persian at http://www.asriran.com/fa/pages/?cid=82975 (accessed February 25, 2010).

253. "Jaryan-e Felestin Emrouz Be Onvan-e Masaleh-ye Avval-e Jahan-e Eslam Matrah Ast" [The Issue of Palestine Has Today Become the Primary Issue of the World of Islam], Sepah News (Tehran), September 19, 2009. Available in Persian ata http://www.sepahnews.com/shownews.Aspx?ID=07b10e80-2948-4de1-b16e-ada0a830ce76 (accessed February 25, 2010).

254. "Showra-ye Rahbari Ba Angizeh-ha-ye Shakhsi Matrah Shodeh Ast" [(The Idea of) Leadership Council Has Been Formulated Because of Personal Motives], Fars News Agency (Tehran), September 18, 2009. Available in Persian at http://www.farsnews.net/newstext.php?nn=8806270314 (accessed February 25, 2010).

255. Ibid.

256. "Ezharat-e Ajib-e Namayandeh-ye Vali-ye Faghigh Dar Sepah Dar Mord-e Man-e Emam Az Dekhalat-e Nezamian Dar Entekhabat" [Curious Statements of the Representative of the Guardian Jurist to the Guards with Regard to the Imam's

Prohibition against Intervention of the Military in Elections], Khabar Online (Tehran), July 28, 2009. Available in Persian at http://khabaronline.ir/news-13477.aspx (accessed February 25, 2010).

257. "Namayandeh-ye Vali-ye Faqih Dar Sepah Dar Goftegou Ba Sobh-e Sadeq" [Representative of the Guardian Jurist to the Guards in Conversation with *Sobh-e Sadeq*], *Sobh-e Sadeq* (Tehran), June 1, 2009. Available in Persian at http://www.sobhesadegh.ir/1388/0401/p08.pdf (accessed November 1, 2011).

258. "Naqsh-e Mardom Dar Nezam-e Dini Mashrouiat-Bakhshi Nist" [In a Religious Regime the Role of the People Is Not to Give Legitimacy], Mehr News (Tehran), July 24, 2009. Available in Persian at http://www.mehrnews.com/fa/newsdetail.aspx?NewsID=917128 (accessed November 1, 2011).

259. "Naghsh-e Mardom Feliyat-Bakhshi Be Hakemiat-e Dini Ast" [The Role of the People Is to Realize Religious Authority], IRNA (Tehran), July 24, 2009. Available in Persian at http://www.irna.ir/View/FullStory/?NewsId=601122 (accessed March 15, 2010).

260. "Ezharat-e Namayandeh-ye Vali-ye Faghih Dar Sepah" [Statements of the Representative of the Guardian Jurist to the Guards], *Aftab-e Yazd* (Tehran), May 31, 2009. Available in Persian at http://www.aftab-yazd.com/pdf/2641/12.pdf (accessed April 1, 2010).

261. "Namayandeh-ye Vali Faghih Dar Sepah: Jaryani Ke Be Donbal-e Tasahol va va Tasamoh Bashad Barandaz Ast" [Representative of the Supreme Leader in the Guards: A Movement Seeking Tolerance and Coexistence Is a Regime Toppling Movement], *Etemad-e Melli* (Tehran), April 29, 2008. Available in Persian at http://etemademeli.com/1387/2/10/EtemaadMelli/908/Page/2 (accessed May 10, 2009).

262. "Vakonesh-e Namayandeh-ye Vali-ye Faqih Dar Sepah Be Didar-e Khatami Ba Pasdaran" [Reaction of the Representative of the Guardian Jurist to Khatami's Meeting with the Guards Commanders], Aftab News (Tehran), May 1, 2009. Available in Persian at http://www.aftabnews.ir/vdcdzj0j.yt05f6a22y.html (accessed November 1, 2011).

263. "Hazrat-e Hojjat al-Eslam Saidi: Kapshen-e Kandida-ye Mored-e Nazar-e Shoma Che Rangi Ast?" [The Honorable Hojjat al-Eslam Saidi: What Is the Color of the Candidate to Your Liking?], Entekhab News Agency (Tehran), May 17, 2009. Available in Persian at http://www.entekhabnews.com/portal/index php?news=4724 (accessed May 20, 2009).

264. "Namayandeh-ye Vali-ye Faqih Dar Sepah: Edeh-I Kouchaktarin Laghzesh-e Dowlat ra Sad Barabar Kardeh va Monakes Mikonand" [There Are Some Who Magnify the Slightest Mistakes of the Government One Hundred Times and Reflect It], Basirat (Tehran), December 14, 2008. Available in Persian at http://www.basirat.ir/news.aspx?newsid=65624 (accessed November 1, 2011).

265. "Na Arman-Garayi-ye Motlaq, Na Maslehat-Garayi-ye Motlaq" [Neither Absolute Idealism, Nor Absolute Pragmatism], *Sobh-e Sadeq* (Tehran), February 28, 2012. Available in Persian at http://www.sobhesadegh.ir/1390/0540/M08.HTM (accessed October 9, 2012).

266. "Sepah Hichgouneh Marzbandi Ba Maraje-e Hami-ye Nezam Nadarad" [The Guards in No Way Dissociates Itself from Sources of Emulation Who Support the Regime], Fars News (Tehran), April 28, 2012. Available in Persian at http://www. farsnews.com/newstext.php?nn=13910209000621 (accessed October 9, 2012).
267. "Hojjat al-Eslam Ali Saidi…" [Hojjat al-Eslam Ali Saidi…], Bashgah-e Khabarnegaran (Tehran), January 3, 2012. Available in Persian at http://www. yjc.ir/129?p_p_id=101_INSTANCE_cxBH&p_p_lifecycle=0&p_p_state= maximized&p_p_mode=view&p_p_col_id=column-1&p_p_col_count=1&_ 101_INSTANCE_cxBH_struts_action=%2Ftagged_content%2Fview_content&_ 101_INSTANCE_cxBH_redirect=%2F129&_101_INSTANCE_cxBHassetId= 209953 (accessed January 3, 2012).

Notes to Table 5-1

1. Moassesseh-ye Tanzim Va Nashr-e Asar-e Emam Khomeini, *Sahifeh-ye Hazrat-e Emam Khomeini* [Pages of His Holiness Imam Khomeini] (Tehran: Moassesseh-ye Tanzim Va Nashr-e Asar-e Emam Khomeini, n.d.), vol. 9, p. 493.
2. Ibid., vol. 11, p. 98.
3. "Hajj Sheikh Fazl-Allah Mahallati" [Hajj Sheikh Fazl-Allah Mahallati], Navid-e Shahed website (Tehran), November 19, 2007. Available in Persian at http://www.navideshahed.com/fa/index.php?Page=definition&UID=35604 (accessed November 10, 2008).
4. Ibid.
5. Ibid.
6. Ibid.
7. Ibid.
8. Khomeini, *Sahifeh-ye Hazrat-e Emam Khomeini*, vol. 12, p. 383.
9. Akbar Hashemi Rafsanjani, *Omid Va Delvapasi. Karnameh Va Khaterat-e Sal-e 1364* [Hope and Concern: Deeds and Memoirs of the Year 1985/1986], 3rd ed., edited by Sarah Lahouti (Tehran: Daftar-e Nashr-e Maaref-e Enqelab, 2008), p. 423.
10. Ayatollah Hassan Taheri Khorram-Abadi, "Khaterat-e Ayatollah Taheri Khorram-Abadi–Fasl-e Dovvom" [Memoirs of Ayatollah Taheri Khorram-Abadi–Chapter Two], Ketabkhaneh-ye Showra-ye Negahban (Tehran), n.d. Available in Persian at http://www.shora-gc.ir/portal/siteold/ketabkhaneh/TAHERI/02.htm (accessed November 10, 2008).
11. Ayatollah Hassan Taheri Khorram-Abadi, "Khaterat-e Ayatollah Taheri Khorram-Abadi–Fasl-e Avval" [Memoirs of Ayatollah Taheri Khorram-Abadi–Chapter One] Ketabkhaneh-ye Showra-ye Negahban (Tehran), n.d. Available in Persian at http://www.shora-gc.ir/portal/siteold/ketabkhaneh/TAHERI/01.htm (accessed November 10, 2008).
12. Ibid.
13. Ibid.

14. In Persian: Majles-e Khobregan-e Qanoun-e Asasi.

15. Taheri Khorram-Abadi, "Khaterat-e Ayatollah Taheri Khorram-Abadi–Fasl-e Dovvom."

16. Khomeini, *Sahifeh-ye Hazrat-e Emam Khomeini*, vol. 15, p. 369.

17. Ibid., vol. 18, section 2.

18. Ibid., vol. 18, section 10.

19. "Namayesh-e Moshakhassat-e Mohammad-Reza Faker" [Display of Information on Mohammad-Reza Faker], Payegah-e Ettelae-Resani-ye Majles-e Hashtom website (Tehran), n.d. Available in Persian at http://www.majlese8.com/Member.asp?nid=184 (accesed November 10, 2008). See also "Zendegi-Nameh-ye Hazrat-e Hojjat al-Eslam Va Al-Moslemin Mohammad-Reza Faker" [Biography of His Holiness Hojjat al-Eslam Mohammad-Reza Faker], Jameeh-ye Modarresin-e Howzeh-ye Elmiyyeh-ye Qom Website (Qom), n.d. Available in Persian at http://www.jameehmodarresin.org/index.php?Itemid=36&id=49&option=com_content&task=view (accessed December 2, 2008).

20. Ibid.

21. Ibid.

22. Ibid.

23. Khomeini, *Sahifeh-ye Hazrat-e Emam Khomeini*, vol. 16, section 14.

24. Ibid., vol. 18, section 2.

25. Ibid., vol. 21, section 3.

26. Ibid.

27. "Nasihat-e Shari'atmadari be Mohsen-e Rezaei" [Recommendations of Shari-atmadari to Mohsen Rezaei], Sharif News (Tehran), April 24, 2008. Available in Persian at http://sharifnews.com/?23720 (accessed November 10, 2008). Tabnak News Agency, close to former commander in chief of the IRGC Mohsen Rezaei, refuted the claims and stressed that Eraqi had served only in an acting capacity.

28. "Hokm-e Entesab-e Namayandeh-ye Vali-ye Faghih Dar Sepah-e Pasdaran" [The Supreme Leader's Decree Appointing the Supreme Leader's Representative in the Revolutionary Guards], News Site of the Institute for Preserving and Publishing Works by Ayatollah Seyyed Ali Khamenei (Tehran), n.d. Available in Persian at http://farsi.khamenei.ir/FA/News/detail.jsp?id=690405A (accessed December 2, 2008).

29. "Ayatollah Movahedi Kermani Khabar-e Estefa-ye Khod ra Tayid Kard" [Ayatollah Movahedi Kermani Verifies the News of His Resignation], Entekhab News (Tehran), December 16, 2005. Available in Persian at http://www.tiknews.net/display/?ID=11131 (accessed November 10, 2008).

30. Ibid.

31. In Persian: Jameeh-ye Rowhaniyat-e Mobarez.

32. "Entesab-e Agha-ye Mohammad-Ali Movahedi Kermani Be Semat-e Namayandegi-ye Vali-ye Faghih Dar Sepah" [Appointment of Mr. Mohammad-Ali Movahedi Kermani as Representative of the Guardian Jurist to the Guards], The

Office of the Supreme Leader website (Tehran), n.d. Available in Persian at http://www.leader.ir/langs/fa/?p=contentShow&id=639 (accessed January 18, 2010).

33. "Ayatollah Movahedi Kermani Khabar-e Estefa-ye Khod ra Tayid Kard."

34. "Entesab-e Namayandeh-ye Rahbari Dar Sepah-e Pasdaran-e Enqelab-e Eslami" [Representative of the Supreme Leader to the Islamic Revolutionary Guards Corps Appointed], Paygah-e Ettelae-Resani-ye Daftar-e Hefz Va Nashr-e Asar-e Hazrat-e Ayatollah Al-Ozma Seyyed Ali Khamenei (Tehran), December 24, 2005. Available in Persian at http://farsi.khamenei.ir/FA/Message/detail.jsp?id=841003A (accessed November 10, 2008).

35. "Hashemi: Sepah Vared-e Eghtesad Shavad" [Hashemi: The Guards Should Enter the Economy], Serat News (Tehran), May 5, 2010. Available in Persian at http://www.seratnews.ir/fa/news/4017%D9%87%D8%A7%D8%B4%D9%85%DB%8C-%D8%B3%D9%BE%D8%A7%D9%87-%D9%88%D8%A7%D8%B1%D8%AF-%D8%A7%D9%82%D8%AA%D8%B5%D8%A7%D8%AF-%D8%B4%D9%88%D8%AF (accessed July 9, 2011).

36. Ibid.

37. "Namayandeh-ye Vali-ye Faqih Dar Sepah Ba Radd-e Edea-ye Yek Sayt-e Interneti: Entesab-e Mohammadi-ye Eraghi Be Onvan-e Namayandeh-ye Emam Dar Sepah Ghabel-e Enkar Nist" [Representative of the Guardian Jurist in the Guards Refutes Claim Made by an Internet Site: Appointment of Mohammadi Eraghi as Representative of the Imam in the Guards Is Irrefutable], Kayhan (Tehran), April 28, 2008. Available in Persian at http://www.kayhannews.ir/870209/3.htm#other303 (accessed November 10, 2008).

38. In Persian: Jameeh-ye Rowhaniyat-e Mobarez.

39. "Az Rowhaniyat-e Mobarez Ta Sepah-e Pasdaran" [From the Combatant Clergy to the Revolutionary Guards], Etemad-e Melli (Tehran), April 27, 2006. Available in Persian at http://www.magiran.com/npview.asp?ID=1047188 (accessed November 10, 2008).

40. "Entesab-e Namayandeh-ye Rahbari Dar Sepah-e Pasdaran-e Enqelab-e Eslami."

Notes to Table 5-2

1. "Ba Hokm-e Magham-e Moazzam-e Rahbari Hojjat al-Eslam Saidi Namayandeh-ye Vali Faqih Dar Sepah Shod" [By The Supreme Leader's Decree Hojjat al-Eslam Saidi Is Appointed the Supreme Leader's Representative in the Guards], Qods (Tehran), December 25, 2005. Available in Persian at http://www.qudsdaily.com/archive/1384/html/10/1384-10-04/page16.html (accessed January 7, 2009).

2. "Mojtaba Zolnour Janeshin-e Namayandeh-ye Vali-ye Faqih Dar Sepah Shod" [Mojtabe Zolnour Appointed Deputy Representative of the Supreme Leader in the Guards], Fars News Agency (Tehran), July 5, 2008. Available in Persian at http://www.farsnews.com/newstext.php?nn=8704150792 (accessed January 7, 2009).

3. "Hojjat al-Eslam Shirazi Masul-e Namayandegi-ye Vali Faqih Dar Sepah-e Qods Shod" [Hojjat al-Eslam Shirazi Was Appointed Representative of the Guardian Jurist to the Quds Force], Fars News Agency (Tehran), September 14, 2011. Available in Persian at http://www.farsnews.com/newstext.php?nn= 13900623001067 (accessed November 9, 2011).

4. "Masoul-e Namayandegi-ye Vali-ye Faqih Dar Nirou-ye Daryayi-e Sepah Mansoub Shod" [Representative of the Guardian Jurist to the Revolutionary Guards Navy Was Appointed], Mehr News (Tehran), October 2, 2011. Available in Persian at http://www.mehrnews.com/fa/NewsDetail.aspx?NewsID=1422564 (accessed November 9, 2011).

5. "Marakez-e Amouzesh-e Sepah Mojahaz Be Sistem-e Modern Va Novin-e Teknolozhi-ye Amouzeshi Ast" [Training Facilities of the Guards Are Equipped with Modern and New Educational Technologies], Fars News Agency (Tehran), October 23, 2007. Available in Persian at http://www.farsnews.net/newstext. php?nn=8608010452 (accessed January 7, 2009).

6. "Dowran-e Eslahat Nabayad Digar Tekrar Shavad" [The Era of Reforms Must Not Be Repeated], IRNA (Tehran), December 22, 2008. Available in Persian at http://www2.irna.ir/fa/news/view/menu-151/8710020815112625.htm (accessed January 7, 2009).

7. "Hadaf-e Konferans-e Annapolis Kharej-kardan-e Iran Az Mehvariat-e Mantagheh Ast" [Goal of the Annapolis Conference Is to Marginalize Iran from the Center of the Region], Rasa News (Qom), November 28, 2007. Available in Persian at http://www.rasanews.com/Negaresh_site/FullStory/?Id=23893 (accessed February 4, 2009).

Notes to Table 5-3

1. "Janeshin-e Namayandah-ye Vali-ye Faqih Dar Sepah-e Ardebil: Amrika Dar Arseh-ye Jahani Tanha Mandeh Ast" [Deputy Representative of the Supreme Leader in the IRGC Unit of Ardebil: The United States Has Become Isolated in International Politics], *Resalat* (Tehran), October 30, 2007. Available in Persian at http://www.magiran.com/npview.asp?ID=1522720 (accessed January 7, 2009).

2. "Namayandeh-ye Vali-ye Faqih Dar Sepah-e Nahiyeh-ye Tabriz Moarrefi Shod" [Representative of the Supreme Leader in Tabriz Area Guards Appointed], RASA News Agency (Tehran), December 30, 2008. Available in Persian at http://www. rasanews.com/Negaresh_Site/FullStory/?Id=44394 (accessed January 7, 2009).

3. "Marasem-e Moarefeh-ye Masoul-e Namayandegi-ye Vali-ye Faqih Dar Sepah-e Shohada-ye Azarbayejan-e Gharbi" [Appointment Ceremony of Representative of the Supreme Leader in Shohada Guard Unit of West Azerbaijan], West Azerbaijan General Governorate Portal (Oroumiyyeh), July 10, 2008. Available in Persian at http://www.ostan-ag.gov.ir/newsite/%D8%B5%D9% 81%D8%AD%D9%87%D8%A7%D8%B5%D9%84%DB%8C/%D8%A2% D8%B1%D8%B4%DB%8C%D9%88%D8%A7%D8%AE%D8%A8%D8%

A7%D8%B1/tabid/135/ctl/Details/mid/630/ItemID/1867/Default.aspx (accessed January 7, 2009).

4. "Marasem-e Towdi va Moaefeh Masoul Namayandegi-ye Vali-ye Faqih Dar Sepah-e Emam Sadeq Bargozar Shod" [Introduction and Farewell Ceremony of the Representative of the Guardian Jurist at the Imam Sadeq Guards Took Place], Eram News (Bushehr), May 25, 2011. Available in Persian at http://www.eramnews. ir/fa/news/51198/%D9%85%D8%B1%D8%A7%D8%B3%D9%85-%D8%AA% D9%88%D8%AF%D9%8A%D8%B9-%D9%88-%D9%85%D8%B9%D8% A7%D8%B1%D9%81%D9%87-%D9%85%D8%B3%D8%A6%D9%88%D9 %84-%D9%86%D9%85%D8%A7%D9%8A%D9%86%D8%AF%DA%AF%D9% 8A-%9%88%D9%84%D9%8A-%D9%81%D9%82%D9%8A%D9%87-%D 8%AF%D8%B1-%D8%B3%D9%BE%D8%A7%D9%87-%D8%A7%D9%85%D8 %A7%D9%85-%D8%B5%D8%A7%D8%AF%D9%82%D8%B9-%D8% A8%D8%B1%DA%AF%D8%B2%D8%A7%D8%B1-%D8%B4%D8%AF (accessed July 9, 2011).

5. "Tajrobeh-ye Defa-e Moghaddas Tavan-e Nirou-ha-ye Mossallah Ra Taghviat Kard" [Experience of the Sacred Defense Strenghtened the Capabilities of the Armed Forces], Hayat News Agency (Tehran), October 22, 2008. Available in Persian at http://www.hayat.ir/?page=showbody_news&row_id=34120 (accessed January 7, 2009).

6. "Namayandeh-ye Vali-ye Faqih Dar Sepah: Mellati Armangar Ast Ke Payband-e Maktab" [Idealist Is the Nation That Remains Truthful to Ideology], Noor Portal (Isfahan), July 7, 2008. Available in Persian at http://noorportal.net/news/ShowNews.aspx?ID=7353 (accessed January 7, 2009).

7. "Zolnour: Eghteshashat-e Bad Az Entekhabat Jebhe-ye Hagh Alyh-e Batel Ra Namayan Kard" [Zolnour: Postelection Unrest Clarified the Front of Right against Wrong], Fars News Agency (Tehran), July 23, 2009. Available in Persian at http://www.farsnews.net/newstext.php?nn=8805010268 (accessed February 16, 2010).

`8. "Resalat-e Asli-ye Emrouz-e Sepah Moghabeleh Ba Tahajom-e Farhangi-ye Doshmanan Ast" [The Main Mission of the Guards Today Is to Counter the Cultural Onslaught of the Enemies], Shabestan (Tehran), July 5, 2011. Available in Persian at http://www.shabestan.ir/NSite/FullStory/News/?Serv=43&Id=49891&Mode (accessed July 9, 2011).

9. "Farmandeh-e Jadid-e Sepah-e Neynava-e Golestan Moarrefi Shod" [New Golestan Guards Chief Appointed], IRNA (Tehran), October 11, 2009. Available in Persian at http://www.irna.ir/View/FullStory/?NewsId=727887 (accessed February 16, 2010).

10. "Masoul-e Howzeh-ye Namayandegi-ye Vali-ye Faghih Dar Sepah-e Hamedan" [Head of the Representation of the Guardian Jurist in Hamedan], Sepah News (Tehran), January 22, 2010. Available in Persian at http://www. sepahnews.com/shownews.Aspx?ID=6fbae5c6-f7e9-4f54-bb43-618c85de4875 (accessed February 16, 2010).

11. "Sedaghat: Houshyari-ye Nokhbegan Dar Jang-e Narm Tain-Konandeh Ast" [Sedaghat: Vigilance of the Elites Is Decisive in Soft Warfare], Fars News Agency (Tehran), November 23, 2009. Available in Persian at http://www.farsnews.net/newstext.php?nn=8809011752 (accessed February 16, 2010).

12. "Nava-ye Allah-o Akbar-e Moazzen-e Aza-Daran-e Ilami Ra Be Setayesh-e Khodavand Fara-Khand" [The Call of "God Is Great" of the Ilam Moazzen Summons the Mourners to Prayer to God], Fars News Agency (Tehran), January 7, 2009. Available in Persian at http://www1.farsnews.com/newstext.php?nn=8710180241 (accessed January 7, 2009).

13. "Namayandeh-ye Vali-ye Faqih Dar Sepah-e Kerman: Ayatollah Nouri Hamedani Hamvareh Ba Salabat az Nezam, Emam va Rahbari Defae Kardeh Ast" [Representative of the Guardian Jurist to the Guards in Kerman: Ayatollah Nouri Hamadani Has Always Forcefully Defended the Regime, the Imam, and the Leader], Parsine (Tehran), July 29, 2010. Available in Persian at http://www.parsine.com/fa/pages/?cid=23464 (accessed July 9, 2011).

14. "Fetnehgaran Sardamdar Ijad-e Shobhe Dar Mossalamat-e Eslam va Enqelab Boudand" [The Seditionists Created Doubt In Certainties of Islam and the Revolution], Fars News Agency (Tehran), June 14, 2010. Available in Persian at http://www.ghatreh.com/news/5355026.html (accessed July 9, 2011).

15. "Shahadat-e Shohada-ye Vahdat-e Basirat Ommat-e Eslami Ra Eregha Dad"[Martyrdom of the Martyrs of Unity of Insight Elevated the Community of Believers], Fars News Agency (Tehran), October 21, 2010. Available in Persian at http://www.ghatreh.com/news/6160288.html (accessed July 9, 2011).

16. "Bazi Ba Velayat Bazi Ba Azemat-e Iran Ast" [Playing with the Guardianship Is Playing with the Greatness of Iran], SNN (Tehran), May 20, 2011. Available in Persian at http://snn.ir/news.aspx?newscode=13900230058 (accessed July 9, 2011).

17. "Basij Majmoueh-I Bara-ye Jam Shodan-e Ommat-e Eslami Bad Az Enqelab Boud" [After the Revolution the Basij Was a Forum for Unity], Fars News Agency (Tehran), November 27, 2008. Available in Persian at http://www.farsnews.com/newstext.php?nn=8509070586 (accessed January 7, 2009).

18. "Namayandeh-ye Vali-ye Faqih Dar Sepah-e Vali-ye Asr-e Khouzestan: Basiji Zahedi Varasteh Va Mojahedi Bi-Bak Ast" [Representative of the Supreme Leader in Vali-ye Asr Guards Unit of Khouzestan: The Basij Member Is a Pious and Fearless Man], Resalat (Tehran), November 27, 2008. Available in Persian at http://magiran.net/npview.asp?ID=1754761 (accessed January 7, 2009).

19. "Janeshin-e Namayandeh-ye Vali-ye Faqih Dar Sepah: Sepah-e Pasdaran Dar Tamam-e Arse-ha Movaffaq Amal Kardeh Ast" [Deputy Representative of the Supreme Leader in the Guards: The Revolutionary Guards Has Performed Well in All Fields], Kayhan (Tehran), July 17, 2008. Available in Persian at http://www.magiran.com/npview.asp?ID=1659934 (accessed January 9, 2009).

20. "Pirouzi Az An-e Mardom-e Ghazzeh Ast" [Victory Belongs to the People of |Ghaza], Fars News Agency (Tehran), January 5, 2009. Available in Persian at http://www1.farsnews.com/newstext.php?nn=8710160813 (accessed January 7, 2009).

21. "Namayandeh-ye Jadid-e Vali-ye Faqih Dar Sepah-e Rouhollah Ostan-e Markazi Moarefeh Shod" [New Representative of the Guardian Jurist to the Rouhollah Guards of Markazi Province Presented], Arak Online (Arak), July 13, 2008. Available in Persian at http://arak-online.blogfa.com/post-85.aspx (accessed July 9, 2011).

22. "Moarefi-ye Masoul-e Jadid-e Namayandegi-ye Vali-ye Faqih Dar Sepah-e Nahiyeh-ye Galougah" [Presentation of the New Head of the Representative of the Guardian Jurist to the Galougah Guards Zone], Kodoom News (Tehran), January 19, 2011. Available in Persian at http://news.kodoom.com/en/iran-politics/%D9%85%D8%B9%D8%B1%D9%81%DB%8C-%D9%85%D8%B3%D8%A6%D9%88%D9%84-%D8%AC%D8%AF%DB%8C%D8%AF-%D9%86%D9%85%D8%A7%DB%8C%D9%86%D8%AF%DA%AF%DB%8C-%D9%88%D9%84%DB%8C-%D9%81%D9%82%DB%8C%D9%87/story/1529330/ (accessed July 9, 2011).

23. "Namayandeh-ye Vali-ye Faqih-e Tip-e Saheb al-Amr: Basij Pishro Dar Defae Az Arzesh-ha-ye Eslami Ast" [Representative of the Supreme Leader in Saheb al-Amr Unit: The Basij Is the Advance Guard in Defense of Islamic Values], IRNA (Tehran), October 18, 2008. Available in Persian at http://www2.irna.ir/en/news/view/line-14/8707278418170021.htm (accessed January 7, 2009).

24. "Masoul-e Namayandegi-ye Vali-ye Faqih Dar Sepah-e Ostan-e Qom" [Representative of the Guardian Jurist to the Guards in Qom], Ayandeh News (Tehran), June 1, 2011. Available in Persian at http://www.aryanews.com/lct/fa-ir/News/20110601/20110601190250796.htm (accessed July 9, 2011).

25. "Bargozari-ye Avvalin Dowreh-ye Mosabeghat-e Qoran Va Azan" [The First Round of Quran Recitation and Calling to Prayer], Basij News Agency (Tehran), December 29, 2008. Available in Persian at http://www.basijnews.net/Ndetail.asp?NewsID=30993 (accessed January 7, 2009).

26. "Namayandeh-ye Vali-ye Faghih Dar Sepah-e Salman-e Sistan Va Balouchestan: Shohada-ye Rowhani Be Aghshar-e Mardom Moarrefi Shavand" [Representative of the Guardian Jurist to the Salman Guards of Sistan va Balouchestan: Clerical Martyrs Should Be Made Known to the Masses], ISNA (Tehran), June 28, 2011. Available in Persian at http://sb.isna.ir/Default.aspx?NSID=5&SSLID=46&NID=24918 (accessed July 9, 2011).

27. "Masoul-e Howzeh-ye Namayandegi-ye Vali-ye Faghih Dar Sepah-e Seyyed al-Shohada-ye Ostan-e Tehran Moarrefi Shod" [Representative of the Guardian Jurist to the Seyyed al-Shohada Guards of Tehran Province Was Presented], Basij-e Tollab (Tehran), May 17, 2011. Available in Persian at http://www.basijtollab.ir/?q=node/1723 (accessed July 9, 2011).

28. "Namayandeh-ye Vali-ye Faqih Dar Sepah-e Mohammad Rasoul-Allah: Shahrdar-e Tehran Shakhs-e Velayatmadari Ast" [Representative of the Guardian

COLLAPSE OF THE COMMISSARIAT 149

Jurist to the Mohammad Rasoul-Allah Guards of Tehran: The Mayor of Tehran Is a Guardian Abiding Individual], Ebrat (Tehran), July 3, 2011. Available in Persian at http://ebrat.ir/?part=news&inc=news&id=33501 (accessed July 9, 2011).

29. "Do Shahid-e Gomnam Be Khak Separdeh Shodand" [Two Unknown Martyrs Are Buried], Hayat News Agency (Tehran), December 29, 2008. Available in Persian at http://hayat.ir/?page=showbody_news&row_id=38000 (accessed January 7, 2009).

30. "Mardom-e Ghazzeh Emrouz Ba Dolar-ha-ye Arab Ghatl-e-Am Mishavand" [Today, the People of Gaza Are Being Massacred by Petrodollars of the Arabs], Fars News Agency (Tehran), December 30, 2008. Available in Persian at http://www1.farsnews.com/newstext.php?nn=8710101396 (accessed January 7, 2009).

6

Dysfunctional Ideological/Political Indoctrination in the IRGC

Apart from the presence of political commissars in the Islamic Revolutionary Guards Corps (IRGC) serving as the eyes and ears of the political leadership as discussed in the previous chapter, the Islamic Republic also has a long tradition of political/ideological indoctrination that theoretically should enable the regime to exert control over the armed forces. This system is not limited to the Islamic Republic: The KGB's commissars, for example, kept an eagle eye on the Red Army, immediately purging any officer who deviated from the Soviet leader's line. Iraqi president Saddam Hussein used a small cadre of his own commissars to keep an eye on his officer corps lest any attempt a coup. In the Islamic Republic, however, indoctrination efforts actually work to strengthen military control over both civilian and clerical centers of power.

The IRGC is, at its core, an ideological organization charged with safeguarding Grand Ayatollah Rouhollah Khomeini's vision for an Islamic Republic.[1] In spring 2008, Supreme Leader Ayatollah Ali Khamenei called for renewed indoctrination of the IRGC.[2] The aim of the indoctrination is to create a "devout and revolutionary man"[3]—or, in the words of Hojjat al-Eslam Mohammad Toyserkani, the chief of the IRGC's Ideological/Political Indoctrination Directorate, to "remake members of the Guards...into true believers with regard to their spiritual, ethical, behavioral adherence to divine values, and even in physical appearance and inner being."[4] The indoctrination effort is based on the four principles of religion, obedience to the Supreme Leader, revolutionary character, and fellowship in a people's army.[5]

6.1. The Legal Framework and Institutions

The 1982 Statute of the Guards argues that ideological guardianship is impossible without proper ideological/political indoctrination. Article 11 of the statute tasks the IRGC with "educating and training members of the Guards in accordance with Islamic values and…ideological, political and military fields in order to obtain the necessary capability to execute the missions it is tasked with."[6]

According to Article 15 of the statute, the Ideological/Political Indoctrination Directorate "decides the content of the ideological/political indoctrination education of the members of the Guards and the Basij, planning and execution of the aforementioned training and recruitment, and training of instructors," although an amendment requires the Supreme Leader or his representatives in the Guards to ratify the unit's programs and publications.[7] The difference between the IRGC chief's role in initiating the ideological and political indoctrination program and the relegation of the representative of the leader to a reactive role is, in practice, significant.

IRGC educational centers host the indoctrination courses and sessions. Martyr Mahallati University in Qom, founded in 1982 and formerly known as the University of Islamic Science and Culture, serves as the most advanced center for training ideological/political instructors of the Guards.[8] Seyyed Al-Shohada Educational Center in Tabriz is the ideological/political training facility of the IRGC Ground Forces,[9] while the IRGC uses a number of provincial centers to host training for IRGC units now organized along a provincial structure. Together, these institutes employ perhaps four thousand "political guides."[10]

Tasking Martyr Mahallati University graduates with indoctrination, however, amounts to asking the IRGC to supervise itself. There are no checks and balances. Political guides compound the problem. Most are likely to be graduates of instructor training programs at Martyr Mahallati University or other IRGC universities and so do not bring an outside element of civilian control. Apart from this, recent statements made by the current representative of the Supreme Leader to the Revolutionary Guards reveal the IRGC's intentions to establish a theological seminary in Qom in which the Guards will train clerics.[11] In the future, the IRGC is likely to infiltrate the ranks of the clergy rather than the reverse, which further weakens civilian control with the IRGC.

6.2. Early Attempts at Ideological/Political Indoctrination in the IRGC

As Grand Ayatollah Khomeini tried to unify different Guards units within the structure of a single IRGC, he paid great attention to the role of ideological indoctrination in the unified corps and was concerned about "deviant" lines of thinking within the Guards.

Grand Ayatollah Khomeini's son, Ahmad Khomeini, in an interview recalled some of the problems with the indoctrination material used in the early days of the establishment of the IRGC:

> At some point some people from a certain city approached the Imam [Grand Ayatollah Khomeini] and told him that in that city the Guards has a publication house of its own which has published materials that are eclectic in their nature. Despite being busy the Imam read all the materials through, disregarding the workload. He told me: "Ahmad, if God forbid there is the slightest deviation in the propaganda effort within the Guards we will receive a most serious blow. We must see to it that the publications of the Guards and all intellectual production which it nourishes is one hundred percent Islamic." After this the Imam tasked Mr. [Hojjat al-Eslam] Taheri [Khorram-Abadi] to attend to the ideological affairs of the Guards prior to which there was none.[12]

Taheri Khorram-Abadi was also tasked with "supervision of the political line of thought of the Guards, which essentially means the Islamic character of this revolutionary organ which has been and is the arm of the Revolution and the Guardian Jurist...which entails purging the Guards of infiltrators nurturing deviating ideologies."[13] As the third part of his duties Taheri Khorram-Abadi mentions disciplinary cases within the Guards.[14]

A survey of Taheri Khorram-Abadi's early interviews reveals valuable information on the state of the clerical educational efforts within the Guards. According to Taheri Khorram-Abadi, Hojjat al-Eslam Jamal al-Din Din-Parvar, a religious scholar from the Elmiyyeh Theological Seminary in Qom, had been appointed head of the internal educational efforts of the IRGC.[15] But surprisingly, Taheri Khorram-Abadi also revealed that it was one of his goals to appoint one "trustworthy cleric informed of Islamic matters as supervisor of the affairs of the IRGC in each [operational] area."[16] This means that by 1982 there were not ideological/political commissars in all provinces. Taheri Khorram-Abadi also revealed that by then, establishment of "a research center in Qom"[17] that would be tasked with the job of producing booklets for the "Islamic ideological/cultural education of the Guards…and [would] evaluate hitherto used materials to cleanse it of deviating lines"[18] was under investigation. This means that until 1982 there had been no control of the publications of the Revolutionary Guards.

Taheri Khorram-Abadi's educational efforts were indeed impressive, and by October 22, 1982, Din-Parvar reported establishment of the IRGC's Imam Sadeq College,[19] educating new cadres for the Guards in military affairs and subjecting them to ideological/political indoctrination.[20] Din-Parvar also explained the need for an IRGC university: "We need professors to teach—both military affairs and ideological/political indoctrination—at our educational centers in ten operational zones of the Guards."[21] Din-Parvar established distance learning for the IRGC members through educational programs on radio and television.[22] He also reported that the Center for Research and Investigations in Qom provided the educational materials for the Imam Sadeq College and for the university.[23] More importantly, Din-Parvar disclosed that censorship of the ideological/political indoctrination materials was done by clerics and Guardsmen, and that the IRGC university reported not to the representative of Grand Ayatollah Khomeini in the Guards but to the IRGC Command Council.[24]

Taheri Khorram-Abadi's apprehensions about the inadequate indoctrination efforts in the IRGC were shared by Din-Parvar. In a later interview with *Payam-e Enqelab*, Din-Parvar conceded that a systematic indoctrination process through class education and speeches by trained clergy had yet to take form,[25] and more seriously, Din-Parvar complained of the heterodox nature of the indoctrination: "Every city and each [operational] zone [of the IRGC] has its own pamphlets. Therefore the Educational Unit [of the Guards] has ordered collection of all those pamphlets for review at the research center in Qom and [that each] be returned [to the units] with a stamp authenticating its approval."[26] Din-Parvar also disclosed that the IRGC did not yet have a university of its own.[27] Another interesting point about Din-Parvar is Taheri Khorram-Abadi's disclosure that he had "suggested" Din-Parvar to the "Command Council of the Guards," after which Din-Parvar was appointed head of the internal ideological educational efforts of the Guards.[28]

Much of Taheri Khorram-Abadi's effort went toward dealing with the factionalism of the IRGC. As discussed before, the unified structure of the IRGC consisted of previously competing militias, and Taheri Khorram-Abadi was the person to repress discord within the ranks of the Guards. As the representative of Khomeini, Taheri Khorram-Abadi for the first time appointed a cleric in each province and all major cities to attend to the ideological/political indoctrination of the IRGC members.[29] Taheri Khorram-Abadi also established the Center for Research and Investigations[30] in Qom, where clerics produced the ideological/political indoctrination materials along with all other publications of the IRGC.[31] In a later interview, Hojjat al-Eslam Mohammadi Eraghi, head of the Educational Bureau of the IRGC, disclosed that Taheri Khorram-Abadi, Hojjat al-Eslam Ebrahim Amini, and Hojjat al-Eslam Parviz Ostadi; Hojjat al-Eslam Mohammad-Mehdi Ahmadi Miyanji and Hojjat al-Eslam Mehdi Rowhani, both members of the Assembly of Experts;[32] and Hojjat al-Eslam Mohammad-Reza Faker and Din-Parvar all supervised the training program for the ideological/political indoctrination teachers at the center in Qom.

Hojjat al-Eslam Hajj Abd al-Nabi Namazi was the head of the ideological/political indoctrination program of the IRGC by 1990, and he explained the nature of the ideological/political effort within the Guards, which apparently changed from before. The ideological/political effort now reported to the representative of the Supreme Leader: "[The] ideological/political [indoctrination apparatus] consists of an organization within the bureau of the representative of the Supreme Leader, who is the patron and supervisor of the intellectual ideological/political affairs of the

Guards and is responsible for increasing and deepening the religious and political knowledge of the force."[33] Discussing the philosophy behind the indoctrination effort, Namazi explained: "Guarding the Revolution is not possible without correct and deep knowledge and an open ideological/political mind about Islam and Islamic values."[34]

According to Namazi, all Guardsmen were required to pass the introductory course, the next level was for more advanced Guardsmen, and the last level was for prospective teachers at the IRGC. The program was designed and developed so that it did not conflict with the military career of the Guardsmen, which explains the extensive use of distance learning.[35] By 1990 the Center for Research and Investigations in Qom had developed into the main center directing the ideological and political currents of the Guards by producing the teaching materials.[36] Namazi also disclosed that a "scientific board" composed of "senior professors at various theological seminaries in Qom read and verify the pamphlets and books."[37] Finally, Namazi disclosed, "some people at the Office of the Representative of the Supreme Leader [in the IRGC] investigate the materials from nonscientific perspectives such as political and military" and issue a final verdict about the materials.[38]

Namazi also provided valuable information on the selection of prospective ideological/political indoctrination instructors. "First, the prospect students must participate in a [French style admission exam, the] *concourse*, [those who pass then have an oral] interview, evaluation of their application with regard to affirmative action for those from unprivileged areas...fourth, membership of the IRGC, and fifth[,] evaluation of their ethics for instructorship."[39]

Namazi disclosed that the IRGC recruited ideological/political indoctrination instructors from various pools of applicants: "The first recruitment effort was from the theological seminaries...the second method...which is the long-term strategy of the Guards[,] is founding instructor training facilities and centers at the top of which is the Higher Education Center [*Markaz-e Amouzesh-e Ali*] or the Department of Ideological/Political Instructor Training—also known as the Martyr Mahallati Instruction and Research Center—in Qom...in the past courses we educated 307 instructors. Now, 500 individuals are being educated at this center."[40] According to Namazi, by 1990 the IRGC had also established smaller centers to educate ideological/political expert instructors[41] in one- and two-year courses.[42] The third method of recruiting ideological/political instructors, according to Namazi, was the recruitment of clerics employed in the IRGC and humanistic graduates who passed the screening process.[43] Namazi also stressed that according to the Statute of the Guards, all ideological/political indoctrination commissars had to be clerics and needed clearance from the Office of the Supreme Leader in the IRGC.[44] According to Namazi, a separate unit within the Office of the Supreme Leader in the IRGC called Authorities' Affairs (*Omour-e Masoulin*) attended to such matters.[45]

Namazi also at length explained the functions of the ideological/ political indoctrination bureau of the IRGC. According to Namazi, the work of the bureau included "production of a news bulletin for the ideological/political instructors of the IRGC. Second part of the job is provision of news to students at IRGC high schools. The third part of the leadership of the political bureau is analysis of international affairs such as spread of religiosity among the nations."[46] Namazi also said that by 1990 "seven such bulletins have been prepared which cover the [Islamic] movements of Kashmir, Islamic movements in Soviet Azerbaijan, combatant Islamic movements in Africa, and separately explanation of the political nature of religion."[47]

6.3. Indoctrinating to Intervene

There have been some changes in the ideological indoctrination courses of the IRGC. The Statute of the Guards mandates that the chiefs of the IRGC's ideological/political, publication, and propaganda bureaus, along with their subsidiaries at various levels of the IRGC, should be chosen from among clergy accepted by the Supreme Leader or his representative in the Guards.[48] Today, these individuals are midrank clerics.[49] Toyserkani has deputies in four of the Guards' five branches: Hojjat al-Eslam Ali-Reza Adyani in the IRGC Navy, Hamid Ghanbari in the IRGC Air Force, Hojjat al-Eslam Ramezan-Ali Kouhestani in the IRGC Ground Forces, and Hojjat al-Eslam Ali Rezaei in the Basij.[50] Public sources do not identify Toyserkani's deputy in the Quds Force, the IRGC unit charged with exporting revolution.

Determining the dominant political current among these individuals is only possible through analysis of those parts of the IRGC indoctrination curriculum available through the Defense and Armed Forces Logistics Ministry website, published in the series *Porsesh Va Pasokh-e Siyasi* (Political Questions and Answers).[51] This series reads like a distance-learning program. The latest edition available on the website, dated April 15, 2008, presents questions such as the following:

- "How effective is the role of the IAEA [International Atomic Energy Agency] director general, and does he act in a deceiving way?"

- "What is the reason behind the delay of presidential elections in Lebanon?"

- "Why does the media refer to a new Cold War?"

- "Why has [French president Nicolas] Sarkozy gotten closer to America (Bush)?"

- "How do you assess statements of [Iraqi president] Jalal Talabani with regard to the 1975 agreement [that delineated the Iran-Iraq border]?"[52]

The November 17, 2007, version focuses on domestic questions and asks the following questions:

- "What is the difference between political and economic privileges? Which has primacy?"

- "What is the role of the Ideological/Political Directorate in crisis management, especially when it comes to sanctions regimes?"

- "What are the characteristics of the internal and external enemies?"

- "Why do some IRGC commanders intervene in politics despite the statements of his holiness the Imam [Ayatollah Khomeini]?"

- "What is the composition of the parties and groupings competing in the next parliamentary elections?"

There are also questions relating to history—"Why did the Islamic
Republic continue the war [against Iraq] after the liberation of Khorramshahr [in 1982]?"—and foreign policy:

- "Are Iran's [close] relations with Iraq and Afghanistan political,
  or are they due to religious and sectarian affinity?"

- "What are the reasons behind the Islamic Republic of Iran's
  support of the Hamas government…and the Lebanese Hezbollah movement?"

- "What is the possibility of cooperation of Arab countries with
  the United States against Iran?"

- "What is the role of Iran in ideological infiltration of the region?"

- "Will Palestine ever be free and will Israel collapse?"

Most of the answers justify rather than deter the Guards' intervention
in politics. For example, the proper answer to the question about why
IRGC commanders intervene in politics despite Khomeini's statements
against the practice is:

Statements of his holiness the Imam [Khomeini] with regard
to nonintervention of the armed forces in politics referred to
membership of military forces in political parties, partisanship
in favor of one party against other parties, and the like. The
activities of the Guards are of a different sort. For example, if
a political group active in the country propagates the idea of
separation between religion and politics, or if another political
party is in favor of providing a foreign government with certain
privileges, the Revolutionary Guards considers itself obliged to
protest and obliged to announce the protest in public since
ideals such as the Guardianship of the Jurist and integrity of
the country have been attacked. Such matters are a part of

guarding the ideals of the Revolution. Therefore one must not consider this as an example of armed forces intervention in politics. It is only within the fields of duties of the Guards.[53]

Similarly, the proper answer to the question about the composition of the parties and groupings competing in the next parliamentary elections is "Political parties have not really been formed and survived. ...The parties and factions center on individuals rather than programs." On such grounds, the indoctrination material expresses concern about survival of the "Islamist nature" of Iran should too much power devolve to ordinary politicians.[54]

The rest of the answers reflect a paranoid worldview in which "Satanic powers" such as the United States and Israel constantly seek to topple the Islamic Republic, and this, in turn, necessitates IRGC intervention in politics to guarantee survival of the regime. Such assertions are, indeed, a constant theme of IRGC publications.[55] Indeed, the first issue of the Defense Ministry's *Negah-e Rouz* (View of the Day) dealt with "cultural and societal strategies of the United States against the Islamic Republic of Iran."[56] The publication continues to label almost every Western academic conference or research institute addressing Iran or Islam as "Zionist."[57]

6.4. Contradictions and Implications

While ambitious, the indoctrination effort suffers from a weak and often contradictory theoretical foundation in several ways. First, there is a contradiction between religion and guardianship. Shia Islam gives each member of the community the right to choose his or her own source of emulation among the ranking Shia clergy. The indoctrination effort deprives individual Guardsmen of their right to choose among sources of emulation and enforces subjugation to Khamenei, who has not achieved the rank of grand ayatollah. In an attempt to address this conflict, the IRGC has developed a cult of the Supreme Leader, which leads to contradiction between serving as a people's army versus simply being Khamenei's militia.

Second, there is also a contradiction between religion and revolutionary character. Traditional Shia Islam is conservative, quietist, and in opposition to the politicization of religion as prescribed by the revolutionary character of the IRGC. This is probably why the IRGC leadership must rely on its own theological universities to train its cadre, as other universities and seminaries may not be in line with the IRGC's own views of religion.

In effect, this deprives the traditional theological seminaries of their monopoly as independent power centers interpreting divine law. Such an attempt also paves the way for the IRGC to infiltrate religious space in Iran. While the traditional religious establishment in Iran may be hostile toward, or, at best, skeptical of, the United States and Western notions of liberalism, it remains hostile to elements of populism and superstition—such as President Mahmoud Ahmadinejad's millenarianism.[58] Should the IRGC universities shut traditional seminaries out of the training of the new generation of clerics, past and present military officials—such as Ahmadinejad—can claim direct contact between themselves and the Hidden Imam in order to receive revelations and bypass traditional clergy and, in theory, the Supreme Leader himself. Indeed, according to traditional Shiite jurisprudence, the Mahdi returns during an era of corruption and chaos[59] and must contend with the opposition of Islamic clerics as he "introduces the 'true Islam.'"[60]

Third, there is a contradiction between religion and the principle of the IRGC being a people's army, especially as the urbanized Iranian population grows more secular in its outlook and values. The IRGC has worked to address this conflict in two ways: by prioritizing the recruitment of members from more traditional rural areas and by using religious police and Basij paramilitaries to impose their interpretation of religion upon the public. Both methods are unsustainable. Iran is increasingly an urbanized society, and the pool of rural recruits is shrinking. Rigid enforcement of IRGC values upon a resistant urbanized population drives a corrosive wedge between the public and the IRGC.

This contradiction is compounded when the role of the Supreme Leader is considered: How can the IRGC be a people's army and be obedient first and foremost to one man? Supporting the personality cult around an unelected Supreme Leader encourages IRGC disrespect for elected offices such as the presidency and the parliament in the Islamic Republic. Mounting popular demand for economic and political reforms in the face of the Supreme Leader's opposition places the IRGC in the middle of a potential conflict, one that will be compounded with the death of the elderly Khamenei, given the lack of any apparent successor.

Paradoxically, the idea of obedience to the Supreme Leader and the preservation of revolutionary values can also be contradictory. The Iranian leadership has often been willing to subjugate revolutionary to practical considerations. It has, for example, supported Christian Armenia in its military conflict with Shiite Azerbaijan, and it has lately provided aid and assistance to the Taliban, a militant Sunni movement, despite the Taliban's ideological and sectarian hostility toward Iran. The IRGC has tried to resolve this problem through the use of vigilante groups such as Ansar-e Hezbollah that operate outside legal channels to pressure the government to conform to revolutionary values, even when the Supreme Leader is willing to compromise.

6.5. Conclusion

Rather than protect Khomeini's vision of clerical rule, IRGC indoctrination has created a cycle of weakening civilian control over the military and a dynamic that threatens the primacy of traditional Shia clergy inside Iran, even those who have conformed to Khomeini's views of clerical rule. Indoctrination materials reinforce a paranoid worldview and encourage involvement in politics. This, in turn, reinforces the trend of militarization within the Islamic Republic as the IRGC stages, in some ways, a slow, creeping coup d'état in which it has become the predominant power within the context of the Islamic Republic in reality, even if not in name.

Notes

1. Constitution of the Islamic Republic of Iran, article 150.
2. "Farmandehi-ye Moazzam-e Koll-e Ghova Farmoudand: 'Sepah Kohansal Mishavad, Laken Nagozarid Kohne Shavad.' In Jomleh-e Besyar Ziba Va Haki-maneh Ast" [Supreme Commander in Chief Stated: "The Guards Is Maturing, But Don't Let It Grow Old." This Is a Very Beautiful and Wise Sentence], *Faslnameh-ye Motaleat-e Siyasi* (Tehran), no. 27 (Spring 2008), pp. 22–24.
3. Ibid.
4. "Reis-e Edareh-ye Amouzesh-ha-ye Aghidati-Siyasi-ye Sepah Dar Goftegou Ba *Sobh-e Sadeq*: Tarbiyat-Mehvari Mabna-ye Harekat-e Mast" [Ideological/

Political Directorate Chief of the Guards in Conversation with *Sobh-e Sadeq*:-Education-Centrism Is the Foundation of Our Movement], *Sobh-e Sadeq* (Tehran), May 8, 2008. Available in Persian at http://www.sobhesadegh.ir/1387/0347/p09. pdf (accessed February 7, 2009).

5. "Mosahebeh Ba Hojjat al-Eslam Val-Moslemin Mohammad-Reza Toyserkani" [Interview with Hojjat al-Eslam Mohammad-Reza Toyserkani], *Fasl-Nameh-ye Morrabian* (Qom), no. 27 (Spring 2008). Available in Persian at http://www.tooba-ir.org/nashr/morabi/mor27/mor27012.htm#link15 (accessed February 7, 2009).

6. "Asasnameh-ye Sepah-e Pasdaran-e Enqelab-e Eslami" [Statute of the Islamic Revolutionary Guards Corps], Tooba Islamic Research Center (Tehran), n.d. Available in Persian at http://www.tooba-ir.org/_Book/BookFehrest.asp?BookID=225&ParentID=61149 (accessed January 14, 2009).

7. Ibid.

8. "Daneshkadeh-ye Aghidatai-Siyasi-ye Shahid Mahallati" [Martyr Mahallati Political/Ideological University], *Aftab* (Tehran), n.d. Available in Persian at http://aftab.ir/companies/company.php?id=34250 (accessed January 14, 2009).

9. "Marakez-e Amouzesh-e Seah Mojjahaz Be Sistem-e Modern Va Novin-e Teknolozhi-ye Amouzeshi Ast" [Educational Centers of the Guards Boast of Modern Educational Technologies], Fars News Agency (Tehran), October 23, 2007. Available in Persian at http://www.farsnews.net/newstext.php?nn=8608010452 (accessed February 7, 2009).

10. "Hamayesh-e Tajlil Az Morabbian-e Aghidati-Siyasi-ye Sepah Bargozar Mishavad" [Conference Celebrating Ideological/Political Instructors of the Guards to Be Held], Fars News Agency, April 22, 2006. Available in Persian at http://www.farsnews.net/newstext.php?nn=8502020598 (accessed February 7, 2009). See also "Farmandeh-ye Koll-e Sepah-e Pasdaran Az Ejrayi-Shodan-e Tarh-e Taala Dar Sepah Khabar Dad" [Revolutionary Guards Commander in Chief Reports That the Ascension Plan of the Guards Has Become Operational], *Kayhan* (Tehran), April 29, 2008. Available in Persian at http://www.kayhannews.ir/870210/14. htm#other1406 (accessed February 17, 2009).

11. "Hojjat al-Eslam Saidi az Rah-Andazi-ye Madreseh-ye Elmiyeh-ye Jadid Khabar Dad" [Hojjat al-Eslam Saidi Announced Establishment of a New Theological Seminary], Revayat-e Hadis (Qom), July 19, 2012. Available in Persian at http://rovatehadis.com/1390/11/25548 (accessed July 19, 2012).

12. "Emam Va Sepah Az Badv-e Tashkil Ta Hal. Mosahebeh Ba Hojjat al-Eslam Seyyed Ahmad Khomeini" [The Imam and the Guards from Establishment until Now: Interview with Hojjat al-Eslam Seyyed Ahmad Khomeini], *Payam-e Enqelab* (Tehran), May 29, 1982, p. 12.

13. "Goftegou Ba Masoulin-e Sepah. In Hafteh: Hojjat al-Eslam Taheri Khorram-Abadi Namayandeh-ye Emam Dar Sepah-e Pasdaran-e Enqelab-e Eslami" [Conversation with Authorities of the Guards. This Week: Hojjat al-Eslam Taheri Khorram-Abadi, Representative of the Imam in the Islamic Revolutionary Guards Corps], *Payam-e Enqelab* (Tehran), January 23, 1982, pp. 46–47.

14. Ibid., p. 47.

15. Ibid.

16. Ibid.

17. Ibid.

18. Ibid.

19. In Persian: Maktab-e Emam Sadeq.

20. "Tarh-e Amouzeshi Va Ahdaf-e Tashkil-e Dabirestan Va Daneshgah-e Sepah" [Educational Plan and Objectives of the University of the Guards], *Payam-e Enqelab* (Tehran), October 22, 1982, pp. 48–49.

21. Ibid., p. 50.

22. "Amouzesh-e Gheir-e Hozouri" [Distance Learning], *Payam-e Enqelab* (Tehran), October 30, 1982, pp. 36–37.

23. "Tarh-e Amouzeshi Va Ahdaf-e Tashkil-e Dabirestan Va Daneshgah-e Sepah," p. 50.

24. Ibid.

25. "Goftegou Ba Masoulin-e Sepah. In Hafteh: Mosahebe Ba Hojjat al-Eslam Din-Parvar Masoul-e Amouzesh-e Sepah-e Pasdaran-e Enqelab-e Eslami" [Conversation with the Authorities of the Guards. This Week: Interview with Hojjat al-Eslam Din-Parvar, Head of Education of the Islamic Revolutionary Guards Corps], *Payam-e Enqelab* (Tehran), October 23, 1981, p. 43.

26. Ibid.

27. Ibid.

28. "Adam-e Tahazzob Va Gorouh-Garayee Dar Sepah" [Nonfactionalism and Lack of Party Politics in the Guards], *Payam-e Enqelab* (Tehran), May 29, 1982, p. 53.

29. Ibid.

30. In Persian: Markaz-e Barresi Va Tahghighat.

31. "Adam-e Tahazzob Va Gorouh-Garayee Dar Sepah," p. 54.

32. In Persian: Majles-e Khobregan.

33. "Sepah Va Amouzesh-e Aghidati/Siyasi" [The Guards and Ideological/Political Indoctrination], *Payam-e Enqelab* (Tehran), May 5, 1990, p. 6.

34. Ibid., p. 7.

35. Ibid.

36. Ibid.

37. Ibid.

38. Ibid.

39. Ibid.

40. Ibid., pp. 8, 9.

41. In Persian: Morrabi-yan-e Kardani-ye Aghidati/Siyasi.

42. "Sepah Va Amouzesh-e Aghidati/Siyasi," p. 8.

43. Ibid.

44. Ibid.

45. Ibid.

46. Ibid.

47. Ibid.

48. "Asasnameh-ye Sepah-e Pasdaran-e Enqelab-e Eslami."

49. "Toyserkani Reis-e Edareh-ye Amouzeh-e Aghidati-Siyasi-ye Sepah Shod" [Toyserkani Was Appointed Ideological/Political Directorate Chief], *Sobh-e Sadeq (Tehran)*, February 4, 2008. Available in Persian at http://www.sobhesadegh. ir/1386/0338/p03.pdf (accessed February 7, 2009).

50. "Masoulan-e Aghidati-Siyasi-ye Sepah Takid Kardand: Baznegari Dar Nezam-e Amouzeshi-Aghidati Ba Rouy-Kard-e Manaviat-Afzayi" [Ideological/ Political Heads of the Guards Stress Reorientation of the Educational System of the Guards toward Added Spirituality], *Sobh-e Sadeq (Tehran)*, April 28, 2008. Available in Persian at http://www.sobhesadegh.ir/1387/0347/p09.pdf (accessed February 7, 2009); and "Basij Vasi-tarin Markaz-e Sazemandehi-ye Morrabian-ye Aghidati-ye Keshvar Ast" [The Basij Is the Most Expansive Center of Organizing Ideological Instructors in the Country], Fars News Agency (Tehran), November 22, 2007. Available in Persian at http://www.farsnews.net/newstext. php?nn=8609010246 (accessed February 7, 2009).

51. The website of Aghidati-Siyasi-e Vezarat-e Defae, the ideological/political unit of the Defense Ministry, is available at http://www.siyasi.ir/ (accessed January 18, 2009).

52. Aghidati-Siyasi-e Vezarat-e Defae, *"Porsesh Va Pasokh-e Siyasi"* [Political Questions and Answers], Aghidati-Siyasi-ye Vezarat-e Defae (Tehran), April 15, 2008. Available in Persian at http://www.siyasi.ir/content/view/2973/1 (accessed January 18, 2009).

53. Ibid.

54. Ibid.

55. See Aghidati-Siyasi-e Vezarat-e Defae, *"Porsesh Va Pasokh-e Siyasi."*

56. Islamic Republic of Iran Ministry of Defense, *"Negah-e Rouz"* [View of the Day], produced 2006, released online November 8, 2007. Available in Persian at http://www.siyasi.ir/component/option,com_remository/func,startdown/id,23 (accessed February 11, 2009).

57. Ibid.

58. Ali Alfoneh, "Ahmadinejad versus the Clergy," *AEI Middle Eastern Outlook Series*, no. 5 (August 2008). Available at http://www.aei.org/publication28494.

59. Mohammad-Javad Mashkour, *Tarikh-e Shie Va Fergheh-he-ye Eslam [History of Shiism and Islamic Sects]*, 5th ed. (Tehran: Ketabforoushi-ye Eshraqi, 1993), p. 132.

60. Mehdi Khalaji, *Apocalyptic Politics: On the Rationality of Iranian Policy* (Washington, DC: Washington Institute for Near East Policy, 2008), p. 3.

7

The Economic Empire of the IRGC

The tale of the transformation of the Islamic Revolutionary Guards Corps (IRGC) into one of the largest business corporations in the Islamic Republic is a tale of what the IRGC's economic activities were meant to be and what they have become over the years.

The constitution of the Islamic Republic granted the IRGC a developmental role in Iran's economy, a role that the IRGC has abused to transform itself into an economic powerhouse beyond the imagination of the fathers of the constitution. Iran's high-tech industry, which aimed at securing Iran's self-sufficiency, has converted its production line to producing consumer goods and outrivals the private sector. The IRGC's social housing projects, which were meant to secure affordable housing for war veterans and their family members, have developed into a major real estate speculator in Dubai and a money-laundering machine in distant Venezuela. The IRGC, which was meant to utilize its means to develop Iran in peacetime, has become a moneymaking machine that impedes growth of the private sector. IRGC chain stores, which were meant to secure basic foodstuff for the family members of the IRGC men in the war, rival the traditional bazaar. The IRGC, which brought the Internet to Iran, has monopolized the country's Internet service and the telecommunications industry. Iran's oil and gas sector, which has hitherto been the monopoly of the National Iranian Oil Company, has become the ultimate prize of the IRGC.

In short, the IRGC is involved in every revenue-generating business —both legal and illegal—in the Islamic Republic and beyond, and is now trying to bypass the international sanctions regime. It benefits from keeping the Islamic Republic in a constant state of crisis in the issue regarding Iran's development of nuclear technology so it can benefit from exit of foreign companies.

7.1. Twisting of the Legal Framework

The IRGC's role in the Iranian economy is constitutionally mandated, and IRGC functionaries often refer to Articles 147, 150, and more recently 44 of the constitution to justify the economic activities of the IRGC. However, the IRGC has managed to twist the legal framework to further its economic interests more than the constitutional fathers of the Islamic Republic had ever dreamt of.

Article 147 of the Iranian constitution states that "in time of peace, the government must utilize the personnel and technical equipment of the Army in relief operations, and for educational and productive ends, and the Construction Jihad, while fully observing the criteria of Islamic justice and ensuring that such utilization does not harm the combat-readiness of the Army."[1] The spirit of Article 147 is also reflected in Article 10 of the founding statute of the IRGC, which states that the IRGC, upon request of the government, can participate in peacetime in "production and the Construction Jihad…to the degree that it does not hinder its military preparedness."[2] IRGC functionaries,[3] as well as the home page of the Construction Base of the Seal of the Prophets (*Gharargah-e Sazandegi-ye Khatam al-Anbia*, or GHORB), the main contracting arm of the IRGC, often reference Article 147 to justify the IRGC's economic activities.[4]

In addition, Article 150 of the constitution assigns the IRGC the "role of guarding the Revolution and its achievements,"[5] a responsibility that IRGC leaders interpret broadly. The IRGC claims the right to involve itself in any project under the guise of "aiding the government in executing parts of the developmental, industrial, agricultural [and] technical assistance [projects], reducing dependency on foreign companies and preparing the grounds for pioneering projects, providing opportunity for the growth of related governmental organizations and especially the private sector, expansion and strengthening of the developmental and industrial infrastructure of the country, development of agricultural land, supporting and expanding the national security—especially in remote and frontier areas through involving the local population in execution of projects," and the like.[6]

More recently, the IRGC has also started referring to Article 44 of the constitution to justify its increasing involvement in the privatization of state-owned enterprises and businesses. According to Article 44, Iran should have a planned economy in which "the state sector is to include all large-scale and mother industries, foreign trade, major minerals, banking, insurance, power generation, dams and large-scale irrigation networks, radio and television, post, telegraph and telephone services, aviation, shipping, roads, railroads and the like; all these will be publicly owned and administered by the state."[7] In addition to the state sector, Article 44 also defines a so-called cooperative sector, which includes "cooperative companies and enterprises concerned with production and distribution, in urban and rural areas," as well as a private sector, which consists of "those activities concerned with agriculture, animal husbandry, industry, trade, and services that supplement the economic activities of the state and cooperative sectors."[8]

A little more than a month before Mahmoud Ahmadinejad's 2005 election victory, Supreme Leader Ali Khamenei issued a decree reinterpreting Article 44 by calling for a smaller government and a 20 percent annual reduction in public-sector economic intervention over five years. Khamenei's directive called for the privatization of large-scale industries to include large-scale oil and low-end gas industries, mines, foreign trade, many banks, shareholder-owned cooperatives, power generation, many postal services, roads, railroads, aviation, and shipping. Khamenei's directive also obliged the government to transfer ownership of 25 percent of Iran's economy to the cooperative sector by the end of the five-year plan and to support expansion of cooperatives with tax rebates and loan guarantees with the aim of encouraging cooperatives to participate in all spheres of the economy, including banking and insurance.[9] As we shall see, the so-called privatization scheme has enabled certain parts of the civilian Iranian leadership to transfer ownership from relatively transparent parts of the public sector to other parts of the public sector shielded from public scrutiny such as the IRGC and its subordinate Basij in exchange for the IRGC's political support.

The IRGC now interprets its operational freedom so broadly that it accepts no constitutional restrictions. Brigadier General Hossein Yasini, deputy chief of human resources of the joint command of the armed forces, argues that the constitutional phrase "economic developmental plans and projects" also encompasses "economic, societal, and cultural developmental programs."[10] IRGC leaders base such a broad mandate upon "orders of the Supreme Leader and Supreme Commander in Chief of the Armed Forces," which they suggest trump Article 147 of the constitution.[11]

In effect, as long as the Supreme Leader supports the IRGC, any action the IRGC takes is legal. And he does. In Iran, the daily newspaper *Kayhan* reflects the thinking of Ayatollah Ali Khamenei, the current Supreme Leader. He appoints the editor of the newspaper in order to ensure that it accurately conveys his thoughts. On October 18, 2006, *Kayhan* editorialized, "At the time of the victory of the Islamic revolution, the founder of the Islamic Revolution proposed development of the country as the most important issue." *Kayhan* supported this argument with a reference to a sermon Khomeini delivered less than a week after his return to Iran. "We must build from scratch a country constructed anew," Khomeini said, "since this government cannot do so."[12] *Kayhan*'s citation, though, twists the context. Khomeini's sermon sought to discredit the Shah's last prime minister, who was still holding onto power. Khomeini's words referred to Iran's political structure, not its physical development.[13] A further reference in the same *Kayhan* editorial to a December 3, 1991, speech by Khamenei is equally amorphous.[14]

7.2. From Military Industries to the Production of Consumer Goods

Today, the IRGC's high-tech companies are the leading companies in the production of electronic consumer goods in the Iranian market, but the history of the armed forces' involvement in the high-tech sector predates the revolution of 1979 and the emergence of the IRGC.

Many historians criticize the Shah's billion-dollar purchases of foreign weaponry, especially at a time of growing economic disparities in Iran.[15] But the Shah also developed a large domestic arms industry in order to reduce Iran's dependence on overseas suppliers. In 1963, he established the Military Industries Organization (*Sazeman-e Sanaye Nezami*), an umbrella group that consisted of such firms as the Iran Electronic Industries (*Sanaye Elektronik-e Iran*) and the Iran Advanced Technology Corporation.[16] After the Shah's ouster and the subsequent creation of the Islamic Republic, Khomeini transferred authority of the renamed Defense

Industries Organization (*Sazeman-e Sanaye Defa*) to the IRGC.[17] According to the memoirs of then parliamentary speaker Akbar Hashemi Rafsanjani, the transfer was being contemplated by the end of November 1982,[18] but the transfer may have taken place earlier. This happened at a time when most countries had embargoed weapons shipments to Iran because of the war with Iraq, although Tehran was able to purchase weaponry from Damascus, and it received some spare parts as a result of the Iran-Contra scheme.[19] But it still needed to manufacture its own arms to carry on its fight. Here, the IRGC's domestic arms production filled the gap.

Following the end of the war with Iraq in 1988, the Defense Industries Organization had more than 65,000 employees.[20] The central units were the munitions unit; the SASAD missile production unit; the chemical industries unit, which worked closely with the missile unit; and the electronics and communications industries unit.[21] After the ceasefire with Iraq, those same companies contemplated converting their production lines over to the production of civilian consumer goods, especially in the electronics and communications industries.[22]

This conversion made good sense for the IRGC. After all, some of the Iranian economy's most advanced technological undertakings occur under the aegis of the IRGC and within the framework of the Iranian arms industry. However, as the IRGC monopolizes the transfer and adaptation of high technology to civilian applications, the military elites leave little room for private producers and service providers. The home pages of the Iran Electronic Industries,[23] its sister organization Integrated Electronic Industries,[24] and their subsidiaries[25] display many consumer goods produced by the arms industry for sale in the Iranian market. The list includes personal computers, scanners, telephones and intercoms, mobile phones, and telephone SIM cards.

7.3. From Social Housing to Real Estate Speculation in Dubai

The IRGC Cooperative Foundation is one of the largest social housing contractors in Iran, constitutes the core of the Mehr Housing Project of the Ahmadinejad government, and has even built 10,000 housing units in faraway Venezuela.[26]

The activities of the Revolutionary Guards in the field of social housing have historically been closely linked with the member profile of the organization. At its emergence, the IRGC members had no real housing needs since the first generation of the Revolutionary Guardsmen consisted of "young people with maximum age of 25 years," and the IRGC Personnel Bureau did not begin its operations before 1988, after the end of the war with Iraq.[27] Other sources provide a different account of the early history of the IRGC's social housing activities. According to Mohsen Rafiqdoust, the first IRGC logistics chief and the sole IRGC minister in the history of the Islamic Republic, the IRGC established a "Cooperatives, Housing and Social Affairs Unit" during the early days of the war with Iraq in order to satisfy the needs of the IRGC members and their families for housing[28] and other social services, the result of thousands of IRGC members' leaving for the front. IRGC commanders such as Mohsen Rezaei,[29] Ali Shamkhani, and Rafiqdoust[30] all reached out to the political leadership to solve the social needs of IRGC family members.

After the end of the war with Iraq, the IRGC's effort to satisfy the housing needs of the families of the war veterans accelerated. *Payam-e Enqelab*'s interview with Mahmoud Rahnema, then personnel general services deputy of the IRGC, clearly shows improvement of the conditions of the Guardsmen. According to Rahnema, the Cooperative Foundation of the IRGC was founded in 1988, and the organization was tasked with providing building materials for the Guardsmen to engage in building their own houses, and providing loans for the IRGC members and their families to secure organizational housing.[31] Rafiqdoust further discloses that the loans were interest free and were provided through the Ansar al-Mojahedin Credit Institute of the Guards.[32] The Ansar al-Mojahedin Credit Institute in turn is funded partially through the voluntary savings of the Guardsmen in the investment company of the Guards,[33] but as we shall see, the credit institute's earnings came from sources other than the savings of the IRGC members.

In Tehran, personnel housing for the Guards is concentrated in Martyr Mahallati City Complex (*Mojtamee Shahid Mahallati*), which is located on land donated by Khomeini. Apartments are sold to the members of the Guards at subsidized prices, and the ownership of the apartment is transferred to the individual Guardsman, who is allowed to sell the house after residing in it for five years.[34] Another city complex, Marlik, also in Tehran, was later added to the social housing stock of the IRGC. The land was donated by the Housing Ministry.[35]

According to IRGC sources, the reward system inherent in the IRGC's housing sector policy reflects the degree of sacrifice made by the individual Guardsman. A Guardsman who held a bachelor's degree prior to entering the IRGC, has lost three family members in the war, has married the wife of a war martyr, has spent at least seventy-two months on the front, or was imprisoned prior to the revolution is entitled to a house with a yard.[36] A diploma earned prior to joining the IRGC and the degree of sacrifice made during the war effort are other factors qualifying individual Guards members for housing privileges.[37] IRGC sources stress that the sale of an apartment is permitted if the house is sold to "any Muslim individual whom they please." The notion of "Muslim individual" in reality limits the sale of personnel housing to ideologically approved individuals.[38]

However, the housing projects of the IRGC have also certain political aims. The IRGC members and families are kept physically separated from the rest of society, they are under surveillance, they are given interest-free loans as long as they are loyal, and if they show signs of disloyalty they lose their privileges. The result of this housing policy is to keep the IRGC family members cordoned off from the rest of society.

7.4. The IRGC as a Contractor: Enemy of the Private Sector

The contracting activities of the IRGC are not limited to the social housing sector. Since the end of the war with Iraq, the priorities of the Islamic Republic authorities, primarily President Rafsanjani, are to keep the IRGC out of politics and provide employment for the hundreds of thousands of soldiers leaving the front and returning to their towns and villages. Therefore, the contracting activities of the IRGC were expanded from establishment of social housing for the IRGC members to general development schemes all over Iran.

During the Iran-Iraq war, the IRGC developed expertise in fortifications and quick construction of shelters.[39] At the conclusion of the war, as its leadership sought to stay relevant, the IRGC engineering corps formed GHORB.[40] GHORB is directed by a council chaired by the IRGC commander in chief. Other board members include the chief of the Joint Forces Command, the chiefs of the five component forces of the IRGC (the IRGC Air Force, the IRGC Ground Force, the IRGC Navy, the IRGC Quds Force, and the volunteer-based Basij), the head of Imam Hossein University, the commanding officer of the IRGC Cooperative Foundation, and the head of the IRGC's Self-Sufficiency Directorate.[41]

The Martyr Bakeri Bridge on Lake Orroummiyeh is one example of an employment project in which the IRGC was invited to participate in development of the infrastructure. According to *Payam-e Enqelab*, West Azerbaijan Governor General Zein al-Abedin Mir-Yousefi Atayi and President Rafsanjani engaged the Engineering Corps of the IRGC Ground Forces as the contractor.[42]

Today, GHORB is "one of the largest and strongest contractors in Iran."[43] GHORB's home page lists activities in sectors ranging from civil engineering, industry, and mines to cultivation and design.[44] It boasts of receiving "750 important contracts in different construction fields such as dams, water diversion system[s], highways, tunnels, buildings, heavy duty structures, three-dimensional trusses, offshore constructions, water supply system[s], water, [and] gas and oil main pipelines." The page claims that GHORB has been a consultant in an additional 170 projects. By June 26, 2005, GHORB said that it had completed 1,220 projects[45] and that it was involved in almost 250 ongoing jobs.[46]

The developmental role of the Guards continues in the aftermath of the war, and in an interview with *Payam-e Enqelab* Mohammad-Bagher Zolghadr reports impressive involvement of GHORB in various development projects.[47] Revolutionary Guards commander in chief Mohsen Rezaei, speaking at the annual conference of the commanders of the Guards, even spoke of the necessity of "the force of God engaging in an economic *Jihad*."[48]

While opportunities for dissent are limited within the Islamic Republic, there are four publicly controversial issues concerning IRGC involvement in the economy. First, the bidding process favors GHORB and other IRGC companies for large and lucrative contracts. Second, GHORB is large enough to underbid private contractors. Third, there are low standards for the work completed by GHORB and its subsidiaries. Finally, GHORB can get capital and hard currency through its connections to publicly owned banks. Absent from much of the public debate are criticism of the IRGC's opaque economic activities, discussion of the fact that GHORB finances are audited by an accounting firm owned by GHORB itself,[49] and talk of GHORB's exemption from taxation.[50]

Rafiqdoust denied that "a single rial" was used for IRGC economic activity under his leadership.[51] While defending current IRGC involvement in infrastructure projects, he is critical of excessive IRGC involvement in economic enterprises. "There are public projects which can be done by the private sector," he said. "Corruption in the bureaucracy, inflation…are all due to the intervention of the state in all economic matters."[52]

The newspaper *Shargh* asked how the private sector could compete with the IRGC, a concern GHORB deputy chief Abd al-Reza Abed dismissed.[53] The Islamic Republic's Management and Planning Organization (MPO; *Sazeman-e Modiriyat va Barnamehrizi-ye Keshvar*) criticized both the bidding process and GHORB's work on the sewage system in the western Iranian town of Kermanshah[54] and on the Sabalan Dam near the Azerbaijan border.[55] Rather than hold GHORB accountable, however, a July 2007 presidential decree incorporated the MPO into the presidency, thereby denying it any further powers of independent audit or evaluation.[56] Because of the number of contracts that Ahmadinejad awarded to GHORB even before he dismantled the MPO, the newspaper *Etemad-e Melli* proclaimed GHORB the real winner of the 2005 presidential elections.[57] GHORB's reputation has indeed become so poor that Bizhan Namdar Zangeneh, a former minister of oil and the longest-serving minister in the history of the Islamic Republic, has rallied against the conglomerate in an attempt to boost his own popularity.[58]

7.5. Chain Stores of the Guards: Competition with the Traditional Bazaar

Providing household goods and basic foodstuff to the members of the IRGC has always been a priority of the IRGC commanders. The Cooperatives, Housing and Social Affairs Unit of the Guards was founded to respond to the needs of the IRGC members.[59] From 1989, this respon-sibility was given to Rafiqdoust, who in his capacity as IRGC coopera-tives chief[60] directed the welfare activities of the IRGC from the Martyr Raiyyat Building in Tehran.[61] Following the end of the war with Iraq, an IRGC Welfare Center was established in each province.[62] In this way the IRGC managed to buy the loyalty of the IRGC members and their family members and reduce the risk of dissidence within the ranks of the corps.

The second part of the services of the Cooperatives, Housing and Social Affairs organization is the distribution of household goods at sub-sidized prices through the network of Association of the Cooperatives of the Army Cadre (*Ettehadiyeh-ye Taavoni-ye Kadr-e Artesh*, or ETKA) chain stores all over Iran.[63] In Tehran alone, there are six major ETKA depart-ment stores at which various household products are sold at subsidized prices to IRGC members and their families.[64]

Some of the products sold at the ETKA stores are produced by the cooperatives of the Guards, providing goods at subsidized prices to which the Guards members have access through coupons and ration cards.[65] In other cases the household goods are imported duty free by the IRGC and distributed at discounted prices through the ETKA chain stores. The household products provided for IRGC members are classified into three classes, the first of which consists of expensive and durable goods such as televisions, refrigerators, twelve-square-meter carpets, washing machines, and the like.[66] Such duty-free imports seem to be a considerable privi-lege for the Guards, and sometimes the items sold at the ETKA stores are indeed smuggled products. According to Rahnema, a refrigerator is imported from the United Arab Emirates to Kish Island, transported to mainland Iran, and provided to the IRGC members at a price of 150,000 rials at a time when the black-market price is 300,000 rials.[67] The IRGC also receives the maximum benefit from the Rafsanjani government's reforms of the tax legislation. In early 1989, the Rafsanjani government provided every Iranian citizen with the right to duty-free imports up to 500,000 rials from the Kish Island Free Trade Zone.[68] According to Rahnema's frank statements, the IRGC organization exploits this citizen's right by importing goods on behalf of all IRGC personnel and is in reality exempted from taxation.[69]

7.6. The IRGC and Telecommunications:
Elimination of Domestic and Foreign Competition

The IRGC has also muscled its way into the Iranian telecommunications sector. In February 2002, the Turkish cell phone company Turkcell—the largest Turkish company traded on the New York Stock Exchange—won a bid to inaugurate a second mobile phone network for Iran,[70] which would end the state's monopoly in the telecom sector. The Iranian government welcomed Turkcell.[71]

That is, Turkcell was welcomed until the IRGC complained. Turkcell would have been in direct competition with IRGC communications technology and electronics firms. The Council of Guardians—an executive body close to the IRGC and the Supreme Leader—protested that Iranians would have only 30 percent ownership in the new company.[72] Even after the National Bank of Iran bought out foreign investors to achieve a 51 percent Iranian stake, the IRGC was not satisfied.[73] The IRGC-operated Iran Electronic Industries and the Foundation of the Oppressed (*Bonyad-e Mostazafan Enqelab-e Eslami*)—an independent financial body traditionally run by a retired IRGC commander and used by the state as a proxy to fund off-the-books IRGC operations—erected a cascade of legal and practical obstacles leading the Turkish investors to retreat from the Iranian market.[74]

The IRGC rooted its rhetoric on Turkcell in national security. How could the Islamic Republic allow foreigners to control an Iranian telephone company? During the 1999 student protests, the Iranian government was able to shut down the cell phone network and close Internet cafés to prevent further organization by the opposition. But regardless of whether the IRGC's concern about Turkcell was security or economic self-interest, the net result is the same: the IRGC expects to maintain its dominant position not only on the battlefield but in civilian sectors as well.

7.7. The IRGC and the Oil and Gas Sector

The Revolutionary Guards smoothly enters the oil and gas sector as other economic actors are persecuted by the Supreme Audit Court (*Divan-e*

Mohasebat) for alleged corruption. One issue is that of the Petropars Company, which is accused of abusing the multiple exchange rates and transfer of an additional $42 million to the company, more than the amount authorized by the government, in order to develop the first phase of the South Pars gas field.[75]

On June 25, 2006, the National Oil Company of Iran gave GHORB a no-bid contract to develop the fifteenth and sixteenth phases of South Pars Gas Field, one of Iran's most valuable gas development projects.[76] Several members of parliament demanded an inquiry into how the grant was awarded.[77] Government spokesman Gholam-Hossein Elham defended the project,[78] and no inquiry occurred.

The South Pars project is not the IRGC's only foray into the oil and gas sector. The National Iranian Gas Company awarded GHORB a contract to build a 600-mile "peace pipeline" from Iran to Pakistan and India.[79] The Supreme Audit Court criticized "extensive irregularities in oil and gas contracts of the country," a concern that Iranian oil minister Kazem Vaziri-Hamaneh brushed aside.[80] Yahya Rahim Safavi, then commander in chief of the IRGC and head of GHORB, defended the IRGC's activity. "The IRGC has a corps of young specialists with the required technical knowledge and full engineering support," he said. Safavi denied the IRGC had ever opposed competition with private industry, but said the IRGC has "gotten involved wherever other contractors were not ready to work."[81]

The IRGC has also expanded its influence in the oil and gas sector by assuming ownership of public enterprises. On July 1, 2006, GHORB acquired the Oriental Kish Company (sometimes called Oriental Oil), a company drilling for oil and gas in various Persian Gulf fields, assuming control over both its activities and $90 million in equipment after Iran's Bank Saderat, in cooperation with Credit Suisse, suspended the financing upon which Oriental Kish depended.[82] The IRGC's involvement changed Oriental Kish's operations. GHORB resolved a commercial dispute with the Romanian-owned Grup Servicii Petroliere by firing on Romanian workers from both military helicopters and ships before boarding the Romanian rig and holding its crew hostage.[83]

On June 9, 2010, in response to Iran's refusal to comply with its international obligations regarding its nuclear program, the United

Nations (UN) Security Council adopted Resolution 1929, imposing the fourth round of sanctions on Iran, including new measures to limit the role of the IRGC and fifteen IRGC-related companies linked to proliferation.[84] The Security Council's initiative follows the same line as the U.S. Treasury Department's February 10, 2010, designation of GHORB and its commander, General Rostam Qasemi, as "proliferators of weapons of mass destruction."[85] The Treasury Department based its designation upon the U.S. government's determination that the IRGC is "assuming greater responsibility" for the Islamic Republic's nuclear program.[86]

Tehran's answer to the Treasury Department's initiative was swift. On February 18, 2010, the state-controlled daily *Kayhan*, whose editor the Supreme Leader appoints to make the newspaper his unofficial mouthpiece, editorialized, "The United States does not even know what the Guards is, let alone how to sanction it," and continued that sanctions would "increase the Guards' popularity."[87] With *Kayhan* preparing the public mind, on February 21, 2010, President Mahmoud Ahmadinejad addressed GHORB commanders and executives and asked them to ready themselves to "enter high-end oil and gas activities in order to satisfy the domestic needs of the country."[88] Sure enough, on March 15, 2010, the Oil Ministry gave GHORB a contract for an $850 million pipeline project.[89] The next month, after Turkish companies said they were withdrawing from the development of the third phase of the South Pars oil and gas field, GHORB was granted—again on a no-bid basis—the $7 billion project.[90] On May 13, 2010, Qasemi told parliamentary speaker Ali Larijani that the IRGC was replacing Shell and Total in South Pars.[91] Larijani praised GHORB as "a model of development" and assured Qasemi of parliamentary support.[92] As the Anglo-Dutch Shell and Spanish Repsol withdrew from development of the thirteenth and fourteenth phases of the South Pars oil and gas field on June 4, 2010, the Petroleum Ministry granted the $5 billion project on a no-bid basis to a certain Khatam al-Owsia Consortium (*Konsersiom-e Khatam al-Owsia*).[93] This consortium consists of GHORB; Iran Shipyard and Offshore Industries Company (*Mojtamae Kashtisazi Va Sanaye Farasahel-e Iran*) and Iran Marine Industrial Company (*Sherkat-e Sanati-ye Daryayi-ye Iran*), both of which are owned by the IRGC; and the private companies Oil Industries Engineering and Construction (*Sherkat-e Sakhteman-e Sanaye Naft*) and Iranian Offshore Engineering and Construction Company (*Sherkat-e Mohandesi Va Sakht-e Tasisat-e Daryayi*).[94]

Ahmadinejad's defiance and Larijani's attempt to ingratiate himself with the IRGC signal the Guards to stay the nuclear course since the Iranian government—as the above examples demonstrate—is ready to compensate the corps for any sanctions-related losses. The Iranian leadership can also be expected to demonstrate a similar pattern of behavior in the wake of the UN Security Council resolution of June 9, 2010. In his first reaction to the fourth round of sanctions against the Islamic Republic, Ahmadinejad said, "These resolutions are not worth a nickel to the Iranian nation. I sent the message to one of them that the resolutions you issue are like a used tissue which must be dumped in a trash can."[95] Also Brigadier General Hossein Salami, IRGC deputy, said the Guards were not concerned about the sanctions.[96] There may be a reason for Ahmadinejad's and the IRGC commanders' self-confidence: Washington has turned a blind eye to the Guards' parallel banking sector through which the IRGC manages its financial activities.

The IRGC's financial activities began during the Iran-Iraq war (1980–1988) as its microbanks provided interest-free loans to war veterans and their families. During the postwar reconstruction, IRGC-owned microbanks laundered money from the IRGC's illicit smuggling enterprise and, in the process, accumulated vast sums. However, these financial activities were very limited compared with the parastatal foundations (*bonyads*) such as the Islamic Revolution's Foundation of the Oppressed (*Bonyad-e Mostazafan-e Enqelab-e Eslami*),[97] Foundation of the Martyrs and Veterans Affairs (*Bonyad-e Shahid Va Omour-e Isargaran*),[98] or Astan-e Ghods-e Razavi Foundation in Mashhad,[99] to mention a few examples. The foundations were established by confiscating real estate, funds, and production units of exiled Iranians connected with the Pahlavi regime, which enabled the foundations to dominate the Iranian economy during the first two decades of the Islamic Republic.[100] Since Ahmadinejad's election, the Guards have used funds accumulated since the 1980s to purchase state enterprises and businesses privatized through the Tehran Stock Exchange. As long as the Guards' financial institutions remain outside the sanctions regime, the IRGC can expand its control over Iran.

7.8. The IRGC on the Tehran Stock Exchange

Ahmad Khomeini also provided the Guards at this early stage with economic powers: "Should our Islamic revolution be endangered economically we will see how the Guards will be engaged in the economy."[101] As noted above, Article 44 of the constitution called for a planned economy in which the state sector included all major industries. In 2005, Supreme Leader Ali Khamenei issued a directive reinterpreting Article 44 to provide for a smaller government and a 20 percent annual reduction in public-sector economic intervention. Khamenei's directive, codified into law on January 28, 2008,[102] effectively meant the privatization of $110–120 billion worth of public assets.[103] Iranian economists worried, however, that the domestic private sector would be barred from the privatization process due to lack of transparency and also expressed concern about Iranian legislation that makes foreign direct investment difficult. In effect, then, any privatization would constitute the transfer of state-owned enterprises to other parts of the state sector.[104] Coupled with a lack of antitrust legislation in Iran, the economists warned that the privatization proposal would actually strengthen state monopolies.[105]

Ahmadinejad, however, embraced Khamenei's privatization schemes. In an April 2010 interview, Ahmadinejad said, "The total sum of [privatizations prior to 2005] was 30 trillion rial [$3 billion], but since then, there has been more than 600 trillion rial [$60 billion] worth of transfers, most of which has been through the [Tehran] Stock Exchange."[106] Ahmadinejad also boasted of Iran's speed of privatization compared with other state-run economies internationally, which, Ahmadinejad said, had taken twenty years to achieve what Iran had.[107]

While the Iran Privatization Organization generally supports Ahmadinejad's claims, reporting 233 trillion rial ($23 billion) worth of privatization conducted through the Tehran Stock Exchange in 2006 alone (see Figure 7-1), the Iranian economists' concerns were valid. Larijani criticized the privatization efforts of the Ahmadinejad government for not involving "the genuine private sector."[108] Similarly, a Strategic Majlis Research Center (*Markaz-e Pazhouhesh-ha-ye Majles-e Showra-ye Eslami*) report found that between 2005 and 2009, only 19 percent of the assets of formerly state-owned enterprises were purchased by the private sector,

FIGURE 7-1

VALUE OF PRIVATIZED STATE-OWNED ENTERPRISES IN IRAN,
1991–2008

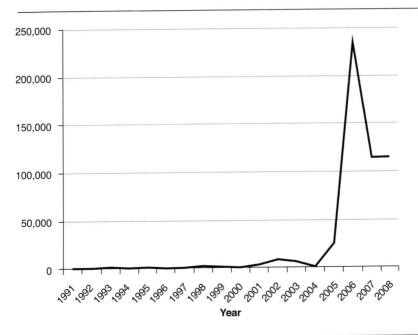

SOURCES: "Vagozari-ye 1970 Ela 1987" [Privatizations from 1970 through 1987], Sazeman-e Khosousi-sazi-ye Keshvar [Iranian Privatization Organization] (Tehran), n.d. Available in Persian at http://www.ipo.ir/index.aspx?siteid=1&pageid=149 (accessed April 19, 2010); and "Amar-ha-ye Asasi-ye Amal-kard-e Moghayseh-i-ye Sazeman-e Khosousisazi" [Basic Comparative Statistics on the Privatization Organization's Performance], Sazeman-e Khosousisazi-ye Keshvar [Iranian Privatization Organization] (Tehran), January 20, 2010. Available in Persian at http://www.ipo.ir/index.aspx?pageid=497&siteid=1 (accessed May 27, 2010).

12.5 percent of the assets were privatized to the so-called public nonstate sector, and 68.5 percent of the assets were purchased by the cooperative sector (see Figure 7-2).

The Strategic Majlis Research Center identified a number of factors detrimental to private-sector participation in privatization. The state sector's privileges, monopolies, and unlimited access to investment capital discourage private-sector involvement, and the government's declared policy of withdrawing $10 billion annually from the foreign-exchange reserve to provide credit for the private sector remains more rhetorical than real.

FIGURE 7-2

PERCENTAGE OF ASSETS PURCHASED THROUGH PRIVATIZATION OF
STATE-OWNED ENTERPRISES IN IRAN, 2005–2009, BY PURCHASING SECTOR

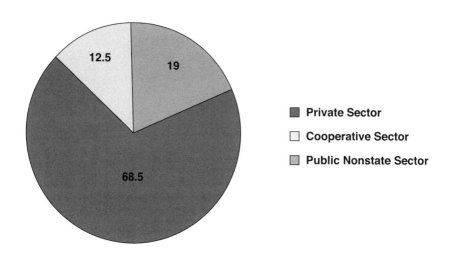

■ Private Sector
□ Cooperative Sector
▨ Public Nonstate Sector

SOURCE: Markaz-e Pazhouhesh-ha-ye Majles-e Showra-ye Eslami [Strategic Majlis Research Center],
"Tavanmandsazi Va Ertegha-ye Bakhsh-ha-ye Gheir-e Dowlati Dar Barnameh-ye Panjom-e Toseeh"
[Empowerment and Elevation of the Nongovernmental Sectors in the Fifth Development Program]
(Tehran: Markaz-e Pazhouhesh-ha-ye Majles-e Showra-ye Eslami, December 2009), pp. 13–14. Avail-
able in Persian at http://rc.majlis.ir/fa/report/download/739036 (accessed May 31, 2010).

Furthermore, the lack of transparency and the presence of state-enterprise
employees with privileged access to information at the Tehran Stock
Exchange impede private-sector involvement in the process.[109]

Larijani and the Strategic Majlis Research Center fail to mention the
most serious problem: the so-called privatization scheme that enables the
Iranian leadership to transfer ownership from relatively transparent parts
of the public sector to other parts of the public sector shielded from public
scrutiny. Purchases of the IRGC and its subordinate volunteer militia, the
Basij, are conducted by their credit and finance institutions, such as
the Mehr Finance and Credit Institution (*Sherkat-e Sarmayehgozari-ye
Mehr-e Eghtesad*). The latter has subsidiaries of its own, including the
IRGC's Cooperative Foundation (*Bonyad-e Taavon-e Sepah*) and the Ansar
Financial and Credit Institute (*Moassesseh-ye Mali/Eghtesadi-ye Ansar*).

These institutions describe themselves as noninterest or Islamic banking institutes, but, according to Hamid Tehranfar, the Central Bank's supervision deputy for banks and credit institutes, "they engage in everything but giving interest-free loans."[110] They function as financial arms of the IRGC and the Basij on the Tehran Stock Exchange and elsewhere, purchasing shares of Iranian companies.

TABLE 7-1

Main Subsidiaries of the Mehr Finance and Credit Institution (Formerly the Basij Cooperative Foundation)

– Basij Housing Foundation (*Moassesseh-ye Tamin-e Maskan-e Basij*)
– Basij No-Interest Loan Institute of the Basij Members (*Moassesseh-ye Gharz al-Hassaneh-ye Basijian*)
– Consumer-Goods Provision Foundation of the Basij Members (*Moassesseh-ye Tamin-e Aghlam-e Masrafi-ye Basijian*)
– Cultural/Artistic Institute of the Warriors of Islam (*Moassesseh-ye Farhangi/Honari-ye Razmandegan-e Eslam*)
– Scientific and Pedagogic Services Institute of the Basij Members (*Moassesseh-ye Khadamat-e Elmi Va Amouzeshi-ye Razmandegan*)

SOURCE: "Vezarat-e Behdasht, Darman Va Amouzesh-e Pezeshki" [Health, Cure and Medical Research Ministry Website], Markaz-e Basij [Basij Center], n.d. Available in Persian at http://basij.behdasht.gov.ir/index.aspx?siteid=121&pageid=18949 (accessed January 9, 2011). (*Moassesseh-ye Khadamat-e Elmi Va Amouzeshi-ye Razmandegan*)

The Mehr Finance and Credit Institution (formerly called the Basij Cooperative Foundation [*Bonyad-e Taavon-e Basij*]), currently headed by Gholam-Hossein Taghi Nattaj, was established in 1991 and has five main subsidiaries (see Table 7-1). The No-Interest Loan Institute of the Basij Members (*Moassesseh-ye Gharz al-Hasaneh-ye Basijian*), established December 14, 1993, performs most of the Basij's financial activities to provide housing and issue job-creating loans to Basij members.[111] Mehr Finance and Credit boasts of more than 700 branches across Iran,[112] making it the largest "private" bank in the Islamic Republic.[113] Its own documents suggest that its goals include "loyalty toward the goals of the sacred regime of the Islamic Republic of Iran," "propagation of the culture of no-interest loan banking," and "propagation and loyalty toward

TABLE 7-2

SUBSIDIARIES OF THE MEHR FINANCE AND CREDIT INSTITUTION

– Azarbaijan Kowsar Company (*Sherkat-e Kowsar-e Azarbaijan*)
– Kousha Paydar Company (*Sherkat-e Kousha Paydar*)
– Mehr Ayandehnegar Commerce Services Company (*Sherkat-e Khadamat-e Bazargani-ye Ayandehnegar*)
– Mehr Housing and Development Investment Company (*Sherkat-e Sarmayehgozari-ye Maskan Va Omran-e Mehr*)
– Mehr-e Eghtesad-e Iranian Investment Company (*Sherkat-e Sarmayehgozari-ye Mehr-e Eghtesad-e Iranian*)
– Tadbirgaran-e Atiyeh Company (*Sherkat-e Tadbirgaran-e Atiyeh*)

SOURCES: Moassesseh-ye Mali Va Etebari-ye Mehr, "Sherkat-e Kowsar-e Azarbaijan" [Azarbaijan Kowsar Company], n.d. Available in Persian at http://www.mehr-fci.ir/index.aspx?siteid=1&pageid=205 (accessed January 9, 2011); "Sherkat-e Kousha Paydar" [Kousha Paydar Company], n.d. Available in Persian at http://www.mehr-fci.ir/index.aspx?siteid=1&pageid=204 (accessed January 9, 2011); Sherkat-e Khadamat-e Bazargani-ye Ayandehnegar-e Mehr, "Sherkat-e Khadamat-e Bazargani-ye Ayandehnegar-e Mehr" [Ayandehnegar-e Mehr Commerce Services Company], n.d. Available in Persian at http://www.anmehr.com/CMS (accessed January 9, 2011); Moassesseh-ye Mali Va Etebari-ye Mehr, "Sherkat-e Sarmayehgozari-ye Maskan Va Omran-e Mehr" [Mehr Investment and Housing Company], n.d. Available in Persian at http://www.mehr-fci.ir/index.aspx?siteid=1&pageid=203 (accessed January 9, 2011); Moassesseh-ye Mali Va Etebari-ye Mehr, "Sherkat-e Sarmayehgozari-ye Mehr-e Eghtesad-e Iranian" [Mehr-e Eghtesad-e Iranian Investment Company], n.d. Available in Persian at http://www.mehr-fci.ir/index.aspx?siteid=1&pageid=202 (accessed January 9, 2011); and Moassesseh-ye Mali Va Etebari-ye Mehr, "Sherkat-e Tadbirgaran-e Atiyeh" [Tadbirgaran-e Atiyeh Company], n.d. Available in Persian at http://www.mehr-fci.ir/index.aspx?siteid=1&pageid=207 (accessed January 9, 2011).

the culture and thought of the Basij." Nowhere is there any mention of profit.[114]

The Iranian press has criticized Mehr Finance and Credit for withholding loans from the poor and needy, those without "credible guarantors,"[115] while engaging in major trades on the Tehran Stock Exchange through its subsidiaries, especially Mehr-e Eghtesad-e Iranian Investment Company (see Table 7-2 for a full list of Mehr Finance and Credit subsidiaries). Mehr-e Eghtesad-e Iranian Investment Company is one of the largest purchasing entities of the IRGC and owns stakes in a number of major Iranian companies (see Table 7-3).

Mehr-e Eghtesad-e Iranian Investment Company has also been involved in various scandals, including the August 2, 2009, purchase of the

TABLE 7-3

COMPANIES ENTIRELY OR PARTIALLY OWNED BY MEHR-E EGHTESAD-E
IRANIAN INVESTMENT COMPANY

– Azerbaijan Development Investment Company (*Sarmayeh-gozari-ye Toseeh-ye Azerbaijan*)

– Iran Aluminum Company (*Sherkat-e Alouminium-e Iran*)

– Iran Marine Industrial Company (*Sherkat-e Sanati-ye Daryayi-ye Iran*)

– Iran Mineral Products Company (*Sherkat-e Faravari-ye Mavad-e Madani-ye Iran*)

– Iran Industrial Development (*Toseeh-ye Sanati-ye Iran*)

– Iran Tractor Factory (*Traktorsazi-ye Iran*)

– Iran Tractor Foundry Company (*Rikhtegariye Traktorsazi-ye Iran*)

– Iran Zinc Mines Development Company (*Touseeh-ye Maaden-e Rouy*)

– Isfahan Mobarakeh Steelwork (*Foulad-e Mobarakeh-ye Esfahan*)

– Jaber Ben Hayan Pharmaceuticals (*Darousazi-ye Jaber Ben Hayan*)

– Middle East Tidewater Company (*Tidewater-e Khavar-e Mianeh*)

– Parsian Bank (*Bank-e Parsian*)

– Sadid Pipe and Equipment Company (*Sherkat-e Louleh Va Tajhizat-e Sadid*)

– Tabriz Tractor Factory (*Teraktorsazi-ye Tabriz*)

– Technotar Engineering Company (*Sherkat-e Mohandesi-ye Teknotar*)

– Tous-Gostar Investment Company (*Sarmayehgozari-ye Tous-Gostar*)

SOURCES: "Ettelaat-e Sahamdaran-e Sherkat-e Sarmayehgozari-ye Toseeh-ye Azarbaijan" [Azerbaijan Development Company's Shareholder Information], Sherkat-e Kargozari-ye Bahman, n.d. Available in Persian at http://www.bahmanbroker.com/groups/shholders/details/?symbol=u%5Dlr (accessed January 9, 2011). (According to the Tehran Stock Exchange, Mehr-e Eghtesad-e Iranian Investment Company has no shares of Azerbaijan Development Company. See "Sherkat-e Sarmayehgozari-ye Toseeh-ye Azarbaijan" [Azerbaijan Development Company], June 1, 2010. Available in Persian at http://market.tse.ir/showins.aspx?symbol=%d9%88%d8%a2%d8%b0%b1 [accessed January 9, 2011].); "Varshekastegi-ye Ghadimitarin Kharkhaneh-ye Alouminium-e Iran" [Bankruptcy of Iran's Oldest Aluminum Factory], Rouznameh-ye Poul (Tehran), April 27, 2010. Available in Persian at http://www.pooldaily.com/Pages/News-4445.html (accessed May 19, 2010); "85 Million Sahm-e SADRA be Mehr-e Eghtesad-e Iranian Vagozar Shod" [Ownership of 85 Million SADRA Shares Transferred to Mehr-e Eghtesad-e Iranian], ECO News (Tehran), May 12, 2009. Available in Persian at http://www.econews.ir/fa/NewsContent.aspx?id=103648 (accessed January 9, 2011); Sherkat-e Kargozari-ye Tadbirgaran-e Farda, "Tahlil-e Sherkat-e Faravari-ye Mavad-e Madani-ye Iran" [Analysis of the Iran Mineral Products Company], n.d. Available in Persian at http://www.google.com/url?sa=t&source=web&ct=res&cd=8&ved=0CD8QFjAH&url=http%3A%2F%2Fwww.tadbirbroker.com%2Fshow.file%3Fmainfile%3Dtrue%26userfile_id%3D6766890%26showType%3D

1&rct=j&q=%D9%81%D8%B1%D8%A2%D9%88%D8%B1%DB%8C+%D9%85%D9%88%D8%A7
%D8%AF+%D9%85%D8%B9%D8%AF%D9%86%DB%8C+%D9%85%D9%87%D8%B1+%D8%A7
%D9%82%D8%AA%D8%B5%D8%A7%D8%AF+%D8%A7%DB%8C%D8%B1%D8%A7%D9%86%
DB%8C%D8%A7%D9%86&ei=YxP0S4fQKMT38Abp6pHcDQ&usg=AFQjCNGtXJKfC8KMIcBtNAz-
KkP2GSbwGpQ&sig2=8WojFFi5foImvdL32r8UBA (accessed January 9, 2011); "Toseeh-ye Sanati-ye
Iran" [Iran Industrial Development], Tehran Stock Exchange, June 2, 2010. Available in Persian at
http://market.tse.ir/ShowIns.aspx?ins=2944500421562364 (accessed January 9, 2011); "Manovr-e
Eghtedar-e Mehr-e Eghtesad Dar Bours Ghabl Az Arzeh-ye Blok-e Mokhaberat" [Mehr-e Eghtesad's
Demonstration of Power in Stock Exchange Prior to Privatization of Communication Shares],
Sarmayeh (Tehran), September 24, 2009; Sherkat-e Toseeh-ye Maaden-e Rouy, "Tasmimat-e Majmae
Omoumi-ye Fowgh al-Adeh" [Decisions of the Extraordinary Public Session], July 7, 2008. Available
in Persian at http://www.seo.ir/Portals/44fa7561-56f7-47e4-a228-477ca071e439/BourseAnnounce-
ments/870417-8.pdf (accessed January 9, 2011); "Foulad-e Mobarakeh-ye Esfahan" [Mobarake
Steel of Isfahan], Tehran Stock Exchange, June 2, 2010. Available in Persian at http://market.tse.
ir/ShowIns.aspx?ins=46348559193224090 (accessed January 9, 2011); "Aya Sarmayehgozari-ha-ye
Mehr-e Eghtesad-e Iranian Dar Bours Soud-avar Ast?" [Are Mehr-e Eghtesad-e Iranian's Investments
in the Stock Exchange Profitable?], Bourse News (Tehran), December 22, 2008. Available in Persian
at http://www.boursenews.ir/fa/pages/?cid=16853 (accessed January 9, 2011); "Ba Tasvib-e Majmae
Omoumi-e Adi-ye Salaneh Tidewater-e Khavar-e Mianeh 1200 Rial Soud Taghsim Kard" [Tidewater
of the Middle East Distributes 1200 Rial Profit Based upon Decision of the Annual General Session],
Donya-ye Eghtesad (Tehran), n.d. Available in Persian at http://www.haftbit.com/fa/hb1253095rd/
P_1253097d.htm (accessed January 9, 2011); "Khabarhayi Ke Bazar Ra That-e Tasir Gharar Khahad
Dad" [News That Will Affect the Market], Boursenegar (Tehran), January 2, 2010. Available in Persian
at http://boursenegar.blogfa.com/post-578.aspx (accessed June 3, 2010); "Foroush-e Teraktorsazi Dar
Se Daghigheh-ye Talayi" [Sale of the Tractor Factory in Three Golden Minutes], Donya-ye Eghtesad
(Tehran), April 17, 2008. Available in Persian at http://www.magiran.com/npview.asp?ID=1603590
(accessed January 9, 2011); "Technotar," Tehran Stock Exchange, June 2, 2010. Available in Persian
at http://market.tse.ir/ShowIns.aspx?ins=3654864906585643 (accessed January 9, 2011); "9.9 Milion
Sahm-e Tous-Gostar Be Foroush Raft" [9.9 Million Tous-Gostar Shares Sold], Fars News Agency
(Tehran), November 5, 2008. Available in Persian at http://xn------nzebtb7bgeenib4x7ax26pia28cga.
eghtesadna.com/T_82977_____9-9-%D9%85%DB%8C%D9%84%DB%8C%D9%88%D9%
86-%D8%B3%D9%87%D9%85-%D8%AA%D9%88%D8%B3-%DA%AF%D8%B3%D8%AA
%D8%B1-%D8%A8%D9%87-%D9%81%D8%B1%D9%88%D8%B4-%D8%B1%D9%81%D8%
AA.htm (accessed January 9, 2011).

Angouran Zinc Mine in Zanjan Province. Iran Zinc Mines Development Company, a subsidiary of Mehr-e Eghtesad-e Iranian Investment Company, purchased the mine for 1.86 trillion rial ($186 million). Following the trade, experts said the real value was closer to 10.55 trillion rial ($1 billion).[116] The acquisition started a wave of criticism against the IRGC. Hojjat al-Eslam Mohammad-Taghi Vaezi, Zanjan Friday prayer leader and representative of the Supreme Leader to the province, raged from the pulpit: "It would have been better if the government had given the mine away for free!"[117] Parliamentarian Jamshid Ansari, and even Reza Abdollahi, the parliament's Plan and Budget Committee chairman, attacked industry and mines minister Ali-Akbar Mehrabian and demanded an investigation into the privatization of the Angouran Zinc Mine.[118]

The investigation, which was conducted by the Supreme Audit Court, disclosed that the three companies competing for ownership—Zinc Production Company (*Sherkat-e Tahiyeh Va Tolid-e Rouy*), Pasargad Company (*Sherkat-e Pasargad*), and Iran Zinc Mines Development Company—all belonged to "the same family."[119] *Etemad-e Melli* reported that "Iran Zinc Mines Development Company owns 100 percent of the shares of Zinc Production Company and 70 percent of the shares of Pasargad Company, while the rest is owned by Mehr-e Eghtesad-e Iranian Investment Company."[120] The Supreme Audit Court's investigation also disclosed that the application forms of each company for ownership of Angouran Mine were signed with the same handwriting.[121] The court promptly declared the trade void.

The Mehr Finance and Credit Institution and its subsidiaries are not the only companies to engage in such shenanigans. The IRGC Cooperative Foundation, established August 23, 1986, has developed into one of Iran's major financial players.[122] (For a list of companies and investment institutes entirely or partially owned by the IRGC Cooperative Foundation, see Table 7-4.) While it does not engage directly in trades on the Tehran Stock Exchange, its front companies and subsidiaries are active players. On September 27, 2009, in its latest major assault against Iran's economy, the IRGC purchased 50 percent plus one of the shares of Iran Telecommunications in the largest trade in the history of the Tehran Stock Exchange, valued around $8 billion.[123] The company completed the trade only after the IRGC disqualified the only genuine private-sector competitor—Pishgaman-e Kavir-e Yazd Cooperative—due to security reasons just hours before.[124] The Mehr-e Eghtesad-e Iranian Investment Company was itself barred from bidding for Iran Telecommunications, but it provided a substantial loan to Toseeh-ye Etemad-e Mobin Consortium to purchase Iran Telecommunications on its behalf.[125] Toseeh-ye Etemad-e Mobin Consortium itself consists of Toseeh-ye Etemad Investment Company (*Sherkat-e Sarmayehgozari-ye Toseeh-ye Etemad*), Shahriar-e Mahestan Investment Company (*Sherkat-e Sarmayehgozari-ye Shahriar-e Mahestan*), and Mobin Iran Electronics Development Company (*Sherkat-e Gostaresh-e Elektronik-e Mobin-e Iran*).[126] Toseeh-ye Etemad Investment Company and Shahriar-e Mahestan Investment Company are both owned by the IRGC Cooperative Foundation,[127] although they both deny this to obfuscate the extent of IRGC

TABLE 7-4

COMPANIES AND INVESTMENT INSTITUTES ENTIRELY OR
PARTIALLY OWNED BY THE IRGC COOPERATIVE FOUNDATION
AS OF MAY 31, 2010

- Alaleh-ye Kavir Samen al-Aemeh Cultural and Service Institution (*Moassesseh-ye Farhangi/Khadamati-ye Samen al-Aemeh-ye Sherkat-e Alaleh-ye Kaboud-e Kavir*)
- Baharan Company (*Sherkat-e Baharan*)
- Bahman Group (*Gorouh-e Bahman*)
- Behinesas Engineering Prefabricated Articles (*Mohandesi-ye Amadeh-ye Behinesaz*)
- Chaharmahal and Bakhtiari Food Products Yeast Company (*Mavad-e Ghazayi-ye Khamir-Mayeh Chaharmahal Va Bakhtiari*)
- Housing Jihad Companies (*Sherkatha-ye Jahad-e Khaneh-sazi*)
- Iran Telecommunications (*Sherkat-e Mokhaberat-e Iran*)
- Isfahan Zowb-rou Company (*Sherkat-e Zowb-ro-ye Esfahan*)
- Kermanshah Petrochemical Industries (*Sanaye Petroshimi-ye Kermanshah*)
- Khorasan ShadabAgricultural and Industrial Company (*Sherkat-e Kesht Va Sanat-e Shadab-e Khorasan*)
- Kish Atlas Commerce and Industrial Company (*Sherkat-e Bazargani Va Sanati-ye Iran Atlas-e Kish*)
- Kish Bahrestan Company (*Sherkat-e Bahrestan-e Kish*)
- Kowsaran Institute (*Moassesseh-ye Kowsaran*)
- Maedeh Food Industries (*Sanaye Ghazayi-ye Maedeh*)
- Misagh-e Basirat Institute (*Moassesseh-ye Misagh-e Basirat*)
- Mowj-e Nasr-Goster Communications Company (*Sherkat-e Mokhaberati-ye Mowj-e Nasr-Gostar*)
- Navid-e Bahman Company (*Sherkat-e Navid-e Bahman*)
- Ofogh-e Toseh-ye Saberin Engineering Company (*Mohandesi-ye Ofogh-e Toseeh-ye Saberin*)
- Omran-e Mohit Consultancy and Development Company (*Sherkat-e Andisheh Va Omran-e Mohit*)
- Pars Air Services (*Sherkat-e Khadamat-e Havayi-ye Pars*)

- Prefabricated Light Structures Consulting Engineering Company
  (*Sherkat-e Mohandesin-e Moshaver-e Sazeh-ha-ye Pishsakhteh-ye Sabok*)

- Rahian-e Komeyl Commercial and Consulting Services Institute
  (*Moassesseh-ye Khadamat-e Bazargani/Moshaverehi-ye Rahian-e Komeyl*)

- Razmandeh Social Housing Company (*Mojtamae
  Khaneh-sazi-ye Razmandeh*)

- Sepahan Social Housing Company (*Sherkat-e Mojtamae
  Khaneh-sazi-ye Sepahan*)

- Shahab-Sang Mining Industries (*Sanaye Madani-ye Shahab-Sang*)

- Shahriar-e Mahestan Investment Company (*Sherkat-e Sarmayehgozari-ye
  Shahriar-e Mahestan*)

- Toseeh-ye Etemad Investment Company (*Sherkat-e Sarmayehgozari-ye To
  seeh-ye Etemad*)

- Yazd Bahar Wool Company (*Sherkat-e Pashmbafi-ye Bahar-e Yazd*)

- Zagros Steel (*Foulad-e Zagros*)

SOURCES: "Bonyad-e Taavon-e Sepah," Sarmayehgozari-ye Khareji Dar Iran (Tehran), n.d. Available in Persian at http://www.foreigninvestment.blogfa.com/post-70.aspx (accessed January 9, 2011); and Masoumeh Taherkhani, "Hame Chiz Darbareh-ye Esm Va Rasm-e Kharidaran-e Moameleh-ye Bozorg" [Everything about Purchasers of the Great Deal], *Donya-ye Eghtesad* (Tehran), September 9, 2009. Available in Persian at http://www.donya-e-eqtesad.com/Default_view.asp?@=173727 (accessed January 9, 2011).

interests in the economy.[128] Toseeh-ye Etemad-e Mobin's executive general Majid Soleymanipour and his wife died under mysterious circumstances in their home as the Iranian parliament demanded an investigation into the "noncompetitive privatization" of Iran Telecommunications.[129]

Another front of the IRGC Cooperative Foundation is Ansar Financial and Credit Institute (*Moassesseh-ye Mali/Eghtesadi-ye Ansar*), previously known as Ansar al-Mojahedin No-Interest Loan Institute (*Sandogh-e Gharz al-Hassaneh-ye Ansar al-Mojahedin*), itself established as a subsidiary of the IRGC Cooperative Foundation in 1986. Its primary task is to provide no-interest loans to Revolutionary Guardsmen, veterans, and active-duty Basij members.[130] According to its director, Gholam-Hossein Taghi Nattaj, Ansar Financial and Credit Institute has 600 branches across Iran, and 6 million Iranians have savings accounts in the bank.[131] Following a long conflict between the Central Bank and no-interest credit and finance institutes, the government reportedly transferred control of Ansar al-Mojahedin to the Central Bank on December 30, 2007, but it is unclear whether the Central Bank is actually in control of the institute.[132]

7.9. The IRGC and Smuggling

The IRGC is also heavily involved in Iran's underground economy. It leverages its control over Iran's borders and airports for financial gain. Take, for example, Payam International Airport near Karaj, northwest of Tehran.[133] Payam is state-owned and IRGC-operated. In theory, it is a post airport, but it has no customs control. In 2005, an Iranian newspaper disclosed that "two thousand tons of goods, mainly cosmetics, performance-enhancing medication [Viagra] and computer electronics," entered Iran on cargo carrier Payam Air, a company owned by the transportation ministry.[134] There may be four smuggling flights each day and as many as twice that number on holidays.[135] The subsequent trial ballooned into a public spectacle.[136] It ended without any accountability for senior leadership but with a single street vendor being found guilty for masterminding the operation.[137]

Payam Air is not alone. Mohammad Ali Moshaffeq, an aide to former speaker of the parliament and 2005 presidential candidate Mehdi Karrubi, said that "more than twenty-five entrance doors of Mehrabad International Airport in Tehran are publicly claimed to be outside customs control, and no measure has been taken to exert control."[138]

Mehrabad, once on the outskirts of Tehran, has, with the capital's expansion, become encompassed by urban sprawl. Even before the Islamic Revolution, officials proposed building a new airport outside the capital. Imam Khomeini International Airport, a new facility in the desert south of Tehran, was meant as a state-of-the-art showplace. The transportation ministry awarded operation of the new airport to a consortium of Austrian and Turkish companies. On May 8, 2004, transportation minister Ahmad Khorram opened the airport. The first plane to land was an airliner from the United Arab Emirates. The second plane had to abort its landing after the IRGC drove tanks onto the runways, stormed the control tower, and demanded that the IRGC—not foreign companies—run the facility.[139] Several hours later, the joint command of the armed forces claimed in a communiqué that the closure was due to "security concerns" and "the presence of foreign firms operating at the Imam Khomeini International Airport."[140] At issue was not national pride or safety, but rather the IRGC's ability to receive equipment and goods illicitly. Any foreign-run operation would have closed the loopholes through which IRGC smuggling is permitted. The IRGC's ploy worked. Iranian officials severed the foreign contracts at significant penalties.

On October 3, 2004, the IRGC forced Khorram's impeachment. The broken contract forced then-president Khatami to delay a state visit to Turkey. It took another six months before Imam Khomeini International Airport could finally reopen under the new IRGC-friendly management.[141] In a head-to-head clash of interests, this episode illustrates the IRGC's ability to trump the power of the cabinet, if not the presidency itself. For the IRGC, though, the move has been profitable. According to the daily newspaper *Iran*, billions of dollars in "luxury goods, mobile phones and cosmetics [were] smuggled through Imam Khomeini International Airport" during the facility's first eighteen months of operation.[142]

The IRGC is also involved in operating a series of what Iranians often call "invisible jetties" (*eskeleh-ha-ye namari*) along Iran's 1,500-mile Persian Gulf and Indian Ocean coastline. While the IRGC may use smaller facilities for low-level smuggling of alcohol and other contraband, larger facilities such as the Martyr Rajai Port Complex in Hormuzgan Province are the linchpin of a lucrative oil-smuggling business.[143] Because the Iranian government subsidizes fuel—a gallon of gasoline may cost only forty cents in Iran—Revolutionary Guardsmen can realize a 200 to 300 percent profit by selling subsidized gasoline abroad. One Iranian parliamentarian suggested that "invisible jetties... and the invisible hand of the mafia control 68 percent of Iran's entire exports."[144] Another parliamentarian estimated that IRGC smuggling might amount to $12 billion per year. "This smuggling business is of such a magnitude that it cannot be done by donkeys or by passengers," he said. "This volume is entering the country through containers and via illegal and unofficial channels [such as] 'invisible jetties' supervised by strongmen and men of wealth."[145]

It is this type of profiteering that antagonizes the more reform-oriented factions within the Islamic Republic's leadership. After Mehdi

Karrubi came in third in the 2005 presidential elections, a poll marked by irregularities and accusations of fraud, he lashed out at the IRGC and its involvement in both the elections[146] and the shadow economy. "We had no money from jetties, no money from smuggled goods, no sugar business, but [my supporters] sacrificed their lives," Karrubi said. "We suffered for months and fought at two to three fronts in order to secure an honorable election,"[147] he added, implying that the IRGC now cared more about material gain than revolutionary principles. Karrubi's aide, Mohammad Ali Moshaffeq, specifically pointed his finger at "sixty jetties with no customs control" that compose "60 percent of the illegal imports to the country."[148]

Another presidential candidate, Mohammad-Baqer Qalibaf, also criticized IRGC smuggling,[149] and Hossein Loghmanian, a parliamentarian from Hamadan disqualified from office by the Council of Guardians, called the IRGC the "mafia of power and wealth."[150]

7.10. Conclusion

The financial activities of the IRGC and the Basij have far-reaching impact on the Iranian economy and society. IRGC intervention distorts the market and marginalizes not only the private sector but also the revolutionary foundations that have dominated the Iranian economy since the revolution. The IRGC also places a burden on the public sector because of the hidden flow of public funds to IRGC companies through generous subsidies. The IRGC distributes some of its profits to keep its officer corps happy, some funds to buy the loyalty of civilians in the political arena, and some funds to elect politicians who then allocate additional national resources to the IRGC or its front companies. In addition, the IRGC's increasing wealth makes it increasingly independent of the state budget. The IRGC's transfer of wealth into these front companies, however, can also make these companies targets for international sanctions. By targeting the economic interests of the IRGC, the international community may force the Guards to recalculate the risk of continuing the Islamic Republic's nuclear program. But absent targeting of these companies, the IRGC can simply continue to play three-card monte.

Notes

1. "Constitution of the Islamic Republic of Iran." Iran Online (Tehran), n.d. Available at http://www.iranonline.com/iran/iran-info/Government/constitution-9-3.html (accessed January 7, 2011).

2. "Asas-nameh-ye Sepah-e Pasdaran-e Enqelab-e Eslami" [Statute of the Islamic Revolutionary Guards Corps], Hafezeh-ye Ghavanin Website (Tehran), n.d. Available in Persian at http://tarh.majlis.ir/?ShowRule&Rid=1D4973FB-9551-4F8D-AEB3-DAEFD52791F1 (accessed September 8, 2010).

3. "Eqtesad-e Sepah" [The Economy of the Guards], *Eqtesad-e Iran Monthly* (Tehran), December 2004. Available at http://www.iraneconomics.net/archive/articles.asp?id=666&magno=70&grid=2 (accessed January 7, 2011); "Dar goftegouye Shargh ba janeshin-e Gharargah Sazandegi barresi shod: Hozour-e Sepah dar gharardad-ha-ye Eqtesadi" [Investigation from the Conversations of *Shargh* with the Deputy Head of the Construction Base: The Presence of the Guards in Economic Contracts], *Shargh* (Tehran), June 26, 2005. Available in Persian at http://www.magiran.com/npview.asp?ID=1117259 (accessed January 9, 2011); "Naghsh-e Sepah Dar Amaliat-e Mardomyari, Bazsazi va Sazandegi-ye Keshvar" [The Role of the Guards in Relief Work, Reconstruction, and Development of the Country], *Javan* (Tehran), April 16, 2008. Available in Persian at http://www.aftab.ir/articles/view/politics/iran/c1c1208342986p1.php/%D9%86%D9%82%D8%B4-%D8%B3%D9%BE%D8%A7%D9%87-%D8%AF%D8%B1-%D8%B9%D9%85%D9%84%DB%8C%D8%A7%D8%AA-%D9%85%D8%B1%D8%AF%D9%85-%DB%8C%D8%A7%D8%B1%DB%8C-%D8%A8%D8%A7%D8%B2%D8%B3%D8%A7%D8%B2%DB%8C-%D9%88-%D8%B3%D8%A7%D8%B2%D9%86%D8%AF%DA%AF%DB%8C-%DA%A9%D8%B4%D9%88%D8%B1 (accessed January 9, 2011).

4. "GHORB Dar Yek Negah" [GHORB at a Glance], Khatam al-Anbia Construction Base Website (Tehran), n.d. Available in Persian at http://khatam.com/?part=menu&inc=menu&id=98 (accessed January 7, 2011).

5. "Constitution of the Islamic Republic of Iran," article 150.

6. "Naghsh-e Sepah Dar Amaliat-e Mardomyari, Bazsazi va Sazandegi-ye Keshvar."

7. "Constitution of the Islamic Republic of Iran," article 44.

8. Ibid.

9. "Matn-e Eblaghiyeh-ye Rahbar-e Moazzam-e Enqelab-e Eslami Dar Khosous-e Siyasat-ha-ye Kolli-ye Asl-e 44" [Text of the Directive of the Supreme Leader of the Islamic Revolution Regarding the General Policies of Article 44], Majma-e Tashkhis-e Maslehat-e Nezam Website (Tehran), May 22, 2005. Available in Persian at http://www.maslehat.ir/Contents.aspx?p=c4eaa3d8-2de0-45c5-8ad9-9004a79af493 (accessed January 7, 2011).

10. Brigadier General Hossein Yasini, "Directive for Guards Participation in Economic, Societal and Cultural Development Schemes of the Country," Sazeman-e

Sanaey Kouchak va Shahrak-ha-ye Sanati-ye Iran (Tehran), April 10, 2006. Available in Persian at http://www.iraniec.ir/FilesArchive/733_mosharekat%20sepah.pdf (accessed September 12, 2007).

11. Ibid.

12. Ahmad-Reza Hedayati, "Razmandegi va Sazandegi" [War-Fighting and Construction], *Kayhan* (Tehran), October 18, 2006. Available in Persian at http://www.magiran.com/npview.asp?ID=1236889 (accessed January 7, 2011).

13. Khomeini's February 6, 1979, sermon is not included in the otherwise extensive online version of Rouhollah Khomeini, *Sahifeh-ye Nour*, vol. 5 (Tehran: Markaz-e Nashr-e Asar-e Emam Khomeini. Ketabkhaneh-ye Tebyan, 2004). Available in Persian at http://library.tebyan.net/books1/5647.htm (accessed October 9, 2007). The quote may be found with no reference to the date of the speech on the official Khomeini website at http://imam-khomeini.com/Didgahha/negahi%20be%20osoul%20toseh.htm (accessed September 21, 2007).

14. Hedayati, "Razmandegi va Sazandegi."

15. Nikki Keddie, *Roots of the Revolution: An Interpretative History of Modern Iran* (New Haven, CT: Yale University Press, 1981), pp. 143–144.

16 A. T. Schulz, "Iran: An Enclave Arms Industry," in Michael Brzoska and Thomas Ohlson (eds.), *Arms Production in the Third World* (Stockholm: Stockholm International Peace Research Institute, 1986), pp. 147–148.

17. Islamic Republic Defense Industries Organization Website (Tehran), n.d. Available at http://www.diomil.ir/en/home.aspx (accessed January 7, 2011).

18. Akbar Hashemi Rafsanjani, *Pas Az Bohran. Karnameh Va Khaterat-e Hashemi Rafsanjani* [After the Crisis: Deeds and Memoirs of Hashemi Rafsanjani], 2nd ed. (Tehran: Daftar-e Nashr-e Maaref-e Enqelab, 2001), p. 323.

19. Anthony H. Cordesman and Abraham R. Wagner, *The Lessons of Modern War: The Iran-Iraq War* (Boulder, CO: Westview; London: Mansell, 1990), vol. 2, p. 53; Shahram Chubin and Charles Tripp, *Iran and Iraq at War* (London: I. B. Tauris, 1988), pp. 180, 221; and Efraim Karsh, *The Iran-Iraq War 1980–1988* (Oxford: Osprey, 2002).

20. "Ashnayi Ba Amal-Kard-e Sazeman-e Sanaye-e Melli-ye Defae" [Overview of the Performance of the National Defense Industry Organization], *Payam-e Enqelab* (Tehran), September 23, 1989, p. 18.

21. Ibid.

22. "Moarrefi-ye Sanaye-e Elektronik Va Mokhaberat-e Sepah-e Pasdaran-e Enqelab-e Eslami" [Presentation of the Electronics and Communications Industries Unit of the Guards], *Payam-e Enqelab* (Tehran), September 23, 1989, p. 40.

23. Iran Electronics Industries Website (Tehran), n.d. Available at http://ieimil.com/main.aspx (accessed August 28, 2007).

24. Integrated Electronic Industries Website (Tehran), n.d. Available at http://www.ieicorp.com (accessed January 7, 2011).

25. Subsidiaries include Shiraz Electronics Industries, established in 1973; Iran Communication Industries; Information Systems of Iran, established in

1971; Electronics Components Industries; Isfahan Optic Industries, established in 1987; and the Iran Electronics Research Institute, established in 1998.

26. "Mosharekat-e Bonyad-e Taavon-e Sepah Dar Maskan-e Mehr" [Participation of the IRGC Cooperative Foundation in Mehr Housing], Tabnak News (Tehran), May 11, 2010. Available in Persian at http://www.tabnak.ir/fa/news/98025/%D9%85%D8%B4%D8%A7%D8%B1%D9%83%D8%AA-%D8%A8%D9%86%D9%8A%D8%A7%D8%AF-%D8%AA%D8%B9%D8%A7%D9%88%D9%86-%D8%B3%D9%BE%D8%A7%D9%87-%D8%AF%D8%B1-%D9%85%D8%B3%D9%83%D9%86%E2%80%8C-%D9%85%D9%87%D8%B1 (accessed January 8, 2011).

27. "Piramoun-e Hal-e Moshkel-e Maskan Va Vam-e Personel-e Sepah" [Regarding Solving the Housing and Loan Problems of the Guards Members], Payam-e Enqelab (Tehran), January 13, 1990, p. 34.

28. "Goft-e-Gou-yi Ba Baradar Mohsen Rafiqdoust" [A Conversation with Brother Mohsen Rafiqdoust], Payam-e Enqelab (Tehran), March 3, 1990, p. 14.

29. Akbar Hashemi Rafsanjani, Be Sou-ye Sarnevesht [Towards Destiny], 3rd ed., edited by Mohsen Hashemi (Tehran: Daftar-e Nashr-e Maaref-e Enqelab, 2004), p. 449.

30. Ibid., p. 467.

31. "Goftegou-yi Ba Masoul-e Khadamat-e Personeli-ye Ostan-e Tehran Piramoun-e Moshkelat-e Refahi-ye Baradaran-e Sepah" [Converstion with Personnel Services Chief of Tehran Province Regarding Welfare Problems of the Brothers of the Guards], Payam-e Enqelab (Tehran), December 30, 1989, p. 26.

32. "Goft-e-Gou-yi Ba Baradar Mohsen Rafiqdoust," p. 15.

33. "Goftegou-yi Ba Masoul-e Khadamat-e Personeli-ye Ostan-e Tehran Piramoun-e Moshkelat-e Refahi-ye Baradaran-e Sepah."

34. "Piramoun-e Hal-e Moshkel-e Maskan Va Vam-e Personel-e Sepah," p. 35.

35. "Goft-e-Gou-yi Ba Baradar Mohsen Rafiqdoust," p. 15.

36. "Piramoun-e Hal-e Moshkel-e Maskan Va Vam-e Personel-e Sepah," p. 35.

37. Ibid.

38. Ibid., pp. 35, 36.

39. "GHORB Dar Yek Negah."

40. "Eqtesad-e Sepah."

41. Yasini, "Directive for Guards Participation in Economic, Societal and Cultural Development Schemes of the Country."

42. "Gozaresh-e Khabarnegaran-e Majjaleh-ye Payam-e Enqelab Az Pol-e Shahid Bakeri" [Report Made by Journalists of Payam-e Enqelab Magazine on Martyr Bakeri Bridge], Payam-e Enqelab (Tehran), December 2, 1989, pp. 14–17.

43. "Eqtesad-e Sepah."

44. "GHORB Dar Yek Negah."

45. Ibid.

46. "Dar goftegouye Shargh ba janeshin-e Gharargah Sazandegi barresi shod: Hozour-e Sepah dar gharardad-ha-ye Eqtesadi."

47. "Goftegou Ba Reis-e Setad-e Moshtarek-e Sepah-e Pasdaran-e Enqelab-e Eslami" [Conversation with Islamic Revolutionary Guards Corps Joint Command Council Chief], *Payam-e Enqelab* (Tehran), April 30, 1992, p. 25.

48. "Javv-e Sepah Javv-e Nouraniyat Ast" [The Atmosphere of the Guards Is an Atmosphere of Light], *Payam-e Enqelab* (Tehran), June 22, 1992, p. 291.

49. For an example, see the GHORB-owned company SEPASAD, which is being supervised by Hesam Accounting Firm, which in turn is owned by Khatam al-Anbia. See Islamic Republic of Iran, "Agahi-ye tasmimat-e sherkat-e mohandesi-ye SEPASAD" [Announcement with Regard to the Resolutions of the SEPASAD Engineering Company], Official Gazette, December 20, 2006. Available in Persian at http://www.rooznamehrasmi.ir/Detail.asp?CurPage=44& NewsID=913423522867907 (accessed October 9, 2007).

50. Kerman Economic and Financial Affairs Organization Website (Kerman), n.d. Available at http://www.kermaneconomic.ir/desktopdefault.aspx?tabid=151 (accessed January 8, 2011).

51. "Sepah-e Pasdaran va Rouz-ha-ye Aghazin-e Faaliyat" [The Guards Corps and the First Days of Operation], ISNA (Tehran), April 21, 2007.

52. Ibid.

53. "Dar goftegouye Shargh ba janeshin-e Gharargah Sazandegi barresi shod: Hozour-e Sepah dar gharardad-ha-ye Eqtesadi." For information on Bank of Industry and Mining financing of GHORB projects, see Amir-Esmail Kazemi, "Motalebat-e Moavvagh-e Bank Sanat va Madan Kahesh yaft" [Fluctuating Rates of the Bank of Industry and Mining Decreased], Jahane Eqtesad (Tehran), February 6, 2007. Available in Persian at http://www.jahaneghtesad.com/Template2/Article.aspx?AID=6429 (accessed October 11, 2007).

54. "Gozaresh-e bazdid az tarh-e Ijad-e tasisat fazelab-e shahr-e Kermanshah" [Inspection Report on Kermanshah Sewage Project], Presidency of Iran, Management and Planning Organization Website (Tehran), n.d. Available in Persian at http://www.mporg.ir/FANNI/PSEB/Omour/shahri/Kermanshah%20W.doc (accessed August 30, 2007).

55. "Gozaresh az bazdid az prozheh-ye Ejrae Sad-e Sabalan" [Inspection Report on the Sabalan Dam Project], Presidency of Iran, Management and Planning Organization Website (Tehran), n.d. Available in Persian at http://www.mporg.ir/fanni/PSEB/Omour/ab/gebeglodam.doc (accessed August 30, 2007).

56. "Sazeman-e Modiriyat va Barnameh-rizi Monhal shod" [Management and Planning Organization Dissolved], BBC Persian, July 10, 2007. Available in Persian at http://www.bbc.co.uk/persian/iran/story/2007/07/070710_ka-mpo.shtml (accessed October 11, 2007). See also "Shenasayi ba Sazeman-e Modiriyat va Barnameh-rizi-ye Keshvar" [Introduction to the Management and Planning Organization], Spokesman of the Islamic Republic of Iran Government Website (Tehran), n.d. Available in Persian at http://www.sokhangoo.net/index.php?option=com_content&task=view&id=3311&Itemid=110 (accessed September 30, 2007).

57. "Yek Mah, Se Gharardad, 7 Milliard Dollar" [One Month, Three Contracts, $7 Billion], *Etemad-e Melli* (Tehran), July 1, 2006.

58. "Zamgeneh khod ra bara-ye voroud be Majles-e hashtom amadeh mikonad" [Zangeneh Prepares Himself for the Eighth Parliament], *Mardomyar* (Tehran), March 26, 2007. Available in Persian at http://www.mardomyar.com/Default_view.asp?@=723 (accessed October 11, 2007).

59. "Goft-e-Gou-yi Ba Baradar Mohsen Rafiqdoust," p. 15.

60. "Goftegou-yi Ba Masoul-e Khadamat-e Personeli-ye Ostan-e Tehran Piramoun-e Moshkelat-e Refahi-ye Baradaran-e Sepah," p. 26.

61. Ibid.

62. Ibid.

63. Ibid.

64. Ibid., p. 27.

65. Ibid.

66. Ibid., p. 28.

67. Ibid.

68. Ibid.

69. Ibid.

70. Fatemeh Mohammad-Nezhad, "Faraz va Nashib-ha-ye Operator-e Dovvom-e Telefon-e Hamrah az Sal-e 82 Ta Konoun—Turkcell; Mandan ya Raftan?" [Ups and Downs of the Second Mobile Phone Operator since 2002—Turkcell: To Stay or to Go?], *Shargh* (Tehran), June 29, 2005.

71. "Gharardad-e Turkcell ghatan amali mishavad" [The Turkcell Contract Will Definitely Be Realized], Iran IT Network, September 1, 2004. Available in Persian at http://www.iritn.com/?action= show&type=news&id=3900 (accessed October 11, 2007).

72. "Faraz va Nashib-ha-ye Operator-e Dovvom-e Telefon-e Hamrah az Sal-e 82 Ta Konoun—Turkcell; Mandan ya Raftan?"

73. "Bank-e Melli be Turkcell Peyvast" [The National Bank Aligned with Turkcell], Aftab News Agency (Tehran), July 22, 2005. Available in Persian at http://www.aftabnews.ir/vdchqkin23n-.html (accessed October 11, 2007).

74. Kaveh Omidvar, "Parvandeh-ye Turkcell, Baztab-e Tiregiye Ofogh-e Eqtesadi-ye Iran" [The Turkcell Case—Reflecting Iran's Dark Economic Horizons], BBC Persian, September 12, 2005. Available in Persian at http://www.bbc.co.uk/persian/business/story/2005/09/050912_ra-iran-turkcell.shtml (accessed October 14, 2007); "Hekayat-e Natamam-e Turkcell, Shoraka va Maghamat-e Mokhaberat" [The Unfinished Story of Turkcell and Partners and the Communications Officials], ITiran.net, September 5, 2005. Available in Persian at http://itiran.net/archives/001916.php (accessed October 11, 2007); and Erfan Anvar (Turkcell spokesman in Iran), interview on ITiran.net, December 3, 2005. Available in Persian at http://www.itiran.com/?type=interview&id=5317 (accessed October 11, 2007).

75. "Bazresi-ye Koll-e Keshvar: Shekayati Dar Mored-e Sherkat-e Petropars Taghdim-e Dadgah Shodeh Ast" [Supreme Audit Court: Complaint Filed against the Petro Pars Company], *Sobh-e Sadeq* (Tehran), February 18, 2002, p. 1. Available in Persian at http://www.sobhesadegh.ir/1380/0041/pdf/P01.pdf (accessed March 29, 2009).

76. "Gharardad-e tosee-ye faz-ha-ye 15 va 16 ba Gharargah-e Khatam al-Anbia emza mishavad" [Development Contracts of the 15th and 16th Phases Are to Be Signed with Khatam al-Anbia Base], Resalat (Tehran), June 25, 2006. Available in Persian at http://www.magiran.com/npview.asp?ID=1115387 (accessed October 11, 2007).

77. Khaneh-ye Mellat Website (Tehran), June 27, 2006. Available in Persian at http://mellat.majlis.ir/archive/1385/04/06/tazakorat.htm (accessed July 25, 2007). See also "Shesh namayandeh dar tazakkor-e katbi khatab be vazir-e naft khastar shodand . . ." [Six Parliamentarians' Demands in a Note of Warning to the Minister of Oil], Fars News Agency, June 27, 2006. Available in Persian at http://www.farsnews.net/newstext.php?nn=8504060095 (accessed October 11, 2007).

78. "Sokhan-gou-ye dowlat: Gharargah-e Khatam al-Anbia raghib-e sherkat-ha-ye dakheli nist" [Government Spokesman: Khatam al-Anbia Is Not a Rival for Domestic Companies], Iranian Labour News Agency, July 3, 2006. See also "Bish az 6 milliard dollar gharar-dad dar Sherkat-e Naft va Gaz-e Pars eneghad gardid" [A Contract Worth More Than $6 Billion Awarded to the Pars Oil and Gas Company], IREXPERT (Tehran), July 8, 2007.

79. "Ba emzae yek moghaveleh-nameh bein Sepah-e Pasdaran va Sherkat-e Melli-ye Gaz-e Iran ehdas-e khat-e louleh-ye gaz Assalouyeh be Sistan va Baluchestan be Sepah-e Pasdaran Sepordeh shod" [With the Signing of a Memorandum of Understanding between the IRGC and the National Gas Company, the Building of a Gas Pipeline from Assalouyeh to Sistan and Baluchestan Was Handed Over to the IRGC], Resalat (Tehran), June 10, 2006. Available in Persian at http://www.barnameh-budjeh.com/npview.asp?ID=1097210 (accessed October 11, 2007); and "Ba 900 kilometr khat-e louleh-ye gaz Assalouyeh be Sistan va Balouchestan miresad" [The 900-Kilometer Gas Pipeline Will Reach Sistan and Baluchestan], *Kayhan* (Tehran), June 8, 2006.

80. "Ba emzae yek moghaveleh-nameh bein Sepah-e Pasdaran va Sherkat-e Melli-ye Gaz-e Iran ehdas-e khat-e louleh-ye gaz Assalouyeh be Sistan va Baluchestan be Sepah-e Pasdaran Sepordeh shod."

81. "Ba 900 kilometr khat-e louleh-ye gaz Assalouyeh be Sistan va Balouchestan miresad."

82. "Sherkat-e Oriental Kish be Gharargah-e Khatam al-anbia vagozar mishavad" [Oriental Oil Kish Will Be Handed Over to Khatam al-Anbia Base], *Kayhan* (Tehran), July 1, 2007.

83. "Rig Hijack Alleged in Persian Gulf: Iran Accuses Romanian Company," *Global Insight*, August 16, 2006; Anca Paduraru, "Iran Denies Attacking Romanian Oil Rig," ISN Security Watch, August 25, 2006. Available at http://www.isn.ethz.

ch/news/sw/details.cfm?ID=16574 (accessed October 14, 2007); and "Mozakerat-e edgham ba Oriental Kish dar Gharargah-e Khatam al-Anbia nahayi mishavad" [Negotiations on Merger with Oriental Kish Are Finalized at the Khatam al-Anbia Base], *Donya-ye Eqtesad* (Tehran), July 3, 2006.

84. "Security Council Imposes Additional Sanctions on Iran, Voting 12 in Favour to 2 Against, with 1 Abstention," United National Security Council Website (New York), June 9, 2010. Available at http://www.un.org/News/Press/docs//2010/sc9948.doc.htm (accessed June 15, 2010).

85. "Treasury Targets Iran's Islamic Revolutionary Guard Corps," U.S. Department of the Treasury Website (Washington, DC), February 10, 2010. Available at http://www.treas.gov/press/releases/tg539.htm (accessed June 14, 2010).

86. Stephen Kaufman, "Iranian Decisions Increasingly Being Made by Revolutionary Guard," America.gov, February 17, 2010. Available at http://www.america.gov/st/peacesec-english/2010/February/20100217145832esnamfuak0.6569178.html (accessed June 14, 2010).

87. "Vaghti Amrika Asabani Mishavad" [When the United States Gets Angry], *Kayhan* (Tehran), February 18, 2010.

88. "Ahmadinejad: Nezam-e Solteh Dar Moghabel-e Mellat-e Iran Be Parakan-deh-Gouyi Oftadeh Ast" [Ahmadinejad: The World Order Speaks Incoherently in the Face of the Iranian Nation], Islamic Republic News Agency (Tehran), February 22, 2010. Available in Persian at http://www.irna.ir/View/FullStory/?NewsId=974074 (accessed March 29, 2010).

89. "Vagozari-ye 850 Melyoun Dolar Prozhehpye Jadid-e Nafti Be Khatam al-Anbia" [$850 Million New Oil Project Given to Khatam al-Anbia], *Abrar* (Tehran), March 16, 2010.

90. "Gharargah-e Khatam al-Anbia Jaygozin-e Torkiyeh Dar 3 Faz-e Pars-e Jonoubi Mishavad" [Khatam al-Anbia Base to Replace Turkey in Three Phases of the South Pars], *Abrar* (Tehran), April 19, 2010.

91. "Gharargah-e Khatam al-Anbia-ye Sepah Mitavanad Olgouyi Baraye Sazandegi-ye Keshvar Bashad" [Khatam al-Anbia Construction Base Can Serve as a Role Model for Development in the Country], Fars News Agency (Tehran), May 13, 2010. Available in Persian at http://www.farsnews.net/newstext.php?nn=8902221585 (accessed May 13, 2010).

92. Ibid.

93. "Jaygozinan-e Dakheli-ye Shell Va Repsol Dar Pars-e Jonoubi" [Domestic Replacements for Shell and Repsol in South Pars], *Poul* (Tehran), June 5, 2010.

94. Ibid.

95. "Ahmadinejad: In Ghatnameh-ha Pashizi Nemiarzand" [Ahmadinejad: These Resolutions Are Not Worth a Nickel], *Poul* (Tehran), June 9, 2010.

96. "Sardar Salami: Negaran-e Tahrim-e Sepah Nistim" [Commander Salami: We Are Not Concerned about Sanctions against the Guards], Tabnak (Tehran), June 14, 2010. Available in Persian at http://tabnak.ir/fa/pages/?cid=104295 (accessed June 16, 2010).

97. "Bonyad Dar Yek Negah" [The Foundation at a Glance], Bonyad-e Mostazafan-e Enqelab-e Eslami Website (Tehran), n.d. Available in Persian at http://www.irmf.ir/About-Us/History.aspx (accessed June 16, 2010).

98. "Moarrefi-ye Bonyad" [Presentation of the Foundation], Bonyad-e Shahid Va Omour-e Isargaran Website (Tehran), n.d. Available in Persian at http://www.isaar.ir/homepage.aspx?site=IsaarPortal&lang=fa-IR&tabid=0 (accessed June 16, 2010).

99. "Astan-e Ghods-e Razavi," Astan-e Ghods-e Razavi Website (Mashhad), n.d. Available in Persian at http://www.aqrazavi.org/index.php?module=pagesett er&func=viewpub&tid=21&pid=110 (accessed June 16, 2010).

100. For a survey of the activities of the foundations, see Suzanne Maloney, "Agents or Obstacles? Parastatal Foundations and Challenges for Iranian Development," in Parvin Alizadeh (ed.), *The Economy of Iran: Dilemmas of an Islamic State* (London: I. B. Tauris, 2000), pp. 145–176.

101. "Emam Va Sepah Az Badv-e Tashkil Ta Hal. Mosahebeh Ba Seyyed Ahmad Khomeini" [The Imam and the Guards from Establishment to Now: Interview with Seyyed Ahmad Khomeini], *Payam-e Enqelab* (Tehran), May 29, 1982, p. 13.

102. "Ghanoun-e Eslahi Az Ghanoun-e Barnameh-ye Chaharom-e Toseeh-ye Eghtesadi, Ejtemai Va Farhangi-ye Jomhouri-ye Eslami-ye Iran Va Ejrae Siasat-ha-ye Kolli-ye Asl-e Chehel Va Chaharom Ghanoun-e Asasi" [Corrective Legislation to the Law on the Fourth Economic, Social, and Cultural Development Program of the Islamic Republic of Iran and Execution of the General Policies of Article Forty-four of the Constitution], Vezarat-e Omour-e Eghtesadi Va Darayi (Tehran), n.d. Available in Persian at http://asl44.mefa.ir/ghanon-matn-fa.html (accessed June 2, 2010).

103. "Kord-e Zangeneh: Khosousisazi Be Nimerah Resid" [Kord Zangeneh: Privatization Has Reached Halfway], *Jam-e Jam* (Tehran), November 29, 2009.

104. Rouzbeh Mehrzad, "Bahs-e Dagh-e Mahafel-e Eghtesadi-ye Iran Darbareh-ye Farman-e Ayatollah Khamenei" [Hot Discussion in Economic Circles about Ayatollah Khamenei's Decree], BBC Persian (London), June 16, 2006. Available in Persian at http://www.bbc.co.uk/persian/business/story/2006/07/060716_ra-rm-article44.shtml (accessed June 3, 2010).

105. Ibid.

106. "Kasi Tavanayi-ye Asib-zadan Be Iran Ra Nadarad" [No One Has the Capacity to Harm Iran], Fars News Agency (Tehran), April 14, 2010. Available in Persian at http://www.farsnews.net/newstext.php?nn=8901250001 (accessed June 2, 2010).

107. Ibid.

108. "Enteghad-e Larijani Az Ravand-e Vagozari-ye Sherkat-ha-ye Dowlati" [Larijani's Criticism of the Trend of Privatization of State Companies], *Jam-e Jam* (Tehran), June 3, 2010.

109. Markaz-e Pazhouhesh-ha-ye Majles-e Showra-ye Eslami [Strategic Majlis Research Center], *Tavanmandsazi Va Ertegha-ye Bakhsh-ha-ye Gheir-e Dowlati*

Dar Barnameh-ye Panjom-e Toseeh [Empowerment and Elevation of the Non-governmental Sectors in the Fifth Development Program] (Tehran: Markaz-e Pazhouhesh-ha-ye Majles-e Showra-ye Eslami, December 2009), p. 19. Available in Persian at http://rc.majlis.ir/fa/report/download/739036 (accessed May 31, 2010).

110. "Akharin Hoshdar-ha-ye Bank-e Markazi Be Moassesseh-ha-ye Gheir-e Mojaz" [The Central Bank's Final Warnings to Nonstandard Institutions], Iranian Students News Agency (Tehran), December 27, 2009. Available in Persian at http://isna.ir/ISNA/NewsView.aspx?ID=News-1462846 (accessed June 2, 2010).

111. "Tarikhcheh Va Amalkard" [History and Performance], Moassesseh-ye Mali Va Etebari-ye Mehr [Mehr Finance and Credit Institution] (Tehran), n.d. Available in Persian at http://www.mehr-fci.ir/index.aspx?siteid=1&pageid=190 (accessed June 2, 2010); and "Modir-Amel Va Showra-ye Moavenin" [Executive Director and the Council of Deputies], Moassesseh-ye Mali Va Etebari-ye Mehr [Mehr Finance and Credit Institution] (Tehran), n.d. Available in Persian at http://www.mehr-fci.ir/index.aspx?siteid=1&pageid=3605 (accessed June 2, 2010).

112. "Mozoue Va Faaliatha" [Fields and Activities], Moassesseh-ye Mali Va Etebari-ye Mehr [Mehr Finance and Credit Institution] (Tehran), n.d. Available in Persian at http://www.mehr-fci.ir/index.aspx?siteid=1&pageid=193 (accessed June 2, 2010).

113. "Shekl-giri-ye Bozorgtarin Bank-e Khosousi Dar Iran" [Formation of the Largest Private Bank in Iran], *Donya-ye Eghtesad* (Tehran), April 9, 2009.

114. "Sanad-e Rahbordi-ye Moassesseh-ye Mali Va Etebari-ye Mehr" [Strategic Document of Mehr Finance and Credit Institution], Moassesseh-ye Mali Va Etebari-ye Mehr [Mehr Finance and Credit Institution] (Tehran), n.d. Available in Persian at http://www.mehr-fci.ir/index.aspx?siteid=1&pageid=425 (accessed June 2, 2010).

115. "Moassessat-e Mali Va Etebari Vam-e Kouchak Be Faghiran Nemidahand" [Credit and Finance Institutes Don't Make Small Loans to the Poor], *Sarmayeh* (Tehran), July 20, 2008.

116. "Ebtal-e Mozayedeh-ye Madan-e Rouy-e Angouran" [Cancelation of Privatization of Angouran Zinc Mine], *Sarmayeh* (Tehran), September 24, 2009.

117. Ibid.

118. Alireza Behdad, "Divan-e Mohasebat Elam Kard: Tabani Dar Bozorgtarin Mozayedeh-ye Madani-ye Keshvar" [Supreme Audit Court Announces: Conspiracy in the Largest Mine Bidding Project in the Country], *Etemad-e Melli* (Tehran), September 29, 2009.

119. Ibid.

120. Ibid.

121. Behdad, "Divan-e Mohasebat Elam Kard: Tabani Dar Bozorgtarin Mozayedeh-ye Madani-ye Keshvar."

122. "Asasnameh-ye Bonyad-e Taavon-e Sepah-e Pasdaran-e Enqelab-e Eslami" [Statute of the Islamic Revolutionary Guards Corps Cooperative], n.d. Available in

Persian at http://www.tooba-ir.org/_book/defa/ghavanin/ghavan12.htm (accessed June 2, 2010).

123. "Anjam-e Movafaghiatamiz-e Bozorgtarin Kharid Va Foroush-e Tarikh-e Bours" [Successful Execution of the Largest Trade in the History of the Stock Exchange], Bourse News (Tehran), September 27, 2009. Available in Persian at http://www.irbourse.com/NewsDetail.aspx?NewsIdn=10607 (accessed June 2, 2010).

124. Masoumeh Taherkhani, "Hame Chiz Darbareh-ye Esm Va Rasm-e Kharidaran-e Moameleh-ye Bozorg" [Everything about Purchasers of the Great Deal], Donya-ye Eghtesad (Tehran), September 9, 2009.

125. "Vam-e 300 Milliard Toumani-ye Moassesseh-ye Mehr Be Kharid-e Mokhaberat" [300 Billion Touman Loan to Mehr Institute in Order to Purchase Telecommunications], Donya-ye Eghtesad (Tehran), November 18, 2009.

126. Taherkhani, "Hame Chiz Darbareh-ye Esm Va Rasm-e Kharidaran-e Moameleh-ye Bozorg."

127. Ibid.

128. "Konsersium-e Kharidar-e Saham-e Mokhaberat: Hich Ertebati Ba Sepah Nadarim" [Consortium Purchasing Communications Shares: We Have No Relationship with the Guards], Jam-e Jam (Tehran), October 4, 2009.

129. "Marg-e Modir-Amel-e Sherkat-e Kharidar-e Saham-e Mokhaberat Bar Asar-e Gaz-Gereftegi!" [Death of Executive Director of the Company Purchasing Communications Shares Because of Gas Poisoning], Aftab (Tehran), December 12, 2009. Available in Persian at http://www.aftab.ir/news/2009/dec/12/c2c1260607089_economy_marketing_business_information_technology_majid_soleimanipoor.php (accessed June 16, 2010).

130. "Sandogh-e Ansar al-Mojahedin Az Radif-e Boudjeh-ye Dowlati Va Sepah Be Hich Onvan Estefadeh Nemikonad" [Ansar Al-Mojahedin Institute Does Not under Any Circumstance Use Governmental Funds of the Guards], Sobh-e Sadeq (Tehran), September 9, 2002.

131. "Pas Az Tasvib-e Showra-ye Poul Va Etebar: Pazireh-nevisi-ye Bank-e Ansar Aghaz Mishavad" [After Passing in the Council of Money and Credit: Ansar Bank to Be Established], Sobh-e Sadeq (Tehran), September 7, 2009.

132. "Dar Pey-e Tasmimi Gheir-e-Montazereh Sepah-e Pasdaran Ekhtiar-e Do Moassesseh-ye Ansar Va Mehr Ra Be Bank-e Markazi Sepord" [Following an Unexpected Decision the Revolutionary Guards Transfers Control of the Ansar and Mehr Institutes to the Central Bank], Sarmayeh (Tehran), December 30, 2007.

133. See the website of Payam Aviation at http://www.payamaviation.ir/farsi_site/darbareh.htm (accessed September 4, 2007).

134. "Majles masaleh-ye Foroudgah-e Payam ra barresi mikonad" [The Parliament Investigates the Payam Airport Case], Iran Daily (Tehran), January 9, 2005; and "Foroudgah-e Payam dekhalati dar gheir-e ghanouni boudan bar nandarad" [Payam Airport Not Implicated in Illegal Goods Transportation], Shargh, November 2, 2004.

135. A. William Samii, "Analysis: Goods Smuggling Highlights Economic Problems in Iran," Radio Free Europe/Radio Liberty, January 7, 2005.

136. "Raye qati-ye Foroudgah-e Payam ba mahkoumiyat-e Abbas Taqizadeh va hamdastanash sader shod" [The Final Ruling in the Payam Airport Case: Conviction of Abbas Taqizadeh and His Accomplices], Islamic Republic News Agency, November 6, 2006. Available in Persian at http://www.irna.com/en/news/view/line-9/8508155245131703.htm (accessed October 11, 2007).

137. "Mottaham-e foroudgah-e payam be etteham-e tahsil mal namashroe mohakemeh mishavad" [Accused in Payam Airport Case Is Prosecuted for Unlawful Possession of Goods], Iran Daily (Tehran), February 7, 2006.

138. "Aya mardom hagh darand bedanand?" [Don't People Have the Right to Know?], website of Hezb-e Etemad-e Melli. Available in Persian at http://www.etemademelli.ir/news/detail.php?ID=1199 (accessed September 4, 2007).

139. "Foroudgah-e Emam Baz-nashodeh Basteh Shod" [Imam Airport Shut Down at Opening Ceremony], Shargh (Tehran), May 9, 2004.

140. Ibid

141. Leyla Khodabakhshi, "Foroudgah-e Emam Saranjam Eftetah Shod" [The Imam Airport Finally Inaugurated], Shargh (Tehran), May 1, 2005.

142. "Ghachagh-e Milliardi az Gomrok-e Foroudgah" [Billions Worth Are Smuggled through Airport Customs], Iran Newspaper, September 29, 2007. Available in Persian at http://www.iran-newspaper.com/1386/860707/html/special4.htm#s754422.

143. "Ghachagh-e Takhassosi" [Specialized Smuggling], Quds Daily (Iran), May 19, 2005. Available in Persian at http://www.qudsdaily.com/archive/1384/html/2/1384-02-29/page29.html#7 (accessed October 11, 2007).

144. "Loghmanian: Mafiya-ye qodrat va servat ejazeh-ye tahhaghogh khast-e mardom ra nemidahad" [Loghmanian: The Mafia of Power and Wealth Does Not Permit the Realization of the Popular Will], Mellat (Tehran), February 8, 2004. For the full text of Loghmanian's speech, see Islamic Republic of Iran, "Mashrouh-e Mozakerat-e Majles-e Showra-ye Eslami —Jalaseh-ye 432" [The Proceedings of the Islamic Consultative Assembly—Session 432], Official Gazette, May 24, 2004. Available in Persian at http://www.rooznamehrasmi.ir/Detail.asp?CurPage=&isParent=0&Level=0&CategoryID=900000&NewsID=917152592894060 (accessed October 11, 2007).

145. "Matn-e kamel-e estefa-ye Armin" [The Complete Text of the Resignation of Armin], Mellat (Tehran), March 14, 2004.

146. "Karrubi: Az Magham-e Moazzam-e Rahbari mikhaham dekhalat konand. Mikhaham posht-e pardeh moshakhas shavad. Vezarat-e Keshvar va Showray-e Negahban ra mottaham midanem. Moshkelat-e ma be Amrika marbout nist" [Karrubi: I Demand the Supreme Leader Intervene. I Want to Expose What Is Behind the Scenes. I Accuse the Ministry of the Interior and the Council of Guardians. Our Problems Are Not Due to America.], Iranian Student News

Agency, June 18, 2005. Available in Persian at http://isna.ir/Main/NewsView. aspx?ID=News-543050 (accessed October 11, 2007).

147. "Eteraz-e Karrubi be shabakeh-ye sazmandeh-ye arae entekhabat" [Karrubi's Protests against the Network Organizing Votes during the Elections], Eqbal, n.d. Available in Persian at http://eqbal.ir/political/news1/last/84329110509.php (accessed September 4, 2007). See also a list of the jetties in Iran in Sharif News on January 4, 2005, at http://www.sharifnews.com/?2025 (accessed October 11, 2007).

148. "Aya mardom hagh darand bedanand?" [Don't People Have the Right to Know?], Etemad-e Melli Website (Tehran), n.d. Available in Persian at http:// www.etemademelli.ir/news/detail.php?ID=1199 (accessed September 4, 2007).

149. "Shirazeh-ye kar-e omour-e ejra-i-ye keshvar az dast rafteh" [Qalibaf: Executive Office of the Country Is Disorganized], Aftab (Tehran), May 29, 2005. Available in Persian at http://www.aftab.ir/news/2005/may/29/c1c1117382863. php (accessed October 11, 2007).

150. Islamic Republic of Iran, "Mashrouh-e Mozakerat-e Majles-e Showra-ye Eslami—Jalaseh-ye 432."

8

The Revolutionary Guards and the Export of the Revolution

8.1. The Ideological Foundations of the Export of the Revolution

The transformation of the Islamic Republic into a military dictatorship dominated by the Islamic Revolutionary Guards Corps (IRGC) is partially rooted in the Islamist ideology of the Islamic Republic. This ideology defines holy war (jihad) as the propelling factor in history, continuing until the Day of Reckoning. Such a messianic ideology maintains the Islamic Republic in a permanent state of crisis in relation to other states and maintains a permanent state of emergency inside of Iran. This state of emergency also paves the way for the involvement of the IRGC, the primary agent of jihad, in the domestic politics of Iran.

The ideological foundation of the Islamic Republic of Iran is derived from Grand Ayatollah Rouhollah Khomeini's revolutionary theory of state, known as *Islamic Government*, which Khomeini conceived during his exile in Najaf, Iraq.[1] Since the revolution in 1979, Khomeini's theory has constituted the ideological foundation of the Islamic Republic and is also enshrined in its Constitution.[2]

Distinct similarities can be identified between Khomeini's ideology and that of the Marxists. Where Karl Marx and Friedrich Engels claimed that the "history of all hitherto existing society is the history of class struggles,"[3] Khomeini identified the holy struggle of the Muslim community of believers (*ummat*) against "Jews,"[4] "imperialists,"[5] their agents,[6] and their machinations as the propelling factor in history. For Khomeini, Islam "is the religion of militant individuals who are committed to truth and

204

justice...those who struggle against imperialism," such as the Shia imams who "put on military dress and went into battle in the wars. ...they killed and they were killed."[7]

There are also similarities between Khomeini's call for a global Islamic revolution and Marxist internationalism. Engels's answer to the question "Will it be possible for this revolution to take place in one country alone?" is "No," and he concludes: "It is a universal revolution and will, accordingly, have a universal range."[8] The same conclusion was drawn by Khomeini, who attacked "tyrannical self-seeking rulers" who "divided the Islamic homeland,"[9] heads of state whom Khomeini accused of separating "various segments of the Islamic believers from each other and artificially creat[ing] separate nations."[10] Hence, Khomeini's revolution was not limited to the political borders of modern Iran, and he desired to mobilize the Muslim community of believers to destroy "those systems of government that are corrupt in themselves and also entail the corruption of others, and to overthrow all treacherous, corrupt, oppressive, and criminal regimes."[11] Khomeini concluded: "This is the duty that all Muslims must fulfill, in every one of the Muslim countries, in order to achieve the triumphant political revolution of Islam."[12]

Khomeini's militant ideology is enshrined in the Constitution of the Islamic Republic of Iran, Article 154, which states: "While scrupulously refraining from all forms of interference in the affairs of other nations, it supports the just struggles of the oppressed [*mustazafun*] against the oppressors [*mostakberoun*] in every corner of the globe."[13] This concept was later termed "export of the revolution."

There is also little doubt that the Revolutionary Guards from the first year of the revolution considered itself the primary agent of the export of the revolution. As apparent in the coat of arms of the Guards, the IRGC is an ideological organization, and the scope of the revolution it advances is global.[14] At the base of the coat of arms, the number 1357 refers to the year 1979, which not only commemorates the year of the revolution in Iran, the establishment of the Islamic Republic, and the emergence of the IRGC but also heralds the beginning of a new era of world revolution. The centerpiece of the logo shows strong arms holding an AK-47, the emblematic weapon of revolutionary armies in the 1960s and 1970s. The arms are shaped in the form of the Arabic word *La*, a reference to the first article of the faith in Islam, *La Ilaha Ilallah* (there is no God but Allah). The Islamist character of the IRGC is further signified by a book that symbolizes the Quran. The Arabic text at the top of the logo reads: "And make ready for them whatever force you can. …" The text is from verse 60 of the sura *al-Anfal*, which—not quoted on the coat of arms—subsequently reads: "to frighten [terrorize] thereby the enemy of Allah and your enemy and others besides them, whom you know not—Allah knows them."[15] There is also an olive branch, which does not play a prominent role in the logo, and a globe, which does. As demonstrated by its coat of arms, the IRGC is clearly a military organization that serves as the vanguard of an Islamist world revolution—a permanent revolution that never managed to seize control over the Islamic world, but helped the IRGC seize control over Iran.

8.2. Practical Foundations of the Export of the Revolution: Iranian Revolutionaries as Members of a World Revolutionary Movement

The concept of a world revolutionary community actually predates Grand Ayatollah Khomeini's concept and can, in its modern form, be traced back to the reactions to the 1953 coup against Prime Minister Mohammad Mossadeq. As the Iranian revolutionaries sought foreign support to advance their revolutionary cause, they became members of an international revolutionary movement that they attempted to support after the victory of the revolution in Iran in 1979. The extensive international network of the Iranian revolutionaries provided the practical foundations for the export of the revolution.

One pamphlet published by the Iran Freedom Movement explains that following the fall of the Mossadeq government, the "defeat of traditional political struggle inside Iran" radicalized political activists in Iran, who reached the conclusion that "the final battle with the Shah's regime and the only way of freedom was through armed struggle."[16] Therefore, both "Islamists and non-Islamic movements" began the preparations for such struggle,[17] inspired by "revolutionary war in Cuba, [and] the victory of the revolution in Algeria."[18]

According to the Iran Freedom Movement, the leftist organizations had much easier access to arms and training because "the Communist states were ready to provide the necessary training to the youth," some of whom went to "China[,]…Cuba or Albania."[19] Islamist groups, on the other hand, looked to newly independent Algeria and Gemal Abdol Nasser's Egypt for support "due to its [Egypt's] anti-imperialist policies."[20] Connection with the Algerians was established through Ali Shariati, whose articles in the Arabic-language weekly *Al-Mojahed* had already made him a known figure to the Algerian students in France, and "after long considerations the Iran Freedom Movement" dispatched "one of the brothers based in Paris" to Algeria.[21] According to the Iran Freedom Movement, the main goal of the contact with the Algerians was to "establish a base for the needed training. The need [was for] experienced instructors who could transfer their revolutionary experiences to the volunteer Iranian youth, revolutionary experiences in the field of clandestine organizational work, training in use of light weapons, instruction in explosives, education in revolutionary warfare and the like."[22] The Iran Freedom Movement also disclosed that the organization had decided that if it were not possible to establish a base in Algeria, they should "at the very least convince the heads of the Liberation Front to teach at camps in the Middle East."[23] But the Algerians welcomed the idea and even expressed their willingness to go to Iran in order to "get the job done."[24]

Another country that expressed its readiness to support the Iran Freedom Movement was Egypt, and in January 1964 the movement sent a delegation headed by Mostafa Chamran to Cairo.[25] Other members of the delegation included Sadeq Qotbzadeh and Ebrahim Yazdi.[26] According to Chamran, he and the rest of the group received "two years of training in partisan warfare…in Egypt."[27] The training activity was monitored by the Iran Freedom Movement Central Committee and was approved by Ayatollah Mahmoud Taleqani and Mehdi Bazargan; a certain Rahim Atayi also monitored the activities of the Egypt-based group.[28] By July 1964 the main cadres of the training program of the Iran Freedom Movement were based in Egypt and had established an organization called the Special Organization of Unity and Action (*Sazeman-e Makhsous-e Ettehad Va Amal*, or SAMAE). A communications network was set up between organizations abroad and in Tehran, and groups of Iranian volunteers from Iran and abroad went to Egypt in order to receive training in "clandestine warfare, the fundamentals of irregular/

partisan warfare, explosives, knowledge of weapons, strategy and tactics, basics of one-on-one fights and the like."[29] Chamran proved to be one of the best recruits at the camps. It was also in training camps in Egypt that Iranian revolutionaries came into contact with Palestinian terrorists of the Fatah movement, which planted the seed for their cooperation in Lebanon in the 1970s.[30]

In addition to the military training, Chamran and Yazdi from the first quarter of 1963 began compiling documents and books analyzing revolutionary wars of the past hundred years, ranging from the civil war in Spain to partisan warfare in the Philippines, China, Cuba, Cyprus, Malaysia, Vietnam, Algeria, and the like.[31] The documents were translated into Persian, taught in classes, and smuggled into Iran as Mohammad Hanif-Nezhad and his friends began preparing for armed struggle.[32] The next phase of the clandestine activities was the deployment of individuals trained in Egypt to Lebanon and Iraq, but eventually most of them returned to Iran.[33] The reason behind the transfer of individuals out of Egypt was difficulties with the Egyptian government encountered beginning in mid-1966. According to the Iran Freedom Movement, the Egyptians insisted upon activating propaganda warfare against the Shah's regime from Radio Cairo, but the Iran Freedom Movement did "not believe in noise and propaganda…did not consider radio propaganda activities expedient…and since a critical number of members had been trained in Egypt the office of the organization was closed and the friends were transferred to Lebanon."[34] The Iran Freedom Movement also mentions Nasser's nationalist and anti-Persian rhetoric as another reason for the move, and Chamran himself explains: "I had some conflicts with extremist Arab nationalist fronts. For example, we protested against the notion of 'the Arab Gulf' or 'Arabestan' [Land of the Arabs] instead of Khouzestan [province]. Nasser recognized our protests but said that Arab nationalism was so strong that one can't deal with it easily."[35]

After leaving Egypt, the Iranian volunteers were based in Lebanon, and in mid-1966 Chamran went to the United States, where he remained until 1970. In the beginning of 1970, Chamran returned to Lebanon and began organizing activities with the charismatic Lebanese Shia leader Imam Mousa Sadr, with whom he had been friends since his days at Tehran University and in Qom.[36] The Iran Freedom Movement and Sadr agreed upon several joint projects, such as the establishment of Jabal al-Amel Technical School in the South, the establishment of a medical center in Beirut, and the establishment of the Supreme Shia Islamic Council of Lebanon.[37] In 1970, when Chamran returned from the United States to Lebanon, he based himself at the technical school in Northern Sour, where he transformed the school into "a political, ideological and military training center."[38]

Chamran contributed to the establishment of both the Supreme Shia Islamic Council of Lebanon, which allegedly was a broad movement for all Shia regardless of their political beliefs, and another institution called Harekat al-Mahroumin (Movement of the Dispossessed), which was established as a consolidated revolutionary movement with an Islamist ideology.[39] A separate organization called Afwaj al-Moghavemat al-Lobnaniyat (AMAL) was established with Chamran's help as the armed wing of Harekat al-Mahroumin, after which the Islamic movement of the Lebanese Shia entered a new phase: "struggle in the ideological dimension, struggle in the political dimension, and struggle in the form of armed jihad."[40]

Chamran explained his activities in Lebanon in a few pamphlets that were later released by the Iran Freedom Movement. In one, Chamran explains that he used Arabic translations of the books of the Iranian radical Ali Shariati to shape the minds of the young Lebanese in AMAL.[41] He propagated Shariati's work through ideological/political indoctrination classes; *Sowt al-Mahroumin* (Voice of the Dispossessed), which discussed theoretical issues; and *Sowt al-AMAL* (Voice of AMAL), which was a news bulletin.[42]

Of course, Chamran's work was not limited to the ideological/political indoctrination of the Lebanese and other Middle Eastern Shia. According to the same pamphlet, by 1970 the Iran Freedom Movement, as well as its offshoot, the Mojahedin-e Khalq organization, had established a vast communications and military training network in the Middle East.[43]

But why Lebanon? In the words of Chamran himself:

> We needed a base in the region from which we could organize our activities against the Iranian regime. At that time the most suitable place was Lebanon, including the fact that Imam Mousa Sadr, the leader of the Lebanese Shia, was opposed to the Shah's regime and was ready to cooperate with us.

Qotbzadeh and Yazdi knew him, and through this channel we
established relations with him until I, in 1970, left the United
States along with my family and went to Lebanon.[44]

The pamphlet continues: "Shia communities in the West and in Africa
were connected with Lebanon more than with Najaf or Qom. Therefore,
Imam Mousa Sadr was not only a Lebanese personality, but was an international personality and made frequent visits to Asian and African countries."[45] The Iran Freedom Movement also disclosed that Sadr, along with
Chamran, traveled to the Soviet Union and Algeria but did not mention
the travel to Libya during which Sadr disappeared.[46]

In one of Chamran's letters to an undisclosed "Professor" and "master"
—possibly a reference to future prime minister Mehdi Bazargan—from
Lebanon, written in 1978, Chamran discussed the issues of Lebanon
in a lengthy report,[47] providing more details on the internal dynamics
of Lebanon.[48]

Simultaneously, Grand Ayatollah Khomeini ran an international
revolutionary network of his own from Najaf. Khomeini's revolutionary
sermons, and particularly his model for a just Islamic society based on
the principle of the Guardianship of the Jurist, found many followers
among the non-Iranian Shia. Most leading members of the Shia clergy
in Iraq and Iran did not subscribe to Khomeini's ideology, but vast numbers of mid- and low-ranking clerics did.

One of Grand Ayatollah Khomeini's Iraqi allies was the Karbala-based
Ayatollah Mohammad al-Shirazi, who aligned himself with Khomeini to
counterbalance the clerical establishment in Najaf.[49] Shirazi tasked his
nephew Hadi al-Modarresi, [50] one of many young Iraqi clerics who had
attended Khomeini's politicizing lectures in Najaf,[51] to collect Khums—
annual taxation of one-fifth of all gain—among the Shia in the Persian
Gulf region. For Shirazi, the publicly announced alliance with Khomeini
meant greater income from the devout Shia living outside of Iraq. For
Khomeini, the alliance meant access to influence over the entire Persian
Gulf region through Shirazi's network.

Another student of Grand Ayatollah Khomeini with a widespread
international network—and a strong connection with Muammar Gaddafi's
regime in Libya—was Hojjat al-Eslam Mohammad Montazeri, son of

Grand Ayatollah Hossein-Ali Montazeri, another radical Islamist leader with an extensive international network. Mohammad Montazeri was politically radicalized by the Shah's suppression of clerical opposition to the White Revolution in 1962 and was imprisoned and severely tortured.[52] Mohammad Montazeri, along with his childhood friend Hojjat al-Eslam Mehdi Hashemi (the brother of the son-in-law of Grand Ayatollah Montazeri), al-Modaressi, and the followers of Shirazi distributed tape recordings of Grand Ayatollah Khomeini's incendiary speeches and organized revolutionary cells in the entire Middle East region;[53] they also dispatched their cadres to undertake military training in Palestine Liberation Organization (PLO) refugee camps in Lebanon.[54]

One interesting account of the revolutionary training programs at PLO camps can be found in the memoirs of Rahim Safavi. Safavi left Iran after February 18, 1978.[55] Because of earlier contacts with Mohammad Montazeri, Safavi sought the help of Ayatollah Ali Meshkini, who helped him to get to Damascus, Syria. In Syria, Mohammad Gharazi instructed Safavi and a fellow Iranian volunteer, Ahmad Fazaeli, in how to fight the prerevolutionary intelligence organization SAVAK and arranged for their training at a Palestinian camp to learn "partisan warfare techniques."[56] The classes included military training and demolition techniques, the use of chemicals, and the like.[57] After a month of military training in the Palestinian camp in Syria, they traveled to Lebanon and were based at the Fatah camp in Nabatia under the command of a certain Raed Abou-Saleh.[58] According to Safavi, he and Fazaeli were both involved in fights against the Israeli forces at the Litani frontlines of Fatah.[59]

It is against the existence of such a vast international revolutionary network even before the victory of the revolution that the post-revolutionary Iranian leadership's desire to export the revolution must be judged.

8.3. Export of the Revolution as a National Security Doctrine and an Instrument of Domestic Power Struggle

As the revolutionaries defeated the Shah's regime, the issue of the export of the revolution and the question of who was in charge of Iranian foreign policy became the highest priority of the new leadership. Already in 1979, the nascent IRGC and Mehdi Bazargan competed to stay at the helm of Iran's foreign policy.

Ahmad Khomeini's recollections of conflicting political and ideological currents among the different Guards provide interesting insights into the revolutionary dynamics of the day: "Whenever they wanted to prepare future plans for the Guards, they would come and make proposals based upon their values. For example, the martyr Sheikh Mohammad Montazeri believed that we should raise a revolutionary mayhem in the region, which would also clarify the role of the Guards in export of the revolution."[60] Ahmad Khomeini also recalled discussing the issue at length with Mohammad Montazeri, explaining: "Well, if you really want to set the entire region ablaze have you any appreciation of our capabilities? He would say: 'We should not wait for them to come and invade and occupy Iran and begin [our struggle] when it is all over. It is a waste of time to be here.'"[61]

The March 19, 1980, issue of the Guards' mouthpiece *Payam-e Enqelab* reflects Mohammad Montazeri's thinking: "Since the colonial and authoritarian powers move into the direction of exploitation and dictatorship, it is in their nature to fight against a justice-seeking and justice-spreading Islamic movement and they will conspire against it in order to preserve themselves."[62] The analysis also claimed that internal ethnic unrest inside Iran, such as the ethnic clashes in "Gonbad, Naghdeh, Sanandaj, Paveh, [and] Bandar Anzali,"[63] were proof of a Western conspiracy against the nascent revolutionary regime in Tehran. The solution provided by *Payam-e Enqelab* was simple and followed Mohammad Montazeri's advice: "In order to achieve ideological, political, security and economic self-reliance we have no other choice but to mobilize all forces loyal toward the Islamic Revolution and through this mobilization plant such a terror into the hearts of the enemies that they abandon the thought of offensive and annihilation of our revolution."[64] Even more directly, the analysis stressed: "If our revolution does not have an offensive and internationalist dimension, the enemies of Islam will again enslave us culturally, politically, and the like and will not abstain from plunder and looting."[65]

Ahmad Khomeini even recalled Mohammad Montazeri's suggestion that Ahmad Khomeini and his father should go elsewhere "since he [Grand Ayatollah Khomeini] has liberated Iran and the work is over. It would be better if you and the Imam [Khomeini] and some other friends go to another retrograde country and begin the work anew by saying *Bism Allah [Al-Rahman Al-Rahim]* [in the name of (the merciful and compassionate) Allah]!"[66] Ahmad Khomeini continued: "Mr. Yazdi, who is a disciplined type, would argue: 'We should not intervene in affairs of the others and we should think of Iran and develop this country, and preserve order. What happens in Kuwait, Bahrain, Pakistan and Afghanistan has nothing to do with us.' Well, both of them were on top of the Guards, two lines with 180-degree difference…"[67] But Ahmad Khomeini also said that "the only difference is with regard to practicalities and methodology. We all desire the establishment of Islamic republics controlled by a central government and there is no one who does not desire this, but in the way of achieving the goals there are differences."[68]

While Ahmad Khomeini's interview leaves the impression that the rivalry was only between Mohammad Montazeri and Bazargan's interim government, Grand Ayatollah Montazeri's memoirs depict Ahmad Khomeini as a part of the rivalry. As Grand Ayatollah Montazeri hosted a delegation from Libya, which had backed Mohammad Montazeri's revolutionary work prior to the victory of the revolution,[69] Ahmad Khomeini spread rumors that the Libyans were attempting to "establish a Communist base in Iran" through the Montazeri household.[70]

Grand Ayatollah Montazeri and his son Mohammad immediately began organizing the Office of the Liberation Movements, which aimed at exporting the revolution abroad, and they even "opened an account in the Melli Bank with the name of the Liberation Movements which enjoyed popular support and the people would transfer money to it. After all they [the Liberation Movements] had certain expectations from the Iranian revolution,"[71] as Grand Ayatollah Montazeri wrote in his memoirs. Montazeri's memoirs also revealed that he expedited a mission to Afghanistan under the supervision of Hojjat al-Eslam Hashem Javaheri to mediate between various Afghan factions, all of whom were fighting against the Soviet Union, and that he too opened an account in Melli Bank to support the liberation movements of Afghanistan.[72]

8.4. Exporting the Revolution

8.4.1. Exporting the Revolution 1979–1980 While Grand Ayatollah Khomeini was inclined to export the revolution abroad, and the Revolutionary Guards already had a network in place to deliver the requirements for the export of the revolution, the revolution in Iran also resonated with many Muslim political groups outside of Iran, who saw the Iranian revolution as the solution to their own political frustrations. Delegations from North America, Sadiq al-Mahdi of the Sudan, Anwar Ibrahim of Malaysia, Nur Misuari of the Philippines, the Muslim Brotherhood and al-Jihad in Egypt, the Muslim Youth Movement of Malaysia and the Party of Islam in Malaysia, and of course Yasir Arafat—who was received in Tehran as the first "foreign head of state" visiting the Islamic Republic—sent their representatives to witness the revolutionary phenomenon firsthand.[73] Apart from their revolutionary tourism in Tehran, they probably also urged the revolutionary regime to support Shia movements outside of Iran.

Iran's neighbors, which hosted the largest part of the world's Shia population, were of course affected more directly, as the local Shia populations saw the revolution as a model to emulate. In Iraq, Ayatollah Mohammad Baqer al-Sadr led Hezb al-Dawa al-Islamiyya (Party of the Islamic Call, commonly known as al-Dawa, a Shia political party that aimed at establishing a Shia Islamic state in Iraq) and directly challenged the authority of the Baath regime. A series of bombings shook the country. The Iraqi government's response was brutal: al-Dawa was banned and Ayatollah Sadr and many other Dawa activists were executed. In Saudi Arabia the Eastern Province was shaken by pro-Khomeini Shia uprisings, and so were Bahrain and Kuwait, both of which had sizable Shia populations. Meanwhile, the revolution gave new energy to the Lebanese Shia, and, apart from the AMAL movement, it also led to the creation of the Lebanese Hezbollah, which benefited from the tireless activities of Mohammad Montazeri. According to *Howzeh*, a quarterly publication of the Theological Seminary in Qom, Mohammad Montazeri deployed a few hundred men in Lebanon as soon as Grand Ayatollah Khomeini seemed to be in control of the situation in Tehran.[74]

holy warriors."[89] Ahmad Khomeini too supported the efforts by first Mohammad Montazeri and then Mehdi Hashemi to export the revolution. In an interview with *Payam-e Enqelab*, Ahmad Khomeini even urged the Revolutionary Guards members to take their line on "how to deal with Kuwait, Pakistan or Central American countries," which echoed Mohammad Montazeri's thoughts of the time.[90]

Grand Ayatollah Montazeri's official statements to *Payam-e Enqelab* disclosed how central the issue of Palestine had become to the Office of the Liberation Movements by mid-1982. Montazeri began his message to the Guards by stating: "I hope that our slogan of 'Today Iran, Tomorrow Palestine' is not only a slogan."[91] Montazeri also expressed hope that members of the Guards who were engaged in the war against Iraq would "not only pursue the path of liberating soil and water, but pursue Islam and martyrdom."[92] He also mentioned "the Philippines, Eritrea, Thailand and many other countries in which the Muslims are truly under pressure, and Afghanistan"[93] as prospective countries ready for the export of the revolution. Montazeri concluded: "The revolution is an Islamic one and Islam is for the entire world. Therefore Islam has no borders and the Guardian of the Revolution also does not recognize borders."[94] *Payam-e Enqelab*, explaining Montazeri's declarations, expressed dissatisfaction that the Revolutionary Guards' duty to export the revolution was not mentioned in the Constitution,[95] and stressed that the peaceful export of the revolution within the framework of diplomacy was not possible and that the Guards must use other means.[96]

Conflicts in the conduct of the export of the revolution peaked on several occasions. Rafsanjani's memoirs of November 19, 1981, reflected Mehdi Hashemi's concern about decisions of the parliament with regard to the Liberation Movements of the Revolutionary Guards.[97] Hashemi's concern may have been warranted since Rafsanjani's December 17, 1981, memoirs revealed the Iranian leadership's discussion of the nature of its relationship with the Liberation Movements. "Early in the evening we went to the home of Mr. Mousavi Ardebili. It was a weekly consultancy meeting. Mr. Khamenei, the Prime Minister [Mir-Hossein Mousavi] and Ahmad [Khomeini]…were also present."[98] Rafsanjani added:

We discussed the arrest of members of the Bahrain Liberation Movement and the claims about their relationship with Iran, expulsion of the Iranian ambassador from Bahrain and the wave of condemnation of Iran by Arab governments. It became clear that if we, because of the Constitution, should want to support the liberation movements, such incidents are unavoidable. But it was decided that the government should have precise control and should not be the secondary player to the Liberation Movements unit of the Guards, which without governmental supervision could make trouble. Good relations with Islamic countries should also be taken into consideration.[99]

The December 19, 1981, note in Rafsanjani's memoirs revealed that the government indeed attempted to control the Office of the Liberation Movements in order to direct it toward the general policies of the government.[100] Rafsanjani's memoirs of the same period shed some light into publications of the Office of the Liberation Movements. According to Rafsanjani, the Office of the Liberation Movements had prepared pamphlets on "the movement of Muslims in the Philippines and the movement of Northern Ireland [the Irish National Army]"[101] and "the Eritrean Movement and the Muslim Brotherhood [of Egypt], which according to the Liberation Movements unit of the Guards are dominated by the Westernizers."[102]

On March 10, 1982, Bahrain's Liberation Movement demonstrated in front of the Iranian parliament as a protest against the trial of seventy-three Bahraini Shia allegedly involved in a coup attempt against the Sunni rulers of the island.[103] The fact that the Islamic Republic allowed such a group to operate in Iran demonstrates the willingness of the regime to intimidate the Persian Gulf monarchies with expatriate groups hostile to their governments.

By June 1982 the Islamic Republic attempted in a more organized manner to unite the Iraqi Shia groups living inside Iran. The Iraqi groups were organized under Mohammad-Ali Hadi Najaf-Abadi, and by June 2, 1982, Rafsanjani and the rest of the Iranian leadership had decided to appoint Mohammad-Baqer Hakim as their spokesman.[104]

8.4.3. Exporting the Revolution 1982–1988

8.4.3.1. Continuation of the war On May 24, 1982, Iran liberated the city of Khorramshahr, ending the Iraqi occupation of the city.[105] But the liberation of Khorramshahr did not end the war with Iraq. The question is why the Islamic Republic leadership chose to continue the war on Iraqi soil after the liberation of Iranian territories. This author considers the continuation of the war with Iraq after May 24, 1982, as the main component of the policy of the export of the revolution at that time. But which bureaucratic institutions pressed for continuation of the war after the liberation of Khorramshahr, and who was to benefit from continuing the war?

Ahmad Khomeini was one of the first senior Islamic Republic authorities to disclose the secret behind the continuation of the war beyond Khorramshahr. In his September 22, 1991, interview with *Payam-e Enqelab*, Ahmad Khomeini said:

> Concerning the issues of Khorramshahr the Imam [Grand Ayatollah Khomeini] believed that it was better to end the war, but those responsible for the war said that we must move toward Shat al-Arab [Arvand-Roud] so that we can demand war reparations from Iraq. The Imam did not at all agree with this issue and used to say that if you want to continue the war, know that should the war continue in the situation that you have now and should you not succeed this war will not come to an end. We must continue this war to a certain point. Now that the…liberation of Khorramshahr has occurred, it is the best time to end the war.[106]

The second high-ranking individual disclosing Grand Ayatollah Khomeini's opposition to the continuation of the war after the liberation of Khorramshahr was Grand Ayatollah Hossein-Ali Montazeri. In his memoirs, Grand Ayatollah Montazeri wrote that "according to one account the Imam himself was inclined to end the war, but those who supported continuation of the war imposed their viewpoint upon him."[107] Grand Ayatollah Montazeri's account of Grand Ayatollah Khomeini's preference seems credible, but when Montazeri's family connections and network and their careers are taken into consideration, it seems highly unlikely that Grand Ayatollah Montazeri himself would have been opposed to continuing the war after the liberation of Khorramshahr.[108] There is also some disagreement among the sources about Grand Ayatollah Montazeri's position with regard to continuation of the war on Iraqi soil. While Grand Ayatollah Montazeri himself claimed to have been opposed to the continuation of the war, Rafsanjani claimed that on May 8, 1982, Grand Ayatollah Montazeri called him and proposed "immediate entrance onto Iraqi soil in order to topple Saddam."[109]

But who were the supporters of the continuation of the war? Rafsanjani's memoirs provide the answer to this question. In his notes on April 18, 1982, Rafsanjani wrote: "The warlike atmosphere of the country and the high expectations of the people and especially the combatants is such that they ridicule such propositions [of peace negotiations] and they do not consider immediate but conditional withdrawal enough and criticize those responsible for the war effort for not immediately entering Iraqi soil."[110] However, consistent with the accounts of Ahmad Khomeini and Grand Ayatollah Montazeri, Rafsanjani's account stressed that Grand Ayatollah Khomeini was opposed to the continuation of the war on Iraqi soil. According to Rafsanjani, Grand Ayatollah Khomeini conveyed his opposition to him through Ahmad Khomeini on March 26, 1982,[111] and at a meeting with military commanders on June 10, 1982.[112] According to Rafsanjani, the military commanders managed to "persuade the Imam" to allow them to enter Iraqi soil in unpopulated or thinly populated areas.[113] Rafsanjani repeated the same account in his conversation with political analyst Sadeq Zibakalam, but also added the arguments Grand Ayatollah Khomeini used—to no avail—against the continuation of the war:

1. After [we enter] Iraqi soil, Arab countries will support Iraq more overtly and will display Arab extremism. 2. The people of Iraq have not supported Saddam until now because Saddam was on our soil. But should we enter Iraqi soil, the people will support [him], and we should not make the people of Iraq oppose us. 3. If we enter Iraqi soil the people will be harmed. In war, the people of Iraq who have not fought us should not

be harmed. 4. Also, the world will present us as invaders and will subject us to propaganda pressure.[114]

These sources show that by May 1982, Grand Ayatollah Khomeini had developed a degree of political maturity that was a world apart from the radicalism he displayed during the first months after the revolution. However, his restraint was of no avail faced with the will of the IRGC to continue the war. Thanks to the war, the IRGC had managed to expand its force from a few thousand undisciplined revolutionaries into the most important security, military, and even political force in the Islamic Republic. This development would not have been possible had it not been for the continuation of the war with Iraq. In this case, the IRGC sacrificed Iran's national interest and hundreds of thousands of Iranian lives for the sake of its expansionist organizational interests.

8.4.3.2. Export of the revolution beyond the war with Iraq Continuation of the war against Iraq did not mean the end of support to foreign terrorist organizations. On the contrary, by 1982 the IRGC increased its presence in Lebanon and helped establish, armed, and supported the Lebanese Hezbollah in an attempt to establish an Islamic state in Lebanon. Apart from military activities, the IRGC also played a political role in Lebanon's Bekaa Valley, proselytizing among the local population and establishing schools, hospitals, mosques, and welfare organizations, thereby creating support for the Islamic revolution and generating recruits for Hezbollah.

As before, the export of the revolution permanently suffered from the lack of coordination among the various bureaucratic organizations of the Islamic Republic. In his conversation with Rafsanjani, Asghar Sabaghian reported on his meetings with the Afghan fighters engaged in the struggle against the Soviet occupation, but the issue is not discussed in Rafsanjani's memoirs.[115] One point of conflict seems to have been the conflict between the Foreign Ministry of the Islamic Republic and the Liberation Movements unit, and Rafsanjani's notes from February 11, 1982, also reflected then Foreign Minister Ali Akbar Velayati's complaints about signals sent by the Office of the Liberation Movements and the Arabic-language journals and weeklies that deviated from the line of the Foreign Ministry.[116] On May 18, 1982, Rafsanjani recorded a meeting with Mehdi Hashemi, who was "distressed about the weakening of his professional position. I told him to wait until the Parliament clarifies the legal relationship between the [Liberation Movements] unit [and] other state organs. For the time being this unit operates under the Guards."[117] Such internal divisions among the revolutionary elites led to a lack of top-level coordination of the policy, but never stopped the export of the revolution.

Efforts to export the revolution to Lebanon suffered from similar disagreements among the civilian leadership. By 1982 Grand Ayatollah Khomeini seems to have become more concerned about the consequences of the policy of exporting the revolution. At the June 22, 1982, meeting of the Supreme Defense Council, Grand Ayatollah Khomeini ordered the IRGC not to expedite forces to Lebanon,[118] a message that he once again communicated to Rafsanjani through his son Ahmad on June 23, 1982.[119] Again, on June 25, 1982, Ahmad Khomeini told Rafsanjani that his father was against deploying forces to Lebanon.[120] When Rafsanjani and Khamenei sought the counsel of Grand Ayatollah Khomeini on June 26, 1982, Grand Ayatollah Khomeini explained that "the Arabs will not put up a serious fight, and our involvement [in a war with Israel] would weaken the effort in the front against Iraq and [there is the risk of] not achieving anything. Finally it was decided that if Syria engages in a serious war we should participate."[121]

Grand Ayatollah Khomeini's fear that increased engagement in Lebanon would weaken the war effort against Iraq must have prevailed since there is no record of the IRGC forces' being engaged in direct clashes with Israeli forces, yet *Payam-e Enqelab* reported that the Revolutionary Guards trained Lebanese forces in the three dimensions of "military training, ideology and politics."[122]

However, the units engaged in the export of the revolution seem to have pressed the leadership in Tehran for an increased IRGC presence in Lebanon. On August 27, 1982, in the Office of the Liberation Movements, some of the members of the corps sought the counsel of Rafsanjani and complained about Hashemi.[123] Another delegation from the Liberation Movements against Hashemi met with Rafsanjani on September 19, 1982.[124] By September 9, 1982, as Rafsanjani's memoirs disclosed, Hashemi himself was concerned about "lack of discipline" among his forces, and Rafsanjani urged him to cooperate with the Foreign Ministry.[125] Rafsanjani spent a great deal of time on the Lebanon portfolio, holding regular meetings with the IRGC commander in Lebanon, an example of which is the meeting on September 22, 1982.[126] The October 11, 1982, meeting of the Lebanese AMAL leaders with Rafsanjani also revealed that the Islamic Republic and the IRGC were shifting their support to Hezbollah, thereby abandoning AMAL.[127]

The Islamic Republic's engagements in Lebanon had already sown the seeds of terror, and on November 11, 1982, in an attack that marked the first case of suicide terrorism in Lebanon, seventeen-year-old Ahmad Qassir plowed his car into a building that served as a major headquarters for the Israeli army in southern Lebanon.[128] An unknown group that called itself the Armed Struggle Organization claimed responsibility, but Hezbollah later boasted of the operation as its first "martyrdom" operation.

Shortly after the attack, on November 17, 1982, the Supreme Council of the Islamic Revolution in Iraq, based in Iran and headed by Mohammad-Baqer Hakim, was established with Iranian support.[129] On December 30, 1982, the Iranian support for "Islamic movements" passed the Iranian parliament, and Iran became an official sponsor of terrorist activities in Iraq with the clear aim of toppling Saddam Hussein's regime.[130] In other words, the war effort against Iraq did not diminish the export of the revolution. Instead, the war effort made the export of the revolution more organized.

On January 1, 1983, the Supreme Defense Council convened in Grand Ayatollah Khomeini's office, where Lebanon was the primary topic of discussion: "A report was presented on the training of the people of Lebanon and it was decided that we should continue our help."[131] On April 17, 1983, the Islamic Republic's continued "help" was translated into the bombing of the American embassy in Beirut, which killed sixty-three people, including seventeen American citizens.[132]

On June 12, 1983, Rafsanjani noted in his memoirs: "The gentlemen Mohsen Rezaei and Rahim Safavi [who according to Rafsanjani had just returned to Iran from Lebanon] came and complained about opaque obligations of the Guards, which is disheartening."[133] In his notes on June 16, 1983, Rafsanjani further commented on a meeting in President Khamenei's office during which the Liberation Movements were discussed.[134] What was the reason behind the increased interest in the activities of the Office of the Liberation Movements? According to U.S. government historian David Crist, Husayn al-Musawi, leader of AMAL, and Imad Mughniyah, head of the Islamic Jihad Organization, met with their IRGC superiors on June 27, 1983, and were "placed under the direct control of Iranian [Revolutionary Guards] officers,"[135] which may explain the increased interest of Rafsanjani, Khamenei, and the IRGC officers in the activities of the Office of the Liberation Movements in the weeks and days prior to the event.

Terrorism against U.S. targets in Lebanon continued. On August 3, 1983, Rafsanjani, an unnamed IRGC commander who had just returned from Lebanon, and Ali-Akbar Mohtashami-Pour met to discuss Iranian strategy in Lebanon.[136] Something was in the making. According to David Crist's study of U.S. government archives, on September 1, 1983, a Revolutionary Guards officer met with Husayn al-Musawi to discuss a "special target."[137] On September 8, 1983, Rafsanjani discussed the latest developments in Lebanon with Mohtashami-Pour and decided "to call the authorities for a meeting,"[138] which could be an evaluation of the conversation between the IRGC officer and Husayn al-Musawi about the "special target." And on September 11, 1983, a certain Sobhi Tofeili of the "Lebanese Council" of Hezbollah complained to Rafsanjani about Mohtashami-Pour's "conservatism" in Lebanon.[139] On September 22, 1983, Husayn al-Musawi's relative Abu-Haydan al-Musawi drove to Damascus to further discuss the Islamic Republic's ambassador Mohtashami-Pour, who encouraged al-Musawi to continue with the plans.[140] On October 23, 1983, a truck loaded with explosives drove into the U.S. Marine barracks, killing 241 American servicemen.[141]

In his entry of October 6, 1983, Rafsanjani noted that Grand Ayatollah Montazeri formally asked Rafsanjani to keep a certain Mr. Kanani as the IRGC chief in Lebanon,[142] and on November 19, 1983,[143] Rafsanjani mentioned the burial of "thirteen of our martyrs from Lebanon," who may have been killed in the retaliatory Israeli bombing of the Nabi Chit base in Lebanon.[144]

Having proven his usefulness in Lebanon, Imad Mughniyah also served as the punishing hand of the Islamic Republic against Kuwait, which, fearing the revolutionary regime in Tehran, had provided financial support to Iraq since the beginning of the Iran-Iraq war. Within two weeks, numerous consecutive bombings rocked the small nation. Some twenty-five individuals were involved in the planning and execution of the attacks on December 12, 1983, yet Mughniyah and a man named Mostafa Badr Al Din played the most violent and important roles.[145]

Badr Al Din utilized his extensive training and Mughniyah's military expertise to lay bombs at the American and French embassies, a Raytheon compound, the control towers of the international airport, the Shuiba industrial center, and the Ministry of Electricity and Water.[146] A truck laden with forty-five large cylinders of gas connected to plastic explosives broke through the front gates of the American embassy in Kuwait City and rammed into the embassy's three-story administrative annex, demolishing half the structure. Five other explosives were attempted within an hour. An hour later, a car parked outside the French embassy blew up, leaving a massive thirty-foot hole in the embassy's security wall.

The twenty-five individuals who were involved in the execution of these extended attacks on Kuwait included seventeen Iraqis from the al-Dawa party, three Lebanese, two Bedouins, and three Kuwaitis.[147] Of the seventeen Iraqis, the most notable figure was Jamal Jaafar Mohammad, who is now in the Iraqi parliament as a part of Nouri al-Malaki's al-Dawa party.[148] An American military probe revealed a continued relationship between the Iraqi politicians and the Islamic Republic, and support of Shia militias throughout the country.[149] Twenty-five youths were rounded up by Kuwaiti authorities, including Badr Al Din. Three men were sentenced to death in absentia, seven to life imprisonment, and seven to terms of five to fifteen years; five men were found not guilty. Badr Al Din was sentenced to life in prison.[150]

What was the purpose of this wave of Iranian-sponsored terror in the region? Rafsanjani's notes of February 14, 1984, are quite interesting in disclosing the strategic calculations of the Iranian leadership. A campaign of suicide bombings had inflicted serious blows to the U.S., French, and Israeli forces: "Interventionist forces in Lebanon are defeated and withdrawing as the Muslims have occupied West Beirut. This is one of the scandalous defeats of the United States and Israel and among the important conquests of the Islamic people."[151] Also, Prime Minister Mir-Hossein Mousavi praised the establishment of "an international front of the oppressed" and continued: "We must remember that our weapon in foreign policy is not the respect of the great powers toward us, but the backing of the innocent and dispossessed nations. Therefore, we must, more than ever before, rely upon the foreign policy of the Islamic combatants. It seems that using the thoughts of the likes of martyr Mohammad Montazeri regarding the export of the revolution is today necessary."[152] On February 15, 1984, Israel retaliated with an assassination attempt on the life of Mohtashami-Pour, the Iranian ambassador to Syria.[153]

Rafsanjani's repeated references to his unhappiness with the conduct of the IRGC and in particular the Office of the Liberation Movements paved the way for his attacks against Grand Ayatollah Montazeri. Rather than taking a direct aim at Grand Ayatollah Montazeri, Rafsanjani directed his attacks against Grand Ayatollah Montazeri's family members who were involved in the Office of the Liberation Movements, particularly Mehdi Hashemi and his brother Hadi Hashemi.

There was also an external reason behind Rafsanjani's attacks against Grand Ayatollah Montazeri and the network of the export of the revolution. In the mid-1980s, the Iranian leadership felt it important to project an impression of pragmatism in its foreign relations. The government tried to rein in extragovernmental bodies such as that of Hashemi and to reach out to former adversaries, including the United States. Hashemi and his followers grew frustrated with what they saw as the Iranian leadership's betrayal of its hard-line principles. To retaliate, they leaked word of the secret contacts between the Reagan administration and Rafsanjani, an episode that developed into the Iran-Contra affair.[154] Arrested by Iranian security in 1986 after the leak, Hashemi and forty followers each "confessed" to a long list of crimes. On September 28, 1987, Hashemi was executed. Hashemi's execution was an integral part of a plot to bring down Grand Ayatollah Montazeri by Ahmad Khomeini and Rafsanjani.

Rahim Safavi later claimed that Hashemi "with the cooperation of groups sharing his views did whatever he pleased and upon his own decision he would train the forces and without coordinating with the central IRGC headquarters would expedite forces to Afghanistan, Lebanon, Syria and other places."[155] Safavi claimed that Hashemi's actions were possible only because of "support of the Montazeri household and the vast network he commanded in Isfahan" and that Hashemi "acted like an independent actor within the body of the Guards."[156] This explanation may be only partially true, because the system tolerated and supported the likes of Rafsanjani, and the former Mohammad Montazeri protégé Rahim Safavi needed to distance himself from the Montazeri household. Furthermore, the Islamic Republic was also interested in distancing itself from the issues that caused the greatest challenges in the foreign policy of the Islamic Republic, those related to the export of the revolution.

By October 1985 the Islamic Republic moderated its policy on the export of the revolution in Lebanon, and Rafsanjani's memoirs reveal that the Lebanese Hezbollah Central Committee visited Tehran to complain about the "return of Hojjat al-Eslam Ali-Akbar Mohtashami-Pour to Iran, [the] lack of IRGC cooperation in Lebanon and insufficient funding."[157] According to Rafsanjani, the Hezbollah Central Committee members even handed over their resignations to Rafsanjani, who persuaded them to return to their positions and provided them with "ten thousand dollars from Kuwait collected for support of their cause."[158] But by March 21, 1986, the Islamic Republic actively mobilized the Iraqi refugees to Iran, organized within the Revolutionary Guards in the war against Iraq.[159]

Rafsanjani's memoirs also reflected that the deal between Iran and the United States involving U.S. spare parts and arms in exchange for Western hostages, later referred to as the Iran-Contra affair, was authorized by Khomeini. In his March 25, 1986, memoirs, Rafsanjani wrote: "I reported [to Khomeini] in continuity with earlier reports with regard to indirect negotiations with the Americans to help free American hostages in Lebanon in return for receiving military possibilities. With regard to the second issue he agrees and orders caution."[160] Rafsanjani implicated not only Khomeini in the secret hostages-for-arms deal with the United States but also the heads of the armed forces of the Islamic Republic, and in his entry of April 2, 1986, he noted that in Khamenei's home, the foreign minister of Oman, who also carried a secret message from the United States, was discussed, but it was decided that the secret negotiations with the United States should continue with engagement of Revolutionary Guards member Mohsen Kangarlou and the IRGC Intelligence Bureau chief, Ahmad Vahidi.[161]

Rafsanjani's memoirs from the later phase of the Iran-Iraq war also included internal problems with the Iraqi Shia organized in Iran. Mohammad-Baqer Hakim, head of the Supreme Council of the Islamic

Revolution in Iraq, allegedly visited Rafsanjani on April 5, 1986, and expressed "deep dissatisfaction" with the Iraq Committee of the President's Office.[162] The Iraq Committee was composed of Mohammad Khatami, Mohammad-Ali Hadi Najaf-Abadi, and Sabbah Zangeneh and was tasked with planning Iraq's future and organizing the cooperation of Iraqi groups in Iran.[163] Rafsanjani also disclosed that Hojjat al-Eslam Ahmad Salek was the person who reported to him with regard to the activities of the Supreme Council of the Islamic Revolution in Iraq, and that the activities of the council were to be directed from Khatam Base of the Revolutionary Guards.[164] On August 27, 1986, Salek discussed some managerial problems with regard to the Iraq portfolio: Grand Ayatollah Montazeri had established a three-man group to direct activities of the Supreme Council of Islamic Revolution in Iraq and other Islamic Iraqi forces, but Khamenei also intervened in the Iraq affairs, thereby creating friction in the line of command.[165] Salek's involvement in the Iraq portfolio in turn signifies that Salek most likely was close to Grand Ayatollah Montazeri and the entire establishment involved in the export of the revolution. Two other individuals involved in the leadership of the IRGC Quds Force at the time were Ahmad Vahidi and Fereydoun Mehdinezhad, who was also known as Verdinezhad.[166]

Rafsanjani did not even hide his happiness about the delivery of American missiles to Iran in his memoirs of August 4, 1986, saying: "At last we managed to humiliate Reagan. Despite their slogans that they will not pay ransom to hostage takers he paid an important ransom. Receiving missiles from an enemy like America is an important issue. We owe this to the holy struggle of the Muslims in Lebanon."[167]

However, the late 1980s also produced a number of setbacks for the Islamic Republic's attempts at exporting the revolution. The disastrous 1987 pilgrimage to Mecca led by Hojjat al-Eslam Mehdi Karrubi provides an interesting case. The Revolutionary Guards planted arms in the luggage of hundreds of Iranian pilgrims in order to instigate unrest in Mecca, which ended with the massacre of Iranian pilgrims at the hands of Saudi authorities. According to Grand Ayatollah Montazeri, "one of the six Guards members in charge of the wrong affair came to me and said that the authorities in the Guards want me to say that this was done on behalf of Seyyed Mehdi Hashemi, and they are spreading the same rumor in the parliament, the cabinet and other places."[168] Grand Ayatollah Montazeri charged: "They commit[ted] this mistake in the Guards, did away with our honor but no one prosecutes them, and Mr. Hassani and Mehdi Hashemi must be prosecuted and punished?"[169] Of course, Mehdi Hashemi had nothing to do with the pilgrimage disaster, and it was the rest of the IRGC organization who was to blame.

8.4.3.3. Ending the war with Iraq Following major setbacks in the war, the Islamic Republic leadership accepted United Nations Security Council Resolution 598, and on August 20, 1988, Iran and Iraq agreed to a ceasefire. Grand Ayatollah Khomeini described acceptance of the ceasefire agreement as being "more deadly than poison," but he assumed complete responsibility for the decision.[170] But what made Grand Ayatollah Khomeini drink from the chalice of poison?

According to Rafsanjani, who was appointed deputy commander in chief on June 3, 1988, the heads of state—meaning Rafsanjani himself, Judiciary Chief Ayatollah Mousavi Ardebili, President Ali Khamenei, Ahmad Khomeini, and Prime Minister Mir-Hossein Mousavi—knew that "they will not allow us to win in the war."[171] Operating under such difficult circumstances, coupled with the U.S. downing of an Iranian airliner, Rafsanjani was fortunate enough to face new demands from IRGC chief Mohsen Rezaei. According to Rafsanjani, toward the end of the war, Rezaei approached Rafsanjani with "a strange list" of military demands in order to continue the war effort.[172] Rafsanjani told Rezaei that he was incapable of providing for such needs and recommended that he write the demands in a letter to Grand Ayatollah Khomeini.[173] The letter, which was written sometime before July 16, 1988, and was first disclosed to the public in 2001 by Grand Ayatollah Montazeri, showed that Rezaei had confessed that there would be no victory in the next five years unless almost unlimited resources were directed to the IRGC and the regular military, Iran developed a nuclear bomb, and Iran managed to force the United States to leave the Persian Gulf.[174] Rezaei's letter was quoted in Grand Ayatollah Khomeini's secret letter to the clerical establishment, which was asked to prepare the public for Iran's acceptance of the end of the war with Iraq. Had it not been for Rafsanjani's manipulation of Rezaei, Grand Ayatollah Khomeini would not have discovered the dire reality of the war, which could not have been won without the unlimited resources requested by the IRGC.

8.4.4. Exporting the Revolution 1988–2003 The end of the war with Iraq did not mean an end to the ambitions of the Revolutionary Guards to continue the export of the revolution. The bureaucracy of the Guards was ready for any opportunity to prove its usefulness to the political leadership. The political leadership, too, saw some reason in keeping the export of the revolution alive. With the war behind him, Rafsanjani, discussing the rationale of the Iraqi invasion of Iran as a way of containing the Iranian revolution,[175] noted that the war also led to improvement of the Iranian forces,[176] and he even claimed that the Afghan resistance and "the resistance in Lebanon [were] due to the self-confidence of our troops."[177] Remarkably, Rafsanjani's statements addressed not only the past but also the future:

> In the great epic of Lebanon in which some countries of the world have deployed troops, there is only one breathing and moving organism, which is the forces that have their roots in the war of the Iranian nation against infidels, and they hope that as soon as we are free of our problems the Basij, the Guards and the Army [will] preserve its cohesion, after which we will become a central axis in the region and prepare for our future moves.[178]

The war in Bosnia provided the Islamic Republic with another opportunity to attempt to export the revolution abroad, this time to the European continent. The Islamic Republic engaged in political, economic, and military support of Bosnia, and three Iranians expedited to Bosnia lost their lives there. Led by Ayatollah Ahmad Jannati, who represented Supreme Leader Ali Khamenei in Bosnian affairs, the IRGC, along with the Imam Khomeini Relief Committee, engaged in arming and training the Bosnian partisans and gathering popular support.[179] According to some sources, Commander Mohammad-Reza Naqdi and Hossein Allah-Karam directed the Islamic Republic's activities in Bosnia within the framework of the Quds Force of the IRGC. The IRGC provided military training to the Bosnian Muslims within the organizational framework of a Mojahedin organization,[180] and the Islamic Republic authorities later admitted their involvement in the export of weapons to Bosnia during the war.[181] It was only after the Dayton peace agreement that the involvement of all the military forces, including Iran's military engagement, came to an end. The Islamic Republic tried hard to preserve its position in Bosnia after the war but does not seem to have had much success.

Despite the setbacks, the Islamic Republic did not entirely give up on Bosnia. During the Ahmadinejad presidency, Allah-Karam was sent to Bosnia, this time as a military attaché. The Islamic Republic also started a Bosnian-language radio station that is still in operation, as is Iran's Sahar Television Station, which broadcasts programs in Bosnian. Iran's radio and television broadcasts add a cultural dimension to the Revolutionary Guards' military export of the revolution to Bosnia. The military and cultural dimensions in turn were complemented by the social dimension added through the work of the Imam Khomeini Relief Committee, which still is active in charitable activities in Bosnia.[182]

The Islamic Republic's competition with Saudi Arabia also paved the way for a major terrorist attack on Saudi soil. After years of patient preparation, a terrorist group called Saudi Hezbollah, the armed wing of which was led by a certain Ahmed al-Mughassil, bombed the Khobar Towers complex in Dhahran on June 25, 1996, killing nineteen American servicemen and wounding many more.[183]

8.4.5. Exporting the Revolution since 2003 Ever since the U.S.-led invasions of Afghanistan and particularly Iraq, Major General Qassem Suleimani has emerged as the face of the Islamic Republic's attempts at exporting its revolution abroad.[184] As commander of Iran's external operations arm, Suleimani is primarily responsible for Iran's covert operations outside of the country's borders. Since 2003, his efforts have largely been consumed by overseeing Iran's support of its surrogate groups in Iraq. Quoting Coalition sources, military historian Kimberly Kagan writes that by August 2007, "Iranian-backed violence account[ed] for roughly half the attacks on Coalition forces."[185]

During a question-and-answer session at the Pentagon in July 2011, the chairman of the Joint Chiefs of Staff, Admiral Mike Mullen, discussed

Iran's actions in Iraq. "Iran is very directly supporting extremist Shia groups [in Iraq], which are killing our troops. ...They are shipping high-tech weapons in there [improvised rocket-assisted munitions and enhanced explosive penetrators]—which are killing our people and the forensics prove that," Mullen said.[186]

While Suleimani and the Quds Force of the IRGC dismiss any involvement in terrorist activities, the Quds Force commander almost boasts of his influence in Lebanon, Iraq, and the rest of the Arabian Gulf region. "You should know that I...control the policy for Iran with respect to Iraq, Lebanon, Gaza and Afghanistan," penned Suleimani in a 2008 message to General David Petraeus, then the commanding general of the Multi-National Force–Iraq.[187]

Neither Suleimani's nor the Quds Force's ties to terrorism are new. The Quds Force has been linked to a number of attacks since the 1990s, including strikes on the Israeli Embassy (1992) and a Jewish community center (1994) in Argentina, as well as the 1996 Khobar Towers attack in Saudi Arabia. While these attacks occurred under Suleimani's predecessor's watch, he has expanded the organization's capabilities to strike its enemies anywhere in the world.

On October 25, 2007, the U.S. Department of the Treasury designated Suleimani "the conduit for Iranian material support to the GID [Syrian General Intelligence Directorate]."[188] Separately, the Treasury cited the Quds Force for "providing lethal support in the form of weapons, training, funding, and guidance to select groups of Iraqi Shi'a militants who target and kill Coalition and Iraqi forces and innocent Iraqi civilians."[189]

Suleimani considered the U.S.-led invasion of Iraq a mixed blessing for the Islamic Republic. On the one hand, the United States was getting rid of a brutal dictator in Saddam Hussein, who had killed thousands of Iranians during the eight-year Iran-Iraq war, but now the United States had thousands of soldiers stationed across the border from Iran. In the words of Brigadier General Mohammad-Ali Rahmani, former commander of the Ramezan Base of the Quds Force (located in northwestern Iran close to the Iraqi border), the invasion "did away with a real menace... [but] the Ba'ath party rule in Iraq was replaced with the US Army. Despite providing some opportunities, their regional presence constitutes a real threat."[190] Iran's central government was concerned that the United

States, which had already toppled the Taliban in Afghanistan, would set its sights on regime change in Iran after leaving Iraq.

To deter the United States from engaging in military actions against the Islamic Republic, Suleimani tasked his men with recruiting Iraqi militant groups to confront foreign troops operating inside Iraq. These Iranian-backed militant groups, referred to as Iran's "Special Groups," received training, weapons, and money from Tehran that were used to attack Coalition forces inside Iraq. Quoting unnamed U.S. military officials, Kagan writes that the Quds Force has provided equipment and funding worth between $750,000 and $3 million in U.S. dollars to the Special Groups every month since 2003.[191]

In addition to operations in Iraq, Suleimani has approved Iranian operations against Israeli interests for their perceived role in a number of attacks against Iranian nuclear scientists. Since 2011, the Quds Force of the IRGC attempted multiple attacks against Israeli diplomats in Azerbaijan, Turkey, Thailand, Georgia, and India. And, if these plots were not aggressive enough, Suleimani likely approved the operation to assassinate the Saudi ambassador to the United States in Washington, DC.

Suleimani clearly considers the Arab Spring as an opportunity to export the revolution. Addressing students at the Haqqani Theological Seminary in Qom on May 22, 2011, Suleimani declared that the social revolutions in the Middle East and North Africa "provide our revolution with the greatest opportunities." He continued, "Today, Iran's victory or defeat no longer takes place in Mehran and Khorramshahr. Our boundaries have expanded and we must witness victory in Egypt, Iraq, Lebanon, and Syria. This is the fruit of the Islamic revolution."[192] Suleimani's words were reminiscent of the late Hojjat al-Eslam Mohammad Montazeri, former chief of the Office of the Liberation Movements of the IRGC, who believed that "keeping the enemy busy abroad" by means of exporting the revolution was the most effective method for "keeping the enemy away from Iran's borders."[193]

In addition to overseeing Iran's terrorist operations, Suleimani ultimately manages the regime's relations with its surrogates, chief among which is the Lebanese Hezbollah, which Tehran helped to establish in the early 1980s. Hezbollah has proven to be a tremendous asset for Iran over the years, but Suleimani also knows the danger a rogue militant group can cause for Tehran, which may explain why Suleimani has to spend more of his energy keeping Iran's most important ally in line.

Suleimani is widely believed to have a close relationship with Hezbollah General Secretary Sheikh Hassan Nasrallah. However, the bond between the two leaders seems to have been damaged by Hezbollah's growing sense of independence. While the two normally hide their disagreements from the public, a report describing a discussion between Suleimani and Nasrallah provided a rare glimpse into the complex relationship between the Quds Force and Hezbollah. According to a Botia News report on May 16, 2012, Suleimani warned Nasrallah against engaging in "any pre-emptive strike against the Zionist regime."[194] Suleimani demanded: "The authority of those who believe in preemptive strikes against the Zionist regime must be restricted."[195] Suleimani also warned Hezbollah against overestimating its own capabilities: "[Your] arms and preparedness to destroy Tel Aviv and even your capacity to engage in continuous strikes against Eilat in southern-occupied Palestine should not make you proud."[196]

Referring to the 2006 war in Lebanon, which Hezbollah is believed to have provoked without authorization from Tehran, Suleimani warned Nasrallah: "Hezbollah's victory in the thirty-three-day war was not because of the power of the weapons but because of the power of faith and divine help."[197] Sticking with the theme of belief in God, Suleimani also referred to Khamenei's new-year address on March 21, 2012: "God guarantees victory of the believers when we are defenders. If we start [a war], the Quran does not guarantee our victory."[198]

Suleimani ended his conversation with Nasrallah by saying:

> Today, the Zionist regime is in total isolation and is facing a serious legitimacy crisis. Any attack would depict them as victims and us as unjust aggressors, which would mobilize the public sympathy for them. This would harm us. ...The claim that in order to relieve Syria of crisis one must create another crisis for the Zionist regime is false and serves as an excuse to prove extremist viewpoints. ...In order to liberate the Al-Aqsa mosque one must stress awakening the people rather than relying on arms.[199]

The report, which can be interpreted as a reaction to Nasrallah's television address of May 11, 2012, in which the Hezbollah leader threatened to annihilate Israel, may indicate that Suleimani believes Israel is waiting for the right moment to strike Iran's nuclear facilities. Suleimani may also fear that the slightest movement by Hezbollah against Israel—in an attempt to divert attention from Syria—could be used by Israel as a pretext to attack Iran. Still, the report reflects a general unhappiness on Suleimani's part with Hezbollah's growing independence and the fact that Hezbollah blatantly ignored Khamenei's new-year message.

8.5. Conclusion: Practical Benefits of the Export of the Revolution for the IRGC

Thirty-three years after the revolution in Iran and the establishment of the Islamic Republic, the desire to export the revolution remains a permanent feature in the foreign and security policy of the regime. The annual Quds [Jerusalem] Day rallies against Israel all over the globe and the regime's rhetorical, logistical, financial, and sometimes armed support to revolutionary movements and terrorist groups should therefore be seen in a broader context of the revolutionary doctrine rather than as the result of a case-by-case cost-benefit analysis that the regime may or may not have contemplated prior to such activities.

There are practical reasons for the longevity of the "export of the revolution" doctrine. In Grand Ayatollah Khomeini's ideal model, external conflict and permanent preparedness would have created the necessary conditions for his monopolization of power inside Iran as well as for broadening Iran's sphere of influence abroad. However, in the longer term, the permanent state of crisis maintained in the Islamic Republic for the past three decades has led to a degree of militarization that ultimately strengthened the IRGC, the very agent tasked with the export of the revolution.

In the immediate aftermath of the revolution, central figures in the early leadership of the Guards seemed to have reached the conclusion that the survival of the revolution inside Iran was not possible without the export of the revolution. Ultimately the opposite proved to be true: Rather than deterring foreign powers from invading Iran, the Islamic

Republic's attempts at exporting the revolution managed to mobilize the entire world against the nascent regime in Tehran. The world revolutionary network to which the IRGC leadership of the time belonged also provided them with real opportunities to attempt to export the revolution beyond the borders of Iran. What the IRGC leadership failed to realize was that foreign revolutionaries desired Iranian support for their own ends and not in order to achieve higher ideals. By answering the call of the "oppressed," the Islamic Republic found itself entangled in multiple international conflicts. Finally, the IRGC leadership realized that the policy of the export of the revolution, with all the hazards it entailed, served the corporate interests of the Guards.

As Iran became engaged in foreign conflicts, the IRGC's political importance and share of the national budget increased, which further motivated the Revolutionary Guards to continue the export of the revolution as a means of strengthening its own position in the struggle for power within the Islamic Republic. The IRGC commanders' wish to continue the war with Iraq after liberation of Khorramshahr in 1982, the engagements of the Quds Force of the IRGC in Bosnia contrary to Rafsanjani's diplomatic opening to the world, the bombing of the Khobar Towers in Saudi Arabia at a time when diplomatic relations with Saudi Arabia had improved, and the plot to kill the Saudi ambassador to Washington may indicate that the Revolutionary Guards and other bureaucracies that engaged in the export of the revolution did so to advance their corporate interests rather than the interests of the Iranian state.

As the Islamic Republic faces adversaries actively engaged in diminishing Iran's nuclear capabilities by the means of cyber warfare and assassination of nuclear scientists, Iran's negotiations with the international community concerning the Islamic Republic's nuclear program seem to have reached an impasse; and as Iran's regional rivals are engaged in subversion against Tehran's longtime ally in Damascus, the regime in Tehran is in ever greater need of the Quds Force of the IRGC. In reality, budgetary limits do not leave any other option for the regime in Tehran but the use of asymmetric warfare. However, as the unsuccessful operations in Washington, DC, the Caucasus, and Asia indicate, even asymmetric operations have become more difficult for the Quds Force of the IRGC to conduct, which must necessarily lead to Tehran's reforming of the agencies involved in such operations. After all, the failed attempt of the Islamic Republic to gain a foothold in Bosnia and the rise of the Taliban threat from Afghanistan made the regime replace Vahidi, the former IRGC Intelligence Bureau chief, with Suleimani as the head of the Quds Force of the IRGC in order to reform the organization and gear it toward the Afghan threat. Only time will show if the regime acts in time to replace Suleimani with another commander capable of reorienting the activities of the Quds Force of the IRGC to the challenges of today. What one can count on is the Revolutionary Guards' continued support for the policy of export of the revolution.

Notes

1. Rouhollah Khomeini, *Islam and Revolution: Writings and Declarations of Imam Khomeini*, trans. Hamid Algar (Berkeley, CA: Mizan Press, 1981), pp. 9, 25.

2. "The Constitution of the Islamic Republic of Iran," Iran Chamber Society website (Tehran), n.d. Available at http://www.iranchamber.com/government/laws/constitution.php (accessed October 12, 2010).

3. Karl Marx and Friedrich Engels, *Marx/Engels Selected Works*, vol. 1 (Moscow: Progress Publishers, 1969), pp. 98–137. Available at http://www.marxists.org/archive/marx/works/1848/communist-manifesto/index.htm (accessed November 1, 2010).

4. Khomeini, *Islam and Revolution*, p. 27.

5. Ibid.

6. Ibid., p. 28.

7. Ibid., pp. 28, 35.

8. Friedrich Engels, *The Principles of Communism*, in Marx and Engels, *Selected Works*, vol. 1, pp. 81–97.

9. Khomeini, *Islam and Revolution*, p. 48.

10. Ibid., pp. 48–49.

11. Ibid., p. 48.

12. Ibid.

13. "The Constitution of the Islamic Republic of Iran."

14. For more information about the IRGC coat of arms, see "Parcham-e Jomhouri-ye Eslami va Chand Arm-e Mandegar Chegouneh Tarahi Shodand?" [How Were the Flag of the Islamic Republic and Some Perdurable Coats of Arms Designed?], Fars News Agency (Tehran), February 4, 2009. Available in Persian at http://www.farsnews.com/newstext.php?nn=8711160991 (accessed December 12, 2010).

15. The Holy Quran, English translation by Maulana Muhammad Ali, Chapter 8, Al-Anfal—Voluntary Gifts. Available at http://aaiil.org/text/hq/trans/ch8.shtml (accessed August 11, 2012).

16. Nehzat-e Azadi-ye Iran, *Zendegi-Nameh-ye Sardar-e Rashid-e Eslam Shahid Doktor Mostafa Chamran* [Biography of the Great Commander of Islam, Martyr Dr. Mostafa Chamran] (N.p.: Iran Freedom Movement, October 1982), pp.19–20.

17. Ibid., p. 20.

18. Ibid., p. 19.

19. Ibid., p. 20.

20. Ibid.

21. Ibid., pp. 20–21.

22. Ibid., p. 21.

23. Ibid., p. 20.

24. Ibid,. p. 21.

25. Ibid.

26. Ibid., p. 22.

27. Ibid.

28. Ibid.

29. Ibid., pp. 22–23.

30. Ibid., p. 27.

31. Ibid., p. 23.

32. Ibid.

33. Ibid.

34. Ibid., p. 24.

35. Ibid.

36. Ibid., p. 26.

37. Ibid.

38. Ibid.

39. Ibid., pp. 27–28.

40. Ibid., p. 28.

41. Ibid., p. 29.

42. Ibid., p. 30.

43. Ibid., p. 19.

44. Ibid.

45. Ibid., p. 31.

46. Ibid.

47. Mostafa Chamran, *Gozareshi Az Lobnan* [A Report from Lebanon] (N.p.: Sher.kat-e Sahami-ye Enteshar, 1982).

48. Ibid., p. 9.

49. For an introduction to the Shiraziyyin, see Laurence Louër, *Transnational Shia Politics: Religious and Political Networks in the Gulf* (New York: Columbia University Press; Paris: Centre d'Etudes et de Recherches Internationales, 2008), pp. 88–99.

50. Amir-Reza Bakhshi, "Jaryan-shenasi-ye Siyasi-ye Shiayan-e Eragh-e Novin" [Shia Political Currents in Modern Iraq], Afkar-e Now (Tehran), January 2012. Available in Persian at http://www.afkarenow.com/mataleb/iraq.htm (accessed May 9, 2012).

51. "Assadollah Jafari, "Maktab-e Feqhi-ye Qom va Chaleshha-ye Qeraat az Velayat-e Faqih" [The Theological School of Thought of Qom and Challenges in Interpreting the Guardianship of the Jurist], Koofi (Herat), December 23, 2009. Available in Persian at http://www.koofi.net/index.php?id=815 (accessed May 13, 2012); and Fatemeh Tabatabaei, Eqlim-e Khaterat [The Realm of Memoirs] (Tehran: Moassesseh-ye Tanzim va Nashr-e Asar-e Emam Khomeini, 2011), p. 247.

52. Shahrbanou Rajabi and Hojjat-Allah Taheri, Shahid Mohammad Montazeri Be Revayat-e Asnad-e SAVAK [Martyr Mohammad Montazeri According to the SAVAK Documents] (Tehran: Markaz-e Asnad-e Enqelab-e Eslami, 1999).

53. "Kholaseh-ye Mabahes-e Neshast-e 'Bohran-e Bahrain'" [Summary of the 'Crisis in Bahrain' Seminar], Basij-e Daneshjouyi-e Daneshgah-e Sanati-ye Sharif (Tehran), May 19, 2011. Available in Persian at http://basij.sharif.ir/?p=550 (accessed May 13, 2012). See also Mahnaz Zahirinejad, Monasebat-e Emam Khomeini Ba Harekat-ha va Mobarezan-e Eslami [Imam Khomeini's Relations with Islamic Movements and Combatants] (Tehran: Markaz-e Asnad Enqelab-e Eslami, 2003), pp. 113, 196–197.

54. Louër, Transnational Shia Politics, p. 158.

55. Rahim Safavi, Az Jonoub-e Lobnan Ta Jonoub-e Iran – Khaterat-e Sardar Seyyed Rahim-e Safavi [From Southern Lebanon to Southern Iran: Memoirs of Commander Seyyed Rahim Safavi], 2nd ed., edited by Majid Najaf-Pour (Tehran: Markaz-e Asnad-e Enqelab-e Eslami, 2006), p. 85.

56. Ibid., p. 100.

57. Ibid., p. 102.

58. Ibid., p. 105.

59. Ibid., p. 106.

60. "Emam Va Sepah Az Badv-e Tashkil Ta Hal. Mosahebeh Ba Seyyed Ahmad Khomeini" [The Imam and the Guards from Establishment to Now: Interview with Seyyed Ahmad Khomeini], Payam-e Enqelab (Tehran), May 29, 1982, p. 10.

61. Ibid.

62. "Tahlili Bar Zarourat-e Tashkil-e Sepah Dar Se Bod-e Ideolozhi, Siyasi, Nezami" [An Analysis of the Necessity of Establishing the Guards in the Three Dimensions of Ideology, Politics, and Military], Payam-e Enqelab (Tehran), March 19, 1980, p. 32.

63. Ibid.

64. Ibid.

65. Ibid.

66. Ibid.

67. Ibid.

68. Ibid.

69. Hossein-Ali Montazeri, *Khaterat-e Hossein-Ali Montazeri* [Memoirs of Hossein-Ali Montazeri] (Los Angeles: Ketab, 2001), p. 241.

70. Ibid.

71. Ibid.

72. Ibid., p. 303.

73. John L. Esposito, "The Iranian Revolution: A Ten-Year Perspective," in John L. Esposito, *The Iranian Revolution: Its Global Impact* (Miami: Florida International University Press, 1990), pp. 32–33.

74. "Ayandeh-ye Mosalmanan Dar Lobnan" [The Future of Muslims in Lebanon], *Howzeh* (Qom), March 1984, p. 91.

75. Montazeri, *Khaterat-e Hossein-Ali Montazeri*, p. 241.

76. "'Enqelab-e Eslami' Ya Eslam-e Amrikayi?" ['An Islamic Revolution' or American Islam?], *Payam-e Enqelab* (Tehran), January 17, 1981, p. 3.

77. "Chegounegi-ye Osoul-e Siyasat-e Khareji-ye Jomhouri-ye Eslami" [Principles of the Foreign Policy of the Islamic Republic], *Payam-e Enqelab* (Tehran), January 17, 1981, p. 64.

78. "Dastavard-ha-ye Sepah Dar Nehzat-ha-ye Azadibakhsh" [Achievements of the Guards with Regard to the Liberation Movements], *Payam-e Enqelab* (Tehran), February 16, 1981, p. 84.

79. "Sokhanan-e Hazrat-e Ayatollah Montazeri Dar Seminar" [Statements of the Honorable Ayatollah Montazeri at the Seminar], *Payam-e Enqelab* (Tehran), February 16, 1981, p. 62.

80. "Mosahebeh-ye Ekhtesasi-ye Payam-e Enqelab Ba Baradar Mohammad-Ali Rajaei Nokhost-Vazir," *Payam-e Enqelab* (Tehran), January 31, 1981, p. 16.

81. Abol-Hassan Bani-Sadr, *Nameh-ha Az Agha-ye Bani-Sadr Be Agha-ye Khomeini Va Digaran...* [Letters from Mr. Bani-Sadr to Mr. Khomeini and Others], edited by Firouzeh Bani-Sadr (Frankfurt, Germany: Entesharat-e Enqelab-e Eslami, 2006), p. 269.

82. Akbar Hashemi Rafsanjani, *Enqelab Dar Bohran. Karnameh Va Khaterat-e Sal-e 1359* [The Revolution in Crisis: Record and Memoirs of the Year 1981], edited by Abbas Bashiri (Tehran: Daftar-e Nashr-e Maaref-e Enqelab, 2005), pp. 176–177.

83. Ibid., p. 177.

84. *Quds Force* seems to have been one of the names of the Office of the Islamic Movements.

85. "Tashkil-e Sepah-e Quds" [Establishment of the Quds Force], *Payam-e Enqelab* (Tehran), December 12, 1981, p. 3.

86. Ibid.

87. Akbar Hashemi Rafsanjani, *Obour Az Bohran. Karnameh Va Khaterat-e Hashemi Rafsanjani* [Through Crisis: Deeds and Memoirs of Hashemi Rafsanjani], edited by Yaser Hashemi (Daftar-e Nashr-e Maaref-e Enqelab, 1999), p. 435.

88. "Esrail Ma Miaim" [Israel, We Are Coming], *Payam-e Enqelab* (Tehran), June 27, 1981, p. 68.

89. Rafsanjani, *Obour Az Bohran*, p. 226.

90. "Emam Va Sepah Az Badv-e Tashkil Ta Hal. Mosahebeh Ba Seyyed Ahmad Khomeini," p. 13.

91. "Hazrat-e Ayatollah Al-Ozma Montazeri: Sepah Pasdar-e Enqelab Ast Va Enqelab Ham Marz Nadarad" [His Holiness Grand Ayatollah Montazeri: The Guards Is the Guardian of the Revolution and the Revolution Has No Borders], *Payam-e Enqelab* (Tehran), May 29, 1982, p. 15.

92. Ibid.

93. Ibid.

94. Ibid.

95. "Sodour-e Amali-ye Enqelab" [Export of the Revolution in Practice], *Payam-e Enqelab* (Tehran), May 29, 1982, p. 71.

96. Ibid.

97. Rafsanjani, *Obour Az Bohran*, p. 373.

98. Ibid., p. 410.

99. Ibid.

100. Ibid., p. 412.

101. Ibid., p. 393.

102. Ibid., p. 394.

103. Ibid., p. 506.

104. Akbar Hashemi Rafsanjani, *Pas Az Bohran. Karnameh va Khaterat-e Hashemi Rafsanjani Sal-e 61* [After the Crisis: Works and Memoirs of Hashemi Rafsanjani of the Year 1982], edited by Fatemeh Hashemi (Tehran: Daftar-e Nashr-e Maaref-e Enqelab, 2000), pp. 107, 129.

105. "Salrouz-e Fath-e Khorramshahr" [Anniversary of Liberation of Khorram-shahr], IRNA (Tehran), n.d. Available in Persian at http://www2.irna.ir/occasion/3khordad86/index.htm (accessed September 13, 2010).

106. Ahmad Khomeini, *Majmou-eh-ye Asar-e Yadegar-e Emam – Hojjat al-Eslam va Al-Moslemin Hajj Seyyed Ahmad Khomeini* [The Complete Works of the Heritage of the Imam Hojjat al-Eslam va Al-Moslemin Hajj Seyyed Ahmad Khomeini] (Tehran: Moassesseh-ye Tanzim va Nashr-e Asar-e Hazrat-e Emam Khomeini, 1996), pp. 716–717.

107. Montazeri, *Khaterat-e Hossein-Ali Montazeri*, p. 330.

108. Ibid., p. 329.

109. Rafsanjani, *Pas Az Bohran*, p. 97.

110. Ibid., pp. 68–69.

111. Ibid., p. 40.

112. Ibid., p. 137.

113. Ibid.

114. Fereshteh Sadatfar and Sadeq Zibakalam, *Hashemi Bedoun-e Routoush* [Hashemi Without Alteration], 3rd ed. (Tehran: Entesharat-e Rozaneh, 2008), pp. 285–286.

115. Ibid., p. 438.

116. Ibid., p. 473.
117. Rafsanjani, *Pas Az Bohran*, p. 107.
118. Ibid., p. 157.
119. Ibid.
120. Ibid., p. 159.
121. Ibid.
122. "Basij-e Sepah-e Pasdaran Dar Lobnan" [Mobilization of the Revolutionary Guards in Lebanon], *Payam-e Enqelab* (Tehran), October 22, 1982, p. 52.
123. Rafsanjani, *Pas Az Bohran*, p. 233.
124. Ibid., p. 252.
125. Ibid., p. 244.
126. Ibid., p. 256.
127. Ibid., p. 274.
128. Jamis Clarity, "Israelis Killed in Blast in Southern Lebanon," *New York Times*, November 12, 1982. For more details, see David Crist, *The Twilight War: The Secret History of America's Thirty-Year Conflict with Iran* (New York: Penguin, 2012), p. 129.
129. Rafsanjani, *Pas Az Bohran*, p. 311.
130. Ibid., p. 349.
131. Ibid., p. 352.
132. Crist, *Twilight War*, p. 132.
133. Rafsanjani, *Pas Az Bohran*, p. 131.
134. Ibid., pp. 138–139.
135. Crist, *Twilight War*, p. 131.
136. Rafsanjani, *Pas Az Bohran*, p. 218.
137. Crist, *Twilight War*, p. 133.
138. Rafsanjani, *Pas Az Bohran*, p. 265.
139. Ibid., p. 267.
140. Crist, *Twilight War*, p. 134.
141. Ibid, p. 138.
142. Rafsanjani, *Pas Az Bohran*, p. 327.
143. Ibid., p. 380.
144. Crist, *Twilight War*, p. 145.
145. Carlyle Murphy, "Bombs, Hostages: A Family Link," *Washington Post*, July 24, 1990.
146. "Mofajjar A'Safarat Fe' l'Kuwait...Qatil Al Hariri" [The Perpetrator of Embassy Bombings in Kuwait: Murderer of Hariri], *Al-Watan* (Kuwait), June 30, 2011. Available in Arabic at http://alwatan.kuwait.tt/articledetails.aspx?id=122160 (accessed on July 3, 2012).
147. Ibid.
148. "Naib Iraqi Motahim Bi Amal Tafjeerat Fee Al Kuwait..." [Iraqi Parliamentarian Accused of Bombing in Kuwait . . .], *Al-Raidah* (Kuwait), July 2, 2007.

Available in Arabic at http://www.alraidiah.com/vb/showthread.php?t=30556 (accessed on July 3, 2012).

149. Ibid.

150. Robin B. Wright, *Sacred Rage: The Wrath of Militant Islam* (New York: Touchstone, 1985), p. 125.

151. Rafsanjani, *Pas Az Bohran*, p. 489.

152. "Tashkil-e Jebhe-ye Jahani-ye Mostazafin" [Establishment of the International Front of the Oppressed], *Pasdar-e Eslam* (Tehran), January 1984, quoted in "Ayeneh-ye Taffakorat, Farhang, Niaz-ha, Rouhiat" [The Mirror of Thought, Culture, Needs, and Spirituality], *Howzeh* (Qom), February 1984, p. 135.

153. Akbar Hashemi Rafsanjani, *Aramesh Va Chalesh. Karnameh Va Khaterat-e Sal-e 1362 Hashemi Rafsanjani* [Calm and Challenge: Deeds and Memoirs of Hashemi Rafsanjani of the Year 1983/1984], 2nd ed., edited by Mehdi Hashemi (Tehran: Daftar-e Nashr-e Maaref-e Enqelab, 2003), p. 491.

154. *Report of the President's Special Review Board* (Tower Commission Report), The White House, Washington, DC, February 26, 1987.

155. Safavi, *Az Jonoub-e Lobnan Ta Jonoub-e Iran – Khaterat-e Sardar Seyyed Rahim-e Safavi*, p. 151.

156. Ibid.

157. Akbar Hashemi Rafsanjani, *Omid Va Delvapasi. Karnameh Va Khaterat-e Sal-e 1364* [Hope and Concern: Deeds and Memoirs of the Year 1985/1986], 3rd ed., edited by Sarah Lahouti (Tehran: Daftar-e Nashr-e Maaref-e Enqelab, 2008), p. 270.

158. Ibid.

159. Akbar Hashemi Rafsanjani, *Owj-e Defae* [The Apex of Defense], edited by Emad Hashemi (Tehran: Daftar-e Nashr-e Maaref-e Enqelab, 2010), p. 33.

160. Ibid., p. 39.

161. Ibid., p. 47.

162. Ibid., p. 51.

163. Ibjd.

164. Ibid., p. 58.

165. Ibid., p. 237.

166. Ibid., pp. 76–77.

167. Ibid., p. 202.

168. Montazeri, *Khaterat-e Ayatollah Hossein-Ali Montazeri*, p. 584.

169. Ibid.

170. Moassesseh-ye Tanzim Va Nashr-e Asar-e Emam Khomeini, *Sahifeh-ye Hazrat-e Emam Khomeini* [Pages of His Holiness Imam Khomeini] (Tehran: Moassesseh-ye Tanzim Va Nashr-e Asar-e Emam Khomeini, n.d.), vol. 21, p. 95.

171. Sadatfar and Zibakalam, *Hashemi Bedoun-e Routoush*, p. 289.

172. Ibid., p. 310.

173. Ibid.

174. Montazeri, *Khaterat-e Ayatollah Hossein-Ali Montazeri*, pp. 571–572.

175. Akbar Hashemi Rafsanjani, *Enqelab Va Defae Moghaddas* [Revolution and the Sacred Defense] (Tehran: Bonyad-e Panzdah-e Khordad, 1989), p. 201.

176. Ibid., p. 213.

177. Ibid., p. 214.

178. Ibid.

179. "Hashemi Rafsanjani: Iran Mossammam Be Mosharekat Dar Bazsazi-ye Bosni Va Herzegovin Boud" [Hashemi Rafsanjani: Iran Insisted upon Participation in Reconstruction of Bosnia and Herzegovina], Fars News Agency (Tehran), August 22, 2004. Available in Persian at http://www.farsnews.net/newstext. php?nn=8306010182 (accessed October 15, 2009).

180 Mohammad-Kazem Rowhaninejad, "Sarnevesht-e Darandeh-I Digar" [Fate of Another Predator], Zan-e Bosniayi Website (Tehran), July 26, 2008. Available in Persian at http://ghalame-khaterat.persianblog.ir/tag/%D8%B2%D9%86+% D8%A8%D9%88%D8%B3%D9%86%DB%8C%D8%A7%DB%8C%DB%8C (accessed August 9, 2012).

181. Mohammad Moeeni, "Khatere-ye Natez Nouri az Ersal-e Aslahe Be Bosni" [Nateq Nouri's Memoirs of Exporting Arms to Bosnia], Mmoeeni Blog (Bandar Abbas), n.d. Available in Persian at http://mmoeeni.blogspot.com/2009/08/blog-post_22.html (accessed August 9, 2012).

182. Kaveh Omidvar, "Jahiziyeh-ye Komiteh-ye Emdad Bara-ye Dokhtaran-e Dam-e Bakht..." [Dowry for Girls at the Age of Marriage...], BBC Persian (London), July 20, 2009. Available in Persian at http://www.bbc.co.uk/persian/ iran/2009/07/090719_ka_relief_foundation_anvari.shtml (accessed August 9, 2012).

183. Crist, *Twilight War*, pp. 404–406.

184 "Tashkil-e Sepah-e Quds" [Establishment of the Quds Force], *Payam-e Enqelab* (Tehran), December 12, 1981, p. 3. Before this date, the Quds Force was known as the Unit of the Liberation Movements of the IRGC. See, for example, "Zarourat-e Tashkil-e Sepah-e Pasdaran-e Enqelab-e Eslami" [The Necessity of Establishing the Islamic Revolutionary Guards Corps], *Payam-e Enqelab* (Tehran), February 16, 1981.

185. Kimberly Kagan, *Iran's Proxy War against the United States and the Iraqi Government* (Washington, DC: Institute for the Study of War and WeeklyStandard. com, May 2006–August 20, 2007), p. 3, note 7.

186. Charley Keyes, "U.S. Military Leader Says Iranian Weapons Killing Americans in Iraq," *CNN World* (July 7, 2011). Available at http://articles.cnn. com/2011-07-07/world/iraq.militias.iran.support_1_iranian-weapons-issue-of-iranian-involvement-baghdad?_s=PM:WORLD (accessed August 15, 2012).

187. "CENTCOM in 2010: Views from General David H. Petraeus," Institute for the Study of War, January 22, 2010. Available at http://www.understandingwar. org/press-media/webcast/centcom-2010-views-general-david-h-petraeus-video (accessed January 4, 2011).

188. U.S. Department of the Treasury, "Administration Takes Additional Steps to Hold the Government of Syria Accountable for Violent Repression against the Syrian People," press release, May 18, 2011. Available at http://www.treasury.gov/press-center/press-releases/Pages/tg1181.aspx (accessed August 14, 2012).
189. Suleimani has received several designations, the latest of which was related to the plot to assassinate the Saudi ambassador to the United States. See U.S. Department of the Treasury, "Treasury Sanctions Five Individuals Tied to Iranian Plot to Assassinate the Saudi Arabian Ambassador to the United States," press release, October 11, 2011. Available at http://www.treasury.gov/press-center/press-releases/pages/tg1320.aspx (accessed August 9, 2012).
190. "Tashkil-e Sepah-e Badr, Amel-e Yekparchegi-ye Amaliat-e Nezami Alayh-e Rezhim-e Bath" [Formation of the Badr Corps, Agent of Unity in Military Operations Against the Bath Regime], Rasekhoon (Tehran), June 2011. Available in Persian at http://www.rasekhoon.net/article/show-86107.aspx (accessed March 7, 2012).
191. Kagan, Iran's Proxy War, p. 5.
192. "Pirouzi-ye Hezbollah Dar Jang-e 33 Rouzeh Samareh-ye Khoun-ha-ye Rikhteh-shodeh Dar 8 Sal Defa-e Moqaddas Boud" [Hezbollah's Victory in the Thirty-Three-Day War Was the Result of Blood Sacrificed during Eight Years of Sacred Defense], Rasa News (Tehran), May 23, 2011. Available in Persian at http://www.rasanews.ir/Nsite/FullStory/?Id=105241 (accessed December 3, 2011).
193. "Emam Va Sepah Az Badv-e Tashkil Ta Hal. Mosahebeh Ba Seyyed Ahmad Khomeini," p. 10.
194. "Sarlashgar Suleimani Hezbollah Ra Az Hargouneh Hamleh-ye Pish-dastaneh Be Rezhim-e Sahyonisti Barhazar Dasth" [Major General Suleimani Warned Hezbollah against Any Preemptive Attack against the Zionist Regime], Botia News (Kerman), May 16, 2012. Available in Persian at http://botianews.com/component/k2/item/3190-%D8%B3%D8%B1%D9%84%D8%B4%DA%A9%D8%B1-%D8%B3%D9%84%DB%8C%D9%85%D8%A7%D9%86%DB%8C-%D8%AD%D8%B2%D8%A8-%D8%A7%D9%84%D9%84%D9%87-%D8%B1%D8%A7-%D8%A7%D8%B2-%D9%87%D8%B1%DA%AF%D9%88%D9%86%D9%87-%D8%AD%D9%85%D9%84%D9%87-%D9%BE%DB%8C%D8%B4-%D8%AF%D8%B3%D8%AA%D8%A7%D9%86%D9%87-%D8%A8%D9%87-%D8%B1%DA%98%DB%8C%D9%85-%D8%B5%D9%87%DB%8C%D9%88%D9%86%DB%8C%D8%B3%D8%AA%DB%8C-%D8%A8%D8%B1%D8%AD%D8%B0%D8%B1-%D8%AF%D8%A7%D8%B4%D8%AA (accessed May 16, 2012).
195. Ibid.
196. Ibid.
197. Ibid.
198. Ibid.
199 Ibid.

9

Conclusion

For much of the last year, political life in the United States has revolved around the result of the presidential election, which secured President Barack Obama's second term in office. So does political life in the Islamic Republic, which is preparing itself for the June 14, 2013, presidential election. However, regardless of the outcome of presidential election in Iran, President Obama is likely to face challenges similar to, if not greater than, those faced by his predecessors in office. In part, those challenges are likely to arise from the changed nature of the regime in Tehran and transformation of the Islamic Republic into a military dictatorship led by the Revolutionary Guards.

Authority in this Islamic Republic has traditionally rested upon a fundamental alliance between the revolutionary Shia clergy headed by the Guardian Jurist, and the Revolutionary Guards: While the revolutionary Shia clergy has ruled Iran since 1979, the Guards were tasked with protecting the clerics against internal and external enemies. Thirty-three years after the revolution of 1979 and establishment of the Islamic Republic, that division of labor is no longer valid, as the Islamic Revolutionary Guards Corps (IRGC) is both ruling and safeguarding the regime against internal and external enemies.

As discussed in this book, the rise of the Guards was deliberate: Facing increasing internal pressures for political and economic liberalization, which the regime is either unwilling to deliver or incapable of delivering to the masses that took to the streets in the wake of the fraudulent June 12, 2009, presidential election, Supreme Leader Ali Khamenei instrumentally uses the Guards and its former officers in an attempt to suppress demands for reform. As the economy of the Islamic Republic deteriorates because of Iranian leaders' incompetence and the international sanctions regime, Ayatollah Khamenei may find further reason to mobilize the IRGC to defend his rule. The IRGC, in turn, uses the domestic political dissidence—coupled with potential bread riots—and external pressure to advance its corporate interests by infiltrating the positions of power and by preying on the polity it was meant to guard against internal and external enemies.

In the short and middle terms, the Guards seem to have prevailed, but in the longer term Iran's prodemocracy movement may resurface as the vanguard of the next revolution. In the meantime, the thirty-three-year-long belief in Iran's Supreme Leader, be it Grand Ayatollah Khomeini, Ayatollah Khamenei or the next clerical head of state who may succeed him in office, is no longer true. Transformation of the Islamic Republic into a military dictatorship led by the Revolutionary Guards has hitherto led to anything but a more democratic and responsible Iran.

In the domestic context, the rise of the Guards has led to further political repression rather than political liberalization and pluralism. The IRGC looks for and finds counterrevolutionaries, saboteurs, and foreign agents among the political elites to terrorize the population. Rafsanjani-era economic liberalization and Khatami-era attempts at opening the political atmosphere have been forgotten, and the IRGC prefers to maintain the society in a state of emergency, which in turn legitimizes the lack of political freedoms under the Guards' domination of the polity. As the Guards instrumentally use the international sanctions regime to eliminate the sorry remains of the private sector, there is also little prospect of genuine liberalization of Iran's economy. Economic liberalization, its champion Ayatollah Rafsanjani, and the traditional bazaar continue an uneasy existence on the verge of total elimination.

As demonstrated in this book, the Guards' domestic need for foreign enemies has also led foreign policy behavior increasingly characterized by risk taking. The attempt on the life of the Saudi ambassador in Washington, DC, terrorist attacks against Israeli diplomats, and support to the armed insurgents in Iraq and Afghanistan seem to be more energetic than earlier policies, which may be a consequence of the Guards' unrestricted power over decision making in Iran.

Also, the Islamic Republic's resilience in the nuclear dispute with the world could be considered as a sign of the preference of the IRGC for the nuclear option. After all, as the engine of the Islamic Republic's nuclear program, the IRGC is also likely to be the institution benefiting most from the nuclear bomb. Should the Islamic Republic also manage to develop the nuclear bomb, which is bound to be under the IRGC's command, such risk-prone behavior could prove catastrophic.

The United States and allies cannot "create" an opposition movement to the militarized regime of the Islamic Republic, but the United States can help create conditions under which a cohesive opposition movement could emerge within Iran. When such an opposition takes form and evolves into a cohesive movement rather than spontaneous rallies, that movement deserves U.S. and allied support. After all, the United States should prefer the development of Iran into a democracy rather than a military dictatorship.

The United States should also use the popular dissatisfaction with the performance of the Revolutionary Guards, and also factionalism within the ranks of the Guards, to its advantage. By providing support to the opposition both within and outside of Iran, the United States could put pressure on the IRGC and engage in a political war of attrition. By appealing to certain factions within the IRGC while imposing sanctions on others, the United States could widen the gap within the Guards. For example, the United States could condemn the Quds Force of the Guards as a terrorist organization, while tentatively leaving the door open to certain IRGC companies. In such a way, the United States could test the degree of cohesion within the IRGC.

The United States and allies have previously devised sanctions targeting leading IRGC personnel and IRGC-owned businesses as a means of changing the Islamic Republic's behavior, particularly regarding the nuclear issue. However, those sanctions should also be imposed for the regime's breach of the human rights of the Iranian people, and sanctions should additionally be a tool to create an environment conducive to emergence of a cohesive opposition movement. Therefore, regime concessions concerning the human rights of the Iranian people should be rewarded by the removal of sanctions.

In the meantime, the United States, like any other government, will find itself in need of conducting negotiations with the regime in Tehran. Those negotiations should take place, but the U.S. authorities should negotiate with Islamic Republic representatives who have the authority to deliver, which for the time being means representatives of the IRGC. The principle of removal of sanctions against IRGC-owned businesses in return for the IRGC's liberalization of the political life of the Islamic Republic could be a new accords process, resembling the one the United State conducted with the Soviet Union.

Granted, this scenario is way too optimistic. The United States must also make its red lines known to the new leadership in Tehran. Rather than changing those red lines, the United States must at all costs demonstrate to the Guards commanders that they will pay a very high price should they ever try to cross those lines. Therefore, credible threats of the use of force and the actual use of force may be necessary to convince the new leadership in Tehran that the United States has certain red lines and, for example, does not tolerate a nuclear-armed Islamic Republic.

Index

Note: Page numbers followed
   by *t* or *f* indicate tables
   or figures.

Abdollahi, Reza, 185
Abdollah-Zadeh, _____, 10
Abed, Abd al-Reza, 173
Abedi, Hassan, 7
Abedi, Mehdi, 85*t*
Abnoush, Salar, 54*t*
Abol-Fazl al-Abbas Brigade, 54*t*, 85*t*
Abou-Hamzeh, Gholam-Ali, 53*t*, 54*t*
Abou-Saleh, Raed, 211
Abou-Sharif (Abbas Aqa-Zamani),
   7, 11, 12, 13, 22–23, 25, 102
Abrisham-Chi, Hassan, 9
Adyani, Ali-Reza, 156
Afghanistan, 161, 230, 237
Afrouz, Gholam-Ali, 92
Afshar, Ali-Reza, 26, 34
Afwaj al-Moghavemat al-Lobnaniyat
   (AMAL), 209, 223
Ahmadi, Abbas-Ali, 9
Ahmadi, Gholam-Reza, 53*t*
Ahmadinejad, Mahmoud,
   2, 16, 30–38, 126–27, 160,
   177, 178, 179
Ajab-Gol, Davoud, 9
Akbari, Hassan, 86*t*
Alam Al-Hoda, Hossein, 7, 10
Alam Al-Hoda, Kazem, 7

Alavi, Javad, 86*t*
Alazmani, Daryoush, 52*t*
Algeria, 207
Al-Ghadir Brigade, 55*t*, 56, 86*t*, 121
Ali Ibn-e Abi-Taleb Brigade, 54*t*,
   56, 86*t*
Alizadeh, Abol-Ghasem, 85*t*
Alizadeh, Nazar-Ali, 51*t*
Allah-Dadi, Mohammad-Ali, 55*t*
Allah-Karam, Hossein, 122, 230–31
Al-Malaki, Nouri, 225
Al-Modarresi, Hadi, 210, 211
Al-Mughassil, Ahmed, 231
Al-Musawi, Abu-Haydan, 224
Al-Musawi, Husayn, 224
Alviri, Mahin, 9
Alviri, Morteza, 7, 9, 12, 13, 14
Al-Zahra Brigade, 47
AMAL (Afwaj al-Moghavemat
   al-Lobnaniyat), 209, 223
Amini, Ebrahim, 154
Amir al-Momenin Brigade, 52*t*, 85*t*
Amiri, Younes, 53*t*
Angouran Zinc Mine, 185–86
Ansar al-Hossein Brigade, 50,
   52*t*, 85*t*
Ansar al-Mojahedin Credit
   Institute, 170
Ansar al-Reza Brigade, 53*t*
Ansar-e Hezbollah organization,
   27, 35, 161

Ansar Financial and Credit Institute, 188–89
Ansari, Jamshid, 185
Anvari, Mohi al-Din, 104
Aqa-Zamani, Abbas (Abou-Sharif), 7, 11, 12, 13, 22–23, 25, 102
Arabpour, Ali, 85t
Arabs in Iran, 22
Arab-Sorkhi, Feiz-Allah, 9
Arab Spring opportunity to export the revolution, 233
Arafat, Yasir, 214
Ardebili, Abd al-Karim Mousavi, 8, 12, 88, 97, 217, 229
Ardebil Province, 50, 51t, 85t
Armenia, 161
Armin, Mohsen, 9
Arms industry, 168–69
Asef, Hossein, 9
Asgari, Ali, 9
Ashoura Brigade, 47, 50, 51t, 85t
Ashtiani, Gholam-Reza Danesh, 92
Association of the Cooperatives of the Army Cadre (ETKA), 174
Astan-e Ghods-e Razavi Foundation, 178
Atayi, Rahim, 207
Atayi, Zein al-Abedin Mir-Yousefi, 172
Aval, Hossein Karimi, 52t
Azadi, Abd al-Reza, 52t
Azerbaijan, 161
Azimi, Mohammad-Nazar, 53t

Babayi, Mohammad-Hossein, 54t
Baba-Zadeh, Jalil, 51t
Babyi, Mohammad-Hossein, 52t
Badeh-Peyma, Reza, 9
Badr Al Din, Mostafa, 225
Badr Divine [Organization], 9
Badr operation, Iran-Iraq War, 110
Bahonar, Mohammad-Javad, 89
Bahrain, 218

Bakeri, Mehdi, 110
Bakhshandeh, Mahmoud, 10
Bani-Sadr, Abol-Hassan, 4, 22–25, 49, 90, 97, 215–16
Banking sector, IRGC's parallel, 178
Barati, Akbar, 9
Basij (paramilitary force), 27, 32, 35, 47, 48–50, 56–57, 83t
Basij of Theological Students, 122
Basir-Zadeh, Gholam-Reza, 10
Bayat, Asadollah, 29
Bazaars vs. IRGC chain stores, 173–74
Bazargan, Mehdi
  destruction of government by IRGC, 19–21
  exporting the revolution, 207, 210, 212, 213
  and IRGC infiltration of National Guard, 11
  and Lahouti Eshkevari, 88, 89, 90
  National Guard's affinity with, 8, 86, 87
Beheshti, Mohammad, 86, 89, 92, 120
Beit al-Moghaddas Brigade, 54t, 85t
Besharati, Ali-Mohammad, 7, 12, 13
Bik-Zadeh, Hadi, 9
Bojnourdi, Mohammad-Kazem Mousavi, 23
Bonyanian, Zohreh, 9
Boroujerdi, Mohammad, 7, 9, 11, 12
Bosnia, war in, 230–31
Bouali, Yadollah, 54t
Bushehr Province, 51t, 85t

Carter, Jimmy, 24
Chahar-Mahal and Bakhtiari Province, 51t, 85t
Chain stores, IRGC's, vs. traditional bazaar, 173–74
Chamran, Mostafa, 207, 208–10
Civilian control over IRGC

foreign policy conflict, 212,
    221–23
ideological/political indoctrination,
    17–18, 20, 32, 90–91, 123–24,
    150–61
IRGC's exploitation of civilian
    factionalism, 24, 36–37, 88, 98,
    105, 112
    in Khamenei's presidency, 118
    See also Commissars;
        Domestic politics
Clergy, ruling
    enhancement of official power of
        Khamenei, 120
    IRGC as poised to infiltrate
        clergy, 152
    IRGC's alliance with, 16, 36–37
    as official instructors to IRGC, 156
    See also Commissars and
        commissariat; Khamenei,
        Ali; Khomeini, Rouhollah
Clinton, Hillary, 1
Command Council, IRGC, 11–12
Commissars and commissariat
    conclusion, 128
    establishment of, 84, 86–87
    introduction, 79
    Khamenei's commissars, 82–83t,
        116–27
    Khomeini's commissars, 81–82t,
        87–117
    legal framework, 79–80, 83–84
    names and associations of, 81–83t,
        85–86t
    organization of commissariat, 80
    provincial level, 85–86t
    relationship to other parts of
        armed forces, 85t
Constitution of the Islamic Republic
    of Iran, 18, 205
Construction Base of the Seal of the
    Prophets (GHORB), 166, 172–73,
    176, 177

Construction industry, IRGC's
    involvement in, 166, 171–73
Consumer goods production, 168–69
Contractor corruption and privilege,
    171–73
Cooperative Foundation, 169, 186,
    187–88t, 188–89
Cooperative sector of economy, 167,
    180, 181f
Cooperatives, Housing and Social
    Affairs Unit, IRGC, 174–75
Council of Guardians, 30–31, 33, 175
Council of the Revolution, 6–7, 11,
    17, 87
Crist, David, 224

Dabbagh, Mrs. Marziyeh
    Hadid-Chi, 93
Dadashi, Habib-Allah, 9
Daghayeghi, Esmail, 10
Damad, Mostafa Mohaghegh, 107,
    108, 120
Defense Industries Organization,
    168–69
Dezfouli, Gholam-Hossein Safati,
    7, 10
Din-Parvar, Jamal al-Din, 153–54
Divine Enlistees' [Organization], 9
Domestic politics, IRGC role in
    Ahmadinejad's support for,
        30–38
    vs. Bani-Sadr, 22–25
    vs. Bazargan, 19–21
    election interference, 1, 31, 32,
        33–35, 123, 125–27, 191
    and exporting the revolution,
        211–13
    future prospects, 246–49
    ideological justification for,
        158–59
    individual vs. institutional
        participation, 18
    introduction, 16–17

in Khamenei's presidency, 25–26
vs. Khatami, 27–30
legal framework, 17–19
precedent for, 19
in Rafsanjani's presidency, 26–27
Saidi's support of, 125–26, 127
Douz-Douzani, Abbas, 7, 12, 23, 93
Douz-Douzani, Mehdi Kazemi,
121–22

East Azerbaijan Province, 51t, 85t
Economy, IRGC's role in
chain stores vs. traditional bazaar,
173–74
consumer goods production,
168–69
contractor corruption and
privilege, 171–73
introduction, 165
oil and gas sector dominance,
175–79
as Rafsanjani's bribe to stay out of
politics, 27
real estate speculation, 169–71
and response to sanctions, 246–47
smuggling operations, 189–91
stock exchange in Tehran,
179–83, 180f, 181f, 184–85t,
185–86, 187–88t, 188–89
subversion of legal framework,
166–68
telecommunications monopoly, 175
Egypt, 207–8
Elections, IRGC interference in, 1, 31,
32, 33–35, 123, 125–27, 191
Elham, Gholam-Hossein, 176
Engels, Friedrich, 204
Eraqi, Abdollah, 35, 55t
Eraqi, Baha al-Din Mohammadi,
112–13
Eraqi, Mahmoud Mohammadi, 82t,
99, 111, 113–14, 115, 118–20,
123, 154

Esfahan Province, 85t
Eshkevari, Hamid Lahouti, 94
Eshkevari, Hassan Lahouti, 13, 81t,
87, 88–98, 100
Eshkevari, Lahouti, 13
Eshkevari, Said Lahouti, 94
Eshkevari, Vahid, 97
Eslami-Mehr, Hassan, 9
Esmaili, Mohammad, 55t
Esmail-Nezhad, _____, 9
Ethnic unrest, Bani-Sadr vs. IRGC
on, 22
ETKA (Association of the
Cooperatives of the Army
Cadre), 174
Exporting the revolution
ideological foundations, 204–6
initial impact of Iran's revolution, 214
and Iran-Iraq War context, 215–30
national security and domestic
power aspects, 211–13
1988–2003, 230–31
practical benefits for IRGC,
235–37
practical foundations and world
revolutionary movement,
206–11
since 2003, 231–35

Factionalism
within commissariat, 104–7, 112
IRGC's exploitation of civilian, 24,
36–37, 88, 98, 105, 112
among militias and within IRGC,
12t, 84, 86–87, 101–2,
107–10, 154, 248
Fada, Mojitaba, 52t
Fadayi, Hossein, 7, 9
Fadayi, Mohammad, 9
Fajr Brigade, 51t, 85t
Faker, Mohammad-Reza, 82t, 99,
104, 105, 112, 154
Fakhri, Nemat, 86t

Fars Province, 51*t*, 85*t*

Farzen, Ali, 92

Fatah, 211

Fatehi, Hamid, 9

Fath al-Mobin operation, Iran-Iraq
    War, 108

Fath Brigade, 53*t*

Faw Peninsula offensive and shooting
    down of Mahallati's plane, 112

Fayazipour, Mohammad-Hossein, 55*t*

Fazaeli, Ahmad, 211

Fazli, Ali, 55*t*

Fereydoun, Abd Al-Rahim, 54*t*

Financial activities, IRGC, 178

Firouzabadi, Hassan, 33, 35

Foreign policy, IRGC vs. civilian
    leadership, 212, 221–23

Foroutan, Yousef, 7, 9, 12, 13

Fotouhi, Akbar, 55*t*

Foundation of the Martyrs and
    Veterans Affairs, 178

Foundation of the Oppressed, 175, 178

Gaddafi, Muammar, 210

Garmeh-i, Ali, 54*t*

Gazani, Abolfazi, 51*t*

Ghadyani, Parviz, 9

Ghalanbar, Hamid, 9

Ghamar Bani-Hashem Brigade, 51*t*, 85*t*

Ghanbari, Hamid, 156

Ghannad-ha, Ali, 9

Gharabi, Alireza, 51*t*

Gharazi, Mohammad, 7, 12, 93, 211

Ghasr-e Firouzeh Garrison, 122

Ghazanfar-Pour, Ahmad, 25

Gheibparvar, Gholam-Hossein, 51*t*

Ghiasi, Hashem, 53*t*

Gholami, Yadollah, 85*t*

GHORB (Construction Base of the
    Seal of the Prophets), 166,
    172–73, 176, 177

Ghotbzadeh, Sadegh, 93

Gilan Province, 51*t*, 85*t*, 97

Golestan Province, 52*t*, 85*t*

Gorbachev, Mikhail, 28

Goudarzi, Mahmoud, 85*t*

Govahi, Abd al-Ali, 86*t*

Governors, regional, influence of, 31

Greater Tehran Province, 55*t*, 86*t*

Green Movement, 34

Grup Servicii Petroliere, 176

Guardians of the Islamic Revolution,
    7*t*, 10, 92

Guards and militias, *See* Militias
    and guards

Habibi, Ali-Asghar, 53*t*

Hafezi, Reza, 54*t*

Haghani, Gholam-Hossein, 104

Haj-Ali-Beygi, _____, 9

Hajizadeh, Mohammad, 85*t*

Hajj-Mohammad-Zadeh, Ebrahim,
    7, 20, 24, 90, 98

Hakim, Mohammad-Baqer, 216–17,
    218, 223, 227–28

Halimi, Nader, 9

Hamadani, Hossein, 55*t*

Hamedan Province, 52*t*, 85*t*

Hamid-Zadeh, Hassan, 10

Hanif-Nezhad, Mohammad, 208

Harekat al-Mahroumin, 209

Hashemi, Hadi, 226–27

Hashemi, Hossein, 9, 217

Hashemi, Mehdi, 107, 211, 216–17,
    222–23, 226–27, 228–29

Hassan-Zadeh, Ayoub, 83*t*

Hazrat-e Abbas Brigade, 50, 51*t*, 85*t*

Hazrat-e Ghaem al-Mohammad
    Brigade, 54*t*, 56, 86*t*

Hejazi, Abrahim, 121

Hejazi, Fakhr al-Din, 111

Hejazi, Mohammad, 48, 50

Hemmati, Ali-Naqi, 54*t*

Heydarian, Mohsen, 85*t*

Hezbollah, Lebanese, 214, 221, 223,
    227, 233–35

Hidden Imam, 29
High-tech economic sector, 168–69
Hojjatiyyeh secret society, 104, 113
Holy war (jihad), 204
Holy Warriors of the Islamic
    Revolution, 7t, 8–10, 12t, 88
Honar-Dar, Mehdi, 10
Hormozgan Province, 52t, 85t
Hormozi, Hassan, 10
Hossein, Sha Soltan, 34
Hosseini, Bahram, 55t
Hosseini, Morteza, 86t
Hostages, taking of U.S. embassy
    personnel as, 20–21, 23–24
Hussein, Saddam, 150, 223

Ideological/Political Indoctrination
    Directorate, 151
Ideology, politics and indoctrination
    A. Khomeini on, 86–87, 212–13
    and civilian control of state,
        17–18, 20, 32, 90–91, 123–24,
        150–61
    contradictions and implications in
        IRGC indoctrination, 159–61
    early attempts to indoctrinate
        IRGC, 90–91, 152–56
    intervention, indoctrination for
        purposes of, 156–59
    Khamenei's role, 118–21
    Khorram-Abadi's role, 103–4
    legal framework and institutions,
        17–18, 151–52
    philosophy behind, 123–24, 150
    R. Khomeini on, 204–5, 214,
        222, 235
    See also Exporting the revolution
Ilam Province, 52t, 85t
Imam Hossein University, 119
Imam Khomeini International
    Airport, 189–90
Imam Reza Brigade, 53t, 85t
Imam Sadeq Brigade, 50, 51t, 85t

Imam Sadeq College, 153
Imam Sajjad Brigade, 52t, 85t
Imperial Guard, 8, 10
Integrated Electronic Industries, 169
Intelligence collection role for IRGC,
    17–18
Intelligence Ministry, Ahmadinejad
    vs. Khamenei, 36
Internal security, IRGC's role in,
    17–18, 31–32, 47–50, 51–55t,
    56–57, 171, 174
    See also Domestic politics
"Invisible jetties" and smuggling
    by sea, 190
Iran-Contra affair, 226, 227, 228
Iran Electronic Industries, 169, 175
Iran Freedom Movement, 8, 102,
    206–10
The Iranian Military in Revolution and
    War (Zabih), 3
The Iranian Military Under the Islamic
    Republic (Schahgaldian), 3
Iranian Offshore Engineering and
    Construction Company, 178
Iranian Regional Presence Offices, 4
Iran-Iraq War
    arms embargo during, 169
    Badr operation, 110
    Basij's role, 49
    debate over continuation of, 108,
        219–21
    ending of, 229–30
    and exporting the revolution,
        215–30
    Faw Peninsula offensive and
        shooting down of Mahallati's
        plane, 112
    IRGC's role, 25, 26, 101–2, 114
    Jafari's role, 47
    Karbala II operation, 114
    Mahallati's operational
        involvement, 108–9
    regular army vs. IRGC, 111

Iran Marine Industrial Company, 177
Iran Privatization Organization, 179
Iran Shipyard and Offshore Industries
    Company, 177
Iran Telecommunications, 186
Iran Zinc Mines Development
    Company, 185–86
Iraq, 214, 223, 231–33
See also Iran-Iraq War
Iraqi Shia groups in Iran, 218,
    227–28
IRGC (Islamic Revolutionary
    Guard Corps)
  ideological/political
    indoctrination in, 17–18,
    90–91, 123–24, 150–61
  ideological symbolism in logo of,
    205–6
  internal security role, 17–18,
    31–32, 47–50, 51–55t, 56–57,
    171, 174
  introduction, 1–5
  origins of, 6–14
  as real power source in Iran,
    246–49
  U.S. hostage situation role,
    20–21
  Western research on, 3–5
  See also Commissars; Domestic
    politics; Economy; Exporting
    the revolution
IRGC Air Force, 83t
IRGC Cooperative Foundation, 169,
    186, 187–88t, 188–89
IRGC Ground Force, 83t
IRGC Navy, 83t
IRGC Strategic Studies Center, 47
IRIB (Islamic Republic of Iran
    Broadcasting), 34
Isfahan Province, 1–7, 52t, 102
Islamic Government, 204
Islamic Republican Party, 86, 89–90,
    91–95, 97

Islamic Republic of Iran Broadcasting
    (IRIB), 34
Islamic Revolutionary Guard Corps,
    See IRGC (Islamic Revolutionary
    Guard Corps)
Islamist world revolution, 205–6
    See also Exporting the revolution
Israel, 159, 216, 226, 233, 234–35

Jabari, Ebrahim, 33, 55t
Jafari, Mohammad Ali ("Aziz" or "Ali")
  criticism of Ahmadinejad, 36
  as IRGC commander in chief,
    31–32, 47–48, 50
  merger of Basij with IRGC, 48–50
  Mosaic Doctrine and IRGC
    restructuring, 50, 51–55t,
    56–57
  at National Guard founding
    convention, 92
  promotion of IRGC's political
    involvement, 35, 36
Jahan-Ara, Ali, 7, 10
Jahed, Ali-Reza Azimi, 55t
Jalali, Yazdan, 51t
Jamiri, Fath-Allah, 51t
Jamshidi, Mehdi, 51t
Jamshidiyeh Garrison, 88
Jannati, Ahmad, 120, 230
Javad al-Aemeh Brigade, 53t, 85t
Javaheri, Hashem, 213
Javani, Yadollah, 34
Jazayeri, Masoud, 32
Jazayeri, Masoumeh, 9
Jomhouri-e Eslami, 25
Judicial system, IRGC's use of to
    quell dissent, 29

Kagan, Kimberly, 231, 233
Kaki, Sadeq, 52t
Kalanki, _____, 9
Kalhor, Vahid, 9
Kameli-Far, Hassan, 85t

Kangarlou, Mohsen, 227
Kani, Mohammad-Reza Mahdavi,
    89–90, 91, 107, 120
Karami, Ali-Reza, 85t
Karami, Jahanbakhsh, 55t
Karbala Brigade, 54t, 85t
Karbala II operation, Iran-Iraq
    War, 114
Karimi, Abbas, 110
Karimnejad, Qanbar, 51t
Karrubi, Mehdi, 29, 34, 189,
    190–91, 228
Katzman, Kenneth, 3
Kayhan, 168, 177
Kazemeini, Mohammad, 53t
Kazemeini, Mohsen, 55t
Kermani, Mohammad-Ali Movahedi,
    82t, 104, 120–23
Kerman Province, 53t, 85t
Kermanshah IRGC Brigade, 53t, 85t
Kermanshah Province, 53t, 85t
Khamenei, Ali
    and Ahmadinejad, 36, 37–38
    and attempted IRGC
        reconstruction (1979), 13
    call for renewed indoctrination of
        IRGC, 150
    commissars of, 82–83t, 116–27
    elections, involvement in, 34–35
    emulation requirement for, 159
    and ending of Iran-Iraq War, 229
    Eshkevari appointment, 89
    and exporting the revolution,
        223–24, 228
    impact of prospective death of on
        IRGC, 160
    Jafari appointment, 47
    vs. Khatami, 28
    as Khomeini's commissar, 81t, 99
    loss of power to IRGC, 1
    and Mahallati, 109
    vs. Montazeri, 116
    as president, 25, 26

    privatization scheme for economy,
        167–68, 179
    and reform suppression role of
        IRGC, 16, 246–47
    Statute of the Guards, 80
    support for Jafari's IRGC/Basij
        merger, 48
    Taeb appointment, 48
Khamenei, Mir-Hossein Mousavi, 217
Khatam al-Owsia Consortium, 177
Khatami, Ahmad, 9, 190
Khatami, Mohammad, 2, 27–30, 31,
    122, 126, 228
Khaziravi, Qasem, 85t
Khobar Towers bombing, Saudi
    Arabia, 231
Khoei, Abu al-Qasim, 120
Khomeini, Ahmad
    on Ayatollah Khomeini's concern
        over armed revolutionary
        groups, 84
    on Bani-Sadr, 23
    and commander/commissar
        conflicts, 105, 107, 112
    and economic role of IRGC, 179
    and ending of Iran-Iraq War, 229
    on Eshkevari affair, 88–89, 90,
        93–94, 95
    and exporting the revolution,
        217, 222
    on initial ideological currents at
        revolution, 86–87, 212–13
    on Khorramshahr and
        continuation of war, 219
    legitimizing of Khamenei's
        power, 117
    and missile firing threat by IRGC
        mutineers, 27
    vs. Montazeri, 116
Khomeini, Mostafa, 100
Khomeini, Rouhollah
    and attempted IRGC
        reconstruction, 13

vs. Bani-Sadr, 22
Basij formation, 49
commissars of, 81–82*t*, 87–117
dealing with armed militias after
    fall of Shah, 84
death of, 26
defense industries transfer to
    IRGC, 168–69
fear of internal threats to
    revolution, 36
ideology and exporting the
    revolution, 204–5, 214, 222, 235
indoctrination strategy for
    IRGC, 152
and Iran-Contra affair, 227
Iran-Iraq War, 219–21, 229–30
and IRGC Command Council
    authority, 12
IRGC's pursuit of own agenda
    under, 17
militias loyal to at time of
    revolution, 6–7, 8–9, 9–10*t*,
    10–11
non-intervention policy of,
    157–59
and opposition suppression role
    for IRGC, 16
Political and Divine Testament,
    26–27, 117–18
and political intervention of IRGC,
    19–20, 21
revolutionary network in exile,
    210–11
secret correspondence with
    Bani-Sadr, 4
Khorram, Ahmad, 85*t*, 189, 190
Khorram-Abadi, Hassan Taheri, 81*t*,
    99, 103–4, 105–7, 112, 120,
    152–54
Khorramshar, liberation of, 108, 219
Khosh-Soulatan, Masoumeh, 9
Khosravi, Homayoun, 9
Khuzestan Province, 53*t*, 85*t*

Kish Island, 174
Kohkilou-ye and Boyer-Ahmad
    Province, 53*t*, 85*t*
Kolahdouz, Yousef, 7, 12, 13, 23
Kordestan Province, 54*t*
Kouhestani, Ramezan-Ali, 156
Kowsari, Mohammad, 32
Kuwait, 27, 224–25

Lajevardi, Assadollah, 98
Lakzaei, Habibollah, 55*t*
Lak-Zayi, Habib, 55*t*
Larijani, Ali, 30, 35, 37, 177, 178,
    179, 181
Larijani, Sadegh, 37
Leader of the Revolution, *See* Khamenei,
    Ali; Khomeini, Rouhollah
Lebanon
    and Basij, 50
    Chamran and Sadr in, 208–10
    early post-revolution presence
        in, 214
    financial assistance to Shia
        groups, 216
    military training with PLO in, 211
    support for insurgent groups, 221,
        222–24, 227, 230
"Liberals," IRGC's war on, 28, 35, 160
Libya, 210, 213
Loghmanian, Hossein, 191
Lorestan Province, 54*t*, 85*t*

Maboudi, Ali, 86*t*
Maddahi, _____, 9
Maghrebi, Hamid Maghfour, 9
Mahallati, Fazl-Allah Mehdi-Zadeh,
    81*t*, 89, 99–112, 114, 115
Mahdavi, Mohammad-Mehdi, 85*t*
Mahdavinejad, Mehdi, 54*t*
Mahdi, Imam of the Era, 113, 160
Majid-Khani, _____, 118
Makhmalbaf, Mohsen, 9
Makouyi, Behrouz, 9

Al-Malaki, Nouri, 225
Maleki, Mohammad-Ali, 10
Management and Planning
    Organization (MPO), 173
Mansouri, Ghodrat-Allah, 53t
Mansouri, Javad, 7, 12, 13
Marani, Mohammad, 52t
Markazi Province, 54t, 85t
Martyr Mahallati City Complex, 170–71
Martyr Mahallati University, 151, 155
Martyr Rajai Port Complex, 190
Marx, Karl, 204
Marxism, and Khomeini's Islamic
    Government theory, 204–5
Mataf, Abdol-Reza, 51t
Mazandaran Province, 54t, 85t
Mecca, massacre of pilgrims in,
    228–29
Media, controls on, 4, 29, 34
Mehdianfar, Mohammad-Reza, 51t
Mehdinezhad, Fereydoun, 228
Mehrabad International Airport, 189
Mehrabian, Ali-Akbar, 185
Mehr-e Eghtesad-e Iranian Investment
    Company, 183, 184–85t, 185–86
Mehr Finance and Credit Institution,
    181–83, 182t, 183t, 184–85t,
    185–86
Mehr Housing Project, 169
Melli Bank, 213
Meshkini, Ali, 211
Milani, Mohammad-Hadi, 120
Military dictatorship, Iran as,
    246–49
    See also IRGC (Islamic
        Revolutionary Guard Corps)
Military forces, See IRGC (Islamic
    Revolutionary Guard Corps);
    Regular military
Military industries, 168–69
Militias and guards
    active at time of revolution, 6–7,
        84, 86–88

multiplicity of at revolution, 6–10
National Guard, 7t, 8, 12t, 84, 86,
    87–88, 90, 91–92
unification of, 10–14
See also IRGC (Islamic Revolutionary
    Guard Corps)
Ministry of Interior, as IRGC tool, 33–34
Mirza-Pour, Ali, 53t
Miyanji, Mohammad-Mehdi
    Ahmadi, 154
Moazzeni, Hassan-Ali, 85t
Al-Modarresi, Hadi, 210, 211
Moffateh, Mohammad, 89
Mohajerani, Ataollah, 28
Mohammad, Jamal Jaafar, 225
Mohammadi, Ali, 83t
Mohammadi, Hamoun, 51t
Mohammadi, Rashid, 53t
Mohammadpour, Gholam-Reza, 53t
Mohammad Rasoul-Allah Brigade,
    55t, 86t
Mohammad-Zadeh, Rajab-Ali, 55t
Mohtashami-Pour, Ali-Akbar, 224,
    226, 227
Moini, Mehdi, 51t
Moinpour, Mahmoud, 53t
Mojahedin-e Khalq organization
    and Bani-Sadr, 24–25
    exporting the revolution, 209
    IRGC's opposition to, 22
    L. Eshkevari's sympathies with, 94
    Montazeri family's connection to,
        10, 116
    revolutionaries' desertion of, 9
    Shamsi's connection to, 12
    V. Eshkevari's connection to, 97
Momen, Mohammad, 120
Money laundering, 178
Monfared, Danesh, 7
Montazer-Ghaem, Hassan, 9
Montazeri, Hossein-Ali
    challenge to IRGC leadership
        (early 1980s), 102, 106, 107, 108

exporting the revolution, 211, 213, 215, 217, 224, 228
on factionalism among military units, 84, 86
fall from grace, 116
as father of Mohammad Montazeri, 10
Iran-Iraq War, 219–20
and IRGC's neutralization of Bani-Sadr, 24
Kermani's purge of supporters of, 121–22
on Mecca pilgrimage massacre, 228–29
memoir of, 3, 4
Montazeri, Mohammad
    as commissar to Palestinian guardsmen, 88
    and conspiracy against Eshkevari, 92
    exporting the revolution, 210–11, 212–13, 214, 215, 217, 226, 233
    factionalism among guards, 84, 86
    as head of Guardians of the Islamic Revolution, 10
    as Khomeini loyalist prior to revolution, 7
    unification of Guards, 11, 12
"Mosaic Doctrine," Jafari's, 50, 51–55t, 56–57
Moshaffeq, Mohammad Ali, 189, 191
Moslehi, Heydar, 36, 37
Mossadeq, Mohammad, 8, 206
Mottahari, Morteza, 88, 89–90, 91, 92, 120
Mousavi, Hajj-Seyyed Naser, 121
Mousavi, Mehdi, 55t
Mousavi, Mir-Hossein, 225–26, 229
Mousavi, Mohammad, 85t
Mousavi, Morteza, 53t
Mowj, 29
Mowlaparast, Mousa, 52t
MPO (Management and Planning Organization), 173

Al-Mughassil, Ahmed, 231
Mughniyah, Imad, 224–25
Mullen, Mike, 231–32
Al-Musawi, Abu-Haydan, 224
Al-Musawi, Husayn, 224
Muslim Students Following the Line of the Imam, 20

Nabavi, Behzad, 7, 9
Naimi, Safar, 9
Najaf-Abadi, Mohammad-Ali Hadi, 218, 228
Naji, Kasra, 31
Nakhli, Ali, 9
Namazi, Abd al-Nabi, 116, 118, 154–56
Namjou, Mousa, 7
Naqdi, Mohammad-Reza, 36, 230–31
Nasiri, Ali, 55t
Nasrallah, Hassan, 234–35
Nasser, Gemal Abdol, 207
National Guard, 7t, 8, 12t, 84, 86, 87–88, 90, 91–92
National Iranian Gas Company, 176
National Oil Company of Iran, 176
National security
    as excuse for IRGC economic control, 175, 189–90
    and exporting the revolution, 211–13
Nattaj, Gholam-Hossein Taghi, 182, 188
Navab, Abol-Hassan, 116–17, 118
Naynava Brigade, 52t
Nazari, Mokhtar, 85t
Nazari, Yaqoub-Ali, 53t
Neynava Brigade, 50, 85t
Nikdel, Mehdi, 9
Nofarasti, Gholam-Hossein, 85t
North Khorasan Province, 53t, 85t
Nour-Allahi, Allah-Nour, 54t
Nour-Allahi, Reza, 85t
Nouri, Abdollah, 82t, 115–17, 118

Nouri, Akbar, 54t
Nouri, Ali-Akbar Nateq, 31, 89, 104
Nouri, Rouhollah, 53t
Nouri-ha, Hassan-Ali, 121
Nowrouzi, Mohammad-Sadegh, 9
Nuclear technology, 165, 176–77,
    178, 233, 247–48, 249

Obama, Barack, 246
Office of the Liberation Movements,
    213, 217–18, 221–24, 226
Office of the Representative of
    the Imam to the Guards,
    See Commissars
Oil and gas sector, 175–79, 190
Oil Industries Engineering and
    Construction, 177
Okhovat, Mohsen, 9
Omid-e Zanjan, 29
Omleshi, Rabbani, 106, 120
Oriental Kish Company, 176
Ossanlou, Mohammad-Taghi, 51t
Ostad-Ebrahim, Amir, 9
Ostadi, Parviz, 154

Pahlavi, Shah Reza, 8, 10, 30, 168,
    178, 211
Pakistan, 104, 106
Palestine, 217
Palestine Liberation Organization
    (PLO), 211
Palestinian guerrillas in revolution, 88
Parvaresh, Ali-Akbar, 7
Pasandideh, Morteza, 25
Payam Air, 189
Payam-e Enqelab, 34, 49
Payam International Airport, 189
Peasant, 9
Petraeus, David, 232
Petropars Company, 176
PLO (Palestine Liberation
    Organization), 211
Police forces, IRGC's relationship to, 17

Political and Divine Testament
    (Khomeini), 26–27, 117–18
Political Bureau of commissariat, 80
Politics, See Domestic politics;
    Ideology, politics and
    indoctrination
Pourjamshidian, Ali-Akbar, 51t
Poushnegar, Hassan, 9
Private sector of economy, 171–73, 181f
Privatization of businesses, IRGB
    takeover of, 167, 172–73, 176,
    179–80
Prodemocracy movement in Iran, 247
Public nonstate sector of
    economy, 181f

Qalibaf, Mohammad-Baqer,
    30, 123, 191
Qasemi, Rostam, 177
Qassemi, Mohammad-Taqi, 52t
Qassemi, Nour-Khoda, 54t
Qassir, Ahmad, 223
Qazvin Province, 54t, 86t
Qods Brigade, 51t, 85t
Qom Province, 54t, 86t
Qorbannejad, Said, 51t
Qotbzadeh, Sadeq, 207, 210
Quds Force, 83t, 216, 228, 230,
    232, 234, 236

Rafii, Karim, 7, 10
Rafiqdoust, Mohsen
    and attempted IRGC
        reconstruction, 13
    on economic role and privileges of
        IRGC, 170, 173, 174
    IRGC formation role, 11, 12,
        92–94
    in Khomeini's decree to Khorram
        Abadi, 105–6
    and Mahallati, 108–10
    on M. Montazeri's view of Guards'
        independence, 87

as pre-revolution Khomeini loyalist, 7
protest of Faker's veto right, 105
Rafsanjani, Akbar Hashemi
  vs. Ali Montazeri, 108, 116, 226
  on Ali Saidi as commissar, 123
  and attempted IRGC reconstruction, 13
  on Bani-Sadr's opposition to IRGC, 23
  as champion of economic liberalization, 247
  as commissar, 81t, 88, 98–99
  on defense industries transfer to IRGC, 169
  economic role and privileges of IRGC, 169, 172, 174
  and Eshkevari affair, 89, 94–95, 96, 97–98
  exporting the revolution, 216–18, 221–24, 225, 227–28, 230, 236
  on fall of Mohsen Rezaei, 110–11
  on Iran-Contra affair, 228
  Iran-Iraq War, 220–21, 229–30
  and Kermani, 120
  and Mahallati, 102, 104–5, 106, 107, 108–12
  memoir of, 3, 4
  and M. Eraqi's campaign for Khomeini's decree, 114
  presidential term, 25–26
Rafsanjani, Faezeh, 94, 98
Rafsanjani, Fatemeh, 94, 98
Rahimi, Naser, 9
Rahim-Mashaei, Esfandiar, 37
Rahmani, _____, 9
Rahmani, Mohammad-Ali, 232
Rahnema, Mahmoud, 170, 174
Rajabi, Mohammad-Hassan, 54t
Rajaei, Mohammad-Ali, 7, 215
Rajavi, Masoud, 24
Rashid, Gholam-Ali, 10

Rastegar, Khalil, 52t
Razaghian, Naser, 52t
Razavi, Mohammad, 9
Razavi Khorasan Province, 53t, 85t
Razavi-Rad, Mohammad-Vali, 85t
Razini, Ebrahim, 116, 118
Reagan, Ronald, 228
Real estate speculation, 169–71
Reformists and reformism
      and criticism of IRGC smuggling operations, 190–91
  IRGC focus on internal security as war against, 47
  IRGC's intimidation/suppression of, 16, 33–34, 246–47
Regular military
  as Bani-Sadr ally, 23, 25
  commissars' relationship to, 85t
  vs. IRGC during Iran-Iraq War, 111
  official vs. practical IRGC relationship to, 83–84
  Rafsanjani's attempt to merge IRGC into, 25
Religion
  and exporting the revolution, 214–15
  and indoctrination contradictions, 159–60
Representative of the Guardian Jurist, See Commissars
Repsol, 177
Rescue mission for IRGC, 18
Revolution, Iran's 1979, 86–87, 212–13, 214
Revolutionary Committee, 91, 94
Revolutionary Guards Strategic Studies Center, 31
Reyhani, Bahman, 53t
Rezaei, Ali, 156
Rezaei, Mohammad-Hadi, 83t
Rezaei, Mohsen
  and early political control of IRGC, 93

and economic role and privileges
  of IRGC, 170, 172
and elections (2009), 35
exporting the revolution, 223
Iran-Iraq War, 229
as IRGC chief, 102, 105–6, 108,
  109–11
and IRGC formation, 10, 12
Khatami's replacement of, 27–28
memoir of, 3
pre-revolution loyalty to
  Khomeini, 7
Saidi on, 125
Rezaei, Morteza, 23, 48, 101–2, 123
Rezvani, Asadollah, 85t
The Rise of the Pasdaran (Wehrey), 3
Roayati, Jafar, 86t
Romanian oil services company,
  IRGC's attack on, 176
Rouh-Allah Brigade, 54t, 85t
Rowhani, Mehdi, 154

Saadati, Mehdi, 53t
Sabaghian, Asghar, 7, 12, 92, 221
Sabzevari, Abd al-Rasoul (Ramin), 9
Sadeqi, Hossein, 7, 9
Sadeqi, Rahmatollah, 54t
Sadr, Mousa, 208–10
Al-Sadr, Mohammad Baqer, 214
Safari, Aziz, 10
Safavi, Rahim, 211, 223, 226–27
Safavi, Salman, 7, 9
Safavi, Yahya Rahim, 28–30, 31, 35,
  109, 176
Safdari, Nour al-Din Shah, 10
Saheb al-Amr Brigade, 54t, 86t
Saheb al-Zaman Brigade, 52t, 85t
Saidi, Ali, 37, 79, 82–83t, 123–27
Saidi, Mohammad-Esmail, 51t
Sakhy, Ali, 9
Salamati, Mohammad, 7, 9
Salamatian, Ahmad, 96
Salami, Hossein, 178

Salek, Ahmad, 228
Salman Brigade, 55t, 86t
Sanctions against Iran, economic,
  165, 177, 178, 248
Sanjaghi, Mohammad-Ebrahim, 92
Sar-Allah Brigade, 53t, 85t
Sarmast, Morteza, 10
Sarraf-Pour, _____, 10
Saudi Arabia, 27, 231
SAVAK, 8, 211
Sazegara, Mohsen, 7, 12, 92
Schahgaldian, Nikola B., 3
Sedaqat, Abd al-Nabi, 83t, 85t
Sediq, Mehdi, 52t
Semnan Province, 54t, 86t
Sepahvandi, Teymour, 54t
Seyf-Allahi, Reza, 107
Seyyed al-Shohada Brigade, 55t, 86t
Seyyed Al-Shohada Educational
  Center, 151
Shafi-Pour, Gholam-Reza, 85t
Shaghaghi, Mohammad, 9
Shah-Abadi, Mohammad-Ali, 89
Shahabi-Far, Avaz, 53t
Shah-Cheraghi, Mohammad-Taghi, 54t
Shah-e-Cheraqi, Mohammad, 54t
Shahroudi, Mahmoud, 120
Shahrvand-e Emrouz, 98
Shahvarpour, Hassan, 53t
Shakarami, Jamal, 52t
Shakeri, Mojtaba, 9
Shakeri, Yousef, 51t
Shakouri, Hossein, 9
Shalikar, Ali, 54t
Shamkhani, Ali, 7, 10, 109, 170
Shamsi, Esmail Davoudi, 12, 13
Shaneh-Saz, Moreza, 55t
Shariati, Ali, 207, 209
Shariatmadari, Mohammad-Kazem, 21
Shariatmadari, Mohsen, 9
Sharifi, Behnam, 9
Sharifi, Javad, 9
Sharokhi, Mohammad, 54t

Sheikh-Attar, Hossein, 9
Shell, 177
Shirazi, Ali, 83t
Al-Shirazi, Mohammad, 210
Shirazi, Sayyad, 111
Shohada Brigade, 50, 51t, 85t
Shojai-Zand, Ali, 9
Sistan and Baluchestan Province, 55t, 86t
Smuggling operations, 174, 178, 189–91
Sobhanian, Abbas, 86t
Sobhani-Nia, Hossein, 215
Sobh-e Sadeq, 34
Social housing services, 169–71
Soleymanipour, Majid, 188
South Khorasan Province, 53t, 85t
South Pars gas field, 176, 177
Special Organization of Unity and Action, 207
Split [Organization], 9
State sector of economy, 167
Statute of the Guards, 18–19, 80, 83, 151, 156
Stock exchange in Tehran, 178–83, 180f, 181f, 184–85t, 185–86, 187–88t, 188–89
Student movement (1999), 28–29
Suleimani, Gholam-Reza, 52t
Suleimani, Qassem, 30, 231–35, 237
Suleimani, Reza-Mohammad, 51t
Supervisory Bureau of commissariat, 80
Suppression of opposition by IRGC, 16, 17, 19, 29, 33–34, 35, 246–47
Supreme Audit Court, 175–76
Supreme Council of the Guards, 80, 83
Supreme Council of the Islamic Revolution in Iraq, 223, 228
Supreme Leader, cult of, 160–61
    See also Khamenei, Ali; Khomeini, Rouhollah

Supreme Shia Islamic Council of Lebanon, 209
Syria, 211, 224

Tabatabai, Ali, 9
Taeb, Hossein, 48
Taghavi-Rad, Mohammad-Ali, 9
Tahayyori, Ali, 9
Tahayyori, Mostafa, 9
Taherkhani, Mehdi, 54t
Taher-Nezhad, Hassan, 9
Tajzadeh, Mostafa, 7, 9
Talabani, Jalal, 157
Taleqani, Mahmoud, 207
Taliban, 161, 237
Tavassoli, Mohammad, 7
Tehranchi, Masoud, 92
Tehranfar, Hamid, 182
Tehran Province, 55t, 86t
Tehran stock exchange, 178–83, 180f, 181f, 184–85t, 185–86, 187–88t, 188–89
Telecommunications monopoly, 175
Terrorism
    Iranian support of terrorist organizations, 221–22, 223–24, 231–33, 247
    National Guard's military training by terrorist groups, 8
Teyrani, Mohammad, 7, 9
Teyyebi-Far, Hossein, 85t
Tofeili, Sobhi, 224
Torshiji, Ahmad, 9
Toseeh-ye Etermad-e Mobin Consortium, 186
Toyserkani, Mohammad, 150
Turkcell, 175
Turkey, 177

United Community of Believers, 9
United Movement of Self-Sacrficers, 122
United Nations, 177, 178, 229

The United Ones, 10
United States
    downing of Iranian airliner, 229
    as evil enemy in IRGC
        indoctrination, 28, 29, 159
    on GHORB as nuclear
        proliferation agent, 177
    hostage crisis, 20–21, 23–24
    Iran-Contra affair, 226, 227, 228
    Iran's sponsoring of terrorism
        against, 223, 224–25
    IRGC's attempted attack on
        Persian Gulf War forces, 27
    IRGC's condemnation of outreach
        after Iraq invasion, 33
    Kermani's blaming of 9/11 attack
        on, 122
    Khomeini's focus on
        confronting, 96
    and negotiations with Iran,
        248–49
    proposed approach for, 248–49
    State department secret
        diplomacy, 4
    threat from Iran during Iraqi
        occupation, 232–33
Urbanization and secularization
    of society, problems for IRGC
    control, 160
Vaezi, Hassan, 7, 9
Vaezi, Mohammad-Taghi, 185
Vafapour, Habibollah, 54t
Vahidi, Ahmad, 227, 228, 237
Vali-ye Asr Brigade, 53t, 85t
Vaziri-Hamaneh, Kazem, 176
Velayati, Ali Akbar, 221
Velvet revolutions, perceived threat
    of, 31, 47, 124
Venezuela, 170

Verdinezhad, Fereydoun, 228
The Victorious, 10

The Warriors of Islam: Iran's
    Revolutionary Guard (Katzman), 3
Weapons industry, 168–69
Weber, Max, 124
Wehrey, Frederic, 124
West Azerbaijan Province, 51t, 85t
World revolutionary movement,
    205–11
    See also Exporting the revolution

Yasini, Hossein, 167–68
Yasini, Javad, 9
Yasini, Mahmoud, 9
Yazdan-Fam, Abbas, 9
Yazdi, Ebrahim, 8, 13, 87, 89, 207,
    208, 210, 213
Yazdi, Mohammad-Taqi Mesbah,
    112–13, 119–20, 123–24
Yazd Province, 55t, 86t
Yousef-Ali-Zadeh, Hossein-Ali, 53t

Zabih, Sepehr, 3
Zamanian, Ahmad, 121
Zangeneh, Bizhan Namdar, 173
Zangeneh, Sabbah, 228
Zanjani, Mirza-Bagher, 120
Zanjan IRGC Brigade, 86t
Zanjan Province, 55t, 86t
Zarei, Mohammad-Mehdi, 52t
Zarghami, Ezzatollah, 34
Zibakalam, Sadeq, 220
Zibayi-Nezhad, Hossein (Nejat), 10
Zolghadr, Mohammad-Bagher,
    7, 10, 172
Zolnour, Mojitaba, 83t, 124
Zolqadr, Ahmad, 55t

About the Author

Ali Alfoneh is a resident fellow at American Enterprise Institute. His research areas include civil-military relations in Iran with a special focus on the role of the Islamic Revolutionary Guards Corps (IRGC). Alfoneh has been a research fellow at the Institute for Strategy at the Royal Danish Defence College and has taught political economy at the Center for Middle Eastern Studies at the University of Southern Denmark.

Sam Peltzman
Ralph and Dorothy Keller
 Distinguished Service Professor
 of Economics
Booth School of Business
University of Chicago

Jeremy A. Rabkin
Professor of Law
George Mason University
 School of Law

Harvey S. Rosen
John L. Weinberg Professor of
 Economics and Business Policy
Princeton University

Richard J. Zeckhauser
Frank Plumpton Ramsey Professor
 of Political Economy
Kennedy School of Government
Harvard University

Research Staff

Joseph Antos
Wilson H. Taylor Scholar in Health
 Care and Retirement Policy

Leon Aron
Resident Scholar; Director,
 Russian Studies

Michael Auslin
Resident Scholar

Claude Barfield
Resident Scholar

Michael Barone
Resident Fellow

Roger Bate
Resident Scholar

Andrew G. Biggs
Resident Scholar

Edward Blum
Visiting Fellow

Dan Blumenthal
Resident Fellow

John R. Bolton
Senior Fellow

Karlyn Bowman
Senior Fellow

Alex Brill
Research Fellow

James Capretta
Visiting Scholar

Timothy P. Carney
Visiting Fellow

Lynne V. Cheney
Senior Fellow

Edward W. Conrad
Visiting Scholar

Sadanand Dhume
Resident Fellow

Thomas Donnelly
Resident Fellow; Co-Director,
 Marilyn Ware Center for
 Security Studies

Mackenzie Eaglen
Resident Fellow

Nicholas Eberstadt
Henry Wendt Scholar in
 Political Economy

Jeffrey A. Eisenach
Visiting Scholar

Jon Entine
Visiting Fellow

Rick Geddes
Visiting Scholar

Jonah Goldberg
Fellow

Aspen Gorry
Research Fellow

Scott Gottlieb, M.D.
Resident Fellow

Michael S. Greve
Visiting Scholar

Kevin A. Hassett
Senior Fellow; Director,
 Economic Policy Studies

Robert B. Helms
Resident Scholar

Arthur Herman
NRI Visiting Scholar

Frederick M. Hess
Resident Scholar; Director,
 Education Policy Studies

Ayaan Hirsi Ali
Visiting Fellow

R. Glenn Hubbard
Visiting Scholar

Frederick W. Kagan
Resident Scholar; Director, AEI
 Critical Threats Project; and
 Christopher DeMuth Chair

Leon R. Kass, M.D.
Madden-Jewett Chair

Andrew P. Kelly
Research Fellow, Jacobs Associate

Desmond Lachman
Resident Fellow

Adam Lerrick
Visiting Scholar

John H. Makin
Resident Scholar

Aparna Mathur
Resident Scholar, Jacobs Associate

Michael Mazza
Research Fellow

Michael Q. McShane
Research Fellow

Thomas P. Miller
Resident Fellow

Charles Murray
W. H. Brady Scholar

Roger F. Noriega
Fellow

Stephen D. Oliner
Resident Scholar

Norman J. Ornstein
Resident Scholar

Pia Orrenius
Visiting Scholar

Richard Perle
Fellow

Mark J. Perry
Scholar

Tomas J. Philipson
Visiting Scholar

Edward Pinto
Resident Fellow

Alex J. Pollock
Resident Fellow

Ramesh Ponnuru
Visiting Fellow

Vincent R. Reinhart
Visiting Scholar

Richard Rogerson
Visiting Scholar

Michael Rubin
Resident Scholar

Sally Satel, M.D.
Resident Scholar

Gary J. Schmitt
Resident Scholar; Director,
 Program on American Citizenship;
 Co-Director, Marilyn Ware Center
 for Security Studies

Mark Schneider
Visiting Scholar

David Schoenbrod
Visiting Scholar

Sita Nataraj Slavov
Resident Scholar

Vincent Smith
Visiting Scholar

Christina Hoff Sommers
Resident Scholar; Director,
 W. H. Brady Program

Michael R. Strain
Research Fellow

Phillip Swagel
Visiting Scholar

Marc A. Thiessen
Fellow

Stan A. Veuger
Research Fellow

Alan D. Viard
Resident Scholar

Peter J. Wallison
Arthur F. Burns Fellow in
 Financial Policy Studies

Paul Wolfowitz
Scholar

John Yoo
Visiting Scholar

Madeline Zavodny
Visiting Scholar

Benjamin Zycher
NRI Visiting Fellow